"BILLY" SUNDAY
THE MAN AND HIS MESSAGE

WITH HIS OWN WORDS
WHICH HAVE WON
THOUSANDS FOR CHRIST

BY

WILLIAM T. ELLIS, LL.D.
AUTHOR OF "MEN AND MISSIONS"

Authorized Edition

Authorized by Mr. Sunday

This work contains the heart of Mr. Sunday's gospel message arranged by subjects, and is published by special agreement with him for the use of copyright material and photographs, which could be used only by his permission.

A WORD FROM THE AUTHOR

Because he is the most conspicuous Christian leader in America today; because he has done an entirely unique and far-reaching work of evangelism; and because his words have a message for all men, I have written, at the request of the publishers, this narrative concerning Rev. William A. Sunday, D.D.

The final appraisal of the man and his ministry cannot, of course, be made while he is alive. "Never judge unfinished work." This book has endeavored to deal candidly, though sympathetically, with its subject. Mr. Sunday has not seen either the manuscript or proofs. He has, however, authorized the use of the messages which he is accustomed to deliver in his meetings, and which comprise more than half the contents of the volume.

The author's hope is that those of us who are just plain "folks" will find the book interesting and helpful. He has no doubt that professional Christian workers will get many suggestions from the story of Mr. Sunday's methods.

I would acknowledge the assistance of Miss Helen Cramp and the Rev. Ernest Bawden in collating and preparing for publication Mr. Sunday's utterances.

WILLIAM T. ELLIS.

SWARTHMORE, PA.

CONTENTS

CONTENTS

CHAPTER XIV

The Service of Society

CHAPTER XV

Giving the Devil His Due

CHAPTER XVI

Critics and Criticism

CHAPTER XVII

A Clean Man on Social Sins

CHAPTER XVIII

"Help Those Women"

CHAPTER XIX

Standing on the Rock

CHAPTER XX

Making a Joyful Noise

CHAPTER XXI

The Prophet and His Own Time

CHAPTER XXII

Those Billy Sunday Prayers

CHAPTER XXIII

The Revival on Trial

CHAPTER XXIV
An Army With Banners

CHAPTER XXV
A Life Enlistment

CHAPTER XXVI
"A Good Soldier of Jesus Christ"

CHAPTER XXVII
A Wonderful Day at a Great University

CHAPTER XXVIII
The Christian's Daily Helper

CHAPTER XXIX

A Victorious Sermon PAGE

CHAPTER XXX

Eternity! Eternity!

CHAPTER XXXI

Our Long Home

CHAPTER XXXII

Glorying in the Cross

CHAPTER I

One of God's Tools

I want to be a giant for God.—Billy Sunday.

HEAVEN often plays jokes on earth's worldly-wise. After the consensus of experience and sagacity has settled upon a certain course and type, lo, all the profundity of the sages is blown away as a speck of dust and we have, say, a shockingly unconventional John the Baptist, who does not follow the prescribed rules in dress, training, methods or message. John the Baptist was God's laugh at the rabbis and the Pharisees.

In an over-ecclesiastical age, when churchly authority had reached the limit, a poor monk, child of a miner's hut, without influence or favor, was called to break the power of the popes, and to make empires and reshape history, flinging his shadow far down the centuries. Martin Luther was God's laugh at ecclesiasticism.

While the brains and aristocracy and professional statesmanship of America struggled in vain with the nation's greatest crisis, God reached down close to the soil of the raw and ignored Middle West, and picked up a gaunt and un-tutored specimen of the common people—a man who reeked of the earth until the earth closed over him—and so saved the Union and freed a race, through ungainly Abraham Lincoln. Thus again Heaven laughed at exalted procedure and conventionality.

In our own day, with its blatant worldly wisdom, with its flaunting prosperity, with its fashionable churchliness, with its flood of "advanced" theology overwhelming the pulpit, God needed a prophet, to call his people back to simple faith and righteousness. A nation imperiled by luxury, greed, love of pleasure and unbelief cried aloud for a deliverer. Surely this crisis required a great man, learned

(15)

in all the ways of the world, equipped with the best preparation of American and foreign universities and theological
seminaries, a man trained in ecclesiastical leadership, and
approved and honored by the courts of the Church? So
worldly wisdom decreed. But God laughed—and produced,
to the scandal of the correct and conventional, Billy Sunday,
a common man from the common people, who, like Lincoln,
so wears the signs and savor of the soil that fastidious folk,
to whom sweat is vulgar and to whom calloused hands are
"bad form," quite lose their suavity and poise in calling
him "unrefined."

That he is God's tool is the first and last word about
Billy Sunday. He is a "phenomenon" only as God is
forever doing phenomenal things, and upsetting men's
best-laid plans. He is simply a tool of God. For a special
work he is the special instrument. God called, and he
answered. All the many owlish attempts to "explain"
Billy Sunday on psychological and sociological grounds fall
flat when they ignore the fact that he is merely a handy
man for the Lord's present use.

God is still, as ever, confounding all human wisdom by
snatching the condemned baby of a Hebrew slave out of
Egypt's river to become a nation's deliverer; by calling a
shepherd boy from his sheep to be Israel's greatest warrior
and king; and by sending his only-begotten Son to earth by
way of a manger, and training him in a workingman's home
and a village carpenter shop. "My ways are not your ways,"
is a remark of God, which he seems fond of repeating and
illustrating.

There is no other explanation of Billy Sunday needed,
or possible, than that he is God's man sent in God's time.
And if God chooses the weak and foolish things of earth to
confound the mighty, is not that but another one of his
inscrutable ways of showing that he is God?

Why are we so confident that Billy Sunday is the Lord's
own man, when so many learned critics have declared the
contrary? Simply because he has led more persons to make

a public confession of discipleship to Jesus Christ than any
other man for a century past. Making Christians is, from
all angles, the greatest work in the world. Approximately
two hundred and fifty thousand persons, in the past twenty-
five years, have taken Sunday's hand, in token that henceforth their lives belong to the Saviour.

That amazing statement is too big to be grasped at
once. It requires thinking over. The huge total of dry
figures needs to be broken up into its component parts of
living human beings. Tens of thousands of those men were
husbands—hundreds of whom had been separated from their
wives and children by sin. Now, in reunited homes, whole
families bless the memory of the man of God who gave them
back husbands and fathers. Other tens of thousands were
sons, over many of whom parents had long prayed and
agonized. It would be hard to convince these mothers,
whose sons have been given back to clean living and to
Christian service, that there is anything seriously wrong with
Mr. Sunday's language, methods or theology. Business
men who find that a Sunday revival means the paying up
of the bad bills of old customers are ready to approve on
this evidence a man whose work restores integrity in commercial relations.

Every conceivable type of humanity is included in that
total of a quarter of a million of Sunday converts. The
college professor, the prosperous business man, the eminent
politician, the farmer, the lawyer, the editor, the doctor, the
author, the athlete, the "man about town," the criminal,
the drunkard, the society woman, the college student, the
workingman, the school boy and girl: the whole gamut of
life is covered by the stream of humanity that has "hit
the sawdust trail"—a phrase which has chilled the marrow
of every theological seminary in the land. But the trail
leads home to the Father's House.

One must reach into the dictionary for big, strong words
in characterizing the uniqueness of Billy Sunday's work.
So I say that another aspect of his success is fairly astound-

ing. He, above all others in our time, has broken through
the thick wall of indifference which separates the Church
from the world. Church folk commonly avoid the subject
of this great fixed gulf. We do not like to face the fact that
the mass of mankind does not bother its head about conventional religious matters. Even the majority of church-
goers are blankly uninterested in the general affairs of
religion. Sad to tell, our bishops and board secretaries and
distinguished preachers are really only local celebrities.
Their names mean nothing in newspaper offices or to newspaper readers: there are not six clergymen in the United
States with a really national reputation. Each in his own
circle, of locality or denomination, may be Somebody with a
big S. But the world goes on unheeding. Great ecclesiastical movements and meetings are entirely unrecorded by the
secular press. The Church's problem of problems is how
to smash, or even to crack, the partition which shuts off the
world from the Church.

Billy Sunday has done that. He has set all sorts and
conditions of men to talking about religion. Go to the
lowest dive in New York's "Tenderloin" or in San Francisco's
"Barbary Coast," and mention the name "Billy Sunday,"
and everybody will recognize it, and be ready to discuss the
man and his message. Stand before a session of the American
Philosophical Society and pronounce the words "Billy
Sunday" and every one of the learned savants present will
be able to talk about the man, even though few of them know
who won last season's base-ball championship or who is the
world's champion prize-fighter.

This is a feat of first magnitude. All levels of society
have been made aware of Billy Sunday and his gospel.
When the evangelist went to New York for an evening
address, early in the year 1914, the throngs were so great
that the police were overwhelmed by the surging thousands.
Even Mr. Sunday himself could not obtain admittance to
the meeting for more than half an hour. Andrew Carnegie
could not get into the hall that bears his name. Probably

a greater number of persons tried to hear this evangelist
that night than were gathered in all the churches of greater
New York combined on the preceding Sunday night.   To
turn thousands of persons away from his meetings is a
common experience of Mr. Sunday.   More than ten thousand,
mostly men, tried in vain to get into the overcrowded Scranton tabernacle at a single session.   Every thoughtful man
or woman must be interested in the man who thus can make
religion interesting to the common people.

The despair of the present-day Church is the modern
urban center.   Our generation had not seen a great city
shaken by the gospel until Billy Sunday went to Pittsburgh.
That he did it is the unanimous report of press and preachers
and business men.   Literally that whole city was stirred to
its most sluggish depths by the Sunday campaign.   No
base-ball series or political campaign ever moved the community so deeply.   Everywhere one went the talk was of
Billy Sunday and his meetings.   From the bell boys in the
hotels to the millionaires in the Dusquesne Club, from the
workmen in the mills and the girls in the stores, to the
women in exclusive gatherings, Sunday was the staple of
conversation.

Day by day, all the newspapers in the city gave whole
pages to the Sunday meetings.   The sermons were reported
entire.   No other topic ever had received such full attention
for so long a time at the hands of the press as the Sunday
campaign.   These issues of the papers were subscribed for
by persons in all parts of the land.   Men and women were
converted who never heard the sound of the evangelist's
voice.   This series of Pittsburgh meetings, more than anything else in his experience, impressed the power of Sunday
upon the metropolitan centers of the nation at large; the
country folk had long before learned of him.

Any tabulation of Mr. Sunday's influence must give a
high place to the fact that he has made good press "copy":
he has put religion on the front pages of the dailies; and has
made it a present issue with the millions.   Under modern

conditions, no man can hope to evangelize America who has not also access to the columns of the newspapers. Within the memory of living men, no other man or agency has brought religion so powerfully and consecutively into the press as William A. Sunday, whom some of his scholarly critics have called "illiterate."

All of which proves the popular interest in vital, contemporaneous religion. Men's ears are dulled by the "shop talk" of the pulpit. They are weary of the worn platitudes of professional piety. Nobody cares for the language of Canaan, in which many ministers, with reverence for the dead past, have tried to enswathe the living truths of the Gospel, as if they were mummies. In the colloquial tongue of the common people, Jesus first proclaimed his gospel, and "the common people heard him gladly," although many of the learned and aristocratic ecclesiastics of his day were scandalized by his free and popular way of putting things, by his "common" stories, and by his disregard for the precedents of the schools. Whatever else may be said about Billy Sunday's much-discussed forms of speech, this point is clear, and denied by nobody: he makes himself and his message clearly understood by all classes of people. However much one may disagree with him, nobody fails to catch his meaning. He harnesses the common words of the street up to the chariot of divine truth. Every-day folk, the uncritical, unscholarly crowd of us, find no fault with the fact that Sunday uses the same sort of terms that we do. In fresh, vigorous, gripping style, he makes his message unmistakable.

College students like him as much as do the farmers and mechanics. In a single day's work at the University of Pennsylvania, when thousands of students crowded his meetings, and gave reverent, absorbed attention to his message, several hundred of them openly dedicated their lives to Christ, and in token thereof publicly grasped his hand. Dr. John R. Mott, the world's greatest student leader, once said to me, in commenting upon Sunday:

"You cannot fool a great body of students. They get a man's measure. If he is genuine, they know it, and if he is not, they quickly find it out. Their devotion to Mr. Sunday is very significant."

This man, who meets life on all levels, and proves that the gospel message is for no one particular class, is a distinctively American type. Somebody has said that the circus is the most democratic of American institutions: it brings all sorts and conditions of people together on a common plane and for a common purpose. The Sunday evangelistic meetings are more democratic than a circus. They are a singular exhibit of American. life—perhaps the most distinctive gathering to be found in our land today. His appeal is to the great mass of the people. The housekeepers who seldom venture away from their homes, the mechanics who do not go to church, the "men about town" who profess a cynical disdain for religion, the "down and outs," the millionaires, the society women, the business and professional men, the young fellows who feel "too big" to go to Sunday school—all these, and scores of other types, may be found night after night in the barn-like wooden tabernacles which are always erected for the Sunday meetings. Our common American life seems to meet and merge in this base-ball evangelist, who once erected tents for another evangelist, and now has to have special auditoriums built to hold his own crowds; and who has risen from a log cabin to a place of national power and honor. Nowhere else but in America could one find such an unconventional figure as Billy Sunday.

Succeeding chapters will tell in some detail the story of the man and his work; and in most of them the man will speak his own messages. But for explanation of his power and his work it can only be said, as of old, "There was a man sent from God, whose name was"—Billy Sunday.

CHAPTER II

Up from the Soil

If you want to drive the devil out of the world, hit him with a cradle instead of a crutch.—BILLY SUNDAY.

SUNDAY must be accepted as a man of the American type before he can be understood. He is of the average, every-day American sort. He is one of the "folks." He has more points of resemblance to the common people than he has of difference from them. His mind is their mind. The keenness of the average American is his in an increased degree. He has the saving sense of humor which has marked this western people. The extravagances and recklessnesses of his speech would be incredible to a Britisher; but we Americans understand them. They are of a piece with our minds.

Like the type, Sunday is not over-fastidious. He is not made of a special porcelain clay, but of the same red soil as the rest of us. He knows the barn-yards of the farm better than the drawing-rooms of the rich. The normal, every-day Americanism of this son of the Middle West, whom the nation knows as "Billy Sunday," is to be insisted upon if he is to be understood.

Early apprenticed to hardship and labor, he has a sympathy with the life of the toiling people which mere imagination cannot give. His knowledge of the American crowd is sure and complete because he is one of them. He understands the life of every-day folk because that has always been his life. While he has obvious natural ability, sharpened on the grindstone of varied experience, his perceptions and his viewpoints are altogether those of the normal American. As he has seen something of life on many levels, and knows city ways as well as country usages, he has never lost his bearings as to what sort of people make up the bulk of this country. To them his sermons are addressed. Because he strikes this medium level of common conduct and thought, it is easy for those in all the ranges of American life to comprehend him.

"Horse-sense," that fundamental American virtue, is Sunday's to an eminent degree. A modern American philosopher defines this quality of mind as "an instinctive something that tells us when the clock strikes twelve." Because he is "rich in saving common sense," Sunday understands the people and trusts them to understand him. His most earnest defenders from the beginning of his public life have been the rank and file of the common people. His critics have come from the extreme edges of society— the scholar, or the man whose business is hurt by righteousness.

The life of William A. Sunday covers the period of American history since the Civil War. He never saw his father, for he was born the third son of pioneer parents on November 19, 1862, four months after his father had enlisted as a private in Company E, Twenty-third Iowa Infantry Volunteers.

There is nothing remarkable to record as to the family. They were one with the type of the middle-western Americans who wrested that empire from the wilderness, and counted poverty honorable. In those mutually helpful, splendidly independent days, Democracy came to its flower, and the American type was born.

Real patriotism is always purchased at a high price; none pay more dearly for war-time loyalty than the women who send their husbands and sons to the front. Mrs. Sunday bade her husband answer the call of his country as only a brave woman could do, and sent him forth to the service and sacrifices which soon ended in an unmarked grave. Four months after she had bidden farewell to her husband, she bade welcome to his son. To this third child she gave the name of her absent soldier husband.

The mother's dreams of the returning soldier's delight

in his namesake child were soon shattered by the tidings
that Private William Sunday had died of disease con-
tracted in service, at Patterson, Missouri, on December
22, 1862, a little more than a month after the birth of the
boy who was to lift his name out of the obscurity of the
hosts of those who gave "the last full measure of devotion"
to their nation.

Then the mother was called upon to take up that
heaviest of all burdens of patriotism—the rearing of an
orphan family in a home of dire poverty. The three children in the Sunday home out at Ames, Iowa—Roy, Edward
and William—were unwitting participants in another aspect
of war, the lot of soldiers' orphans. For years, Mrs. Sunday,
who at this writing is still living and rejoicing in the successes
of her son, was able to keep her little family together under
the roof of the two-roomed log cabin which they called home.
In those early days their grandfather, Squire Corey, was
of unmeasured help in providing for and training the three
orphan boys.

Experience is a school teacher who carries a rod, as
Sunday could well testify. He learned life's fundamental
lessons in the school of poverty and toil. To the part which
his mother played in shaping his life and ideals he has borne
eloquent tribute on many platforms. When the youngest
son was twelve years old, he and his older brother were sent
off to the Soldiers' Orphanage at Glenwood, Iowa. Later
they were transferred to the Davenport Orphanage, which
they left in June of 1876, making two years spent in the
orphanages. Concerning this experience Sunday himself
speaks:

"I was bred and born (not in old Kentucky, although
my grandfather was a Kentuckian), but in old Iowa. I
am a rube of the rubes. I am a hayseed of the hayseeds, and
the malodors of the barnyard are on me yet, and it beats
Pinaud and Colgate, too. I have greased my hair with
goose grease and blacked my boots with stove blacking.
I have wiped my old proboscis with a gunny-sack towel;

I have drunk coffee out of my saucer, and I have eaten with my knife; I have said 'done it,' when I should have said 'did it,' and I 'have saw' when I should 'have seen,' and I expect to go to heaven just the same. I have crept and crawled out from the university of poverty and hard knocks, and have taken postgraduate courses.

"My father went to the war four months before I was born, in Company E, Twenty-third Iowa. I have butted and fought and struggled since I was six years old. That's one reason why I wear that little red, white and blue button. I know all about the dark and seamy side of life, and if ever a man fought hard, I have fought hard for everything I have ever gained.

"The wolf scratched at the cabin door and finally mother said: 'Boys, I am going to send you to the Soldiers' Orphans' Home.' At Ames, Iowa, we had to wait for the train, and we went to a little hotel, and they came about one o'clock and said: 'Get ready for the train.'

"I looked into mother's face. Her eyes were red, her hair was disheveled. I said: 'What's the matter, mother?' All the time Ed and I slept mother had been praying. We went to the train; she put one arm about me and the other about Ed and sobbed as if her heart would break. People walked by and looked at us, but they didn't say a word.

"Why? They didn't know, and if they had they wouldn't have cared. Mother knew; she knew that for years she wouldn't see her boys. We got into the train and said, 'Good-bye, mother,' as the train pulled out. We reached Council Bluffs. It was cold and we turned up our coats and shivered. We saw the hotel and went up and asked the woman for something to eat. She said: 'What's your name?'

"'My name is William Sunday, and this is my brother Ed.'

"'Where are you going?'

"'Going to the Soldiers' Orphans' Home at Glenwood.'

"She wiped her tears and said: 'My husband was a

soldier and he never came back. He wouldn't turn any one away and I wouldn't turn you boys away.' She drew her arms about us and said: 'Come on in.' She gave us our breakfast and our dinner, too. There wasn't any train going out on the 'Q' until afternoon. We saw a freight train standing there, so we climbed into the caboose.

"The conductor came along and said: 'Where's your money or ticket?'

"'Ain't got any.'

"'I'll have to put you off.'

"We commenced to cry. My brother handed him a letter of introduction to the superintendent of the orphans' home. The conductor read it, and handed it back as the tears rolled down his cheeks. Then he said: 'Just sit still, boys. It won't cost a cent to ride on my train.'

"WHERE'S YOUR MONEY OR TICKET?"

"It's only twenty miles from Council Bluffs to Glenwood, and as we rounded the curve the conductor said: 'There it is on the hill.'

"I want to say to you that one of the brightest pictures that hangs upon the walls of my memory is the recollection of the days when as a little boy, out in the log cabin on the frontier of Iowa, I knelt by mother's side.

"I went back to the old farm some years ago. The scenes had changed about the place. Faces I had known and loved had long since turned to dust. Fingers that used to turn the pages of the Bible were obliterated and the old trees beneath which we boys used to play and swing had been felled by the woodman's axe. I stood and thought. The man became a child again and the long weary nights of sin and of hardships became as though they never had been.

"Once more with my gun on my shoulder and my favorite dog trailing at my heels I walked through the pathless wood and sat on the old familiar logs and stumps, and as I sat and listened to the wild, weird harmonies of nature, a vision of the past opened. The squirrel from the limb of the tree barked defiantly and I threw myself into an interrogation point, and when the gun cracked, the squirrel fell at my feet. I grabbed him and ran home to throw him down and receive compliments for my skill as a marksman. And I saw the tapestry of the evening fall. I heard the lowing herds and saw them wind slowly o'er the lea and I listened to the tinkling bells that lulled the distant fowl. Once more I heard the shouts of childish glee. Once more I climbed the haystack for the hen's eggs. Once more we crossed the threshold and sat at our frugal meal. Once more mother drew the trundle bed out from under the larger one, and we boys, kneeling down, shut our eyes and clasping our little hands, said: 'Now I lay me down to sleep; I pray the Lord, my soul to keep. If I should die before I wake, I pray thee, Lord, my soul to take. And this I ask for Jesus' sake, Amen.'

> " 'Backward, turn backward, O time in thy flight,
> Make me a child again, just for tonight,
> Mother, come back from that echoless shore,
> Take me again to your heart as of yore.
> Into the old cradle I'm longing to creep,
> Rock me to sleep, mother, rock me to sleep.'

"I stood beneath the old oak tree and it seemed to carry on a conversation with me. It seemed to say:

" 'Hello Bill. Is that you?'

" 'Yes, it's I, old tree.'

" 'Well, you've got a bald spot on the top of your head.

" 'Yes, I know, old tree.'

" 'Won't vou climb up and sit on my limbs as you used to?'

" 'No, I haven't got time now. I'd like to, though, awfully well.'

" 'Don't go, Bill. Don't you remember the old swing you made?'

" 'Yes, I remember; but I've got to go.'

" 'Say Bill, don't you remember when you tried to play George Washington and the cherry tree and almost cut me down? That's the scar you made, but it's almost covered over now.'

" 'Yes, I remember all, but I haven't time to stay.'

" 'Are you comin' back, Bill?'

" 'I don't know, but I'll never forget you.'

"Then the old apple tree seemed to call me and I said: 'I haven't time to wait, old apple tree.'

" ' I want to go back to the orchard,
    The orchard that used to be mine,
  The apples are reddening and filling
    The air with their wine.
  I want to run on through the pasture
    And let down the dusty old bars,
  I want to find you there still waiting,
    Your eyes like the twin stars.
  Oh, nights, you are weary and dreary,
    And days, there is something you lack;
  To the farm in the valley,
    I want to go back.'

"I tell it to you with shame, I stretched the elastic bands of my mother's love until I thought they would break. I went far into the dark and the wrong until I ceased to hear her prayers or her pleadings. I forgot her face, and I went so far that it seemed to me that one more step and the elastic bands of her love would break and I would be lost. But, thank God, friends, I never took that last step.   Little by little I yielded to the tender memories and recollections of my mother; little by little I was drawn away from the yawning abyss, and twenty-seven years ago, one dark and stormy night in Chicago, I groped my way out of darkness into the arms of Jesus Christ and I fell on my knees and cried 'God be merciful to me a sinner!' "

Of formal education the boy Sunday had but little. He went to school intermittently, like most of his playmates, but he did get into the high school, although he was never graduated. Early in life he began to work for his living, even before he went off to the Soldiers' Orphanage. Concerning these periods of early toil he himself has spoken as follows:

"When I was about fourteen years old, I made application for the position of janitor in a school.

"I used to get up at two o'clock, and there were fourteen stoves and coal had to be carried for all them. I had to keep the fire up and keep up my studies and sweep the floors. I got twenty-five dollars a month salary. Well, one day I got a check for my salary and I went right down to the bank to get it cashed. Right in front of me was another fellow with a check to be cashed, and he shoved his in, and I came along and shoved my check in, and he handed me out forty dollars. My check called for twenty-five dollars. I called on a friend of mine who was a lawyer in Kansas City and told him. I said: 'Frank, what do you think, Jay King handed me forty dollars and my check only called for twenty-five dollars.' He said, 'Bill, if I had your luck, I would buy a lottery ticket.' But I said, 'The fifteen dollars is not mine.' He said, 'Don't be a chump. If you were shy ten dollars and you went back you would not get it, and if they hand out fifteen dollars, don't be a fool, keep it.'

"Well, he had some drag with me and influenced me. I was fool enough to keep it, and I took it and bought a suit of clothes. I can see that suit now; it was a kind of brown, with a little green in it and I thought I was the goods, I want to tell you, when I got those store clothes on. That was the first suit of store clothes I had ever had, and I bought that suit and I had twenty-five dollars left after I did it.

"Years afterwards I said, 'I ought to be a Christian,' and I got on my knees to pray, and the Lord seemed to touch me on the back and say, 'Bill, you owe that Farmers' Bank fifteen dollars with interest,' and I said, 'Lord, the bank don't know that I got that fifteen dollars,' and the Lord said 'I know it'; so I struggled along for years, probably like some of you, trying to be decent and honest and right some wrong that was in my life, and every time I got down to pray the Lord would say, 'Fifteen dollars with interest, Nevada County, Iowa; fifteen dollars, Bill.' So years afterwards I sent that money back, enclosed a check, wrote a letter and acknowledged it, and I have the peace of God from that day to this, and I have never swindled anyone out of a dollar."

There are other kinds of education besides those which award students a skeepskin at the end of a stated term. Sunday has no sheepskin—neither has he the sheep quality which marks the machine-made product of any form of training. His school has been a diversity of work, where he came face to face with the actualities of life. He early had to shift for himself. He learned the priceless lesson of how to work, regardless of what the particular task might be, whether it was scrubbing floors (and he was an expert scrubber of floors!), or preaching a sermon to twenty thousand persons. He had a long hard drill in working under authority: that is why he is able to exercise authority like a major-general. Because personally he has experienced, with all of the sensitiveness of an American small boy, the bitter injustice of over-work and under-pay under an oppressive task-master, he is a voice for the toilers of the world. In this same diversified school of industry he learned the lesson of thoroughness which is now echoed by every spike in his tabernacle and every gesture in his sermons. Such a one as he could not have come from a conventional educational course. It needed this hard school to make such a hardy man.

It was while a youth in Marshalltown, Iowa, playing base ball on the lots, that Sunday came to his own. Captain A. C. Anson, the famous leader of the Chicago "White Sox," chanced to see the youth of twenty, whose phenomenal base-running had made him a local celebrity. It is no new experience for Sunday to be a center of public interest. He has known this since boyhood. The local base-ball "hero" is as big a figure in the eyes of his own particular circle as ever a great evangelist gets to be in the view of the world. Because his ears early became accustomed to the huzzahs of the crowd, Sunday's head has not been turned by much of the foolish adulation which has been his since he became an evangelist.

A level head, a quick eye, and a body which is such a finely trained instrument that it can meet all drafts upon it, is part of Sunday's inheritance from his life on the base-ball diamond.

Most successful base-ball players enter the major leagues by a succession of steps. With Sunday it was quite otherwise. Because he fell under the personal eye of "Pop" Anson he was borne directly from the fields of Marshall-town, Iowa, to the great park of the Chicago team. That was in 1883, when Sunday was not yet twenty-one years of age. His mind was still formative—a quality it retains to this day—and his entrance into the larger field of base ball trained him to think in broad terms. It widened his horizon and made him reasonably indifferent to the comments of the crowds.

A better equipment for the work he is doing could not have been found; for above all else Sunday "plays ball." While others discuss methods and bewail conditions he keeps the game going. Such a volume of criticism as no other evangelist, within the memory of living men, has ever received, has fallen harmless from his head, because he has not turned aside to argue with the umpire, but has "played ball."

There is no call for tears or heroics over the early experiences of Sunday. His life was normal; no different from that of tens of thousands of other American boys. He himself was in no wise a phenomenon. He was possessed of no special abilities or inclinations. He came to his preaching gift only after years of experience in Christian work. It is clear that a Divine Providence utilized the very ordinariness of his life and training to make him an ambassador to the common people.

CHAPTER III

A Base-Ball "Star"

Don't get chesty over success.—BILLY SUNDAY.

SOMETIMES the preacher tells his people what a great journalist he might have been, or what a successful business man, had he not entered the ministry; but usually his hearers never would have suspected it if he had not told them. Billy Sunday's eminence as a base-ball player is not a shadow cast backward from his present pre-eminence. His success as a preacher has gained luster from his distinction as a base-ball player, while his fame as a base-ball player has been kept alive by his work as an evangelist.

All the world of base-ball enthusiasts, a generation ago, knew Billy Sunday, the speediest base-runner and the most daring base-stealer in the whole fraternity. Wherever he goes today veteran devotees of the national game recall times they saw him play; and sporting periodicals and sporting pages of newspapers have been filled with reminiscences from base-ball "fans," of the triumphs of the evangelist on the diamond.

A side light on the reality of his religion while engaged in professional base ball is thrown by the fact that sporting writers always speak of him with pride and loyalty, and his old base-ball associates who still survive, go frequently to hear him preach. The base-ball world thinks that he reflects distinction on the game.

Now base ball in Marshalltown and base ball in Chicago had not exactly the same standards. The recruit had to be drilled. He struck out the first thirteen times he went to bat. He never became a superior batter, but he could always throw straight and hard. At first he was inclined to take too many chances and his judgment was rather unsafe. One base-ball writer has said that "Sunday

probably caused more wide throws than any other player
the game has ever known, because of his specialty of going
down to first like a streak of greased electricity.   When he
hit the ball infielders yelled 'hurry it up.'   The result was
that they often threw them away."   He was the acknowledged champion sprinter of the National League.   This once
led to a match race with Arlie Latham, who held like honors
in the American League.   Sunday won by fifteen feet.

Sunday was the sort of figure the bleachers liked.   He
was always eager—sometimes too eager— to"take a chance."
What was a one-base hit for another man was usually good
for two bases for
him.   His slides and
stolen bases were
adventures beloved
of the "fans"—the
spice of the game.
He also was apt in
retort to the com-
ments from the
bleachers, but al-
ways good-natured.
The crowds liked
him, even as did his
team mates.

HIS SLIDES WERE ADVENTURES BELOVED
OF THE "FANS"

Sunday was a man's man, and so continues to this day.
His tabernacle audiences resemble base-ball crowds in the
proportion of men present, more nearly than any other
meetings of a religious nature that are regularly being held.
Sunday spent five years on the old Chicago team, mostly
playing right or center field.   He was the first man in the
history of base ball to circle the bases in fourteen seconds.
He could run a hundred yards from a standing start in ten
seconds flat.   Speed had always been his one distinction.
As a lad of thirteen, in the Fourth of July games at Ames,
he won a prize of three dollars in a foot-race, a feat
which he recalls with pleasure.

Speed is a phase of base ball that, being clear to all eyes, appeals to the bleachers. So it came about that Sunday was soon a base-ball "hero," analogous to "Ty" Cobb or "Home-Run" Baker, or Christy Mathewson of our own day. He himself tells the story of one famous play, on the day after his conversion:

"That afternoon we played the old Detroit club. We were neck and neck for the championship. That club had Thompson, Richardson, Rowe, Dunlap, Hanlon and Bennett, and they could play ball.

"I was playing right field. Mike Kelly was catching and John G. Clarkson was pitching. He was as fine a pitcher as ever crawled into a uniform. There are some pitchers today, O'Toole, Bender, Wood, Mathewson, Johnson, Marquard, but I do not believe any one of them stood in the class with Clarkson.

"Cigarettes put him on the bum. When he'd taken a bath the water would be stained with nicotine.

"We had two men out and they had a man on second and one on third and Bennett, their old catcher, was at bat. Charley had three balls and two strikes on him. Charley couldn't hit a high ball: but he could kill them when they went about his knee.

"I hollered to Clarkson and said: 'One more and we got 'em.'

"You know every pitcher puts a hole in the ground where he puts his foot when he is pitching. John stuck his foot in the hole and he went clean to the ground. Oh, he could make 'em dance. He could throw overhanded, and the ball would go down and up like that. He is the only man on earth I have seen do that. That ball would go by so fast that the batter could feel the thermometer drop two degrees as she whizzed by. John went clean down, and as he went to throw the ball his right foot slipped and the ball went low instead of high.

"I saw Charley swing hard and heard the bat hit the ball with a terrific boom. Bennett had smashed the ball on the nose. I saw the ball rise in the air and knew that it was going clear over my head.

"I could judge within ten feet of where the ball would light. I turned my back to the ball and ran.

"The field was crowded with people and I yelled, 'Stand back!' and that crowd opened as the Red Sea opened for the rod of Moses. I ran on, and as I ran I made a prayer; it wasn't theological, either, I tell you that. I said, 'God, if you ever helped mortal man, help me to get that ball, and you haven't very much time to make up your mind, either.' I ran and jumped over the bench and stopped.

"I thought I was close enough to catch it. I looked back and saw it was going over my head and I jumped and shoved out my left hand and the ball hit it and stuck. At the rate I was going the momentum carried me on and I fell under the feet of a team of horses. I jumped up with the ball in my hand. Up came Tom Johnson. Tom used to be mayor of Cleveland. He's dead now.

"'Here is $10, Bill. Buy yourself the best hat in Chicago. That catch won me $1,500. Tomorrow go and buy yourself the best suit of clothes you can find in Chicago.'

"An old Methodist minister said to me a few years ago, 'Why, William, you didn't take the $10, did you?' I said, 'You bet your life I did.' "

After his five years with the Chicago base-ball team, Sunday played upon the Pittsburgh and the Philadelphia teams, his prestige so growing with the years that after he had been eight years in base ball, he declined a contract at five hundred dollars a month, in order to enter Christian work.

For most of his base-ball career Sunday was an out-and-out Christian. He had been converted in 1887, after four years of membership on the Chicago team. He had worked at his religion; his team mates knew his Christianity for the real thing. On Sundays, because of his eminence as a base-ball player, he was in great demand for Y. M. C. A.

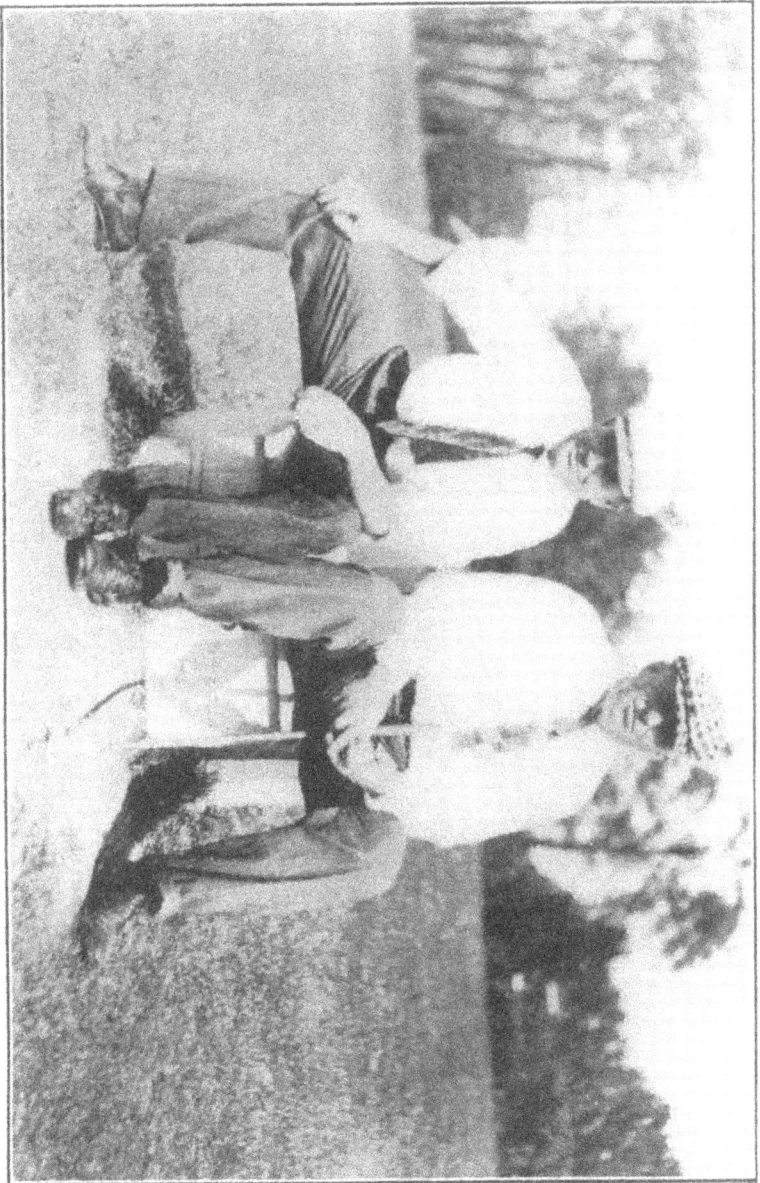

BILLY SUNDAY AND "POP" ANSON, FORMER CAPTAIN OF THE FAMOUS CHICAGO "WHITE SOX" BASEBALL TEAM, ON THE GOLF LINKS.

BILLY SUNDAY IN NATIONAL LEAGUE UNIFORM.

talks.   The sporting papers all alluded frequently to his religious interests and activities.   Because of his Christian scruples he refused to play base ball on Sunday.   During the four years of his experience as a Christian member of the base-ball profession it might have been clear to anybody who cared to study the situation carefully that the young man's interest in religion was steadily deepening and that he was headed toward some form of avowedly Christian service.

"I had a three-year contract with Philadelphia.   I said to God, 'Now if you want me to quit playing ball and go into evangelistic work, then you get me my release,' and so I left it with God to get my release before the 25th day of March and would take that as an evidence that he wanted me to quit playing ball.

"On the 17th day of March, St. Patrick's day—I shall never forget it—I was leading a meeting and received a letter from Colonel Rogers, president of the Philadelphia club, stating I could have my release.

"In came Jim Hart, of the Cincinnati team, and up on the platform and pulled out a contract for $3,500.   A player only plays seven months, and he threw the check down for $500, the first month's salary in advance.   He said, 'Bill, sign up!'   But I said, 'No!'   I told him that I told God if he wanted me to quit playing ball to get my release before the 25th day of March and I would quit.

"There I was up against it.   I went around to some of my friends and some said, 'Take it!'   Others said, 'Stick to your promise.'   I asked my father-in-law about it, and he said, 'You are a blank fool if you don't take it.'   I went home and went to bed, but could not sleep, and prayed that night until five o'clock, when I seemed to get the thing straight and said, 'No, sir, I will not do it.'

"I went to work for the Y. M. C. A. and had a very hard time of it.   It was during those hard times that I hardly had enough to pay my house rent, but I stuck to my promise."

It was in March of 1891 that Sunday made the decision
which marked the parting of the ways for him.   He abandoned base ball forever as a profession, although not as an
interest, and entered upon definite religious work.   He
accepted a position in the Chicago Y. M. C. A. as a subordi-
nate secretary at $83.33 per month—and sometimes this
was six months overdue.

The stuff of which the young man's moral character
was made is revealed by the fact that he deliberately rejected
a $500-a-month base-ball contract in order to serve Christ
at a personal sacrifice.   This incident reveals the real
temper of Sunday, and is to be borne in mind when discussion is raised concerning the large offerings which are made
to him now in his successful evangelistic work.   That act
was not the deed of a money-loving man.   If it does not
spell consecration, it is difficult to define what it does mean.

Doubtless there were many who thought this ending
of a conspicuous base-ball career an anti-climax, even as
the flight of Moses into the wilderness of Sinai apparently
spelled defeat.   Out of such defeats and sacrifices as these
grow the victories that best serve the world and most honor
God.

CHAPTER IV

A Curbstone Recruit

You've got to sign your own Declaration of Independence before you can celebrate your Fourth of July victory.—BILLY SUNDAY.

NOBODY this side of heaven can tell to whom the credit belongs for any great life or great work. But we may be reasonably sure that the unsung and unknown women of the earth have a large part in every achievement worth while.

Mrs. Clark, saintly wife of Colonel Clark, the devoted founder of the Pacific Garden Rescue Mission in Chicago, is one of that host of women who, like the few who followed Jesus in his earthly ministry, have served in lowly, inconspicuous ways, doing small tasks from a great love. Night after night, with a consecration which never flagged, she labored in the gospel for a motley crowd of men and women, mostly society's flotsam and jetsam, many of whom found this hospitable building the last fort this side of destruction.

A single visit to a down-town rescue mission is romantic, picturesque and somewhat of an adventure—a sort of sanctified slumming trip. Far different is it to spend night after night, regardless of weather or personal feelings, in coming to close grips with sin-sodden men and women, many of them the devil's refuse. A sickening share of the number are merely seeking shelter or lodging or food: sin's wages are not sufficient to live upon, and they turn to the mercy of Christianity for succor. Never to be cast down by unworthiness or ingratitude, to keep a heart of hope in face of successive failures, and to rejoice with a shepherd's joy over the one rescued—this is the spirit of the consecrated rescue-mission worker.

Such a woman was Mrs. Clark, the spiritual mother to a

multitude of redeemed men. Of all the trophies which she has laid at the feet of her Lord, the redemption of Billy Sunday seems to human eyes the brightest. For it was this woman who persuaded him to accept Christ as his Saviour: he whose hand has led perhaps a quarter of a million persons to the foot of the Cross was himself led thither by this saintly woman.

When we contemplate the relation of that one humble rescue mission in Chicago, the monument of a business man's consecration to Christ, to the scores of Sunday Taber- nacles over the land; and when we connect the streams of penitents on the "sawdust trail" with that one young man of twenty-five going forward up the aisle of the rude mission room, we realize afresh that God uses many workers to carry on his one work; and that though Paul may plant and Apollos water, it is God alone who giveth the increase.

It was one evening in the fall of 1887 that Sunday, with five of his base-ball team mates, sat on the curbstone of Van Buren Street and listened to the music and testimonies of a band of workers from the Pacific Garden Rescue Mission. The deeps of sentiment inherited from a Christian mother, and the memories of a Christian home, were stirred in the breast of one of the men; and Sunday accepted the invitation of a worker to visit the mission. Moved by the vital testimonies which he heard, he went again and again; and at length, after conversation and prayer with Mrs. Clark, he made the great decision which committed him to the Christian life.

Sunday's own story of his conversion is one of the most thrilling of all the evangelist's messages. It is a human document, a leaf in that great book of Christian evidences which God is still writing day by day.

"Twenty-seven years ago I walked down a street in Chicago in company with some ball players who were famous in this world—some of them are dead now—and we went into a saloon. It was Sunday afternoon and we got tanked up and then went and sat down on a corner. I never go by

that street without thanking God for saving me.   It was a
vacant lot at that time.   We sat down on a curbing.   Across
the street a company of men and women were playing on
instruments—horns, flutes and slide trombones—and the
others were singing the gospel hymns that I used to hear
my mother sing back in the log cabin in Iowa and back in
the old church where I used to go to Sunday school.

"And God painted on the canvas of my recollection
and memory a vivid picture of the scenes of other days and
other faces.

"Many have long since turned to dust.   I sobbed and
sobbed and a young man stepped out and said, 'We are
going down to the Pacific Garden Mission.   Won't you come
down to the mission?   I am sure you will enjoy it.   You
can hear drunkards tell how they have been saved and girls
tell how they have been saved from the red-light district.'

"I arose and said to the boys, 'I'm through.   I am going
to Jesus Christ.   We've come to the parting of the ways,'
and I turned my back on them.   Some of them laughed and
some of them mocked me; one of them gave me encouragement; others never said a word.

'Twenty-seven years ago I turned and left that little
group on the corner of State and Madison Streets and walked
to the little mission and fell on my knees and staggered out
of sin and into the arms of the Saviour.

"The next day I had to get out to the ball park and
practice.   Every morning at ten o'clock we had to be out
there.   I never slept that night.   I was afraid of the horse-
laugh that gang would give me because I had taken my stand
for Jesus Christ.

"I walked down to the old ball grounds.   I will never
forget it.   I slipped my key into the wicket gate and the
first man to meet me after I got inside was Mike Kelly.

"Up came Mike Kelly; he said, 'Bill, I'm proud of
you!   Religion is not my long suit, but I'll help you all I
can.'   Up came Anson, the best ball player that ever played
the game; Pfeffer, Clarkson, Flint, Jimmy McCormick,

Burns, Williamson and Dalrymple. There wasn't a fellow in that gang who knocked; every fellow had a word of encouragement for me.

"Mike Kelly was sold to Boston for $10,000. Mike got half of the purchase price. He came up to me and showed me a check for $5,000. John L. Sullivan, the champion fighter, went around with a subscription paper and the boys raised over $12,000 to buy Mike a house.

"They gave Mike a deed to the house and they had $1,500 left and gave him a certificate of deposit for that.

"His salary for playing with Boston was $4,700 a year. At the end of that season Mike had spent the $5,000 purchase price and the $4,700 he received as salary and the $1,500 they gave him and had a mortgage on the house. And when he died in Pennsylvania they went around with a subscription to get money enough to put him in the ground, and each club, twelve in all, in the two leagues gave a month a year to his wife. Mike sat here on the corner with me twenty-seven years ago, when I said, 'Good-bye, boys, I'm going to Jesus Christ.'

"BILL, I'M PROUD OF YOU!"

"A. G. Spalding signed up a team to go around the world. I was the second he asked to sign a contract and Captain Anson was the first. I was sliding to second base one day. I always slid head first, and hit a stone and cut a ligament loose in my knee.

"I got Dr. Magruder, who attended Garfield when he was shot, and he said:

" 'William, if you don't go on that trip I will give you a good leg.' I obeyed and have as good a leg today as I ever had. They offered to wait for me at Honolulu and Australia. Spalding said, 'Meet us in England, and play with us through England, Scotland and Wales.' I didn't go.

"Ed Williamson, our old short-stop, a fellow weighing 225 pounds, was the most active big man you ever saw. He went with them, and while they were on the ship crossing the English channel a storm arose and the captain thought the ship would go down. Williamson tied two life-preservers on himself and one on his wife and dropped on his knees and prayed and promised God to be true. God spoke and the waves were stilled. They came back to the United States and Ed came back to Chicago and started a saloon on Dearborn Street. I would go through there giving tickets for the Y. M. C. A. meetings and would talk with them and he would cry like a baby.

"I would get down and pray for him, and would talk with him. When he died they put him on the table and cut him open and took out his liver and it was so big it would not go in a candy bucket. Kidneys had shriveled until they were like two stones.

"Ed Williamson sat there on the street corner with me, drunk, twenty-seven years ago when I said, 'Good-bye, I'm going to Jesus Christ.'

"Frank Flint, our old catcher, who caught for nineteen years, drew $3,200 a year on an average. He caught before they had chest protectors, masks and gloves. He caught bare-handed. Every bone in the ball of his hand was broken. You never saw such a hand as Frank had. Every bone in his face was broken, and his nose and cheek bones, and the shoulder and ribs had all been broken. He got to drinking, his home was broken up and he went to the dogs.

"I've seen old Frank Flint sleeping on a table in a stale beer joint and I've turned my pockets inside out and said, 'You're welcome to it, old pal.' He drank on and on, and one day in winter he staggered out of a stale beer joint and stood on a corner, and was seized with a fit of coughing. The blood streamed out of his nose, mouth and eyes. Down the street came a wealthy woman. She took one look and said, 'My God, is it you, Frank?' and his wife came up and kissed him.

"She called two policemen and a cab and started with him to her boarding house. They broke all speed regulations. She called five of the best physicians and they listened to the beating of his heart, one, two, three, four, five, six, seven, eight, nine, ten, eleven, twelve, and the doctors said, 'He will be dead in about four hours.' She told them to tell him what they had told her. She said, 'Frank, the end is near,' and he said, 'Send for Bill.'

"They telephoned me and I came. He said, 'There's nothing in the life of years ago I care for now. I can hear the bleachers cheer when I make a hit that wins the game. But there is nothing that can help me out now; and if the umpire calls me out now, won't you say a few words over me, Bill?' He struggled as he had years ago on the diamond, when he tried to reach home, but the great Umpire of the universe yelled, 'You're out!' and waved him to the club house, and the great gladiator of the diamond was no more.

"He sat on the street corner with me, drunk, twenty-seven years ago in Chicago, when I said, 'Good-bye, boys, I'm through.'

"Did they win the game of life or did Bill?"

"First—Are You Kindly Disposed Toward Me?"

"GOD LIKES A LITTLE HUMOR, AS EVIDENCED BY THE FACT THAT HE MADE THE MONKEY, THE PARROT—AND SOME OF YOU PEOPLE."

CHAPTER V

Playing the New Game

It is not necessary to be in a big place to do big things.—BILLY SUNDAY.

IF Billy Sunday had not been an athlete he would not today be the physical marvel in the pulpit that he is; if he had not been reared in the ranks of the plain people he would not have possessed the vocabulary and insight into life which are essential parts of his equipment; if he had not served a long apprenticeship to toil he would not display his present pitiless industry; if he had not been a cog in the machinery of organized base ball, with wide travel and much experience of men, he would not be able to perfect the amazing organization of Sunday evangelistic campaigns; if he had not been a member and elder of a Presbyterian church he could not have resisted the religious vagaries which lead so many evangelists and immature Christian workers astray; if he had not been trained in three years of Y. M. C. A. service he would not today be the flaming and insistent protagonist of personal work that he now is; if he had not been converted definitely and consciously and quickly in a rescue mission he could not now preach his gospel of immediate conversion.

All of which is but another way of saying that Sunday was trained in God's school. God prepared the man for the work he was preparing for him. Only by such uncommon training could this unique messenger of the gospel be produced. A college course doubtless would have submerged Sunday into the level of the commonplace. A theological seminary would have denatured him. Evidently Sunday has learned the lesson of the value of individuality; he prizes it, preaches about it, and practices it. He probably does not know what *"sui generis"* means, but he is it. Over and over again he urges that instead of railing at what we have

not enjoyed, we should magnify what we already possess.
The shepherd's rod of Moses, rightly wielded, may be might-
ier than a king's scepter.

As we approach the development of the unique work of
Billy Sunday, which is without a parallel in the history of
evangelism, we must reckon with those forces which
developed his personality and trace the steps which led him
into his present imperial activity. For he has gone forward
a step at a time.

He followed the wise rule of the rescue mission, that
the saved should say so. At the very beginning he began
to bear testimony to his new faith. Wherever opportunity
offered he spoke a good word for Jesus Christ. In many
towns and cities his testimony was heard in those early
days; and there was not a follower of the base-ball game who
did not know that Billy Sunday was a Christian.

The convert who does not join a church is likely soon
to be in a bad way; so Sunday early united with the Jefferson
Park Presbyterian Church, Chicago. He went into religious activity with all the ardor that he displayed on the
base-ball field. He attended the Christian Endeavor
society, prayer-meeting and the mid-week church service.
This is significant; for it is usually the church members who
are faithful at the mid-week prayer-meetings who are the
vital force in a congregation.

Other rewards than spiritual awaited Sunday at the
prayer-meeting; for there he met Helen A. Thompson, the
young woman who subsequently became his wife. Between
the meeting and the marriage altar there were various
obstacles to be overcome. Another suitor was in the way,
and besides, Miss Thompson's father did not take kindly
to the idea of a professional base-ball player as a possible
son-in-law, for he had old-fashioned Scotch notions of things.
"Love conquers all," and in September, 1888, the young
couple were married, taking their wedding trip by going
on circuit with the base-ball team.

Mrs. Sunday's influence upon her husband has been

extraordinary.   It is a factor to be largely considered in any estimate of the man.   He is a devoted husband, of the American type, and with his ardent loyalty to his wife has complete confidence in her judgment.   She is his man of affairs.   Her Scotch heritage has endowed her with the prudent qualities of that race, and she is the business manager of Mr. Sunday's campaigns.   She it is who holds her generous, careless husband down to a realization of the practicalities of life.

He makes no important decisions without consulting her, and she travels with him nearly all of the time, attending his meetings and watching over his work and his personal well-being like a mother.   In addition Mrs. Sunday does yeoman service in the evangelistic campaigns.

The helplessness of the evangelist without his wife is almost ludicrous: he dislikes to settle any question, whether it be an acceptance of an invitation from a city or the employment of an additional worker, without Mrs. Sunday's counsel.   Frequently he turns vexed problems over to her, and abides implicitly by her decision, without looking into the matter himself at all.

Four children—Helen, George, William and Paul— have been born to the Sundays, two of whom are themselves married.   The modest Sunday home is in Winona Lake, Indiana.   When Mrs. Sunday is absent with her husband, the two younger children are left in the care of a trusted helper.   The evangelist himself is home for only a short period each summer.

Mrs. Sunday was the deciding factor in determining her husband to abandon base ball for distinctively religious work.   A woman of real Scotch piety, in the time of decision she chose the better part.   Her husband had been addressing Y. M. C. A. meetings, Sunday-schools and Christian Endeavor societies.   He was undeniably a poor speaker. No prophet could have foreseen the present master of platform art in the stammering, stumbling young man whose only excuse for addressing public meetings was the eagerness of men to hear the celebrated base-ball player's story.   His speech was merely his testimony, such as is required of all mission converts.

If Sunday could not talk well on his feet he could handle individual men.   His aptness in dealing with men led the Chicago Young Men's Christian Association to offer him an assistant secretaryship in the department of religious work.   It is significant that the base-ball player went into the Y. M. C. A. not as a physical director but in the distinctively spiritual sphere.   He refused an invitation to become physical director; for his religious zeal from the first outshone his physical prowess.

Those three years of work in the Chicago Association bulk large in the development of the evangelist.   They were not all spent in dealing with the unconverted, by any means. · Sunday's tasks included the securing of speakers for noon-day prayer-meetings, the conducting of office routine, the raising of money, the distribution of literature, the visiting of saloons and other places to which invitations should be carried, and the following up of persons who had displayed an interest in the meetings.   Much of it was sanctified drudgery: but it was all drill for destiny. The young man saw at close range and with particular detail what sin could do to men; and he also learned the power of the Gospel to make sinners over.

The evangelist often alludes to those days of personal work in Chicago.   Such stories as the following have been heard by thousands.

A Father Disowned

"While I was in the Y. M. C. A. in Chicago I was standing on the corner one night and a man came along with his toes sticking out and a ragged suit on and a slouch hat and asked me for a dime to get something to eat.   I told him I wouldn't give him a dime because he would go and get a drink.   He said, 'You wouldn't let me starve, would you?' I told him no, but that I wouldn't give him the money.   I asked him to come to the Y. M. C. A. with me and stay until after the meeting and I would take him out and get him a good supper and a bed. He wanted me to do it right away before going to the Y. M. C. A., but I told him that I was working for someone until ten o'clock. So he came up to the meeting and stayed through the meeting and was very much interested. I saw that he used excellent language and questioned him and found that he was a man who had been Adjutant General of one of the Central States and had at one time been the editor of two of the biggest newspapers.

"I went with him after the meeting and got him a supper and a bed and went to some friends and we got his clothes. I asked him if he had any relatives and he said he had one son who was a bank cashier but that he had disowned him and his picture was taken from the family album and his name was never spoken in the house, all because he was now down and out, on account of booze.

"I wrote to the boy and said, 'I've found your father. Send me some money to help him.'

"He wrote back and said for me never to mention his father's name to him again, that it wasn't ever spoken around the house and that his father was forgotten.

"I replied: 'You miserable, low-down wretch. You can't disown your father and refuse to help him because he is down and out. Send me some money or I will publish the story in all of the papers.' He sent me five dollars and that's all I ever got from him. I took care of the old man all winter and in the spring I went to a relief society in Chicago and got him a ticket to his home and put him on the train and that was the last I ever saw of him."

Redeeming a Son

"I stood on the street one Sunday night giving out tickets inviting men to the men's meeting in Farwell Hall. Along came a young fellow, I should judge he was thirty, who looked prematurely old, and he said, 'Pard, will you give me a dime?'

"I said, 'No, sir.'

"'I want to get somethin' to eat.'

"I said, 'You look to me as though you were a booze-fighter.'

"'I am.'

" 'I'll not give you money, but I'll get your supper.'

"He said, 'Come on. I haven't eaten for two days.'

"'My time is not my own until ten o'clock. You go upstairs until then and I'll buy you a good supper and get you a good, warm, clean bed in which to sleep, but I'll not give you the money.'

"He said, 'Thank you, I'll go.' He stayed for the meeting. I saw he was moved, and after the meeting I stood by his side. He wept and I talked to him about Jesus Christ, and he told me this story:

"There were three boys in the family. They lived in Boston. The father died, the will was probated, he was given his portion, took it, started out drinking and gambling. At last he reached Denver, his money was gone, and he got a position as fireman in the Denver and Rio Grande switchyards. His mother kept writing to him, but he told me that he never read the letters. He said that when he saw the postmark and the writing he threw the letter into the firebox, but one day, he couldn't tell why, he opened the letter and it read:

"'Dear —— : I haven't heard from you directly, but I am sure that you must need a mother's care in the far-off West, and unless you answer this in a reasonable time I'm going to Denver to see you.' And she went on pleading, as only a mother could, and closed it: 'Your loving mother.'

"He said, 'I threw the letter in the fire and paid no more heed to it. One day about two weeks later I saw a woman coming down the track and I said to the engineer: "That looks like my mother." She drew near, and I said: "Yes, that's mother." What do you think I did?'

"I said, 'Why you climbed out of your engine, kissed her and asked God to forgive you.'

"He said, 'I did nothing of the kind. I was so low-down, I wouldn't even speak to my mother. She followed me up and down the switchyard and even followed me to my boarding house. I went upstairs, changed my clothes, came down, and she said, "Frank, stay and talk with me." I pushed by her and went out and spent the night in sin. I came back in the morning, changed my clothes and went to work. For four days she followed me up and down the switchyards and then she said, "Frank, you have broken my heart, and I am going away tomorrow."

"'I happened to be near the depot with the engine when she got on the train and she raised the window and said, "Frank, kiss me good-bye." I stood talking with some of my drinking and gambling friends and one man said, "Frank Adsitt, you are a fool to treat your mother like that. Kiss her good-bye." I jerked from him and turned back. I heard the conductor call "All aboard." I heard the bell on the engine ring and the train started out, and I heard my mother cry, "Oh,.Frank, if you won't kiss me good-bye, for God's sake turn and look at me!"

"'Mr. Sunday, when the train on the Burlington Railroad pulled out of Denver, I stood with my back to my mother. That's been nine years ago and I have never seen nor heard from her.'

"I led him to Jesus. I got him a position in the old

"FRANK, KISS ME GOOD-BYE!"

Exposition building on the lake front.   He gave me the money he didn't need for board and washing.   I kept his money for months.   He came to me one day and asked for it.

"He used to come to the noon meetings every day. Finally I missed him, and I didn't see him again until in June, 1893, during the World's Fair he walked into the Y. M. C. A.   I said, 'Why, Frank, how do you do?'

"He said, 'How do you know me?'

"I said, 'I have never forgotten you; how is your mother?'

"He smiled, then his face quickly changed to sadness, and he said, 'She is across the street in the Brevoort House. I am taking her to California to fill her last days with sunshine.'

"Three months later, out in Pasadena, she called him to her bedside, drew him down, kissed him, and said, 'Good-bye; I can die happy because I know my boy is a Christian.'"

The Gambler

"I have reached down into the slime, and have been privileged to help tens of thousands out of the mire of sin— and I believe that most of them will be saved, too.   I've helped men in all walks of life.   When I was in Chicago I helped a man and got him a position, and so was able to restore him to his wife and children.   One night a fellow came to me and told me that the man was playing faro bank down on Clark Street.   I said: 'Why that can hardly be—I took dinner with him only a few hours ago.'

"But my informant had told me the truth, so I put on my coat and went down LaSalle Street and past the New York Life Building and along up the stairway to the gambling room.   I went past the big doorkeeper, and I found a lot of men in there, playing keno and faro bank and roulette and stud and draw poker.   I saw my man there, just playing a hand.   In a moment he walked over to the bar and ordered a Rhine wine and seltzer.

THE PACIFIC GARDEN MISSION IN CHICAGO, WHERE BILLY SUNDAY WAS CONVERTED.

"I'll Fight till Hell Freezes Over."

"I walked over and touched him on the shoulder, and he looked and turned pale. I said, 'Come out of this. Come with me.' He said, 'Here's my money,' and pulled $144 from his pocket and handed it to me. 'I don't want your money.' He refused at first, and it was one o'clock in the morning before I got him away from there. I took him home and talked to him, then I sent down into Ohio for an old uncle of his, for he had forged notes amounting to $2,000 or so, and we had to get him out of trouble. We got him all fixed up and we got him a job selling relief maps, and he made $5,000 a year.

"I didn't hear from him for a long time; then one day Jailor Whitman called me up and told me that Tom Barrett, an old ball player I knew well, wanted me to come up and see a man who had been sentenced to the penitentiary. I went down to the jail and the prisoner was my friend. I asked him what was the matter, and he said that he and some other fellows had framed up a plan to stick up a jewelry store. He was caught and the others got away. He wouldn't snitch, and so he was going down to Joliet on an indeterminate sentence of from one to fourteen years. He said: 'You are the only man that will help me. Will you do it?'

"I said: 'I won't help you, I won't spend so much as a postage stamp on you if you are going to play me dirt again!' He promised to do better as soon as he got out, and I wrote a letter to my friend, Andy Russell, chairman of the board of pardons. He took up the case and we got my friend's sentence cut down to a maximum of five years.

"Time passed again, and one day he came in dressed fit to kill. He had on an $80 overcoat, a $50 suit, a $4 necktie, a pair of patent leather shoes that cost $15, shirt buttons as big as hickory nuts and diamond cuff buttons. He walked up to my desk in the Y. M. C. A. and pulled out a roll of bills. There were a lot of them—yellow fellows. I noticed that there was one for $500. There was over $4,500 in the roll. He said: 'I won it last night at faro bank.' He asked me to go out to dinner with him and I went.   We had everything on the bill of fare, from soup to nuts, and the check was $7.60 apiece for two suppers.   I've never had such a dinner since.

"We talked things over.   He said he was making money hand over fist—that he could make more in a week than I could in a year.   I was working at the Y. M. C. A. for $83 a month, and then not getting it, and base-ball managers were making me tempting offers of good money to go back into the game at $500 to $1,000 a month to finish the season.   But I wouldn't do it.   Nobody called me a grafter then.   'Well,' I said to my friend, 'old man, you may have more at the end of the year than I've got— maybe I won't have carfare—but I'll be ahead of you.'

"Where is he now?   Down at Joliet, where there is a big walled institution and where the stripes on your clothes run crossways."

A Living Testimony

"I had a friend who was a brilliant young fellow.   He covered the Chino-Japanese war for a New York paper. He was on his way home when he was shipwrecked, and the captain and he were on an island living on roots for a week and then they signaled a steamer and got started home.   He got word from the New York *Tribune* and they told him to go to Frisco, so he went, and they told him to come across the arid country and write up the prospects of irrigation.   And as he walked across those plains, he thought of how they would blossom if they were only irrigated.   Then he thought of how his life was like that desert, with nothing in it but waste.

"He got to Chicago and got a job on the *Times* and lost it on account of drunkenness, and couldn't get another on account of having no recommendation.   So he walked out one winter night and took his reporter's book, addressed it to his father, and wrote something like this: 'I've made a miserable failure of this life.   I've disgraced you and sent mother to a premature grave.   If you care to look for me you'll find my body in the Chicago River.' He tossed aside the book and it fell on the snow.

"He leaped to the rail of the bridge, but a policeman who had been watching him sprang and caught him. He begged him to let him leap, but the policeman wouldn't do it and got his story from him. Then the policeman said, 'Well, I don't know whether you're stringing me or not, but if half of what you say is true you can make a big thing out of life. I'm not much on religion, but I'll show you a place where they will keep you,' and he took him to the Pacific Garden Mission at 100 East Van Buren Street, which for 13,000 nights has had its doors open every night.

"He went in and sat down by a bum. He read some of the mottos, like 'When did you write to mother last?' and they began to work on him and he asked the bum what graft they got out of this. The bum flared right up and said there was no graft, that Mrs. Clark had just mortgaged her home for $3,000 to pay back rent. Then he told him he could sleep right there and go down in the morning and get something to eat free, and if he could not land a bed by next night he could come back to one of the benches. Then my friend got up and told him the story of Jesus Christ, and the young man went down and accepted Christ. He was so full of gold bromide cures that he tingled when he talked and he jingled when he walked.

"He started out to give his testimony and he was a marvelous power. I met him some time later in an elevator in Chicago, and he was dressed to kill with a silk lid and a big diamond and the latest cut Prince Albert, and he said, 'Bill, that was a great day for me. I started out with not enough clothes to make a tail for a kite or a pad for a crutch and now look at me.' He was secretary in the firm of Morgan & Wright, and was drawing $175 a month. He is an expert stenographer. A newspaper in New York had written him to take an associate editorship, but I told him not to do it, to stay where he was and tell his story."

The next class in the University of Experience which Sunday entered was that of professional evangelistic work, in association with Rev. J. Wilbur Chapman, D.D., the well-known Presbyterian evangelist. This invitation came after three years of service in the Chicago Y. M. C. A. Not yet to platform speaking as his chief task was Sunday called. Far from it. He was a sort of general roustabout for the evangelist. His duties were multifarious. He was advance agent, going ahead to arrange meetings, to organize choirs, to help the local committee of arrangements with its advertising or other preparations, and, in general, tying up all loose ends. When tents were used he would help erect them with his own hands; the fists that so sturdily beat pulpits today, have often driven home tent pegs. Sunday sold the evangelist's song books and sermons at the meetings; helped take up the collection, and, when need arose, spoke from the platform. The persons who wonder at the amazing efficiency for organization displayed by Sunday overlook this unique apprenticeship to a distinguished evangelist. He is a "practical man" in every aspect of evangelistic campaigns, from organizing a local committee and building the auditorium, to handling and training the converts who come forward.

The providence of all this is clear in retrospect: but as for Sunday himself, he was being led by a way that he knew not.

CHAPTER VI

A Shut Door—and an Open One

Faith is the beginning of something of which you can't see the end but in which you believe.—BILLY SUNDAY.

DESTINY'S door turns on small hinges. Almost everybody can say out of his own experience, "If I had done this, instead of that, the whole course of my life would have been changed." At many points in the career of William A. Sunday we see what intrinsically small and unrelated incidents determined his future course in life.

If he had not been sitting on that Chicago curbstone one evening, and if the Pacific Garden Mission workers had failed on that one occasion alone to go forth into the highways, Billy Sunday might have been only one of the multitude of forgotten base-ball players. If he had not gone to prayer-meeting in his new church home he would not have met the wife who has been so largely a determining factor in his work. If he had not joined the Y. M. C. A. forces in Chicago he would not have become Peter Bilhorn's friend and so Dr. Chapman's assistant.

And—here we come to a very human story—if Dr. J. Wilbur Chapman had not suddenly decided to abandon the evangelistic field and return to the pastorate of Bethany Presbyterian Church in Philadelphia, Sunday would doubtless still be unknown to the world as a great religious leader. The story came to me from the lips of the evangelist himself one morning. We were discussing certain current criticisms of his work and he showed himself frankly bewildered as well as pained by the hostility displayed toward him on the part of those up to whom he looked as leaders and counselors. Off the platform Sunday is one of the most childlike and guileless of men. He grew reminiscent and confidential as he said to me: "I don't see why they hammer me so. I have just gone on, as the Lord opened the way, trying to do his work. I had no plan for this sort of thing. It is all the Lord's doings. Just look how it all began, and how wonderfully the Lord has cared for me.

"I had given up my Y. M. C. A. work, and was helping Chapman, doing all sorts of jobs—putting up tents, straightening out chairs after the meetings and occasionally speaking. Then, all of a sudden, during the holidays of 1895–96, I had a telegram from Chapman saying that our work was all off, because he had decided to return to Bethany Church.

"There I was, out of work, knowing not which way to turn. I had a wife and two children to support. I could not go back to base ball. I had given up my Y. M. C. A. position. I had no money. What should I do? I laid it before the Lord, and in a short while there came a telegram from a little town named Garner, out in Iowa, asking me to come out and conduct some meetings. I didn't know anybody out there, and I don't know yet why they ever asked me to hold meetings. But I went.

"I only had eight sermons, so could not run more than ten days, and that only by taking Saturdays off. That was the beginning of my independent work; but from that day to this I have never had to seek a call to do evangelistic work. I have just gone along, entering the doors that the Lord has opened one after another. Now I have about a hundred sermons and invitations for more than two years in advance. I have tried to be true to the Lord and to do just what he wants me to do."

That naïve bit of autobiography reveals the real Billy Sunday. He has gone forward as the doors have been providentially opened. His career has not been shrewdly planned by himself. Nobody has been more surprised at his success than he. Of him may be recorded the lines that are inscribed on Emerson's tombstone in Sleepy Hollow Cemetery, Concord:

"The passive master lent his hand
To the vast Soul that o'er him planned."

From Garner, Iowa, to Philadelphia, with its most
eminent citizens on the committee of arrangements, seems a
far cry; but the path is plainly one of Providence. Sunday
has added to his addresses gleanings from many sources,
but he has not abated the simplicity of his message. The
gospel he preaches today is that which he heard in the Pacific
Garden Rescue Mission a quarter of a century ago.

In childlike faith, this man of straight and unshaded
thinking has gone forward to whatever work has offered
itself. Nobody knows better than he that it is by no powers
of his own that mighty results have been achieved: "This
is the Lord's doing; it is marvelous in our eyes."

While the Sunday meetings have swung a wide orbit
they have centered in the Middle West. That typically
American section of the country was quick to appreciate
the evangelist's character and message. He was of them,
"bone of their bone, flesh of their flesh," mind of their mind.

When news of the triumphs of this evangelist's uncon-
ventionally-phrased gospel began to be carried over the
country a few years ago, the verdict of religious leaders was,
"Billy Sunday may do for the Middle West, but the East
will not stand him." Since then, again, to the confusion
of human wisdom, his most notable work has been achieved
in the East, in the great cities of Pittsburgh and Scranton;
and at this writing the city of Philadelphia is in the midst
of preparations for a Sunday campaign; while the Baltimore
churches have also invited him to conduct meetings with
them. Billy Sunday is now a national figure—and the
foremost personality on the day's religious horizon. A
recent issue of The American Magazine carried the results
of a voting contest, "Who's the Greatest Man in America."
Only one other clergyman (Bishop Vincent, of Chautauqua)
was mentioned at all, but Billy Sunday was tied with
Andrew Carnegie and Judge Lindsey for eighth place.

To tell the stories of the Sunday campaigns in detail would be needless repetition; with occasional exceptions they continue to grow in scope and efficiency and results. The record of independent campaigns extends over nearly twenty years, and in that time the evangelist has gone on from strength to strength.

BURNING WORDS OF MR. SUNDAY THAT REACH THE HEART.

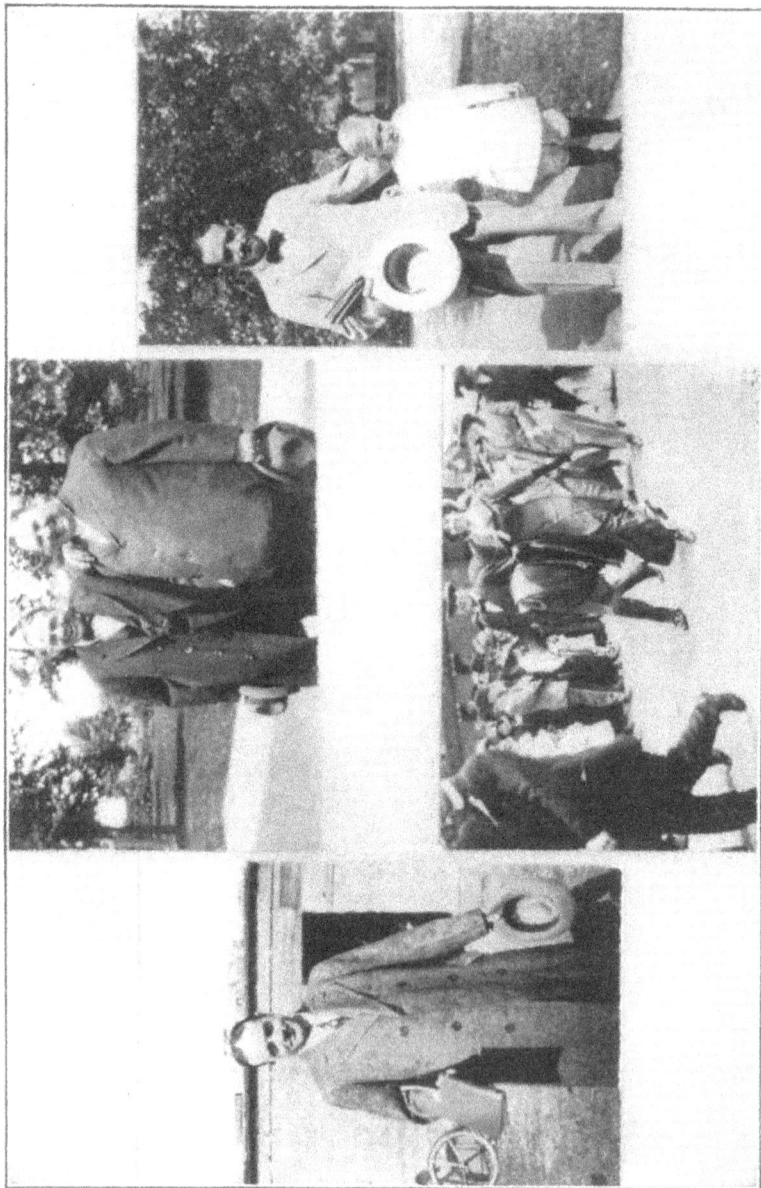

SUNDAY POSING IN FRONT   BILLY'S SMILE.   SUNDAY AND HIS
  OF TABERNACLE.   MR. AND MRS. SUNDAY IN A REVIVAL PARADE.   YOUNGEST SON PAUL.

CHAPTER VII

Campaigning for Christ

Let's quit fiddling with religion and do something to bring the world to Christ.—BILLY SUNDAY.

HIS American birthright of plain common sense stands Sunday in stead of theological training. He is "a practical man," as mechanics say. Kipling's poem on "The American" hits off Sunday exactly:

> "He turns a keen, untroubled face
> Home to the instant need of things."

So a Sunday evangelistic campaign is a marvel of organization. It spells efficiency at every turn and is a lesson to the communities which do Christian work in haphazard, hit-or-miss fashion. Work and faith are written large over every series of Sunday meetings.

Sunday never took a course in psychology, but he understands the crowd mind. He knows how to deal with multitudes. He sees clearly where the masses must come from, and so he sets to work to bring them out of the homes of the working people. He goes beyond the church circles for his congregations, and makes his appeal to the popular taste. He frankly aims to strike the average of the common people. For he is after that host which too often the preacher knows nothing about.

People must be set to talking about religion and about the Sunday campaign if the latter is to succeed. Indifference is the foe of all foes to be feared by an evangelist. Even hostile criticism really serves a religious purpose, for it directs attention to the messenger and the message. Knowledge of this is the reason why Sunday always devotes his earliest sermons in a campaign to the subjects likeliest to

create comment.   These are the discourses that contain
the largest proportion of startling views and language.

Part of the task of a man who would move a city for
Christ is to consolidate Christian sentiment and to create
a Church consciousness.   Sunday is at great pains to get
his own "crowd" behind him.   He evokes that loyalty
which alone makes organized work and war effective.

So he insists that churches must unite before he will
visit a city.   Also he asks that they surrender their Sunday
services, all uniting in common worship in the Tabernacle.
For these campaigns are not Billy Sunday meetings: they
are an effort toward a revival of religion on the part of the
united Christian forces of a community.   If anybody thinks
the evangelist disparages the Church, he need but recall the
particular effort Sunday makes to solidify the Church folk:
that reveals his real estimate of the Church.   He would no
more attempt a revival without church co-operation than a
general would besiege a city without an army.   This
Christian unity which he requires first of all is a sermon in
itself.

Before one has looked very deeply into the work of
Evangelist Sunday he perceives that it is no new message
the man speaks, but that it is his modernization of language
and of methods that makes possible the achieving of great
results by the old Gospel.

The preacher of a generation ago would have counted
it indecorous to make use of the public press.   Sunday
depends largely upon the newspapers for spreading his
message and promoting interest in the meetings.   He does
not employ a press agent; he simply extends to the local
press all the facilities and co-operation in his power.   He is
always accessible to the reporters and ever ready to assist
in their work in any proper fashion.   He makes public
announcements frequently in his meetings of the cordial
assistance he has received from the newspapers.

Without any expense to anybody and without any
scientific experience in this particular field, Sunday has

demonstrated the power of Christian publicity. The newspapers carry his messages all over the world. The Pittsburgh dailies published special "Sunday Editions." They had thousands of subscribers for the issues containing the evangelist's sermons and many persons have been converted by reading the newspaper accounts of the Sunday meetings. One cherished story tells of a young man in China who had been converted thirteen thousand miles away from the spot where the evangelist was speaking. Sunday makes religion "live news." Editors are glad to have copy about him and his work, and about anything that pertains to the campaigns. The uniform experience of the communities he has visited is that the Church has had more publicity through his visit than on any other occasion.

After Sunday has accepted a city's invitation and a date has been fixed for the meetings, and the time has drawn near, he·gets the Church people to organize. Before ever a hammer has struck a blow in the building of the Sunday Tabernacle,·the people have been meeting daily in the homes of the city for concerted prayer for the Divine favor upon the campaign.

By the Sunday system of work, every few blocks in the city is made a center for cottage prayer-meetings. No politician ever divided a community more carefully than do the Sunday workers in arranging for these prayer-meetings. Every section of the city is covered and every block and street. By preference, the meetings are held in the homes of the unconverted, and it is a normal experience for conversions to be reported before ever the evangelist arrives. In Scranton the city was divided into nine districts besides the suburbs and these districts were again sub-divided so that one had as many as eighty-four prayer groups. The total proportions of this kind of work are illustrated by the Pittsburgh figures: Between December 2 and December 26, 4,137 prayer meetings in private houses were held, having a combined attendance of 68,360 persons. The following table covers eight meetings, as follows:

	No. of Meetings	Attendance	Prayers	Men	Women
December 2...	562	8,394	3,362	1,658	6,736
December 5..	579	8,909	3,667	1,931	6,978
December 9..	586	10,667	4,271	2,221	8,446
December 12..	410	6,532	2,753	1,410	5,122
December 16..	705	16,257	5,588	3,489	12,617
December 19..	590	8,580	4,602	2,027	6,553
December 23..	398	6,014	2,347	2,381	3,633
December 26..	307	5,388	1,983	1,179	4,209

When tens of thousands of earnest Christians are meeting constantly for united prayer a spirit of expectancy and unity is created which makes sure the success of the revival. Incidentally, there is a welding together of Christian forces that will abide long after the evangelist has gone. These preliminary prayer-meetings are a revelation of the tremendous possibilities inherent in the churches of any community. With such a sea of prayer buoying him up any preacher could have a revival.

Sagaciously, Sunday throws all responsibility back on the churches. While he takes command of the ship when he arrives, yet he does all in his power to prevent the campaign from being a one-man affair. The local committee must underwrite the expenses; for these campaigns are not to be financed by the gifts of the wealthy, but by the rank and file of the church membership accepting responsibility of the work. The guarantees are underwritten in the form of shares and each guarantor receives a receipt for his shares to be preserved as a memento of the campaign. True, no guarantor ever had to pay a dollar on his Billy Sunday campaign subscription, for the evangelist himself raises all of the expense money in the early meetings of the series.

John the Baptist was only a voice: but Billy Sunday is a voice, plus a bewildering array of committees and assistants and organized machinery. He has committees galore to co-operate in his work: a drilled army of the Lord. In the list of Scranton workers that is before me I see tabulated an executive committee, the directors, a prayer-meeting committee, an entertainment committee, an usher committee, a dinner committee, a business women's committee, a building committee, a nursery committee, a personal workers' committee, a decorating committee, a shop-meetings committee—and then a whole list of churches and religious organizations in the city as ex-officio workers!

Wherever he goes Sunday erects a special tabernacle for his meetings. There are many reasons for this. The very building of a tabernacle dedicated to this one special use helps create an interest in the campaign as something new come to town. But, primarily, the evangelist's purposes are practical. In the first place, everything has to be on the ground floor. Converts cannot come forward from a gallery. In addition, existing big buildings rarely have proper acoustics. Most of all Sunday, who has a dread of panics or accidents happening in connection with his meetings, stresses the point that in his tabernacle people have their feet on the ground. There is nothing to give way with them. The sawdust and tan bark is warm, dustless, sanitary, fireproof and noiseless. "When a crowd gets to walking on a wooden floor," said Sunday—and then he made a motion of sheer disgust that shows how sensitive he is to any sort of disturbance—"it's the limit."

One of his idiosyncrasies is that he must have a perfectly still audience. He will stop in the midst of a sermon to let a single person walk down the aisle. When auditors start coughing he stops preaching. He never lets his crowd get for an instant out of hand. The result is that there probably never were so many persons gathered together in one building at one time in such uniform quietness.

The possibilities of panic in a massed multitude of thousands are best understood by those who have had most to do with crowds. Sunday's watchfulness against this marks the shrewd American caution of the man. His tabernacles, no matter whether they seat five, eight, ten, fifteen, or twenty thousand persons, are all built under the direction of his own helper, who has traveled with him for years. He knows that nothing will break down, or go askew. His tabernacles are fairly panic-proof. Thus every aisle, lengthwise and crosswise, ends in a door.

So careful is he of the emergency that might arise for a quick exit that no board in the whole tabernacle is fastened with more than two nails; so that one could put his foot through the side of the wall if there was need to get out hurriedly. Describing the building of the choir platform Sunday says, with a grim shutting of his jaws: "You could run a locomotive over it and never faze it." His own platform, on which he does amazing gymnastic stunts at every meeting, is made to withstand all shocks. About the walls of the tabernacle are fire extinguishers, and a squad of firemen and policemen are on duty with every audience.

There is nothing about a Sunday tabernacle to suggest a cathedral. It is a big turtle-back barn of raw, unfinished timber, but it has been constructed for its special purpose, and every mechanical device is used to assist the speaker's voice. Sunday can make twenty-five thousand persons hear perfectly in one of his big tabernacles. A huge sounding board, more useful than beautiful, hangs like an inverted sugar scoop over the evangelist's platform.

Behind the platform is the post office, to which the names of converts are sent for the city pastors every day; and here also are the telephones for the use of the press. Adjoining the tabernacle is a nursery for babies, and an emergency hospital with a nurse in attendance. It seems as if no detail of efficient service has been overlooked by this practical westerner. So well organized is everything that the collection can be taken in an audience of eight thousand persons within three minutes.

While touching upon collections, this is as good a place as any to raise the point of Mr. Sunday's own compensation. He receives a free-will offering made on the last day. The offerings taken in the early weeks are to meet the expenses of the local committee. Mr. Sunday has nothing to do with this. This committee also pays approximately half of the expenses of his staff of workers, and it also provides a home for the Sunday party during their sojourn.   Mr. Sunday himself pays the balance of the expenses of his workers out of the free-will offering which he receives on the last day.   These gifts have reached large figures—forty-four thousand dollars in the Pittsburgh campaign.

There is a quality in human nature which will not associate money with religion, and while we hear nobody grumble at a city's paying thousands of dollars a night for a grand opera performance;   yet an evangelist who has sweetened up an entire city, lessened the police expense, promoted the general happiness and redeemed hundreds of thousands of lives from open sin to godliness, is accused of mercenariness, because those whom he has served give him a lavish offering as he departs.

Although much criticized on the subject of money, Mr. Sunday steadfastly refuses to make answer to these strictures or to render an accounting, insisting that this is entirely a personal matter with him.   Nobody who knows him doubts his personal generosity or his sense of stewardship.   Intimate friends say that he tithes his income.

Three important departments of the Sunday organization are the choir, the ushers, and the personal-work secretaries. Concerning the first more will be said in a later chapter. The ushers are by no means ornamental functionaries. They are a drilled regiment, each with his station of duty and all disciplined to meet any emergency that may arise. In addition to seating the people and taking the collection, they have the difficult task of assisting the officers to keep out the overflow crowds who try to press into the building that has been filled to its legal capacity.   For it is quite a normal condition in the Sunday campaigns for thousands of persons to try to crowd their way into the tabernacle after the latter is full.   Sometimes it takes foot-ball tactics to keep them out.

Without the assistance of the personal-work secretaries the rush forward when the invitation is extended would

mean a frantic mob. The recruits have to be formed
into line and directed to the pulpit where they take Mr.
Sunday's hand. Then they must be guided into the front
benches and the name and address and church preference
of each secured. While the invitation is being given personal
workers all over the building are busy gathering converts.
The magnitude of the Sunday evangelistic meetings in their
results is revealed by the necessity for systematically handling the converts as vividly as by any other one factor.

The tabernacle by no means houses all of the Sunday
campaign. There are noon shop meetings, there are noon
meetings for business women and luncheon meetings, there
are services in the schools, in the jails, in the hospitals, and
there are special afternoon parlor meetings where social
leaders hear the same message that is given to the men of
the street. In a phrase, the entire community is combed by
personal activity in order to reach everybody with the
Sunday evangelistic invitation.

The personnel of the Sunday party has varied during
the years. The first assistant was Fred G. Fischer, a soloist
and choir leader who continued with the evangelist for
eight years. At present the staff numbers about a dozen
workers. Among past and present helpers have been Homer
A. Rodeheaver, the chorister; Charles Butler, the soloist;
Elijah J. Brown ("Ram's Horn" Brown); Fred. R. Seibert,
an ex-cowboy and a graduate of the Moody School, who is
the handy man of the tabernacle; Miss Frances Miller,
Miss Grace Saxe, Miss Anna MacLaren, Mrs. Rae Muirhead,
Rev. L. K. Peacock, B. D. Ackley, Albert G. Gill, Joseph
Speice, the builder, Mrs. and Mr. Asher and Rev. I. E.
Honeywell. As the magnitude of the work increases this
force is steadily augmented, so that the evangelist must
not only be a prophet but a captain of industry.

The Sunday Campaign clearly reveals that as Kipling's
old engineer, McAndrew, says,

"Ye'll understand, a man must think o' things."

Billy Sunday and His Staff at Scranton. From Left to Right: (standing) F. R. Seibert, A. G. Gill; (sitting) B. D. Ackley, Miss Frances Miller, Miss Grace Saxe, Mr. Sunday.

"I'll Fight to the Last Ditch, this Hellish Traffic."

CHAPTER VIII

" Speech—Seasoned with Salt "

I want to preach the gospel so plainly that men can come from the factories and not have to bring along a dictionary.—BILLY SUNDAY.

SUNDAY is not a shepherd, but a soldier; not a husbandman of a vineyard, but a quarryman. The rôle he fills more nearly approximates that of the Baptist, or one of the Old Testament prophets, than any other Bible character. The word of the Lord that has come to him is not "Comfort ye! comfort ye!" but "Arouse ye! arouse ye!" and "Repent! repent!"

Evangelist Sunday's mission is not conventional, nor may it be judged by conventional standards. He is not a pastor; probably he would be a failure in the pastorate. Neither would any sensible person expect pastors to resemble Billy Sunday; for that, too, would be a calamity.

Taking a reasonable view of the case, what do we find? Here is a man whose clear work it is to attract the attention of the heedless to the claims of the gospel, to awaken a somnolent Church, and to call men to repentance. To do this a man must be sensational, just as John the Baptist was sensational—not to mention that Greater One who drew the multitudes by his wonderful works and by his unconventional speech.

In the time of Jesus, as now, religion had become embalmed in petrified phrases. The forms of religious speech were set. But Christ's talk was not different from everyday speech. The language of spirituality, which once represented great living verities, had become so conventionalized that it slipped easily into cant and "shop talk." It is a fact which we scarcely like to admit that myriads of persons who attend church regularly do not expect really to understand what the preacher is talking about.

They admire his "zeal" or "unction," but as for understanding him as clearly and definitely as they understand a neighbor talking over the back fence—that is not to be thought of.

When God called this man whom the common people should hear gladly, he took him straight out of the walks of common life with no other vocabulary than that of ordinary "folks." We Americans use the most vivid language of any people. Our words are alive, new ones being born every hour. "Slang" we call these word pictures, and bar them from polite speech until the crowbar of custom has jimmied a way for them into the dictionary. And the most productive slang factory of our time is the realm of sports in which Sunday was trained.

So he talks religion as he talked base ball. His words smack of the street corners, the shop, the athletic field, the crowd of men. That this speech is loose, extravagant and undignified may be freely granted: but it is understandable. Any kind of a fair play that will get the runners to the home plate is good base ball; and any speech that will puncture the shell of human nature's complacency and indifference to religion is good preaching. Neither John the Baptist nor Jesus was dignified, and highly correct Pharisees despised them as vulgarians; "but the common people heard him gladly." With such examples before him on one side, and a Church waterlogged with dignity on the other, Sunday has "gone the limit" in popularized speech.

Perhaps he is not as polite as is professionally proper for a preacher. He seems to have recovered some of the prophet's lost art of denunciation. He dares call sin by its proper name. He excoriates the hypocrite. He cares not for feelings of the unfaithful preacher or of the double-living church member. As for the devil and all his lieutenants, Sunday has for them a sizzling, blistering vocabulary that helps men to loathe sin and all its advocates. His uncompromising attitude is shown by this gem, culled from one of his sermons:

"They say to me, 'Bill, you rub the fur the wrong way.' I don't; let the cats turn 'round."

Again, "It isn't a good thing to have synonyms for sin. Adultery is adultery, even though you call it affinity."

Again, "Paul said he would rather speak five words that were understood than ten thousand words in an unknown tongue. That hits me. I want people to know what I mean, and that's why I try to get down where they live. What do I care if some puff-eyed, dainty little dibbly-dibbly preacher goes tibbly-tibbling around because I use plain Anglo-Saxon words."

Two important points are to be considered in connection with Sunday's vigorous vocabulary; the first is that what he says does not sound as bad as it seems in cold type. Often he is incorrectly reported. The constant contention of his friends is that he should be heard before being criticized. The volume of testimony of all the men who have heard him—preachers, professors and purists—is that his addresses which seem shocking when reported are not shocking when heard.

On the public square in Scranton a great sign was displayed by the local committee:

BE FAIR!

DON'T JUDGE BILLY SUNDAY UNTIL YOU

HAVE HEARD HIM YOURSELF.

NO REPORT, VERBAL OR PRINTED, CAN

DO HIM PERFECT JUSTICE.

One Scranton business man put it this way: "Type is cold; his sermons are hot."

Sunday speaks with his eyes, with his gestures and with every muscle of his body; and all this must be taken into account in weighing his words.   Assuredly his message in its totality does not shock anybody.   That is why preachers sit through his arraignment of a deficient church and ministry and applaud him.   They find in his severest utterances a substantial volume of undoubted truth.

The second point is that the most vigorous speech is used earliest in an evangelistic campaign.   That is one way of stirring up the Church, and of attracting attention to the meetings.   Sunday goads Christians to an interest. Apparently he purposely speaks to arouse resentment, if no other form of interest is awakened in his hearers.   The latter part of a Sunday campaign is singularly free from his denunciations, from his invective and from his slang. There is a clear method in his procedure, which is always followed in about the same course.

Sunday would be the last man to expect everybody to approve all that he says, either in form or in substance. I don't; and I know no other thinking observer of his meetings who does.   No more do I expect him to approve all that is said in this book.   Nevertheless, there remains the unanswerable rejoinder to all criticism of Evangelist Sunday's utterances and message: he "delivers the goods." He does arouse communities to an interest in religion as no other preacher of our generation.   He helps people "get right with God."   His campaigns promote righteousness, diminish wickedness and strengthen the Church.

As samples of the pungent sort of speech with which Sunday's discourses are flavored I have selected these shakings from his salt-celler:

Live so that when the final summons comes you will leave something more behind you than an epitaph on a tombstone or an obituary in a newspaper.

You can find anything in the average church today, from a humming bird to a turkey buzzard.

The Lord is not compelled to use theologians.   He can take snakes, sticks or anything else, and use them for the advancement of his cause.

The Lord may have to pile a coffin on your back before he can get you to bend it.

Don't throw your ticket away when the train goes into a tunnel. It will come out the other side.

The safest pilot is not the fellow that wears the biggest hat, but the man who knows the channels.

If a man goes to hell he ought to be there, or he wouldn't be there.

I am preaching for the age in which I live. I am just recasting my vocabulary to suit the people of my age instead of Joshua's age.

The Church gives the people what they need; the theater gives them what they want.

Death-bed repentance is burning the candle of life in the service of the devil, and then blowing the smoke into the face of God.

Your reputation is what people say about you. Your character is what God and your wife know about you.

When your heart is breaking you don't want the dancing master or saloon-keeper. No, you want the preacher.

Don't you know that every bad man in a community strengthens the devil's mortgage?

Pilate washed his hands. If he had washed his old black heart he would have been all right.

It takes a big man to see other people succeed without raising a howl.

It's everybody's business how you live.

Bring your repentance down to a spot-cash basis.

I believe that cards and dancing are doing more to dam the spiritual life of the Church than the grog-shops—though you can't accuse me of being a friend of that stinking, dirty, rotten, hell-soaked business.

If you took no more care of yourself physically than spiritually, you'd be just as dried up physically as you are spiritually.

We place too much reliance upon preaching and upon singing, and too little on the living of those who sit in the pews.

The carpet in front of the mirrors of some of you people is worn threadbare, while at the side of your bed where you should kneel in prayer it is as good as the day you put it down.

Some persons think they have to look like a hedgehog to be pious.

Look into the preaching Jesus did and you will find it was aimed straight at the big sinners on the front seats.

If you live wrong you can't die right.

"You are weighed in the balance"—but not by Bradstreet's or Dun's—you are weighed in God's balance.

A revival gives the Church a little digitalis instead of an opiate.

It isn't the sawdust trail that brings you to Christ, it's the Christ that is in the trail, the Christ that is in your public confession of sins.

Some sermons instead of being a bugle call for service, are nothing more than showers of spiritual cocaine.

Theology bears the same relation to Christianity that botany does to flowers.

Morality isn't the light; it is only the polish on the candlestick.

Some homes need a hickory switch a good deal more than they do a piano.

Churches don't need new members half so much as they need the old bunch made over.

God's work is too often side-tracked, while social, business and domestic arrangements are thundering through on the main line.

A lot of people, from the way they live, make you think they've got a ticket to heaven on a Pullman parlor car and have ordered the porter to wake 'em up when they get there. But they'll get side-tracked almost before they've started.

I believe that a long step toward public morality will have been taken when sins are called by their right names.

The bars of the Church are so low that any old hog with two or three suits of clothes and a bank roll can crawl through.

You will not have power until there is nothing questionable in your life.

You can't measure manhood with a tape line around the biceps.

The social life is the reflex of the home life.

There are some so-called Christian homes today with books on the shelves of the library that have no more business there than a rattler crawling about on the floor, or poison within the child's reach.

Home is the place we love best and grumble the most.

I don't believe there are devils enough in hell to pull a boy out of the arms of a godly mother.

To train a boy in the way he should go you must go that way yourself.

The man who lives for himself alone will be the sole mourner at his own funeral.

Don't try to cover up the cussedness of your life, but get fixed up.

Wrong company soon makes everything else wrong. An angel would never be able to get back to heaven again if he came down here for a week and put in his time going with company that some church members would consider good.

The devil often grinds the axe with which God hews.

I wish the Church were as afraid of imperfection as it is of perfection.

Whisky is all right in its place—but its place is in hell.

A pup barks more than an old dog.

Character needs no epitaph. You can bury the man, but character will beat the hearse back from the graveyard and it will travel up and down the streets while you are under the sod.   It will bless or blight long after your name is forgotten.

Some people pray like a jack-rabbit eating cabbage.

If you put a polecat in the parlor you know which will change first—the polecat or the parlor?

A church is not dropped down on a street corner to decorate the corner and be the property of a certain denomination.

Many preachers are like a physician—strong on diagnosis, but weak on therapeutics.

Your religion is in your will, not in your handkerchief.

It won't save your soul if your wife is a Christian.   You have got to be something more than a brother-in-law to the Church.

If every black cloud had a cyclone in it, the world would have been blown into tooth-picks long ago.

No man has any business to be in a bad business.

When you quit living like the devil I will quit preaching that way.

You can't raise the standard of women's morals by raising their pay envelope.   It lies deeper than that.

The seventh commandment is not: "Thou shalt not commit affinity."

A saloon-keeper and a good mother don't pull on the same rope.

The presumptive husband should be able to show more than the price of a marriage license.

Put the kicking straps on the old Adam, feed the angel in you, and starve the devil.

When a baby is born, what do you do with it?   Put it in a refrigerator?   That's a good place for a dead chicken, and cold meat, but a poor place for babies.   Then don't put these new converts, 'babes in Christ,' into refrigerator churches.

"Billy" and "Ma" Sunday.

Copyright, 1908, by C. U. Williams.
"You Old Hypocrite!"

Copyright, 1908, by C. U. Williams.
"It's Up to You."

Nobody can read the Bible thoughtfully, and not be impressed with the way it upholds the manhood of man. More chapters in the Bible are devoted to portraying the manhood of Caleb than to the creation of the world.

Home is on a level with the women; the town is on a level with the homes.

You will find lots of things in Shapespeare which are not fit for reading in a mixed audience and call that literature. When you hear some truths here in the tabernacle you will call it vulgar. It makes all the difference in the world whether Bill Shakespeare or Bill Sunday said it.

The more oyster soup it takes to run a church, the faster it runs to the devil.

The reason you don't like the Bible, you old sinner, is because it knows all about you.

Bob Ingersoll wasn't the first to find out that Moses made mistakes. God knew about it long before Ingersoll was born.

"A SALOON-KEEPER AND A GOOD MOTHER DON'T PULL ON THE SAME ROPE"

All that God has ever done to save this old world, has been done through men and women of flesh and blood like ourselves.

Nearly everybody is stuck up about something. Some people are even proud that they aren't proud.

The average young man is more careful of his company than the average girl.

Going to church doesn't make a man a Christian, any more than going to a garage makes him an automobile.

If we people were able to have panes of glass over our hearts, some of us would want stained glass, wouldn't we?

To see some people, you would think that the essential orthodox Christianity is to have a face so long they could eat oatmeal out of the end of a gas pipe.

God likes a little humor, as is evidenced by the fact that he made the monkey, the parrot—and some of you people.

Wouldn't this city be a great place to live in if some people would die, get converted, or move away?

The normal way to get rid of drunkards is to quit raising drunkards—to put the business that makes drunkards out of business.

You can't shine for God on Sunday, and then be a London fog on Monday.

I don't believe that God wants any man to be a hermit. Jesus Christ did not wear a hair shirt and sleep upon a bed of spikes. He went among the people and preached the Gospel.

If you only believe things that you can understand you must be an awful ignoramus.

There is more power in a mother's hand than in a king's scepter.

I have no doubt that there are men looking into my face tonight who will have "1914" carved on their tombstones.

If God had no more interest in this world than some of you church members have in Johnstown, this city would have been in hell long ago.

I hate to see a man roll up to church in a limousine and then drop a quarter in the collection plate.

Give your face to God and he will put his shine on it.

No fountain under the sun can hold enough to satisfy an immortal spirit.

Jesus Christ came among the common people. Abraham Lincoln said that God must have loved the common people: he made so many of them.

Yank some of the groans out of your prayers, and shove in some shouts.

The Bible says forgive your debtors; the world says "sue them for their dough."

The race will appear as far above us as we are above the harem when godly girls marry godly men.

It is impossible for a saloon-keeper to enjoy a good red-hot prayer-meeting.

I'm no spiritual masseur or osteopath. I'm a surgeon, and I cut deep.

A prudent man won't swallow a potato bug, and then take Paris green to kill it.

If you want milk and honey on your bread, you'll have to go into the land where there are giants.

There is nothing in the world of art like the songs mother used to sing.

God pays a good mother. Mothers, get your names on God's payroll.

The man who can drive a hog and keep his religion will stand without hitching.

The right preaching of the Gospel will never hurt anything good.

If you would have your children turn out well, don't turn your home into a lunch counter and lodging house.

Man was a fool in the Garden of Eden, and he has taken a good many new degrees since.

The backslider likes the preaching that wouldn't hit the side of a house, while the real disciple is delighted when the truth brings him to his knees.

There would be more power in the prayers of some folks if they would put more white money in the collection basket.

What have you given the world it never possessed before you came?

Temptation is the devil looking through the keyhole. Yielding is opening the door and inviting him in.

CHAPTER IX

Battling with "Booze"

The man who votes for the saloon is pulling on the same rope with the devil, whether he knows it or not.—BILLY SUNDAY.

THERE is a tremendous military advantage in having a definite enemy. The sermons that are aimed at nothing generally hit it. Billy Sunday is happiest and most successful when attacking the liquor evil. Down among the masses of men he learned for himself the awful malignity of strong drink, which he deems the greatest evil of our day.

So he fights it. Everybody will admit—the saloon-keeper first of all—that Billy Sunday is the most effective foe of the liquor business in America today. Small wonder the brewers spend large sums of money in circulating attacks upon him, and in going before him to every town where he conducts meetings, spreading slanders of many sorts.

There is a ghastly humor in the success the brewers have in enlisting the preachers to make common cause with them in discrediting this evangelist. Shrewd men have come quite generally to the conclusion that they will not give aid and comfort to the enemies of righteousness whose interests are best served by criticism of Billy Sunday. All incidental questions aside, Sunday does the Lord's work and is on the Lord's side. It is a pitiable spectacle to see the Lord's servants attacking him; though it is quite understandable why the liquor interest should spend large sums of money in antagonizing Sunday. It would be worth a million dollars to them any day if he could be put out of action.

Wherever Sunday goes a great temperance awakening follows. In eleven of fifteen Illinois towns where he campaigned "dry" victories were won at the next election. Fifteen hundred saloons were put out of business in a single day in Illinois, largely as the result of his work. With characteristic indifference to figures and tabulated results, Sunday has kept no record of the communities which have gone "dry" following his meetings. That consequence is common. His recent presence in Pennsylvania is the surest token that the Keystone State will not much longer be the boasted Gibraltar of the liquor interests. Even up in Pennsylvania's coal regions, with their large foreign population, many communities are going "dry," while individual saloons are being starved out. Within about a year of Sunday's visit there, the number of saloons was reduced by more than two hundred.

So intense is Sunday's zest for temperance that he will go anywhere possible to deliver a blow against the saloon. He has toured Illinois and West Virginia in special trains, campaigning for temperance. During the Sunday campaign in Johnstown ten thousand men in a meeting organized themselves into a Billy Sunday Anti-Saloon League. In Iowa literally scores of towns and counties are reported as having gone dry as a direct result of the Sunday meetings. Muscatine, Ottumwa, Marshalltown, Linwood and Centerville are communities in point. Thirteen out of fifteen towns in Illinois visited by Sunday voted out the saloon. West Virginia's temperance leaders utilized Sunday in a whirlwind campaign through the state. He spoke in ten towns in five days, traveling from point to point in a special car. It is now history that West Virginia went dry by ninety thousand majority. His latest work in the West has been timed to precede elections where the temperance question was an issue. Next to his passion for the conversion of men and women is this consuming antagonism to rum.

More important than his own valiant blows against the saloon is the fact that Sunday makes enemies for the liquor business. Practically all of his converts and friends become enthusiastic temperance workers. In western Pennsylvania he converted practical machine politicians to the old time Gospel and to the temperance cause.

Every campaign is full of incidents like that of the blacksmith, a part of whose business came from a large brewery. When this man became a Sunday convert and a temperance "fanatic," as they termed him, the brewers' business was withdrawn. But the loyalty which Sunday infuses into his followers, rallied to the man's help, and such a volume of Christian business was turned his way that his conversion and the loss of the brewery trade turned out to his profit.

In the *Outlook* of August 8, 1914, Lewis Edwin Theiss introduces a powerful article, "Industry versus Alcohol," with this Billy Sunday story:

" We were discussing Billy Sunday and the economic effect of his work.

" 'The vice-president of the C—— Iron Works told me,' said a manufacturer of railway cars, 'that his company could have afforded to pay its employees a quarter of a million dollars more than their wages during the period that Billy Sunday was working among them.'

'The corporation concerned is one of the great steel companies of the country. It employs thousands of men.

" 'Why was that?' I asked.

" 'Because of the increased efficiency of the men. They were steadier. Accidents decreased remarkably. They produced enough extra steel to make their work worth the quarter million additional.'

" 'It is interesting to find that religion has such an effect on every-day life,' I observed.

" 'Religion as such had little to do with it,' replied the car-maker, 'except that it started it. The thing that made those men efficient was cutting out the drink. Billy Sunday got them all on the water wagon. They became sober and stayed sober. They could run their machines with steady hands and true eyes. The men themselves realize what a difference it makes. They are strong for prohibition. If the people of Pittsburgh and its vicinity could vote on the temperance question today, the saloons would be wiped out there.'

" 'The manufacturers are strong for prohibition, too. They never gave much thought to the matter before. But this demonstration of Billy Sunday's has made us all strong for prohibition. We *know* now that most of our accidents are due to whisky. For years we have been trying to find a way to secure a high degree of efficiency among our men. We never succeeded. Along comes this preacher and accomplishes more in a few weeks than we have ever been able to do.

" 'We know now that until booze is banished we can never have really efficient workmen. We're fools if we don't profit by what he has shown us. Take it from me, booze has got to go. We are not much interested in the moral side of the matter as such. It is purely a matter of dollars and cents. They say corporations have no souls. From this time forth corporations are going to show mighty little soul toward the man who drinks.' "

A great parade of men marks the close of a Sunday campaign. In Scranton the line of march was broken into by a brewer's wagon. The driver was not content with trying to break the line of parade, but he also hurled offensive epithets at Sunday and his converts. Perhaps passive endurance was the virtue called for on this occasion; but it was certainly not the virtue practiced. For those husky mill workers stepped out of line for a moment, bodily overturned the brewer's wagon, and sent the beer kegs rolling in the street, all to the tune of the Sunday war song, "De Brewer's Big Horses Can't Run Over Me."

This song, written by H. S. Taylor, is the most popular one in the Sunday campaign. It is by no means a hymn of worship, but rather a battle-cry. When thousands of

De Brewer's Big Hosses.

(SOLO AND CHORUS.)

H. S. Taylor.   J. B. Herbert.

1. Oh de Brew-er's big hoss-es, com-in' down de road,
2. Oh de lick-er men's act-in' like dey own dis place,
3. Oh I'll har-ness dem hoss-es to de temp-'rance cart,

Tot-in' all a-round ole Lu-ci-fer's load; Dey step so high,
Liv-in' on de sweat ob de po' man's face. Dey's fat and sas-
Hit 'em wid a gad to gib 'em a start, I'll teach 'em how

an' dey step so free, But dem big hoss-es can't run o-ver me.
sy as dey can be, But dem big hoss-es can't run o-ver me.
for to haw and gee, For dem big hoss-es can't run o-ver me.

CHORUS.

Oh, no! boys, oh, no! De turnpike's free wherebber I go, I'm a temperance

Oh, no! boys, no, no, no!

in-gine, don't you see, And de Brewer's big hoss-es can't run o-ver me!

* A good effect can be obtained if the male voices will imitate escaping steam and whistle while the female voices sing the two following measures.

men lift their voices in this militant refrain, with whistles
blowing and bells ringing in the chorus, the effect is
fairly thrilling. Words and music are beneath the
consideration of the scholarly musician; but they strike
the common mind of the American who wants a battle
hymn.

DE BREWER'S BIG HOSSES.*

Oh, de Brewer's big hosses, comin' down de road,
Totin' all around ole Lucifer's load;
Dey step so high, an' dey step so free,
But dem big hosses can't run over me.

CHORUS.

Oh, no! boys, oh, no!
De turnpike's free wherebber I go,
I'm a temperance ingine, don't you see,
And de Brewer's big hosses can't run over me.

Oh, de licker men's actin' like dey own dis place,
Livin' on de sweat ob de po' man's face,
Dey's fat and sassy as dey can be,
But dem big hosses can't run over me.—CHO.

Oh, I'll harness dem hosses to de temp'rance cart,
Hit 'em wid a gad to gib 'em a start,
I'll teach 'em how for to haw and gee,
For dem big hosses can't run over me.—CHO.

Sunday is the Peter the Hermit of the temperance
crusade. He inflames men's passions for this righteous war.
Most critics call his sermon on "booze" his greatest achievement. He treats the theme from all angles—economic,
social, human, and religious. When he puts a row of boys
up on the platform and offers them as one day's contribution
to the saloon's grist of manhood which must be maintained,
the result is electric; all the militant manhood of the men
before him is urged to action.

*Reproduced by permission. Copyright, 1887, by Fillmore Bros. Homer A. Rodeheaver
owner. International copyright secured.

THE FAMOUS "BOOZE" SERMON

Here we have one of the strangest scenes in all the Gospels. Two men, possessed of devils, confront Jesus, and while the devils are crying out for Jesus to leave them, he commands the devils to come out, and the devils obey the command of Jesus. The devils ask permission to enter into a herd of swine feeding on the hillside. This is the only record we have of Jesus ever granting the petition of devils, and he did it for the salvation of men.

Then the fellows that kept the hogs went back to town and told the peanut-brained, weasel-eyed, hog-jowled, beetle-browed, bull-necked lobsters that owned the hogs, that "a long-haired fanatic from Nazareth, named Jesus, has driven the devils out of some men and the devils have gone into the hogs, and the hogs into the sea, and the sea into the hogs, and the whole bunch is dead."

And then the fat, fussy old fellows came out to see Jesus and said that he was hurting their business. A fellow says to me, "I don't think Jesus Christ did a nice thing."

You don't know what you are talking about.

Down in Nashville, Tennessee, I saw four wagons going down the street, and they were loaded with stills, and kettles, and pipes.

"What's this?" I said.

"United States revenue officers, and they have been in the moonshine district and confiscated the illicit stills, and they are taking them down to the government scrap heap."

Jesus Christ was God's revenue officer. Now the Jews were forbidden to eat pork, but Jesus Christ came and found that crowd buying and selling and dealing in pork, and confiscated the whole business, and he kept within the limits of the law when he did it. Then the fellows ran back to those who owned the hogs to tell what had befallen them and those hog-owners said to Jesus: "Take your helpers and hike. You are hurting our business." And they looked into the sea and the hogs were bottom side up, but Jesus said, "What is the matter?"

And they answered, "Leave our hogs and go." A fellow says it is rather a strange request for the devils to make, to ask permission to enter into hogs. I don't know—if I was a devil I would rather live in a good, decent hog than in lots of men. If you will drive the hog out you won't have to carry slop to him, so I will try to help you get rid of the hog.

And they told Jesus to leave the country. They said: "You are hurting our business."

Interest in Manhood

"Have you no interest in manhood?"

"We have no interest in that; just take your disciples and leave, for you are hurting our business."

That is the attitude of the liquor traffic toward the Church, and State, and Government, and the preacher that has the backbone to fight the most damnable, corrupt institution that ever wriggled out of hell and fastened itself on the public.

I am a temperance Republican down to my toes. Who is the man that fights the whisky business in the South? It is the Democrats! They have driven the business from Kansas, they have driven it from Georgia, and Maine and Mississippi and North Carolina and North Dakota and Oklahoma and Tennessee and West Virginia. And they have driven it out of 1,756 counties. And it is the rock-ribbed Democratic South that is fighting the saloon. They started this fight that is sweeping like fire over the United States. You might as well try and dam Niagara Falls with toothpicks as to stop the reform wave sweeping our land. The Democratic party of Florida has put a temperance plank in its platform and the Republican party of every state would nail that plank in their platform if they thought it would carry the election. It is simply a matter of decency and manhood, irrespective of politics. It is prosperity against poverty, sobriety against drunkenness, honesty against thieving, heaven against hell. Don't you want to see men sober? Brutal, staggering men transformed into respectable citizens? "No," said a saloonkeeper, "to hell with men. We are interested in our business, we have no interest in humanity."

After all is said that can be said upon the liquor traffic, its influence is degrading upon the individual, the family, politics and business, and upon everything that you touch in this old world. For the time has long gone by when there is any ground for arguments as to its ill effects. All are agreed on that point. There is just one prime reason why the saloon has not been knocked into hell, and that is the false statement that "the saloons are needed to help lighten the taxes." The saloon business has never paid, and it has cost fifty times more than the revenue derived from it.

Does the Saloon Help Business?

I challenge you to show me where the saloon has ever helped business, education, church, morals or anything we hold dear.

The wholesale and retail trade in Iowa pays every year at least $500,000 in licenses. Then if there were no drawback it ought to reduce the taxation twenty-five cents per capita. If the saloon is necessary to pay the taxes, and if they pay $500,000 in taxes, it ought to reduce them twenty-five cents a head. But no, the whisky business has increased taxes $1,000,000 instead of reducing them, and I defy any whisky man on God's dirt to show me one town that has the saloon where the taxes are lower than where they do not have the saloon. I defy you to show me an instance.

Listen! Seventy-five per cent of our idiots come from intemperate parents; eighty per cent of the paupers, eighty-two per cent of the crime is committed by men under the influence of liquor; ninety per cent of the adult criminals are whisky-made. The Chicago *Tribune* kept track for ten years and found that 53,556 murders were committed by men under the influence of liquor.

Archbishop Ireland, the famous Roman Catholic, of St. Paul, said of social crime today, that "seventy-five per cent is caused by drink, and eighty per cent of the poverty."

I go to a family and it is broken up, and I say, "What caused this?" Drink! I step up to a young man on the scaffold and say, "What brought you here?" Drink! Whence all the misery and sorrow and corruption? Invariably it is drink.

Five Points, in New York, was a spot as near like hell as any spot on earth. There are five streets that run to this point, and right in the middle was an old brewery and the streets on either side were lined with grog shops. The newspapers turned a searchlight on the district, and the first thing they had to do was to buy the old brewery and turn it into a mission.

The Parent of Crimes

The saloon is the sum of all villanies. It is worse than war or pestilence. It is the crime of crimes. It is the parent of crimes and the mother of sins. It is the appalling source of misery and crime in the land. And to license such an incarnate fiend of hell is the dirtiest, low-down, damnable business on top of this old earth. There is nothing to be compared to it.

The legislature of Illinois appropriated $6,000,000 in 1908 to take care of the insane people in the state, and the whisky business produces seventy-five per cent of the insane. That is what you go down in your pockets for to help support. Do away with the saloons and you will close these institutions. The saloons make them necessary, and they make the poverty and fill the jails and the penitentiaries. Who has to pay the bills? The landlord who doesn't get the rent because the money goes for whisky; the butcher and the grocer and the charitable person who takes pity on the children of drunkards, and the taxpayer who supports the insane asylums and other institutions, that the whisky business keeps full of human wrecks. .

Do away with the cursed business and you will not have to put up to support them.   Who gets the money?   The saloon-keepers and the brewers, and the distillers, while the whisky fills the land with misery, and poverty, and wretchedness, and disease, and death, and damnation, and it is being authorized by the will of the sovereign people.

You say that "people will drink anyway."   Not by my vote.   You say, "Men will murder their wives anyway." Not by my vote.   "They will steal anyway."   Not by my vote.   You are the sovereign people, and what are you going to do about it?

Let me assemble before your minds the bodies of the drunken dead, who crawl away "into the jaws of death, into the mouth of hell," and then out of the valley of the shadow of the drink let me call the appertaining mother- hood, and wifehood, and childhood, and let their tears rain down upon their purple faces.   Do you think that would stop the curse of the liquor traffic?   No! No!

In these days when the question of saloon or no saloon is at the fore in almost every community, one hears a good deal about what is called "personal liberty."   These are fine, large, mouth-filling words, and they certainly do sound first rate; but when you get right down and analyze them in the light of common old horse-sense, you will discover that in their application to the present controversy they mean just about this: "Personal liberty" is for the man who, if he has the inclination and the price, can stand up at a bar and fill his hide so full of red liquor that he is transformed for the time being into an irresponsible, dangerous, evil- smelling brute.   But "personal liberty" is not for his patient, long-suffering wife, who has to endure with what fortitude she may his blows and curses; nor is it for his children, who, if they escape his insane rage, are yet robbed of every known joy and privilege of childhood, and too often grow up neglected, uncared for and vicious as the result of their surroundings and the example before them.   "Per- sonal liberty" is not for the sober, industrious citizen who

from the proceeds of honest toil and orderly living, has to
pay, willingly or not, the tax bills which pile up as a direct
result of drunkenness, disorder and poverty, the items
of which are written in the records of every police court and
poor-house in the land; nor is "personal liberty" for the good
woman who goes abroad in the town only at the risk of being
shot down by some drink-crazed creature. This rant about
"personal liberty" as an argument has no leg to stand
upon.

The Economic Side

Now, in 1913 the corn crop was 2,373,000,000 bushels,
and it was valued at $1,660,000,000. Secretary Wilson says
that the breweries use less than two per cent; I will say that
they use two per cent. That would make 47,000,000
bushels, and at seventy cents a bushel that would be about
$33,000,000. How many people are there in the United
States? Ninety millions. Very well, then, that is thirty-
six cents per capita. Then we sold out to the whisky
business for thirty-six cents apiece—the price of a dozen
eggs or a pound of butter. We are the cheapest gang this
side of hell if we will do that kind of business.

Now listen! Last year the income of the United States
government, and the cities and towns and counties, from the
whisky business was $350,000,000. That is putting it
liberally. You say that's a lot of money. Well, last year
the workingmen spent $2,000,000,000 for drink, and it cost
$1,200,000,000 to care for the judicial machinery. In other
words, the whisky business cost us last year $3,400,000,000.
I will subtract from that the dirty $350,000,000 which we
got, and it leaves $3,050,000,000 in favor of knocking the
whisky business out on purely a money basis. And listen!
We spend $6,000,000,000 a year for our paupers and criminals
insane, orphans, feeble-minded, etc., and eighty-two per
cent of our criminals are whisky-made, and seventy-five
per cent of the paupers are whisky-made. The average
factory hand earns $450 a year, and it costs us $1,200 a year

to support each of our whisky criminals.   There are 326,000
enrolled criminals in the United States and 80,000 in jails
and penitentiaries.   Three-fourths were sent there because
of drink, and then they have the audacity to say the saloon
is needed for money revenue.   Never was there a baser lie.

"But," says the whisky fellow, "we would lose trade;
the farmer would not come to town to trade."   You lie.
I am a farmer.   I was born and raised on a farm and I have
the malodors of the barnyard on me today.   Yes, sir.   And
when you say that you insult the best class of men on God's
dirt.   Say, when you put up the howl that if you don't
have the saloons the farmer won't trade—say, Mr. Whisky
Man, why do you dump money into politics and back the
legislatures into the corner and fight to the last ditch to
prevent the enactment of county local option?   You know
if the farmers were given a chance they would knock the
whisky business into hell the first throw out of the box.
You are afraid.   You have cold feet on the proposition.
You are afraid to give the farmer a chance.   They are scared
to death of you farmers.

I heard my friend ex-Governor Hanly, of Indiana, use
the following illustrations:

"Oh, but," they say, "Governor, there is another danger
to the local option, because it means a loss of market to the
farmer.   We are consumers of large quantities of grain in
the manufacture of our products.   If you drive us out of
business you strike down that market and it will create a
money panic in this country, such as you have never seen,
if you do that."   I might answer it by saying that less than
two per cent of the grain produced in this country is used for
that purpose, but I pass that by.   I want to debate the merit
of the statement itself, and I think I can demonstrate in
ten minutes to any thoughtful man, to any farmer, that the
brewer who furnishes him a market for a bushel of corn is
not his benefactor, or the benefactor of any man, from an
economic standpoint.   Let us see.   A farmer brings to the
brewer a bushel of corn.   He finds a market for it.   He

gets fifty cents and goes his way, with the statement of the brewer ringing in his ears, that the brewer is the benefactor. But you haven't got all the factors in the problem, Mr. Brewer, and you cannot get a correct solution of a problem without all the factors in the problem. You take the farmer's bushel of corn, brewer or distiller, and you brew and distill from it four and one-half gallons of spirits. I don't know how much he dilutes them before he puts them on the market. Only the brewer, the distiller and God know. The man who drinks it doesn't, but if he doesn't dilute it at all, he puts on the market four and a half gallons of intoxicating liquor, thirty-six pints. I am not going to trace the thirty-six pints. It will take too long. But I want to trace three of them and I will give you no imaginary stories plucked from the brain of an excited orator. I will take instances from the judicial pages of the Supreme Court and the Circuit Court judges' reports in Indiana and in Illinois to make my case.

Tragedies Born of Drink

Several years ago in the city of Chicago a young man of good parents, good character, one Sunday crossed the street and entered a saloon, open against the law. He found there boon companions. There were laughter, song and jest and much drinking. After awhile, drunk, insanely drunk, his money gone, he was kicked into the street. He found his way across to his mother's home. He importuned her for money to buy more drink. She refused him. He seized from the sideboard a revolver and ran out into the street and with the expressed determination of entering the saloon and getting more drink, money or no money. His fond mother followed him into the street. She put her hand upon him in a loving restraint. He struck it from him in anger, and then his sister came and added her entreaty in vain. And then a neighbor, whom he knew, trusted and respected, came and put his hand on him in gentleness and friendly kindness, but in an insanity of drunken rage he raised the revolver and shot his friend dead in his blood upon the street. There was a trial; he was found guilty of murder. He was sentenced to life imprisonment, and when the little mother heard the verdict—a frail little bit of a woman—she threw up her hands and fell in a swoon. In three hours she was dead.

In the streets of Freeport, Illinois, a young man of good family became involved in a controversy with a lewd woman of the town. He went in a drunken frenzy to his father's home, armed himself with a deadly weapon and set out for the city in search of the woman with whom he had quarreled. The first person he met upon the public square in the city, in the daylight, in a place where she had a right to be, was one of the most refined and cultured women of Freeport. She carried in her arms her babe—motherhood and babyhood, upon the streets of Freeport in the day time, where they had a right to be—but this young man in his drunken insanity mistook her for the woman he sought and shot her dead upon the streets with her babe in her arms. He was tried and Judge Ferand, in sentencing him to life imprisonment said: "You are the seventh man in two years to be sentenced for murder while intoxicated."

In the city of Anderson, you remember the tragedy in the Blake home. A young man came home intoxicated, demanding money of his mother. She refused it. He seized from the wood box a hatchet and killed his mother and then robbed her. You remember he fled. The officer of the law pursued him and brought him back. An indictment was read to him charging him with the murder of the mother who had given him his birth, of her who had gone down into the valley of the shadow of death to give him life, of her who had looked down into his blue eyes and thanked God for his life. And he said, "I am guilty; I did it all." And Judge McClure sentenced him to life imprisonment.

Now I have followed probably three of the thirty-six pints of the farmer's product of a bushel of corn and the three of them have struck down seven lives, the three boys

who committed the murders, the three persons who were
killed and the little mother who died of a broken heart.
And now, I want to know, my farmer friend, if this has been
a good commercial transaction for you? You sold a bushel
of corn; you found a market; you got fifty cents; but a
fraction of this product struck down seven lives, all of whom
would have been consumers of your products for their life
expectancy. And do you mean to say that is a good economic transaction to you? That disposes of the market
question until it is answered; let no man argue further.

More Economics

And say, my friends, New York City's annual drink bill
is $365,000,000 a year, $1,000,000 a day. Listen a minute.
That is four times the annual output of gold, and six times
the value of all the silver mined in the United States. And
in New York there is one saloon for every thirty families.
The money spent in New York by the working people for
drink in ten years would buy every working man in New
York a beautiful home, allowing $3,500 for house and lot.
It would take fifty persons one year to count the money in
$1 bills, and they would cover 10,000 acres of ground. That
is what the people in New York dump into the whisky hole
in one year. And then you wonder why there is poverty
and crime, and that the country is not more prosperous.

The whisky gang is circulating a circular about Kansas
City, Kansas. I defy you to prove a statement in it. Kansas
City is a town of 100,000 population, and temperance went
into effect July 1, 1905. Then they had 250 saloons,
200 gambling hells and 60 houses of ill fame. The population was largely foreign, and inquiries have come from
Germany, Sweden and Norway, asking the influence of
the enforcement of the prohibitory law.

At the end of one year the president of one of the largest
banks in that city, a man who protested against the enforcement of the prohibitory law on the ground that it would
hurt business, found that his bank deposits had increased

$1,700,000, and seventy-two per cent of the deposits were from men who had never saved a cent before, and forty-two per cent came from men who never had a dollar in the bank, but because the saloons were driven out they had a chance to save, and the people who objected on the grounds that it would injure business found an increase of 209 per cent in building operations; and, furthermore, there were three times as many more people seeking investment, and court expenses decreased $25,000 in one year.

Who pays to feed and keep the gang you have in jail? Why, you go down in your sock and pay for what the saloon has dumped in there. They don't do it. Mr. Whisky Man, why don't you go down and take a picture of wrecked and blighted homes, and of insane asylums, with gibbering idiots. Why don't you take a picture of that?

At Kansas City, Kansas, before the saloons were closed, they were getting ready to build an addition to the jail. Now the doors swing idly on the hinges and there is nobody to lock in the jails. And the commissioner of the Poor Farm says there is a wonderful falling off of old men and women coming to the Poor House, because their sons and daughters are saving their money and have quit spending it for drink. And they had to employ eighteen new school teachers for 600 boys and girls, between the ages of twelve and eighteen, that had never gone to school before because they had to help a drunken father support the family. And they have just set aside $200,000 to build a new school house, and the bonded indebtedness was reduced $245,000 in one year without the saloon revenue. And don't you know another thing: In 1906, when they had the saloon, the population, according to the directory, was 89,655. According to the census of 1907 the population was 100,835, or an increase of twelve per cent in one year, without the grog-shop. In two years the bank deposits increased $3,930,000.

You say, drive out the saloon and you kill business— Ha! ha! "Blessed are the dead that die in the Lord."

I tell you, gentlemen, the American home is the dearest

heritage of the people, for the people, and by the people, and when a man can go from home in the morning with the kisses of wife and children on his lips, and come back at night with an empty dinner bucket to a happy home, that man is a better man, whether white or black. Whatever takes away the comforts of home—whatever degrades that man or woman—whatever invades the sanctity of the home, is the deadliest foe to the home, to church, to state and school, and the saloon is the deadliest foe to the home, the church and the state, on top of God Almighty's dirt. And if all the combined forces of hell should assemble in conclave, and with them all the men on earth that hate and despise God, and purity, and virtue—if all the scum of the earth could mingle with the denizens of hell to try to think of the deadliest institution to home, to church and state, I tell you, sir, the combined hellish intelligence could not conceive of or bring an institution that could touch the hem of the garment of the open licensed saloon to damn the home and manhood, and womanhood, and business and every other good thing on God's earth.

In the Island of Jamaica the rats increased so that they destroyed the crops, and they introduced a mongoose, which is a species of the coon. They have three breeding seasons a year and there are twelve to fifteen in each brood, and they are deadly enemies of the rats. The result was that the rats disappeared and there was nothing more for the mongoose to feed upon, so they attacked the snakes, and the frogs, and the lizards that fed upon the insects, with the result that the insects increased and they stripped the gardens, eating up the onions and the lettuce and then the mongoose attacked the sheep and the cats, and the puppies, and the calves and the geese. Now Jamaica is spending hundreds of thousands of dollars to get rid of the mongoose.

The American Mongoose

The American mongoose is the open licensed saloon. It eats the carpets off the floor and the clothes from off your back, your money out of the bank, and it eats up character, and it goes on until at last it leaves a stranded wreck in the home, a skeleton of what was once brightness and happiness.

There were some men playing cards on a railroad train, and one fellow pulled out a whisky flask and passed it about, and when it came to the drummer he said, "No." "What," they said, "have you got on the water wagon?" and they all laughed at him. He said, "You can laugh if you want to, but I was born with an appetite for drink, and for years I have taken from five to ten glasses per day, but I was at home in Chicago not long ago and I have a friend who has a pawn shop there. I was in there when in came a young fellow with ashen cheeks and a wild look on his face. He came up trembling, threw down a little package and said, 'Give me ten cents.' And what do you think was in that package? It was a pair of baby shoes.

"My friend said, 'No, I cannot take them.'

"'But,' he said, 'give me a dime. I must have a drink.'

"'No, take them back home, your baby will need them.'

"And the poor fellow said, 'My baby is dead, and I want a drink.'"

Boys, I don't blame you for the lump that comes up in your throat. There is no law, divine or human, that the saloon respects. Lincoln said, "If slavery is not wrong, nothing is wrong." I say, if the saloon, with its train of diseases, crime and misery, is not wrong, then nothing on earth is wrong. If the fight is to be won we need men— men that will fight—the Church, Catholic and Protestant, must fight it or run away, and thank God she will not run away, but fight to the last ditch.

Who works the hardest for his money, the saloon man or you?

Who has the most money Sunday morning, the saloon man or you?

The saloon comes as near being a rat hole for a wage-earner to dump his wages in as anything you can find.

The only interest it pays is red eyes and foul breath, and the loss of health. You can go in with money and you come out with empty pockets. You go in with character and you come out ruined. You go in with a good position and you lose it. You lose your position in the bank, or in the cab of the locomotive. And it pays nothing back but disease and damnation and gives an extra dividend in delirium tremens and a free pass to hell. And then it will let your wife be buried in the potter's field, and your children go to the asylum, and yet you walk out and say the saloon is a good institution, when it is the dirtiest thing on earth. It hasn't one leg to stand on and has nothing to commend it to a decent man, not one thing.

"But," you say, "we will regulate it by high license." Regulate what by high license? You might as well try and regulate a powder mill in hell. Do you want to pay taxes in boys, or dirty money? A man that will sell out to that dirty business I have no use for. See how absurd their arguments are. If you drink Bourbon in a saloon that pays $1,000 a year license, will it eat your stomach less than if you drink it in a saloon that pays $500 license? Is it going to have any different effect on you, whether the gang pays $500 or $1,000 license? No. It will make no difference whether you drink it over a mahogany counter or a pine counter—it will have the same effect on you; it will damn you. So there is no use talking about it.

In some insane asylums, do you know what they do? When they want to test some patient to see whether he has recovered his reason, they have a room with a faucet in it, and a cement floor, and they give the patient a mop and tell him to mop up the floor. And if he has sense enough to turn off the faucet and mop up the floor they will parole him, but should he let the faucet run, they know that he is crazy.

Well, that is what you are trying to do. You are trying to mop it up with taxes and insane asylums and jails and Keeley cures, and reformatories. The only thing to do is to shut off the source of supply.

A man was delivering a temperance address at a

fair grounds and a fellow came up to him and said: "Are you the fellow that gave a talk on temperance?"

"Yes."

"Well, I think that the managers did a dirty piece of business to let you give a lecture on temperance. You have hurt my business and my business is a legal one."

"You are right there," said the lecturer, "they did do a mean trick; I would complain to the officers." And he took up a premium list and said: "By the way, I see there is a premium of so much offered for the best horse and cow and butter. What business are you in?"

"I'm in the liquor business."

"Well, I don't see that they offer any premium for your business. You ought to go down and compel them to offer a premium for your business and they ought to offer on the list $25 for the best wrecked home, $15 for the best bloated bum that you can show, and $10 for the finest specimen of broken-hearted wife, and they ought to give $25 for the finest specimens of thieves and gamblers you can trot out. You can bring out the finest looking criminals. If you have something that is good trot it out. You ought to come in competition with the farmer, with his stock, and the fancy work, and the canned fruit."

"SHOULD HE LET THE FAUCET RUN, THEY KNOW THAT HE IS CRAZY"

The Saloon a Coward

As Dr. Howard said: "I tell you that the saloon is a coward. It hides itself behind stained-glass doors and opaque windows, and sneaks its customers in at a blind door, and it keeps a sentinel to guard the door from the officers of the law, and it marks its wares with false bills-of-lading, and offers to ship green goods to you and marks them with the name of wholesome articles of food so people won't know what is being sent to you. And so vile did that business get that the legislature of Indiana passed a law forbidding a saloon to ship goods without being properly labeled. And the United States Congress passed a law forbidding them to send whisky through the mails.

I tell you it strikes in the night. It fights under cover of darkness and assassinates the characters that it cannot damn, and it lies about you. It attacks defenseless womanhood and childhood. The saloon is a coward. It is a thief; it is not an ordinary court offender that steals your money, but it robs you of manhood and leaves you in rags and takes away your friends, and it robs your family. It impoverishes your children and it brings insanity and suicide. It will take the shirt off your back and it will steal the coffin from a dead child and yank the last crust of bread out of the hand of the starving child; it will take the last bucket of coal out of your cellar, and the last cent out of your pocket, and will send you home bleary-eyed and staggering to your wife and children. It will steal the milk from the breast of the mother and leave her with nothing with which to feed her infant. It will take the virtue from your daughter. It is the dirtiest, most low-down, damnable business that ever crawled out of the pit of hell. It is a sneak, and a thief and a coward.

It is an infidel. It has no faith in God; has no religion. It would close every church in the land. It would hang its beer signs on the abandoned altars. It would close every public school. It respects the thief and it esteems the blasphemer; it fills the prisons and the penitentiaries. It despises heaven, hates love, scorns virtue. It tempts the passions. Its music is the song of a siren. Its sermons are a collection of lewd, vile stories. It wraps a mantle about the hope of this world and that to come. Its tables are full of the vilest literature. It is the moral clearing house for rot, and damnation, and poverty, and insanity, and it wrecks homes and blights lives today.

God's Worst Enemy

The saloon is a liar. It promises good cheer and sends sorrow. It promises health and causes disease. It promises prosperity and sends adversity. It promises happiness and sends misery. Yes, it sends the husband home with a lie on his lips to his wife; and the boy home with a lie on his lips to his mother; and it causes the employee to lie to his employer. It degrades. It is God's worst enemy and the devil's best friend. It spares neither youth nor old age. It is waiting with a dirty blanket for the baby to crawl into the world. It lies in wait for the unborn.

It cocks the highwayman's pistol. It puts the rope in the hands of the mob. It is the anarchist of the world and its dirty red flag is dyed with the blood of women and children. It sent the bullet through the body of Lincoln; it nerved the arm that sent the bullets through Garfield and William McKinley. Yes, it is a murderer. Every plot that was ever hatched against the government and law, was born and bred, and crawled out of the grog-shop to damn this country.

I tell you that the curse of God Almighty is on the saloon. Legislatures are legislating against it. Decent society is barring it out. The fraternal brotherhoods are knocking it out. The Masons and Odd Fellows, and the Knights of Pythias and the A. O. U. W. are closing their doors to the whisky sellers. They don't want you wriggling your carcass in their lodges. Yes, sir, I tell you, the curse of God is on it. It is on the down grade. It is headed for hell, and, by the grace of God, I am going to give it a push, with a whoop, for all I know how. Listen to me! I am going to show you how we burn up our money. It costs twenty cents to make a gallon of whisky; sold over the counter at ten cents a glass, it will bring four dollars.

"But," said the saloon-keeper, "Bill, you must figure on the strychnine and the cochineal, and other stuff they put in it, and it will bring nearer eight dollars."

Yes; it increases the heart beat thirty times more in a minute, when you consider the licorice and potash and logwood and other poisons that are put in. I believe one cause for the unprecedented increase of crime is due to the poison put in the stuff nowadays to make it go as far as they can.

I am indebted to my friend, George B. Stuart, for some of the following points:

I will show you how your money is burned up. It costs twenty cents to make a gallon of whisky, sold over the counter at ten cents a glass, which brings four dollars. Listen, where does it go? Who gets the twenty cents? The farmer for his corn or rye. Who gets the rest? The United States government for collecting revenue, and the big corporations, and part is used to pave our streets and pay our police. I'll show you. I'm going to show you how it is burned up, and you don't need half sense to catch on, and if you don't understand just keep still and nobody will know the difference.

I say, "Hey, Colonel Politics, what is the matter with the country?"

He swells up like a poisoned pup and says to me, "Bill, why the silver bugbear. That's what is the matter with the country."

The total value of the silver produced in this country in 1912 was $39,000,000. Hear me! In 1912 the total value of the gold produced in this country was $93,000,000, and we dumped thirty-six times that much in the whisky hole and didn't fill it. What is the matter? The total value of all the gold and silver produced in 1912 was $132,000,000, and we dumped twenty-five times that amount in the whisky hole and didn't fill it.

What is the matter with the country, Colonel Politics? He swells up and says, "Mr. Sunday, Standpatism, sir."

I say, "You are an old windbag."

"Oh," says another, "revision of the tariff." Another man says, "Free trade; open the doors at the ports and let them pour the products in and we will put the trusts on the side-track."

Say, you come with me to every port of entry. Listen! In 1912 the total value of all the imports was $1,812,000,000, and we dumped that much in the whisky hole in twelve months and did not fill it.

"Oh," says a man, "let us court South America and Europe to sell our products. That's what is the matter; we are not exporting enough."

Last year the total value of all the exports was $2,362,-000,000, and we dumped that amount in the whisky hole in one year and didn't fill it.

One time I was down in Washington and went to the United States treasury and said: "I wish you would let me go where you don't let the general public." And they took us around on the inside and we walked into a room about twenty feet long and fifteen feet wide and as many feet high, and I said, "What is this?"

"This is the vault that contains all of the national bank stock in the United States."

I said, "How much is here?"

They said, "$578,000,000."

And we dumped nearly four times the value of the national bank stock in the United States into the whisky hole last year, and we didn't fill the hole up at that. What is the matter? Say, whenever the day comes that all the Catholic and Protestant churches—just when the day comes when you will say to the whisky business: "You go to hell," that day the whisky business will go to hell. But you sit there, you old whisky-voting elder and deacon and vestry-man, and you wouldn't strike your hands together on the proposition. It would stamp you an old hypocrite and you know it.

Say, hold on a bit. Have you got a silver dollar? I am going to show you how it is burned up. We have in this country 250,000 saloons, and allowing fifty feet frontage for each saloon it makes a street from New York to Chicago, and 5,000,000 men, women and children go daily into the saloon for drink. And marching twenty miles a day it would take thirty days to pass this building, and marching five abreast they would reach 590 miles. There they go; look at them!

On the first day of January, 500,000 of the young men of our nation entered the grog-shop and began a public career hellward, and on the 31st of December I will come back here and summon you people, and ring the bell and raise the curtain and say to the saloon and breweries: "On the first day of January, I gave you 500,000 of the brain and muscle of our land, and I want them back and have come in the name of the home and church and school; father mother, sister, sweetheart; give me back what I gave you. March out."

I count, and 165,000 have lost their appetites and have become muttering, bleary-eyed drunkards, wallowing in their own excrement, and I say, "What is it I hear, a funeral dirge?" What is that procession? A funeral procession 3,000 miles long and 110,000 hearses in the procession. One hundred and ten thousand men die drunkards in the land of the free and home of the brave. Listen! In an hour twelve men die drunkards, 300 a day and 110,000 a year. One man will leap in front of a train, another will plunge from the dock into a lake, another will throw his hands to his head and life will end. Another will cry, "Mother," and his life will go out like a burnt match.

I stand in front of the jails and count the whisky criminals. They say, "Yes, Bill, I fired the bullet." "Yes, I backed my wife into the corner and beat her life out. I am waiting for the scaffold; I am waiting." "I am waiting," says another, "to slip into hell." On, on, it goes. Say, let me summon the wifehood, and the motherhood, and the childhood and see the tears rain down the upturned faces. People, tears are too weak for that hellish business. Tears are only salty backwater that well up at the bidding of an occult power, and I will tell you there are 865,000 whisky orphan children in the United States, enough in the world to belt the globe three times around, punctured at every fifth point by a drunkard's widow.

Like Hamilcar of old, who swore young Hannibal to eternal enmity against Rome, so I propose to perpetuate this feud against the liquor traffic until the white-winged dove of temperance builds her nest on the dome of the capitol of Washington and spreads her wings of peace, sobriety and joy over our land which I love with all my heart.

What Will a Dollar Buy?

I hold a silver dollar in my hand. Come on, we are going to a saloon. We will go into a saloon and spend that dollar for a quart. It takes twenty cents to make a gallon of whisky and a dollar will buy a quart. You say to the saloon-keeper, "Give me a quart." I will show you, if you wait a minute, how she is burned up. Here I am John, an old drunken bum, with a wife and six kids. (Thank God, it's all a lie.) Come on, I will go down to a saloon and throw down my dollar. It costs twenty cents to make a gallon of whisky. A nickel will make a quart. My dollar will buy a quart of booze. Who gets the nickel? The farmer, for corn and apples. Who gets the ninety-five cents? The United States government, the big distillers, the big corporations. I am John, a drunken bum, and I will spend my dollar. I have worked a week and got my pay. I go into a grog-shop and throw down my dollar. The saloon-keeper gets my dollar and I get a quart of booze. Come home with me. I stagger, and reel, and spew in my wife's presence, and she says:

"Hello, John, what did you bring home?"

"A quart."

What will a quart do? It will burn up my happiness and my home and fill my home with squalor and want. So there is the dollar. The saloon-keeper has it. Here is my quart. There you get the whisky end of it. Here you get the workingman's end of the saloon.

But come on; I will go to a store and spend the dollar for a pair of shoes. I want them for my son, and he puts them on his feet, and with the shoes to protect his feet he goes out and earns another dollar, and my dollar becomes a silver thread in the woof and warp of happiness and joy, and the man that owns the building gets some, and the clerk that sold the shoes gets some, and the merchant, and the traveling man, and the wholesale house gets some, and the factory, and the man that made the shoes, and the man that tanned the hide, and the butcher that bought the calf, and the little colored fellow that shined the shoes, and my dollar spread itself and nobody is made worse for spending the money.

I join the Booster Club for business and prosperity. A man said, "I will tell you what is the matter with the country: it's over-production." You lie, it is undercon-sumption.

Say, wife, the bread that ought to be in your stomach to satisfy the cravings of hunger is down yonder in the grocery store, and your husband hasn't money enough to carry it home. The meat that ought to satisfy your hunger hangs in the butcher shop. Your husband hasn't any money to buy it. The cloth for a dress is lying on the shelf in the store, but your husband hasn't the money to buy it. The whisky gang has his money.

What is the matter with our country? I would like to do this. I would like to see every booze-fighter get on the water wagon. I would like to summon all the drunkards in America and say: "Boys, let's cut her out and spend the money for flour, meat and calico; what do you say?" Say! $500,000,000 will buy all the flour in the United States; $500,000,000 will buy all the beef cattle, and $500,000,000 will buy all the cotton at $50 a bale. But we dumped more money than that in the whisky hole last year, and we didn't fill it. Come on; I'm going to line up the drunkards. Everybody fall in. Come on, ready, forward, march. Right, left, here I come with all the drunkards. We will line up in front of a butcher shop. The butcher says, "What do you want, a piece of neck?"

"No; how much do I owe you?"   "Three dollars." "Here's your dough. Now give me a porterhouse steak and a sirloin roast."

"Where did you get all that money?"

"Went to hear Bill and climbed on the water wagon."

"Hello! What do you want?"

"Beefsteak."

"What do you want?"

"Beefsteak."

We empty the shop and the butcher runs to the telephone. "Hey, Central, give me the slaughter house. Have you got any beef, any pork, any mutton?"

They strip the slaughter house, and then telephone to Swift, and Armour, and Nelson Morris, and Cudahy, to send down trainloads of beefsteaks.

"The whole bunch has got on the water wagon."

And Swift and the other big packers in Chicago say to their salesmen: "Buy beef, pork and mutton."

The farmer sees the price of cattle and sheep jump up to three times their value. Let me take the money you dump into the whisky hole and buy beefsteaks with it. I will show what is the matter with America. I think the liquor business is the dirtiest, rottenest business this side of hell.

Come on, are you ready? Fall in! We line up in front of a grocery store.

"What do you want?"

"Why, I want flour."

"What do you want?"

"Flour."

"What do you want?"

"Flour."

"Pillsbury, Minneapolis, 'Sleepy Eye'?"

"Yes, ship in trainloads of flour; send on fast mail schedule, with an engine in front, one behind and a Mogul in the middle."

"What's the matter?"

"Why, the workingmen have stopped spending their money for booze and have begun to buy flour."

The big mills tell their men to buy wheat and the farmers see the price jump to over $2 per bushel. What's the matter with the country? Why, the whisky gang has your money and you have an empty stomach, and yet you will walk up and vote for the dirty booze.

Come on, cut out the booze, boys. Get on the water wagon; get on for the sake of your wife and babies, and hit the booze a blow.

Come on, ready, forward, march! Right, left, halt! We are in front of a dry goods store.

"What do you want?"

"Calico."

"What do you want?"

"Calico."

"What do you want?"

"Calico."

"Calico; all right, come on." The stores are stripped.

Marshall Field, Carson, Pirie, Scott & Co., J. V. Farrell, send down calico. The whole bunch has voted out the saloons and we have such a demand for calico we don't know what to do. And the big stores telegraph to Fall River to ship calico, and the factories telegraph to buy cotton, and they tell their salesmen to buy cotton, and the cotton plantation man sees cotton jump up to $150 a bale.

What is the matter? Your children are going naked and the whisky gang has got your money. That's what's the matter with you. Don't listen to those old whisky-soaked politicians who say "stand pat on the saloon."

Come with me. Now, remember, we have the whole bunch of booze fighters on the water wagon, and I'm going home now. Over there I was John, the drunken bum.

The whisky gang got my dollar and I got the quart. Over here I am John on the water wagon. The merchant got my dollar and I have his meat, flour and calico, and I'm going home now. "Be it ever so humble, there's no place like home without booze."

Wife comes out and says, "Hello, John, what have you got?"

"Two porterhouse steaks, Sally."

"What's that bundle, Pa?"

"Clothes to make you a new dress, Sis. Your mother has fixed your old one so often, it looks like a crazy quilt."

"And what have you there?"

"That's a pair of shoes for you, Tom; and here is some cloth to make you a pair of pants. Your mother has patched the old ones so often, they look like the map of United States."

What's the matter with the country? We have been dumping into the whisky hole the money that ought to have been spent for flour, beef and calico, and we haven't the hole filled up yet.

A man comes along and says: "Are you a drunkard?"

"Yes, I'm a drunkard."

"Where are you going?"

"I am going to hell."

"Why?'

"Because the Good Book says: 'No drunkard shall inherit the kingdom of God,' so I am going to hell."

Another man comes along and I say: "Are you a church member?"

"Yes, I am a church member."

"Where are you going?"

"I am going to heaven."

"Did you vote for the saloon?"

"Yes."

"Then you shall go to hell."

Say, if the man that drinks the whisky goes to hell, the man that votes for the saloon that sold the whisky to him will go to hell. If the man that drinks the whisky goes to hell, and the man that sold the whisky to the men that drank it, goes to heaven, then the poor drunkard will have the right to stand on the brink of eternal damnation and put his arms around the pillar of justice, shake his fist in the face of the Almighty and say, "Unjust! Unjust!" If you vote for the dirty business you ought to go to hell as sure as you live, and I would like to fire the furnace while you are there.

Some fellow says, "Drive the saloon out and the buildings will be empty." Which would you rather have, empty buildings or empty jails, penitentiaries and insane asylums? You drink the stuff and what have you to say? You that vote for it, and you that sell it? Look at them painted on the canvas of your recollection.

The Gin Mill

What is the matter with this grand old country? I heard my friend, George Stuart, tell how he imagined that he walked up to a mill and said:

"Hello, there, what kind of a mill are you?"

"A sawmill."

"And what do you make?"

"We make boards out of logs."

"Is the finished product worth more than the raw material?"

"Yes."

"We will make laws for you. We must have lumber for houses."

He goes up to another mill and says:

"Hey, what kind of a mill are you?"

"A grist mill."

"What do you make?"

"Flour and meal out of wheat and corn."

"Is the finished product worth more than the raw material?"

"Yes."

"Then come on. We will make laws for you. We will protect you."

He goes up to another mill and says:

"What kind of a mill are you?"

"A paper mill."

"What do you make paper out of?"

"Straw and rags."

"Well, we will make laws for you. We must have paper on which to write notes and mortgages."

He goes up to another mill and says:

"Hey, what kind of a mill are you?"

"A gin mill."

"I don't like the looks nor the smell of you. A gin mill; what do you make? What kind of a mill are you?"

"A gin mill."

"What is your raw material?"

"The boys of America."

The gin mills of this country must have 2,000,000 boys or shut up shop. Say, walk down your streets, count the homes and every fifth home has to furnish a boy for a drunkard. Have you furnished yours? No. Then I have to furnish two to make up.

"What is your raw material?"

"American boys."

"Then I will pick up the boys and give them to you."

A man says, "Hold on, not that boy, he is mine."

Then I will say to you what a saloon-keeper said to me when I protested, "I am not interested in boys; to hell with your boys."

"Say, saloon gin mill, what is your finished product?"

"Bleary-eyed, low-down, staggering men and the scum of God's dirt."

Go to the jails, go to the insane asylums and the penitentiaries, and the homes for feeble-minded. There you will find the finished product for their dirty business. I tell you it is the worst business this side of hell, and you know it.

Listen! Here is an extract from the *Saturday Evening Post* of November 9, 1907, taken from a paper read by a brewer. You will say that a man didn't say it: "It appears from these facts that the success of our business lies in the creation of appetite among the boys. Men who have formed the habit scarcely ever reform, but they, like others, will die, and unless there are recruits made to take their places, our coffers will be empty, and I recommend to you that money spent in the creation of appetite will return in dollars to your tills after the habit is formed."

What is your raw material, saloons? American boys. Say, I would not give one boy for all the distilleries and saloons this side of hell. And they have to have 2,000,000 boys every generation. And then you tell me you are a man when you will vote for an institution like that. What do you want to do, pay taxes in money or in boys?

I feel like an old fellow in Tennessee who made his living by catching rattlesnakes. He caught one with fourteen rattles and put it in a box with a glass top. One day when he was sawing wood his little five-year old boy, Jim, took the lid off and the rattler wriggled out and struck him in the cheek. He ran to his father and said, "The rattler has bit me." The father ran and chopped the rattler to pieces, and with his jack-knife he cut a chunk from the boy's cheek and then sucked and sucked at the wound to draw out the poison. He looked at little Jim, watched the pupils of his eyes dilate and watched him swell to three times his normal size, watched his lips become parched and cracked, and eyes roll, and little Jim gasped and died.

The father took him in his arms, carried him over by the side of the rattler, got on his knees and said, "O God, I would not give little Jim for all the rattlers that ever crawled over the Blue Ridge mountains."

And I would not give one boy for every dirty dollar you get from the hell-soaked liquor business or from every brewery and distillery this side of hell.

In a Northwest city a preacher sat at his breakfast

8

table one Sunday morning. The door-bell rang; he answered it; and there stood a little boy, twelve years of age. He was on crutches, right leg off at the knee, shivering, and he said, "Please, sir, will you come up to the jail and talk and pray with papa? He murdered mamma. Papa was good and kind, but whisky did it, and I have to support my three little sisters. I sell newspapers and black boots. Will you go up and talk and pray with papa? And will you come home and be with us when they bring him back? The governor says we can have his body after they hang him."

The preacher hurried to the jail and talked and prayed with the man. He had no knowledge of what he had done. He said, "I don't blame the law, but it breaks my heart to think that my children must be left in a cold and heartless world. Oh, sir, whisky did it."

The preacher was at the little hut when up drove the undertaker's wagon and they carried out the pine coffin. They led the little boy up to the coffin, he leaned over and kissed his father and sobbed, and said to his sister, "Come on, sister, kiss papa's cheeks before they grow cold." And the little hungry, ragged, whisky orphans hurried to the coffin, shrieking in agony. Police, whose hearts were adamant, buried their faces in their hands and rushed from the house, and the preacher fell on his knees and lifted his clenched fist and tear-stained face and took an oath before God, and before the whisky orphans, that he would fight the cursed business until the undertaker carried him out in a coffin.

A Chance for Manhood

You men have a chance to show your manhood. Then in the name of your pure mother, in the name of your manhood, in the name of your wife and the poor innocent children that climb up on your lap and put their arms around your neck, in the name of all that is good and noble, fight the curse. Shall you men, who hold in your hands the ballot, and in that ballot hold the destiny of womanhood and childhood and manhood, shall you, the sovereign power, refuse to rally in the name of the defenseless men and women and native land? No.

I want every man to say, "God, you can count on me to protect my wife, my home, my mother and my children and the manhood of America."

By the mercy of God, which has given to you the unshaken and unshakable confidence of her you love, I beseech you, make a fight for the women who wait until the saloons spew out their husbands and their sons, and send them home maudlin, brutish, devilish, stinking, blear-eyed, bloated-faced drunkards.

You say you can't prohibit men from drinking. Why, if Jesus Christ were here today some of you would keep on in sin just the same. But the law can be enforced against whisky just the same as it can be enforced against anything else, if you have honest officials to enforce it. Of course it doesn't prohibit. There isn't a law on the books of the state that prohibits. We have laws against murder. Do they prohibit? We have laws against burglary. Do they prohibit? We have laws against arson, rape, but they do not prohibit. Would you introduce a bill to repeal all the laws that do not prohibit? Any law will prohibit to a certain extent if honest officials enforce it. But no law will absolutely prohibit. We can make a law against liquor prohibit as much as any law prohibits.

Or would you introduce a bill saying, if you pay $1,000 a year you can kill any one you don't like; or by paying $500 a year you can attack any girl you want to; or by paying $100 a year you can steal anything that suits you? That's what you do with the dirtiest, rottenest gang this side of hell. You say for so much a year you can have a license to make staggering, reeling, drunken sots, murderers and thieves and vagabonds. You say, "Bill, you're too hard on the whisky." I don't agree. Not on your life. There was a fellow going along the pike and a farmer's dog ran snapping at him. He tried to drive it back with a pitchfork he carried, and failing to do so he pinned it to the ground with the prongs. Out came the farmer: "Hey, why don't you use the other end of that fork?" He answered "Why didn't the dog come at me with the other end?"

Personal Liberty

Personal liberty is not personal license. I dare not exercise personal liberty if it infringes on the liberty of others. Our forefathers did not fight and die for personal license but for personal liberty bounded by laws. Personal liberty is the liberty of a murderer, a burglar, a seducer, or a wolf that wants to remain in a sheep fold, or the weasel in a hen roost. You have no right to vote for an institution that is going to drag your sons and daughters to hell.

If you were the only persons in this city you would have a perfect right to drive your horse down the street at breakneck speed; you would have a right to make a race track out of the streets for your auto; you could build a slaughter house in the public square; you could build a glue factory in the public square. But when the population increases from one to 600,000 you can't do it. You say, "Why can't I run my auto? I own it. Why can't I run my horse? I own it. Why can't I build the slaughter house? I own the lot." Yes, but there are 600,000 people here now and other people have rights.

So law stands between you and personal liberty, you miserable dog. You can't build a slaughter house in your front yard, because the law says you can't. As long as I am standing here on this platform I have personal liberty. I can swing my arms at will. But the minute any one else steps on the platform my personal liberty ceases. It stops just one inch from the other fellow's nose.

When you come staggering home, cussing right and left and spewing and spitting, your wife suffers, your children suffer. Don't think that you are the only one that suffers. A man that goes to the penitentiary makes his wife and children suffer just as much as he does. You're placing a shame on your wife and children. If you're a dirty, low-down, filthy, drunken, whisky-soaked bum you'll affect all with whom you come in contact. If you're a God-fearing man you will influence all with whom you come in contact. You can't live by yourself.

I occasionally hear a man say, "It's nobody's business how I live." Then I say he is the most dirty, low-down, whisky-soaked, beer-guzzling, bull-necked, foul-mouthed hypocrite that ever had a brain rotten enough to conceive such a statement and lips vile enough to utter it. You say, "If I am satisfied with my life why do you want to interfere with my business?"

'If I heard a man beating his wife and heard her shrieks and the children's cries and my wife would tell me to go and see what was the matter, and I went in and found a great, big, broad-shouldered, whisky-soaked, hog-jowled, weasel-eyed brute dragging a little woman around by the hair, and two children in the corner unconscious from his kicks and the others yelling in abject terror, and he said, "What are you coming in to interfere with my personal liberty for? Isn't this my wife, didn't I pay for the license to wed her?" You ought, or you're a bigamist. "Aren't these my children; didn't I pay the doctor to bring them into the world?" You ought to, or you're a thief. "If I want to beat them, what is that your business, aren't they mine?" Would I apologize? Never! I'd knock seven kinds of pork out of that old hog.

The Moderate Drinker

I remember when I was secretary of the Y. M. C. A. in Chicago, I had the saloon route. I had to go around and give tickets inviting men to come to the Y. M. C. A. services. And one day I was told to count the men going into a certain saloon. Not the ones already in, but just those going in. In sixty-two minutes I could count just 1,004 men going in there. I went in then and met a fellow who used to be my side-kicker out in Iowa, and he threw down a mint julep while I stood there, and I asked him what he was doing.

"Oh, just come down to the theater," he said, "and came over for a drink between acts."

"Why, you are three sheets in the wind now," I said, and then an old drunken bum, with a little threadbare coat, a straw hat, no vest, pants torn, toes sticking out through his torn shoes, and several weeks' growth of beard on his face, came in and said to the bartender: "For God's sake, can't you give an old bum a drink of whisky to warm up on?" and the bartender poured him out a big glass and he gulped it down. He pulled his hat down and slouched out.

I said to my friend, "George, do you see that old drunken bum, down and out? There was a time when he was just like you. No drunkard ever intended to be a drunkard. Every drunkard intended to be a moderate drinker."

"Oh, you're unduly excited over my welfare," he said. "I never expect to get that far."

"Neither did that bum," I answered. I was standing on another corner less than eight months afterward and I saw a bum coming along with head down, his eyes bloodshot, his face bloated, and he panhandled me for a flapjack before I recognized him. It was George. He had lost his job and was on the toboggan slide hitting it for hell. I say if sin weren't so deceitful it wouldn't be so attractive. Every added drink makes it harder.

Some just live for booze. Some say, "I need it. It keeps me warm in winter." Another says, "It keeps me cool in summer." Well, if it keeps you warm in winter and cool in summer, why is it that out of those who freeze to death and are sun-struck the greater part of them are booze-hoisters? Every one takes it for the alcohol there is in it. Take that out and you would as soon drink dish water.

I can buy a can of good beef extract and dip the point of my knife in the can and get more nourishment on the point of that knife than in 800 gallons of the best beer. If the brewers of this land today were making their beer in Germany, ninety per cent of them would be in jail. The extract on the point of the knife represents one and three-quarter pounds of good beefsteak.   Just think, you have to make a swill barrel out of your bellies and a sewer if you want to get that much nourishment out of beer and run 800 gallons through.   Oh, go ahead, if you want to, but I'll try to help you just the same.

Every man has blood corpuscles and their object is to take the impurities out of your system.   Perspiration is for the same thing.   Every time you work or I preach the impurities come out.   Every time you sweat there is a destroying power going on inside.   The blood goes through the heart every seventeen seconds.   Oh, we have a marvelous system.   In some spots there are 4,000 pores to the square inch and a grain of sand will cover 150 of them. I can strip you and cover you with shellac and you'll be dead in forty-eight hours.   Oh, we are fearfully and wonderfully made.

What Booze Does to the System

Alcohol knocks the blood corpuscles out of business so that it takes eight to ten to do what one ought to do. There's a man who drinks.   Here's a fellow who drives a beer wagon.   Look how pussy he is.   He's full of rotten tissue.   He says he's healthy.   Smell his breath.   You punch your finger in that healthy flesh he talks about and the dent will be there a half an hour afterwards.   You look like you don't believe it.   Try it when you go to bed tonight. Pneumonia has a first mortgage on a booze-hoister.

Take a fellow with good, healthy muscles, and you punch them and they bound out like a rubber band.   The first thing about a crushed strawberry stomach is a crushed strawberry nose.   Nature lets the public on the outside know what is going on inside.   If I could just take the stomach of a moderate drinker and turn it wrong side out for you, it would be all the temperance lecture you would need.   You know what alcohol does to the white of an egg. It will cook it in a few minutes.   Well, alcohol does the same thing to the nerves as to the white of an egg. That's why some men can't walk. They stagger because their nerves are partly paralyzed.

The liver is the largest organ of the body. It takes all of the blood in the body and purifies it and takes out the poisons and passes them on to the gall and from there they go to the intestines and act as oil does on machinery. When a man drinks the liver becomes covered with hob nails, and then refuses to do the work, and the poisons stay in the blood. Then the victim begins to turn yellow. He has the jaundice. The kidneys take what is left and purify that. The booze that a man drinks turns them hard.

That's what booze is doing for you. Isn't it time you went red hot after the enemy? I'm trying to help you. I'm trying to put a carpet on your floor, pull the pillows out of the window, give you and your children and wife good clothes. I'm trying to get you to save your money instead of buying a machine for the saloon-keeper while you have to foot it.

By the grace of God I have strength enough to pass the open saloon, but some of you can't, so I owe it to you to help you.

I've stood for more sneers and scoffs and insults and had my life threatened from one end of the land to the other by this God-forsaken gang of thugs and cutthroats because I have come out uncompromisingly against them. I've taken more dirty, vile insults from this low-down bunch than from any one on earth, but there is no one that will reach down lower, or reach higher up or wider, to help you out of the pits of drunkenness than I.

CHAPTER X

"Give Attendance to Reading"

There are some so-called Christian homes today with books on the shelves of the library that have no more business there than a rattler crawling about on the floor, or poison within the child's reach.—BILLY SUNDAY.

"I NEVER heard Billy Sunday use an ungrammatical sentence," remarked one observer. "He uses a great deal of slang, and many colloquialisms, but not a single error in grammar could I detect. Some of his passages are really beautiful English."

Sunday has made diligent effort to supplement his lack of education. He received the equivalent of a high-school training in boyhood, which is far more than Lincoln ever had. Nevertheless he has not had the training of the average educated man, much less of a normal minister of the gospel. He is conscious of his limitations: and has diligently endeavored to make up for them. When coaching the Northwestern University base-ball team in the winter of '87 and '88 he attended classes at the University. He has read a great deal and to this day continues his studies. Of course his acquaintance with literature is superficial: but his use of it shows how earnestly he has read up on history and literature and the sciences. He makes better use of his knowledge of the physical sciences, and of historical allusions, than most men drilled in them for years. He displays a proneness for what he himself would call "high-brow stuff," and his disproportionate display of his "book learning" reveals his conscious effort to supply what does not come to him naturally.

Sunday has an eclectic mind. He knows a good thing when he sees it. He is quick to incorporate into his discourses happenings or illustrations wherever found. Moody also was accustomed to do this: he circulated among his friends interleaved Bibles to secure keen comments on Scripture passages. All preachers draw on the storehouses of the past: the Church Fathers speak every Sunday in the pulpits of Christendom. Nobody originates all that he says. "We are the heirs of all the ages."

At the opening of every one of his campaigns Sunday repeatedly announces that he has drawn his sermon material from wherever he could find it, and that he makes no claim to originality. So the qualified critic can detect, in addition to some sermon outlines which were bequests from Dr. Chapman, epigrams from Sam Jones, flashes from Talmage, passages from George Stuart, paragraphs from the religious press, apothegms from the great commentators. It is no news to say that Sunday's material is not all original; he avows this himself. In his gleanings he has had help from various associates. Elijah P. Brown's hand can be traced in his sermons: the creator of the "Ram's Horn" proverbs surely is responsible for Sunday's penchant for throwing stones at the devil.

Sunday is not an original thinker. He has founded no school of Scriptural interpretation. He has not given any new exposition of Bible passages, nor has he developed any fresh lines of thought. Nobody hears anything new from him. In every one of his audience there are probably many persons who have a more scholarly acquaintance with the Bible and with Christian literature.

Temperamentally a conservative, Sunday has taken the truth taught him by his earliest teachers and has adapted and paraphrased and modernized it. In the crucible of his intense personality this truth has become Sundayized. His discourses may have a variety of origin, but they all sound like Billy Sunday when he delivers them.

A toilsome, painstaking worker, he has made elaborate notes of all his sermons, and these he takes with him in leather-bound black books to the platform and follows more or less closely as he speaks. No other man than himself could use these rough notes. Often he interjects into one sermon parts of another. He has about a hundred discourses at his command at present, and his supply is constantly growing.

The early copies of Sunday's sermons were taken down more or less correctly in shorthand, and these have been reproduced in every city where he has gone: consequently they lack the tang and flavor of his present deliverances.

He is alert to glean from all sources. In conversation one morning in Scranton I told him how on the previous day a lawyer friend had characterized a preacher with whom I had been talking by saying, "How much like a preacher he looks, and how little like a man." That afternoon Sunday used this in his sermon and twiddled it under his fingers for a minute or two, paraphrasing it in characteristic Sunday fashion. Doubtless it is now part of his permanent oratorical stock in trade.

The absolute unconventionality of the man makes all this possible. He is not afraid of the most shocking presentation of truth. Thus when speaking at the University of Pennsylvania, he alluded to a professor who had criticized the doctrine of hell, saying, "That man will not be in hell five minutes before he knows better." Of course that thrust caught the students. A more discreet and diplomatic person than Sunday would not have dared to say this.

The gospel preached by Sunday is the same that the Church has been teaching for hundreds of years. He knows no modifications. He is fiercely antagonistic to "modern" scholarship. He sits in God's judgment seat in almost every sermon and frequently sends men to hell by name.

All this may be deplorable, but it is Sunday. The Bible which he uses is an interpreted and annotated edition by one of the most conservative of Bible teachers: this suits Sunday, for he is not of the temperament to be hospitable to new truths that may break forth from the living word.

This state of mind leads him to be extravagant and intolerant in his statements. His hearers are patient with all of this because the body of his teachings is that held by all evangelical Christians.   If he were less cock-sure he would not be Billy Sunday; the great mass of mankind want a religion of authority.

After all, truth is intolerant.

Although lacking technical literary training Sunday is not only a master of living English and of terse, strong, vivid and gripping phrase, but he is also capable of extraordinary flights of eloquence, when he uses the chastest and most appropriate language.   He has held multitudes spellbound with such passages as these:

God's Token of Love

"Down in Jacksonville, Florida, a man, Judge Owen, quarreled with his betrothed and to try to forget, he went off and worked in a yellow-fever hospital.   Finally he caught the disease and had succumbed to it.   He had passed the critical stage of the disease, but he was dying.   One day his sweetheart met the physician on the street and asked about the judge.   'He's sick,' he told her.

"'How bad?' she asked.

"'Well, he's passed the critical stage, but he is dying,' the doctor told her.

"'But I don't understand,' she said, 'if he's passed the critical stage why isn't he getting well?'

"'He's dying, of undying love for you, not the fever,' the doctor told her.   She asked him to come with her to a florist and he went and there she purchased some smilax and intertwined lilacs and wrote on a card, 'With my love,' and signed her given name.

"The doctor went back to the hospital and his patient was tossing in fitful slumber.   He laid the flowers on his breast and he awoke and saw the flowers and buried his head in them.   'Thanks for the flowers, doctor,' he said, but the doctor said, 'They are not from me.'

"'Then who are they from?'

"'Guess!'

"'I can't; tell me.'

"'I think you'll find the name on the card,' the doctor told him, and he looked and read the card, 'With my love.'

"'Tell me,' he cried, 'did she write that of her free will or did you beg her to do it?' The doctor told him she had begged to do it herself.

"Then you ought to have seen him. The next day he was sitting up. The next day he ate some gruel. The next day he was in a chair. The next day he could hobble on crutches. The next day he threw one of them away. The next day he threw the cane away and the next day he could walk pretty well. On the ninth day there was a quiet wedding in the annex of the hospital. You laugh; but listen: This old world is like a hospital. Here are the wards for the libertines. Here are the wards for the drunkards. Here are the wards for the blasphemers. Everywhere I look I see scarred humanity.

"Nineteen hundred years ago God looked over the battlements of heaven and he picked a basket of flowers, and then one day he dropped a baby into the manger at Bethlehem. 'For God so loved the world that he gave his only begotten Son that whosoever believeth on him should not perish but have everlasting life.' What more can he do?

"But God didn't spare him. They crucified him, but he burst the bonds of death and the Holy Spirit came down. They banished John to the isle of Patmos and there he wrote the words: 'Behold, I stand at the door and knock; if any man hear my voice and open the door I shall come in to him and sup with him and he with me.'"

The Sinking Ship

"Years ago there was a ship on the Atlantic and a storm arose. The ship sprung a leak and in spite of all the men could do they could not pump out the water fast enough. The captain called the men to him and told them that he had taken observations and bearings and said unless the leak was stopped in ten hours the boat would be at the bottom of the sea. 'I want a man who will volunteer his life to stay the intake. It's in the second hold and about the size of a man's arm and some one can place his arm in the hole and it will hold back the water until we can get it pumped out enough.'

"Not a man stirred. They said they would go back to the pumps and they did. They worked hard and when a man dropped they would drag him away and revive him and bring him back. The captain called them again and told them it was no use unless it was changed. They would be at the bottom before ten hours unless some one volunteered and in less time than that if a storm arose. Then one stepped back. 'What! My boy!'

"'Yes, father, I'll go.'

"He sent some endearing words to his mother, took one last look at the sky and kissed his father and bade the sailors good-bye, and went below. He found the leak and placed his arm in it and packed rags around it and the men went back to the pumps. When day broke they saw the body floating and swaying in the water, but the arm was still in the hole. And the vessel sailed into port safe. There on the coast today stands a monument to perpetuate the deed.

"Nineteen hundred years ago this old world sprung a leak. God asked for volunteers to stop it, and all of the angels and seraphim stood back, Noah, Abraham, Elijah, Isaiah, David, Jeremiah, Solomon, none would go, and then forth stepped his Son and said: 'Father, I'll go,' and descended, and died on the cross; but

.'' 'Up from the grave he arose,
   With a mighty triumph o'er his foes.
   He arose a victor from the dark domain
   And he lives forever with his saints to reign.
   Hallelujah, Christ arose!'

He burst the bonds of death, and the gates of heaven, while the angels sang and would crown him yet. 'Let me stand between God and the people,' and there he stands today, the Mediator, with the salvation, full, free, perfect, and eternal in one hand and the sword of inflexible justice in the other. The time will come when he'll come with his angels; some day he will withdraw his offer of salvation.

"Come and accept my Christ! Who'll come and get under the blood with me?"

"What If It Had Been My Boy?"

"'Say, papa, can I go with you?' asked a little boy of his father. 'Yes, son, come on,' said the father, as he threw the axe over his shoulder and accompanied by a friend, went to the woods and felled a tree.

"The little fellow said: 'Say, papa, can I go and play in the water at the lagoon?' 'Yes, but be careful and don't get into deep water; keep close to the bank.' The little fellow was playing, digging wells, picking up stones and shells and talking to himself, when pretty soon the father heard him cry, 'Hurry, papa, hurry.'

"The father leaped to his feet, grabbed the axe and ran to the lagoon and saw the boy floundering in deep water, hands outstretched, a look of horror on his face as he cried, 'Hurry, papa; hurry; the alligator has got me.' The hideous amphibious monster had been hibernating and had come out, lean, lank, hungry, voracious, and seized the boy.

"The father leaped into the lagoon and was just about to sink the axe through the head of the monster when he turned and swished the water with his huge tail like the screw of an ocean steamer, and the little fellow cried out: 'Hurry, papa; hurry, hurry, hur——' The water choked him. The blood-flecked foam told the story. The father went and got men and they plunged in and felt around and all they ever carried home to his mother was just two handfuls of crushed bones.

"When I read that, for days I could not eat, for nights I could not sleep. I said, 'Oh, God, what if that had been my boy?'

"There are influences worse than an alligator and they are ripping and tearing to shreds your virtue, your morality.

Young men are held by intemperance, others by vice, drunkards crying to the Church, 'Hurry, faster,' and the church members sit on the bank playing cards, sit there drinking beer and reading novels. 'Hurry.' They are splitting hairs over fool things, criticizing me or somebody else, instead of trying to keep sinners out of hell, and they are crying to the Church, 'Faster! Faster! Faster!' 'Lord, is it I?'

"How many will say, 'God, I want to be nearer to you than I have ever been before. I want to renew my vows. I want to get under the cross.' How many will say it?

"Who'll yield his heart to Christ? Who'll take his stand for the Lord? Who'll come out clean-cut for God?"

A Dream of Heaven

"Some years ago, after I had been romping and playing with the children, I grew tired and lay down, and half awake and half asleep, I had a dream.

· "I dreamed I was in a far-off land; it was not Persia, but all the glitter and gaudy raiment were there; it was not India, although her coral strands were there; it was not Ceylon, although all the beauties of that island of paradise were there; it was not Italy, although the soft dreamy haze of the blue Italian skies shone above me. I looked for weeds and briars, thorns and thistles and brambles and found none. I saw the sun in all its regal splendor and I said to the people, 'When will the sun set and it grow dark?'

"They all laughed and said: 'It never grows dark in this land; there is no night here.'

"I looked at the people, their faces wreathed in a simple halo of glory, attired in holiday clothing. I said: 'When will the working men go by clad in overalls? and where are the brawny men who work and toil over the anvil?'

"They said, 'We toil not, neither do we spin; there remaineth a rest for the people of God.'

"I strolled out in the suburbs. I said, 'Where are the graveyards, the grave-diggers? Where do you bury your dead?'

"They said, 'We never die here.'

"I looked out and saw the towers and spires; I looked at them, but I did not see any tombstones, mausoleums, green or flower-covered graves. I said, 'Where, where are the hearses that carry your dead? Where are the under-takers that embalm the dead?'

"They said, 'We never die in this land.'

"I said, 'Where are the hospitals where they take the sick? Where is the minster, and where are the nurses to give the gentle touch, the panacea?'

"They said, 'We never grow sick in this land.'

"I said, 'Where are the homes of want and squalor? Where live the poor?'

"They said, 'There is no penury; none die here; none ever cry for bread in this land.' I was bewildered. I strolled along and heard the ripple of the waters as the waves broke against the jeweled beach. I saw boats with oars dipped with silver, bows of pure gold. I saw multitudes that no man could number. We all jumped down through the violets and varicolored flowers, the air pulsing with bird song, and I cried,

"'Are—all—here?' And they echoed,

"'All—are—here.'

"And we went leaping and shouting and vied with bower and spire, and they all caroled and sung my welcome, and we all bounded and leaped and shouted with glee, 'Home—Home—Home.'"

The Battle With Death

"Just one thing divides you people. You are either across the line of safety, or you are outside the kingdom of God. Old or young, rich or poor, high or low, ignorant or educated, white or colored, each of you is upon one side or upon the other.

"The young man who talked to Jesus didn't let an infidel persuade him, and neither should you.

"The time will come when his head will lie on his pillow and his fevered head will toss from side to side.

9

"The time will come when there will be a rap on the door.

" 'Who are you?'

" 'Death.'

" 'I didn't send for you. Why do you come here?'

" 'Nobody sends for me. I choose my own time. If I waited for people to send for me I would never come.'

" 'But don't come in now, Death.'

" 'I am coming in. I have waited for a long time. I have held a mortgage on you for fifty years, and I've come to foreclose.'

" 'But, ah, Death, I'm not ready.'

" 'Hush! Hush! I've come to take you. You must come.'

" 'Death ! Death! Go get my pocketbook, there! Go get my bankbook! Go get the key to my safety deposit box! Take my gold watch, my jewelry, my lands, my home, everything I've got, I'll give all to you if you'll only go.'

"But Death Says, 'I've Come for You' "

"But Death says, 'I've come for you. I don't want your money or your land or anything that you have. You must come with me.'

" 'Death! Death! Don't blow that icy breath upon me. Don't crowd me against the wall!'

" 'You must come! You have a week—you have five days—you have one day—you have twelve hours—you have one hour—you have thirty minutes—you have ten minutes—you have one minute—you have thirty seconds—

you have ten seconds! I'll count them—one—two—three—four—five—six—ha! ha!—seven—eight—nine—ten!'

"He's gone. Telephone for the undertaker. Carry him to the graveyard. Lay him beside his mother. She died saying, 'I'm sweeping through the gates, washed in the blood of the Lamb.' He died shrieking, 'Don't blow that cold breath in my face! Don't crowd me against the wall!' Oh! God, don't let that old infidel keep you out of the kingdom of God.

"Who'll come into the kingdom of God? Come quick—quick—quick!"

"Christ or Nothing"

"'And whatsoever ye shall ask the Father in my name, that will I do, that the Father may be glorified in the Son.' No man can be saved without Jesus Christ. There's no way to God unless you come through Jesus Christ. It's Jesus Christ or nothing.

"At the close of the Battle of Gettysburg the country roundabout was overrun by Federals or Confederates, wounded or ill, and the people helped both alike. Relief corps were organized in all the little towns. In one of them—I think it was York—a man who had headed the committee, resigned as chairman and told his clerk not to send any more soldiers to him. There came a Union soldier with a blood-stained bandage and with crutches that he had made for himself, and asked to see this man. 'I am no longer chairman of the committee,' said the man, 'and I cannot help you, for if I were to make any exception to the rule, I would be overrun with applicants.'

"'But,' said the soldier, 'I don't want to ask you for anything. I only want to give you a letter. It is from your son, who is dead. I was with him, when he died. When he was wounded I got him a canteen of water and propped him up against a tree and held his hand when he wrote. I know where he lies.' The father took the letter, and he read it. It said, 'Treat this soldier kindly for my sake.'

Then it told how he had helped the writer—the dying boy. The father said, 'You must come with me to his mother.' She saw them coming and cried out, 'Have you any news of my boy?' The father said, 'Here is a letter—read it.' She read it and shrieked. They took the wounded soldier into their home, 'Won't you stay with us and be our son? You were his friend, you were with him at the last, you look like him, your voice reminds us of him. When you speak and we turn our faces away, we can almost think he is here. Let us adopt you. Won't you do it?' He heard their plea, and he was touched and he stayed. So heaven will hear your prayer if it is in the name of Christ.

"When I go in the name of Jesus Christ, God will stop making worlds to hear me.

"Lord, teach us how to pray."

Calvary

"There comes Judas, leading the devil's crowd, the churchly gang. Don't forget that Jesus was crucified by church members whose sins he rebuked. Judas said, 'The fellow that I kiss, that's Jesus.' Look at the snake on his sanctimonious countenance. He said, 'Hail, Master,' and he kissed him.

"Jesus said, 'Judas, betrayest thou the Son of Man with a kiss?'

"And they staggered back. 'Whom seek ye?'

"'We are all looking for Jesus of Nazareth.'

"'All right, I am he.' They staggered again, and Judas led them on.

"They rushed up and seized Jesus Christ. When starting for Calvary they put a cross on his back. He was tired and he staggered and stumbled, then fell, but he climbed up and a fellow smote him and said, 'Ha, ha,' and the young fellow spat upon him. They cursed him and damned him. What for? Because he came to open up a plan of redemption to keep you and me out of hell; and yet you live a life of disgrace. On he went and along came a colored man

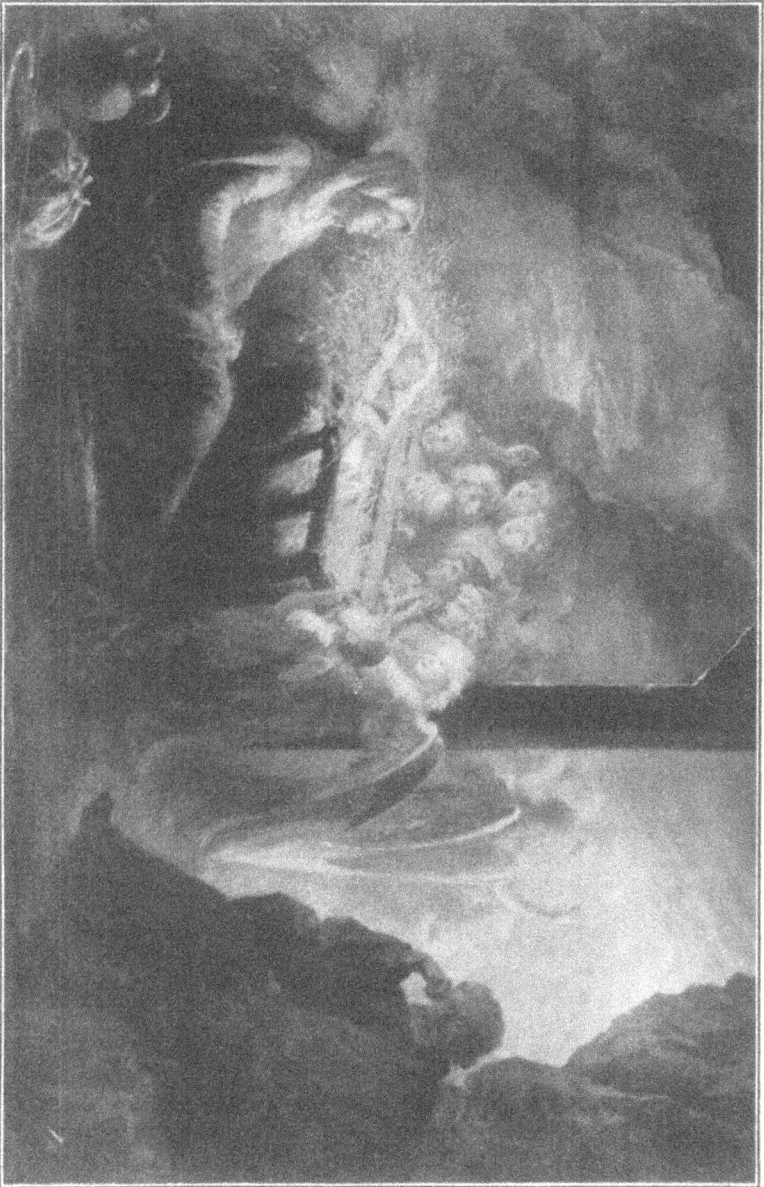

"The Ideal Mother is the Product of a Civilization that Rose from the Manger of Bethlehem."

BILLY JR., MR. AND MRS. SUNDAY AND PAUL.

named Simon and they put the cross on his back and he went dragging if for Jesus. The colored race has borne many a burden in the advancement of civilization, but a grander burden has never been on the back of black or white, than when Simon bore the Master's cross.

"On they went and seized him, and I can see his arms as they pounded the nails through his hands and his feet. Another fellow digs a hole, and I can hear the cross as it 'chugs' in the hole, and they lift him between heaven and earth. Then the disciples forsook him and fled. Left him all alone. How many will go with Jesus to the last ditch? Thousands will die for him, but there is another set that will not.

"The disciples followed him to the garden, but forsook him at the cross.

"If we had been there we might have seen the hill-tops and the tree-tops filled and covered with angels, and houses crowded. As Jesus hung on the cross and cried, 'I thirst,' a Jew ran and dipped a sponge in wormwood and gall and vinegar and put it on a reed and put it up to his lips. Then Jesus cried, 'My God, why hast thou forsaken me?' There he hung, feeling the burden of your guilt, you booze-fighter, you libertine, you dead-beat. 'My God, hast thou forsaken me?' he cried, and I imagine that the archangel cried, "Oh, Jesus, if you want me to come and sweep the howling, blood-thirsty mob into hell, lift your head and look me in the face and I will come.'

"But Jesus gritted his teeth and struggled on, and the archangel again cried, 'Oh, Jesus, if you want me to come, tear your right hand loose from the cross and wave it, and I will come.' But Jesus just clenched his fist over the nails. What for? To keep you out of hell. Then tell me why you are indifferent. And soon he cried, 'It is finished.'

"The Holy Spirit plucked the olive branch of peace back through the gates of heaven from the cross and winged his way and cried, 'Peace! Peace has been made by his death on the cross.' That is what he had to do. That was his duty."

The World for God

"A heathen woman named Panathea was famous for her great beauty, and King Cyrus wanted her for his harem. He sent his representatives to her and offered her money and jewels to come, but she repulsed them and spurned their advances. Again he sent them, this time with offers still more generous and tempting; but again she sent them away with scorn. A third time they were sent, and a third time she said, 'Nay.' Then King Cyrus went in person to see her, and he doubled and trebled and quadrupled the offers his men had made, but still she would not go. She told him that she was a wife, and that she was true to her husband.

"He said, 'Panathea, where dwellest thou?'

"'In the arms and on the breast of my husband,' she said.

"'Take her away,' said Cyrus. 'She is of no use to me.' Then he put her husband in command of the charioteers and sent him into battle at the head of the troops. Panathea knew what this meant—that her husband had been sent in that he might be killed. She waited while the battle raged, and when the field was cleared she shouted his name and searched for him and finally found him wounded and dying. She knelt and clasped him in her arms, and as they kissed, his lamp of life went out forever. King Cyrus heard of the man's death, and came to the field. Panathea saw him coming, careening on his camel like a ship in a storm. She called, 'Oh, husband! He comes—he shall not have me. I was true to you in life, and will be true to you in death!' And she drew her dead husband's poniard from its sheath, drove it into her own breast and fell dead across the body.

"King Cyrus came up and dismounted. He removed his turban and knelt by the dead husband and wife, and thanked God that he had found in his kingdom one true and virtuous woman that his money could not buy, nor his power intimidate.

"Oh, preachers, the problem of this century is the pro-

blem of the first century. We must win the world for God
and we will win the world for God just as soon as we have
men and women who will be faithful to God and will not lie
and will not sell out to the devil."

A Word Picture

"Every day at noon, while Ingersoll was lecturing,
Hastings would go to old Farwell Hall and answer Ingersoll's statements of the night before. One night Ingersoll
painted one of those wonderful word pictures for which he
was justly famous. He was a master of the use of words.
Men and women would applaud and cheer and wave their
hats and handkerchiefs, and the waves of sound would rise
and fall like great waves of the sea. As two men were
going home from his lecture, one of them said to the other:
'Bob certainly cleaned 'em up tonight.' The other man
said: 'There's one thing he didn't clean up. He didn't
clean up the religion of my old mother.'

"This is the word picture Ingersoll painted:

"'I would rather have been a French peasant and worn
wooden shoes; I would rather have lived in a hut, with a
vine growing over the door and the grapes growing and
ripening in the autumn sun; I would rather have been that
peasant, with my wife by my side and my children upon my
knees twining their arms of affection about me; I would
rather have been that poor French peasant and gone down
at least to the eternal promiscuity of the dust, followed by
those who loved me; I would a thousand times rather have
been that French peasant than that imperial incarnation of
force and murder (Napoleon); and so I would ten thousand
times.'

"What was that? Simply a word picture. It was only
the trick of an orator.

"Let me paint for you a picture, and see if it doesn't
make you feel like leaping and shouting hallelujahs. ,

"Infidelity has never won a drunkard from his cups.
It has never redeemed a fallen woman from her unchastity.

It has never built a hospital for the crushed and sick. It has never dried tears. It has never built a mission for the rescue of the down-and-out. It wouldn't take a ream, or a quire, or a sheet, or even a line of paper to write down what infidelity has done to better and gladden the world.

"What has infidelity done to benefit the world? What has it ever done to help humanity in any way? It never built a school, it never built a church, it never built an asylum or a home for the poor. It never did anything for the good of man. I challenge the combined forces of unbelief. They have failed utterly.

"Well may Christianity stand today and point to its hospitals, its churches and its schools with their towers and the spires pointing to the source of their inspiration and say: 'These are the works that I do.'

"I would rather have been a French peasant and worn wooden shoes; I would rather have lived in a hut, with a vine growing over the door and grapes growing and ripening in the autumn sun; I would rather have been that peasant, with my wife and children by my side and the open Bible on my knees, at peace with the world and at peace with God; I would rather have been that poor peasant and gone down at least in the promiscuity of the dust, with the certainty that my name was written in the Lamb's book of life than to have been that brilliant infidel whose tricks of oratory charmed thousands and sent souls to hell."

The Faithful Pilot

"Some years ago a harbor pilot in Boston, who had held a commission for sixty-five years (you know the harbor pilots and the ocean pilots are different). For sixty-five years he had guided ships in and out of the Boston harbor, but his time to die had come. Presently the watchers at his bedside saw that he was trying to sit up, and they aided him. 'I see a light,' he said.

"'Is it the Minot light?' they asked him.

"'No, that is first white and then red; this one is all

white all the time,' and he fell back. After a few moments he struggled to rise again. 'I see a light,' he gasped.

"'Is it the Highland light?'

"'No, that one is red and then black; this one is white all the time.' And he fell back again and they thought certainly he was gone, but he came back again as if from the skies and they saw his lips moving. 'I see a light.'

"'Is it the Boston light; the last as you pass out?' they asked.

"'No, that one is red all the time; this one is white all the time.' And his hands trembled and he reached out his feeble arms. His face lighted up with a halo of glory. 'I see a light,' he gasped, 'and it is the light of glory. Let the anchor drop.'

"'And he anchored his soul in the haven of rest,
 To sail the wild seas no more:
 Tho' the tempest may beat o'er the wild stormy deep,
 In Jesus I'm safe evermore.'

"That's where you ought to be. Will you come?"

CHAPTER XI

Acrobatic Preaching

If nine-tenths of you were as weak physically as you are spiritually, you couldn't walk.—BILLY SUNDAY.

IF, as has been often said, inspiration is chiefly perspiration, then there is no doubting the inspiration of Rev. William A. Sunday, D.D. Beyond question he is the most vigorous speaker on the public platform today. One editor estimates that he travels a mile over his platform in every sermon he delivers. There is no other man to liken him to: only an athlete in the pink of condition could endure the gruelling exertions to which he subjects himself every day of his campaigns. The stranger who sees him for the first time is certain that he is on the very edge of a complete collapse; but as that same remark has been made for years past, it is to be hoped that the physical instrument may be equal to its task for a long time to come.

People understand with their eyes as well as with their ears; and Sunday preaches to both. The intensity of his physical exertions—gestures is hardly an adequate word—certainly enhances the effect of the preacher's earnestness. No actor on the dramatic stage works so hard. Such passion as dominates Sunday cannot be simulated; it is the soul pouring itself out through every pore of the body.

Some of the platform activities of Sunday make spectators gasp. He races to and fro across the platform. Like a jack knife he fairly doubles up in emphasis. One hand smites the other. His foot stamps the floor as if to destroy it. Once I saw him bring his clenched fist down so hard on the seat of a chair that I feared the blood would flow and the bones be broken. No posture is too extreme for this restless gymnast. Yet it all seems natural. Like his speech,

it is an integral part of the man.   Every muscle of his body
preaches in accord with his voice.

Be it whispered, men like this unconventional sort of
earnestness.   Whenever they are given a chance, most men
are prone to break the trammels of sober usage.   I never
yet have met a layman who has been through a Billy Sunday
campaign who had a single word of criticism of the platform
gymnastics of the evangelist.   Their reasoning is something
like this: On the stage, where men undertake to represent
a character or a truth, they use all arts and spare themselves
not at all.   Why should not a man go to greater lengths
when dealing with living
realities of the utmost importance?

Sunday is a physical
sermon.   In a unique sense
he glorifies God with his
body.   Only a physique
kept in tune by clean living
and right usage could re-
spond to the terrific and
unceasing demands which
Sunday makes upon it.
When in a sermon he
alludes to the man who acts

SUNDAY IS FOR AN INSTANT DOWN ON
ALL FOURS.

no better than a four-footed brute, Sunday is for an instant
down on all fours on the platform and you see that brute.
As he pictures a man praying he sinks to his knees for a
single moment.   When he talks of the death-bed penitent
as a man waiting to be pumped full of embalming fluid, he
cannot help going through the motions of pumping in the
fluid.   He remarks that death-bed repentance is "burning
the candle of life in the service of the devil, and then blowing
the smoke in God's face"—and the last phrase is accompanied by "pfouff!"   In a dramatic description of the
marathon he pictures the athlete falling prostrate at the
goal and—thud!—there lies the evangelist prone on the

platform. Only a skilled base-ball player, with a long drill in sliding to bases, could thus fling himself to the floor without serious injury. On many occasions he strips off his coat and talks in his shirt sleeves. It seems impossible for him to stand up behind the pulpit and talk only with his mouth.

The fact is, Sunday is a born actor. He knows how to portray truth by a vocal personality. When he describes the traveler playing with a pearl at sea, he tosses an imaginary gem into the air so that the spectators hold their breath lest the ship should lurch and the jewel be lost. Words without gesture could never attain this triumph of oratory.

A hint of Sunday's state of mind which drives him to such earnestness and intensity in labor is found in quotations like the following:

"You will agree with me, in closing, that I'm not a crank; at least I try not to be. I have not preached about my first, second, third or hundredth blessing. I have not talked about baptism or immersion. I told you that while I was here my creed would be: 'With Christ you are saved; without him you are lost.' Are you saved? Are you lost? Going to heaven? Going to hell? I have tried to build every sermon right around those questions; and also to steer clear of anything else, but I want to say to you in closing, that it is the inspiration of my life, the secret of my earnestness. I never preach a sermon but that I think it may be the last one some fellow will hear or the last I shall ever be privileged to preach. It is an inspiration to me that some day He will come.

> " 'It may be at morn, when the day is awaking,
>   When darkness through sunlight and shadow is breaking,
>   That Jesus will come, in the fullness of glory,
>   To receive from the world his own.
>
> " 'Oh joy, Oh delight, to go without dying,
>   No sickness, no sadness, no sorrow, no crying!
>   Caught up with the Lord in the clouds of glory
>   When he comes to receive from the world his own.' "

"Now—the servant of Naaman entered the hut of the Prophet Elisha and found him sitting perched upon a stool, writing on Papyrus, and he explained how Naaman had the leprosy —and the old prophet never got up, but just said, 'Tell him to bathe in the Jordan seven times—now BEAT IT! BEAT IT!'

—oo—

So the servant went back, and Naaman said, 'Well did you see him?'

And the servant said, 'Yes, but he's a queer old duck—he said for you to bathe in the Jordan seven times.'

—But he went right ahead! First he stuck one toe in— and shivered—but finally—

—And nothing had happened except that his sores began to itch—but when he had dipped seven times—his flesh was made whole—

—He held onto his nose and shut his eyes and down he went—in all over!

WELL—

Naaman thought he'd take a chance —so he went down to the river bank and got off his clothes and probably about the first thing he did was to stub his toe against a big rock! O-o-o-o-o-o-o!—

—And then—like as not —one of those big sand flies sat right down between his shoulder blades! We-e-e-e-e-e!!!

—And then up he came and stamped and pounded and spluttered and got the water out of his ears—

HIS LEPROSY WAS HEALED!

A CARICATURE OF BILLY SUNDAY'S EMPHATIC WAY OF PREACHING.

BITING, BLISTERING, BLASTING CONDEMNATION OF SIN. THIS RARE PHO-
TOGRAPH SHOWS THE TREMENDOUS EARNESTNESS OF MR. SUNDAY AND
THE ENERGY, ZEAL AND FIRE HE PUTS INTO HIS MESSAGE WHICH
HAS WARMED THIS COLD WORLD MORE THAN THAT OF ANY
OTHER APOSTLE OF RIGHTEOUSNESS IN THIS GENERATION.

"Go straight on and break the lion's neck and turn it into a beehive, out of which you will some day take the best and sweetest honey ever tasted, for the flavor of a dead lion in the honey beats that of clover and buckwheat all to pieces. Be a man, therefore, by going straight on to breathe the air that has in it the smoke of battle.

"Don't spend much time in looking for an easy chair, with a soft cushion on it, if you would write your name high in the hall of fame where the names of real men are found. The man who is willing to be carried over all rough places might as well have wooden legs. 'He is not worthy of the honeycomb who shuns the hive because the bees have stings.' The true value of life lies in the preciousness of striving. No tears are ever shed for the chick that dies in its shell.

> " 'Did you tackle the trouble that came your way
> With a resolute heart and cheerful?
> Or hide your face from the light of day
> With a craven soul and fearful?
> Oh, a trouble is a ton, or a trouble is an ounce,
> Or a trouble is what you make it,
> And it isn't the fact that you're hurt that counts—
> But only—How did you take it?' "

"This poem is by Paul Lawrence Dunbar, the negro poet:

" 'The Lord had a job for me, but I had so much to do,
I said: "You get somebody else—or, wait till I get through.
I don't know how the Lord came out, but he seemed to get along—
But I felt kinda sneakin' like, 'cause I know'd I done him wrong—
One day I needed the Lord, needed him myself—needed him right away—
And he never answered me at all, but I could hear him say—
Down in my accusin' heart—"Nigger, I'se got too much to do,
You get somebody else, or wait till I get through."
Now when the Lord he have a job for me, I never tries to shirk;
I drops what I have on hand and does the good Lord's work;
And my affairs can run along, or wait till I get through,
Nobody else can do the job that God's marked out for you.' "

"I will tell you many young people are good in the beginning, but they are like the fellow that was killed by falling off a skyscraper—they stop too quick. They go one day like a six-cylinder automobile with her carbureters working; the next day they stroll along like a fellow walking through a graveyard reading the epitaphs on the tombstones. It is the false ideals that strew the shores with wrecks, eagerness to achieve success in realms we can not reach that breeds half the ills that curse today. One hundred years from tonight what difference will it make whether you are rich or poor; whether learned or illiterate.

"'It matters little where I was born,
  Whether my parents were rich or poor;
Whether they shrunk from the cold world's scorn,
  Or lived in pride of wealth secure.
But whether I live an honest man,
  And hold my integrity firm in my clutch;
I tell you—my neighbor—as plain as I can,
  That matters much.'

"The engineer is bigger than the locomotive, because he runs it.

"Do your best and you will never wear out shoe leather looking for a job. Do your best, and you will never become blind reading 'Help Wanted' ads in a newspaper. Be like the fellow that went to college and tacked the letter V up over his door in his room. He was asked what that stood for, and he said valedictorian, and he went out carrying the valedictory with him.

" 'If I were a cobbler, best of all cobblers I would be.
  If I were a tinker, no tinker beside should mend an old tea kettle for me.'"

In dealing with the unreality of many preachers, Sunday pictures a minister as going to the store to buy groceries for his wife, but using his pulpit manner, his pulpit tone of voice and his pulpit phraseology. This is so true to life that it convulses every congregation that hears it. In these few minutes of mimicry the evangelist does more to argue for reality and genuineness and unprofessionalism on the part of the clergy than could be accomplished by an hour's lecture.

Another of his famous passages is his portrayal of the society woman nursing a pug dog. You see the woman and you see the dog, and you love neither one. Likewise, Sunday mimics the skin-flint hypocrite in a way to make the man represented loathe himself.

This suggests a second fact about Sunday's preaching. He often makes people laugh, but rarely makes them cry. His sense of humor is stronger than his sense of pathos. Now tears and hysterics are supposed to be part of the stock in trade of the professional evangelist. Not so with Sunday. He makes sin absurd and foolish as well as wicked; and he makes the sinner ashamed of himself. He has recovered for the Church the use of that powerful weapon, the barb of ridicule. There are more instruments of warfare in the gospel armory than the average preacher commonly uses. Sunday endeavors to employ them all, and his favorites seem to be humor, satire and scorn.

As a physical performance the preaching to crowds of from ten to twenty-five thousand persons every day is phenomenal. Sunday has not a beautiful voice like many great orators. It is husky and seems strained and yet it is able to penetrate every corner of his great tabernacles. Nor is he possessed of the oratorical manner, "the grand air" of the rhetorician. Mostly he is direct, informal and colloquial in his utterances. But he is so dead in earnest that after every address he must make an entire change of raiment—and, like most base-ball players, and members of the sporting fraternities, he is fond of good clothes, even to the point of foppishness. He carries about a dozen different suits with him and I question whether there is a single Prince Albert or "preacher's coat" in the whole outfit.

A very human figure is Billy Sunday on the platform. During the preliminaries he enjoys the music, the responses of the delegations, and any of the informalities that are common accessories of his meetings. When he begins to speak he is an autocrat and will brook no disturbance. He is less concerned about hurting the feelings of some fidgety, restless usher or auditor than he is about the comfort of the great congregation and its opportunity to hear his message.

Any notion that Sunday loves the limelight is wide of the mark. The fact is, he shuns the public gaze. It really makes him nervous to be pointed out and stared at. That is one reason why he does not go to a hotel, but hires a furnished house for himself and his associates. Here they "camp out" for the period of the campaign, and enjoy something like the family life of every-day American folk. Their hospitable table puts on no more frills than that of the ordinary home. The same cook has accompanied the party for months; and when a family's religion so commends itself to the cook, it is likely to grade "A No. 1 Hard," like Minnesota wheat.

"Ma," as the whole party call Mrs. Sunday, is responsible for the home, as well as for many meetings. Primarily, though, she looks after "Daddy." Sunday is the type of man who is quite helpless with respect to a dozen matters which a watchful wife attends to. He needs considerable looking after, and all his friends, from the newspaper men to the policeman on duty at the house, conspire to take care of him.

The Pittsburgh authorities assigned a couple of plain clothes men to safeguard Sunday; of course he "got them" early, as he gets most everybody he comes into touch with. So these men took care of Sunday as if he were the famous "millionaire baby" of Washington and Newport. Not a sense of official duty, but affectionate personal solicitude animated those two men who rode in the automobile with us from the house to the Tabernacle.

This sort of thing is one of the most illuminating phases of the Sunday campaign. Those who come closest to the man believe most in his religion. As one of the newspaper men covering the meetings said to me, "The newspaper boys have all 'hit the trail.' " Then he proved his religion by offering to do the most fraternal services for me. From Mrs. Sunday, though, I learned that there was one bright reporter who had worked on aspects of the revival who had not gone forward. He avoided the meetings, and evaded the personal interviews of the Sunday party. The evangelist's wife was as solicitous over that one young man's spiritual welfare as if he had been one of her own four children.

Ten of the policemen stationed at the Tabernacle went forward the night before I arrived in Pittsburgh. I was told that twenty others were waiting to "hit the trail" in a group, taking their families with them.

The personal side of Sunday is wholesome and satisfactory. He is a simple, modest chap, marked by the ways of the Middle West. Between meetings he goes to bed, and there friends sometimes visit him. Met thus intimately, behind the scenes, one would expect from him an unrestrained display of personality, even a measure of egotism. Surely, it is sometimes to be permitted a man to recount his achievements. Never a boast did I hear from Sunday. Instead, he seemed absurdly self-distrustful. These are his times for gathering, and he wanted me to tell him about Bible lands!

CHAPTER XII

"The Old-Time Religion"

I am an old-fashioned preacher of the old-time religion, that has warmed this cold world's heart for two thousand years.—BILLY SUNDAY.

MODERN to the last minute Sunday's methods may be, but his message is unmistakably the "old-time religion." He believes his beliefs without a question. There is no twilight zone in his intellectual processes; no mental reservation in his preaching. He is sure that man is lost without Christ, and that only by the acceptance of the Saviour can fallen humanity find salvation. He is as sure of hell as of heaven, and for all modernized varieties of religion he has only vials of scorn.

In no single particular is Sunday's work more valuable than in its revelation of the power of positive conviction to attract and convert multitudes. The world wants faith. "Intolerant," cry the scholars of Sunday; but the hungry myriads accept him as their spiritual guide to peace, and joy, and righteousness. The world wants a religion with salvation in it; speculation does not interest the average man who seeks deliverance from sin in himself and in the world. He does not hope to be evoluted into holiness; he wants to be redeemed.

"Modernists" sputter and fume and rail at Sunday and his work: but they cannot deny that he leads men and women into new lives of holiness, happiness and helpfulness. Churches are enlarged and righteousness is promoted, all by the old, blood-stained way of the Cross. The revivals which have followed the preaching of Evangelist Sunday are supplemental to the Book of the Acts. His theology is summed up in the words Peter used in referring to Jesus: "There is none other Name under heaven given among men whereby we must be saved."

One of Sunday's favorite sayings is: "I don't know any more about theology than a jack-rabbit does about ping-pong, but I'm on the way to glory." That really does not fully express the evangelist's point. He was arguing that "theology bears the same relation to Christianity that botany does to flowers, or astronomy to the stars. Botany is re-written, but the flowers remain the same. Theology changes (I have no objection to your new theology when it tries to make the truths of Christianity clearer), but Christianity abides. Nobody is kept out of heaven because he does not understand theology. It isn't theology that saves, but Christ; it is not the saw-dust trail that saves, but Christ in the motive that makes you hit the trail.

"I believe the Bible is the word of God from cover to cover. I believe that the man who magnifies the word of God in his preaching is the man whom God will honor. Why do such names stand out on the pages of history as Wesley, Whitefield, Finney and Martin Luther? Because of their fearless denunciation of all sin, and because they preach Jesus Christ without fear or favor.

"But somebody says a revival is abnormal. You lie! Do you mean to tell me that the godless, card-playing conditions of the Church are normal? I say they are not, but it is the abnormal state. It is the sin-eaten, apathetic condition of the Church that is abnormal. It is the 'Dutch lunch' and beer party, card parties and the like, that are abnormal. I say that they lie when they say that a revival is an abnormal condition in the Church.

"What we need is the good old-time kind of revival that will cause you to love your neighbors, and quit talking about them. A revival that will make you pay your debts, and have family prayers. Get that kind and then you will see that a revival means a very different condition from what people believe it does.

"Christianity means a lot more than church member-ship. Many an old skin-flint is not fit for the balm of Gilead until you give him a fly blister and get after him with a currycomb. There are too many Sunday-school teachers who are godless card-players, beer, wine and champagne drinkers. No wonder the kids are going to the devil. No wonder your children grow up like cattle when you have no form of prayer in the home.".

THE GOSPEL ACCORDING TO SUNDAY

What does converted mean? It means completely changed. Converted is not synonymous with reformed. Reforms are from without—conversion from within. Conversion is a complete surrender to Jesus. It's a willingness to do what he wants you to do. Unless you have made a complete surrender and are doing his will it will avail you nothing if you've reformed a thousand times and have your name on fifty church records.

Believe on the Lord Jesus Christ, in your heart and confess him with your mouth and you will be saved. God is good. The plan of salvation is presented to you in two parts. Believe in your heart and confess with your mouth. Many of you here probably do believe. Why don't you confess? Now own up. The truth is that you have a yellow streak. Own up, business men, and business women, and all of you others. Isn't it so? Haven't you got a little saffron? Brave old Elijah ran like a scared deer when he heard old Jezebel had said she would have his head, and he beat it.¶ And he ran to Beersheba and lay down under a juniper tree and cried to the Lord to let him die. The Lord answered his prayer, but not in the way he expected. If he had let him die he would have died with nothing but the wind moaning through the trees as his funeral dirge. But the Lord had something better for Elijah. He had a chariot of fire and it swooped down and carried him into glory without his ever seeing death.

So he says he has something better for you—salvation if he can get you to see it. You've kept your church membership locked up. You've smiled at a smutty story. When God and the Church were scoffed at you never peeped, and when asked to stand up here you've sneaked out the back way and beat it. You're afraid and God despises a coward—a mutt. You cannot be converted by thinking so and sitting still.

Maybe you're a drunkard, an adulterer, a prostitute, a liar; won't admit you are lost; are proud. Maybe you're even proud you're not proud, and Jesus has a time of it.

Jesus said: "Come to me," not to the Church; to me, not to a creed; to me, not to a preacher; to me, not to an evangelist; to me, not to a priest; to me, not to a pope; "Come to me and I will give you rest." Faith in Jesus Christ saves you, not faith in the Church.

You can join church, pay your share of the preacher's salary, attend the services, teach Sunday school, return thanks and do everything that would apparently stamp you as a Christian—even pray—but you won't ever be a Christian until you do what God tells you to do.

That's the road, and that's the only one mapped out for you and for me. God treats all alike. He doesn't furnish one plan for the banker and another for the janitor who sweeps out the bank. He has the same plan for one that he has for another. It's the law—you may not approve of it, but that doesn't make any difference.

Salvation a Personal Matter

The first thing to remember about being saved is that salvation is a personal matter. "Seek ye the Lord"—that means every one must seek for himself. It won't do for the parent to seek for the children; it won't do for the children to seek for the parent. If you were sick all the medicine I might take wouldn't do you any good. Salvation is a personal matter that no one else can do for you; you must attend to it yourself.

Some persons have lived manly or womanly lives, and they lack but one thing—open confession of the Lord Jesus Christ. Some men think that they must come to him in a certain way—that they must be stirred by emotion or something like that.

Some people have a deeper conviction of sin before they are converted than after they are converted. With some it is the other way. Some know when they are converted and others don't.

Some people are emotional. Some are demonstrative. Some will cry easily. Some are cold and can't be moved to emotion. A man jumped up in a meeting and asked whether he could be saved when he hadn't shed a tear in forty years. Even as he spoke he began to shed tears. It's all a matter of how you're constituted. I am vehement, and I serve God with the same vehemence that I served the devil when I went down the line.

Some of you say that in order to accept Jesus you must have different surroundings. You think you could do it better in some other place. You can be saved where you are as well as any place on earth. I say, "My watch doesn't run. It needs new surroundings. I'll put it in this other pocket, or I'll put it here, or here on these flowers." It doesn't need new surroundings. It needs a new mainspring; and that's what the sinner needs. You need a new heart, not a new suit.

What can I do to keep out of hell? "Believe on the Lord Jesus Christ and thou shalt be saved."

The Philippian jailer was converted. He had put the disciples into the stocks when they came to the prison, but after his conversion he stooped down and washed the blood from their stripes.

Now, leave God out of the proposition for a minute. Never mind about the new birth—that's his business. Jesus Christ became a man, bone of our bone, flesh of our flesh. He died on the cross for us, so that we might escape the penalty pronounced on us. Now, never mind about anything but our part in salvation. Here it is: "Believe on the Lord Jesus Christ, and thou shalt be saved."

You say, "Mr. Sunday, the Church is full of hypocrites." So's hell. I say to you if you don't want to go to hell and live with that whole bunch forever, come into the Church, where you won't have to associate with them very long. There are no hypocrites in heaven.

You say, "Mr. Sunday, I can be a Christian and go to heaven without joining a church." Yes, and you can go to Europe without getting on board a steamer. The swimming's good—but the sharks are laying for fellows who take that route. I don't believe you. If a man is truly saved he will hunt for a church right away.

You say, "It's so mysterious. I don't understand." You'll be surprised to find out how little you know. You plant a seed in the ground—that's your part. You don't understand how it grows. How God makes that seed grow is mysterious to you.

Some people think that they can't be converted unless they go down on their knees in the straw at a camp-meeting, unless they pray all hours of the night, and all nights of the week, while some old brother storms heaven in prayer. Some think a man must lose sleep, must come down the aisle with a haggard look, and he must froth at the mouth and dance and shout. Some get it that way, and they don't think that the work I do is genuine unless conversions are made in the same way that they have got religion.

I want you to see what God put in black and white; that there can be a sound, thorough conversion in an instant; that man can be converted as quietly as the coming of day and never backslide. I do not find fault with the way other people get religion. What I want and preach is the fact that a man can be converted without any fuss.

If a man wants to shout and clap his hands in joy over his wife's conversion, or if a wife wants to cry when her husband is converted, I am not going to turn the hose on them, or put them in a strait-jacket. When a man turns to God truly in conversion, I don't care what form his conversion takes. I wasn't converted that way, but I do not rush around and say, with gall and bitterness, that you are not saved because you did not get religion the way I did. If we all got religion in the same way, the devil might go to sleep with a regular Rip Van Winkle snooze and still be on the job.

Look at Nicodemus. You could never get a man with the temperament of Nicodemus near a camp meeting, to kneel down in the straw, or to shout and sing. He was a quiet, thoughtful, honest, sincere and cautious man. He wanted to know the truth and he was willing to walk in the light when he found it.

Look at the man at the pool of Bethesda. He was a big sinner and was in a lot of trouble which his sins had made for him. He had been in that condition for a long time. It didn't take him three minutes to say "Yes," when the Lord spoke to him. See how quietly he was converted.

"And He Arose and Followed Him".

Matthew stood in the presence of Christ and he realized what it would be to be without Christ, to be without hope, and it brought him to a quick decision. "And he arose and followed him."

How long did that conversion take? How long did it take him to accept Christ after he had made up his mind? And you tell me you can't make an instant decision to please God? The decision of Matthew proves that you can. While he was sitting at his desk he was not a disciple. The instant he arose he was. That move changed his attitude toward God. Then he ceased to do evil and commenced to do good. You can be converted just as quickly as Matthew was.

God says: "Let the wicked man forsake his way." The instant that is done, no matter if the man has been a life-long sinner, he is safe. There is no need of struggling for hours—or for days—do it now. Who are you struggling with? Not God. God's mind was made up long before the foundations of the earth were laid. The plan of salvation was made long before there was any sin in the world. Electricity existed long before there was any car wheel for it to drive. "Let the wicked man forsake his way." When?

Within a month, within a week, within a day, within an hour? No! Now! The instant you yield, God's plan of salvation is thrown into gear. You will be saved before you know it, like a child being born.

Rising and following Christ switched Matthew from the broad to the narrow way. He must have counted the cost as he would have balanced his cash book. He put one side against the other. The life he was living led to all chance of gain. On the other side there was Jesus, and Jesus outweighs all else. He saw the balance turn as the tide of a battle turns and then it ended with his decision. The sinner died and the disciple was born.

I believe that the reason the story of Matthew was written was to show how a man could be converted quickly and quietly. It didn't take him five or ten years to begin to do something—he got busy right away.

You don't believe in quick conversions? There have been a dozen men of modern times who have been powers for God whose conversion was as quiet as Matthew's. Charles G. Finney never went to a camp meeting. He was out in the woods alone, praying, when he was converted. Sam Jones, a mighty man of God, was converted at the bedside of his dying father. Moody accepted Christ while waiting on a customer in a boot and shoe store. Dr. Chapman was converted as a boy in a Sunday school. All the other boys in the class had accepted Christ, and only Wilbur remained. The teacher turned to him and said, "And how about you, Wilbur?" He said, "I will," and he turned to Christ and has been one of his most powerful evangelists for many years. Gipsy Smith was converted in his father's tent. Torrey was an agnostic, and in comparing agnosticism, infidelity and Christianity, he found the scale tipped toward Christ. Luther was converted as he crawled up a flight of stairs in Rome.

Seemingly the men who have moved the world for Christ have been converted in a quiet manner. The way to judge a tree is by its fruit. Judge a tree of quiet conversion in this way.

Another lesson. When conversion compels people to forsake their previous calling, God gives them a better job. Luke said, "He left all." Little did he dream that his influence would be world-reaching and eternity-covering. His position as tax-collector seemed like a big job, but it was picking up pins compared to the job God gave him. Some of you may be holding back for fear of being put out of your job. If you do right God will see that you do not suffer. He has given plenty of promises, and if you plant your feet on them you can defy the poor-house. Trust in the Lord means that God will feed you. Following Christ you may discover a gold mine of ability that you never dreamed of possessing. There was a saloon-keeper, converted in a meeting at New Castle, who won hundreds of people to Christ by his testimony and his preaching.

You do not need to be in the church before the voice comes to you; you don't need to be reading the Bible; you don't need to be rich or poor or learned. Wherever Christ comes follow. You may be converted while engaged in your daily business. Men cannot put up a wall and keep Jesus away. The still small voice will find you.

At the Cross-roads

Right where the two roads through life diverge God has put Calvary. There he put up a cross, the stumbling block over which the love of God said, "I'll touch the heart of man with the thought of father and son." He thought that would win the world to him, but for nineteen hundred years men have climbed the Mount of Calvary and trampled into the earth the tenderest teachings of God.

You are on the devil's side. How are you going to cross over?

So you cross the line and God won't issue any extradition papers. Some of you want to cross. If you believe, then say so, and step across. I'll bet there are hundreds that are on the edge of the line and many are standing straddling it. But that won't save you. You believe in your heart—confess him with your mouth. With his heart man believes and with his mouth he confesses. Then confess and receive salvation full, free, perfect and external. God will not grant any extradition papers. Get over the old line. A man isn't a soldier because he wears a uniform, or carries a gun, or carries a canteen. He is a soldier when he makes a definite enlistment. All of the others can be bought without enlisting. When a man becomes a soldier he goes out on muster day and takes an oath to defend his country. It's the oath that makes him a soldier. Going to church doesn't make you a Christian any more than going to a garage makes you an automobile, but public definite enlistment for Christ makes you a Christian.

"Oh," a woman said to me out in Iowa, "Mr. Sunday, I don't think I have to confess with my mouth." I said: "You're putting up your thought against God's."

M-o-u-t-h doesn't spell intellect. It spells mouth and you must confess with your mouth. The mouth is the biggest part about most people, anyhow.

What must I do?

Philosophy doesn't answer it. Infidelity doesn't answer it. First, "believe on the Lord Jesus Christ and thou shalt be saved." Believe on the Lord. Lord—that's his kingly name. That's the name he reigns under. "Thou shalt call his name Jesus." It takes that kind of a confession. Give me a Saviour with a sympathetic eye to watch me so I shall not slander. Give me a Saviour with a strong arm to catch me if I stumble. Give me a Saviour that will hear my slightest moan.

Believe on the Lord Jesus Christ and be saved. Christ is his resurrection name. He is sitting at the right hand of the Father interceding for us.

Because of his divinity he understands God's side of it and because of his humanity he understands our side of it. Who is better qualified to be the mediator? He's a mediator. What is that? A lawyer is a mediator between the jury and the defendant. A retail merchant is a mediator between the wholesale dealer and the consumer. Therefore, Jesus Christ is the Mediator between God and man. Believe on the Lord. He's ruling today. Believe on the Lord Jesus. He died to save us. Believe on the Lord Jesus Christ. He's the Mediator.

Her majesty, Queen Victoria, was traveling in Scotland when a storm came up and she took refuge in a little hut of a Highlander. She stayed there for an hour and when she went the good wife said to her husband, "We'll tie a ribbon on that chair because her majesty has sat on it and no one else will ever sit on it." A friend of mine was there later and was going to sit in the chair when the man cried: "Nae, nae, mon. Dinna sit there. Her majesty spent an hour with us once and she sat on that chair and we tied a ribbon on it and no one else will ever sit on it." They were honored that her majesty had spent the hour with them. It brought unspeakable joy to them.

It's great that Jesus Christ will sit on the throne of my heart, not for an hour, but here to sway his power forever and ever.

"He Died for Me"

In the war there was a band of guerillas—Quantrell's band—that had been ordered to be shot on sight. They had burned a town in Iowa and they had been caught. One long ditch was dug and they were lined up in front of it and blindfolded and tied, and just as the firing squad was ready to present arms a young man dashed through the bushes and cried, "Stop!" He told the commander of the firing squad that he was as guilty as any of the others, but he had escaped and had come of his own free will, and pointed to one man in the line and asked to take his place. "I'm single," he said, "while he has a wife and babies." The commander of that firing squad was an usher in one of the cities in which I held meetings, and he told me how the young fellow was blindfolded and bound and the guns rang out and he fell dead.

Time went on and one day a man came upon another in a graveyard in Missouri weeping and shaping the grave into form. The first man asked who was buried there and the other said, "The best friend I ever had." Then he told how he had not gone far away but had come back and got the body of his friend after he had been shot and buried it; so he knew he had the right body. And he had brought a withered bouquet all the way from his home to put on the grave. He was poor then and could not afford anything costly, but he had placed a slab of wood on the pliable earth with these words on it: "He died for me."

Major Whittle stood by the grave some time later and saw the same monument. If you go there now you will see something different. The man became rich and today there is a marble monument fifteen feet high and on it this inscription:

SACRED TO THE MEMORY OF
WILLIE LEE
HE TOOK MY PLACE IN THE LINE
HE DIED FOR ME

Sacred to the memory of Jesus Christ. He took our place on the cross and gave his life that we might live, and go to heaven and reign with him.

"Believe on the Lord Jesus Christ, confess him with thy mouth, and thou shalt be saved and thy house."

It is a great salvation that can reach down into the quagmire of filth, pull a young man out and send him out to hunt his mother and fill her days with sunshine. It is a great salvation, for it saves from great sin.

The way to salvation is not Harvard, Yale, Princeton, Vassar or Wellesley. Environment and culture can't put you into heaven without you accept Jesus Christ.

It's great. I want to tell you that the way to heaven is a blood-stained way. No man has ever reached it without Jesus Christ and he never will.

CHAPTER XIII

"Hitting the Sawdust Trail"

Come and accept my Christ.—BILLY SUNDAY.

PIONEERS are necessarily unconventional. America has done more than transform a wilderness into a nation: in the process she has created new forms of life and of speech. Back from the frontier has come a new, terse, vigorous and pictorial language. Much of it has found its way into the dictionaries. The newer West uses the word "trail"—first employed to designate the traces left by traveling Indians—to designate a path. The lumbermen commonly call the woods roads "trails."

Imagine a lumberman lost in the big woods. He has wandered, bewildered, for days. Death stares him in the face. Then, spent and affrighted, he comes to a trail. And the trail leads to life; it is the way home.

There we have the origin of the expression "Hitting the sawdust trail," used in Mr. Sunday's meetings as a term similar to the older stereotyped phrases: "Going forward"; "Seeking the altar." The more conventional method, used by the other evangelists, is to ask for a show of hands.

Out in the Puget Sound country, where the sawdust aisles and the rough tabernacle made an especial appeal to the woodsmen, the phrase "Hitting the sawdust trail" came into use in Mr. Sunday's meetings. The figure was luminous. For was not this the trail that led the lost to salvation, the way home to the Father's house?

The metaphor appealed to the American public, which relishes all that savors of our people's most primitive life. Besides, the novel designation serves well the taste of a nation which is singularly reticent concerning its finer feelings, and delights to cloak its loftiest sentiments beneath slang phrases. The person who rails at "hitting the trail" as an irreverent phrase has something to learn about the mind of Americans. Tens of thousands of persons have enshrined the homely phrase in the sanctuary of their deepest spiritual experience.

The scene itself, when Mr. Sunday calls for converts to come forward and take his hand, in token of their purpose to accept and follow Christ, is simply beyond words. Human speech cannot do justice to the picture. For good reason. This is one of those crises in human life the portrayal of which makes the highest form of literature. A Victor Hugo could find a dozen novels in each night's experience in the Sunday Tabernacle.

This is an hour of bared souls. The great transaction between man and his Maker is under way. The streams of life are here changing their course. Character and destiny are being altered. The old Roman "Sacramentum," when the soldiers gave allegiance with uplifted hand, crying, "This for me! This for me!" could not have been more impressive than one of these great outpourings of human life up the sawdust aisle to the pulpit, to grasp the preacher's hand, in declaration that henceforth their all would be dedicated to the Christ of Calvary.

The greatness of the scene is at first incomprehensible. There are no parallels for it in all the history of Protestantism. This unschooled American commoner, who could not pass the entrance examinations of any theological seminary in the land, has publicly grasped the hands of approximately a quarter of a million persons, who by that token have said, in the presence of the great congregation, that they thereby vowed allegiance to their Saviour and Lord. Moody, Whitefield, Finney, have left no such record of converts as this.

A dramatic imagination is needed to perceive even a fragment of what is meant by this army of Christian recruits. The magnitude of the host is scarcely revealed by the statement that these converts more than equal the number of inhabitants of the states of Delaware or Arizona at the last census, and far surpass those of Nevada and Wyoming. Imagine a state made up wholly of zealous disciples of Christ! Of the one hundred largest cities in the United States there are only nineteen with more inhabitants than the total number of persons who have "hit the trail" at the Sunday meetings.

Break up that vast host into its component parts. Each is an individual whose experience is as real and distinctive as if there never had been another human soul to come face to face with God. To one the act means a clean break with a life of open sin. To another it implies a restored home and a return to respectability. To this young person it signifies entrance upon a life of Christian service; to that one a separation from all old associations. Some must give up unworthy callings. Other must heal old feuds and make restitution for ancient wrongs. One young woman in accepting Christ knows that she must reject the man she had meant to marry. To many men it implies a severance of old political relations. Far and wide and deep this sawdust trail runs; and the record is written in the sweat of agonizing souls and in the red of human blood.

The consequences of conversion stagger the imagination: this process is still the greatest social force of the age.

Little wonder that persons of discernment journey long distances to attend a Sunday meeting, and to witness this appeal for converts to "hit the trail." I traveled several hundred miles to see it for the first time, and would go across the continent to see it again. For this is vital religion. If a wedding casts its dramatic spell upon the imagination; if a political election stirs the sluggish deeps of the popular mind; if a battle calls for newspaper "extras"; if an execution arrests popular attention by its element of the mystery of life becoming death—then, by so much and more, this critical, decisive moment in the lives of living men and women grips the mind by its intense human interest. What issues, for time and eternity, are being determined by this step! The great romance is enacted daily at the Sunday meetings.

For these converts are intent upon the most sacred experience that ever comes to mortal. Through what soul struggles they have passed, what renunciations they have made, what futures they front, only God and heaven's hosts know. The crowd dimly senses all this. There is an instinctive appreciation of the dramatic in the multitude. So the evangelist's appeal is followed by an added tenseness, a straining of necks and a general rising to behold the expected procession.

A more simple and unecclesiastical setting for this tremendous scene could scarcely be devised. The plain board platform, about six feet high, and fifteen feet long, is covered by a carpet. Its only furniture is a second-hand walnut pulpit, directly under the huge sounding board; and one plain wooden chair, "a kitchen chair," a housewife would call it. Then the invitation is given for all who want to come out on the side of Christ to come forward and grasp Sunday's hand.

See them come! From all parts of the vast building they press forward. Nearly everyone is taking this step before the eyes of friends, neighbors, work-fellows. It calls for courage, for this is a life enlistment. Behold the young men crowding toward the platform, where the helpers form them into a swiftly moving line—dozens and scores of boys and men in the first flush of manhood. Occasionally an old person is in the line; oftener it is a boy or girl. There goes a mother with her son.

How differently the converts act. Some have streaming eyes. Others wear faces radiant with the light of a new hope. Still others have the tense, set features of gladiators entering the arena. For minute after minute the procession continues. When a well-known person goes forward, the crowd cheers.

11

As I have studied Mr. Sunday in the act of taking the hands of converts—one memorable night more than five hundred at the rate of fifty-seven a minute—the symbolism of his hand has appealed to my imagination.

Surprisingly small and straight and surprisingly strong it is. Base-ball battles have left no scars upon it. The lines are strong and deep and clear. The hand is "in condition"; no flabbiness about it. There are no rings on either of Mr. Sunday's hands, except a plain gold wedding ring on the left third finger.

No outstretched hand of military commander ever pointed such a host to so great a battle. Is there anywhere a royal hand, wielding a scepter over a nation, which has symbolized so much vital influence as this short, firm hand of a typical American commoner? The soldier sent on a desperate mission asked Wellington for "one grasp of your conquering hand." A conquering hand, a helping hand, an uplifting hand, an upward-pointing hand, is this which once won fame by handling a base ball.

Conceive of the vast variety of hands that have been reached up to grasp this one, and what those hands have since done for the world's betterment! Two hundred thousand dedicated right hands, still a-tingle with the touch of this inviting hand of the preacher of the gospel! The picture of Sunday's right hand belongs in the archives of contemporary religious history.

No stage manager could ever set so great a scene as this. The vastness of it—sixteen or seventeen thousand eyes all centered on one ordinary-looking American on a high green-carpeted platform, a veritable "sea of faces"— is not more impressive than the details which an observer picks out.

The multitudes are of the sort who thronged the Galilean; plain people, home-keeping women, seldom seen in public places; mechanics, clerks, the great American commonalty. Again and again one is impressed from some fresh angle with the democracy of it all; this man somehow appeals to that popular sense wherein all special tastes and interests merge.

The *débâcle* is a sight beyond words. The ice of conventionality breaks up, and the tide of human feeling floods forth. From every part of the great tabernacle—from the front seats, where you have been studying the personalities, and from the distant rear, where all the faces merge into an impersonal mass—persons begin to stream forward. See how they come. The moment is electric. Everybody is on the *qui vive*.

The first to take the evangelist's hand is a young colored boy. The girl who follows may be a stenographer. Young men are a large part of the recruits; here come a dozen fine-looking members of an athletic club in a body, while the crowd cheers; evidently somebody has been doing personal work there.

Contrasts are too common to mention. There is a delicate lady's kid-gloved hand reached up to that of the evangelist; the next is the grimy, calloused hand of a blue-shirted miner. The average is of young men and women, the choice and the mighty members of a community. Is the world to find a new moral or religious leader in the person of some one of these bright-faced youth who tonight have made this sign of dedication?

And here comes an old man, with a strong face; evidently a personality of force. Twice the evangelist pats the head bowed before him, in pleasure over this aged recruit. He seems reluctant to let the old man go; but, see the children crowd behind him, and no convert can have more than a handclasp and a word.

All around the platform the crowd resembles a hive of bees just before swarming. Stir, motion, animation seem to create a scene of confusion. But there is order and purpose in it all. The occupants of the front seats are being moved out to make way for the converts, who are there to be talked with, and to sign the cards that are to be turned over to the local pastors.

Personal workers are getting into action. See the ministers streaming down into the fray! There goes the Young Men's Christian Association secretary, and the Salvation Army soldiers, and the members of the choir, wearing Christian Endeavor and Bible class badges. This is religion in action. Can these church members ever again lapse into dead conventionality?

Meanwhile, Rodeheaver, the chorister, leans upon the piano and softly leads the great choir in "Almost Persuaded." The musical invitation continues while the work goes on in front. It is undisturbed by an occasional appeal from the evangelist. The song quickly changes to "Oh, Where Is My Wandering Boy Tonight?" and then, as the volume of penitents increases, into "I Am Coming Home" and "Ring the Bells of Heaven, There is Joy Today!" All this is psychological; it fosters the mood which the sermon has created. Music mellows as many hearts as spoken words.

All the while Sunday is shaking hands. At first he leans far over, for the platform is more than six feet high. Sometimes it seems as if he will lose his balance. To reach down he stands on his left foot, with his right leg extended straight behind him, the foot higher than his head. No one posture is retained long. Often he dips down with a swinging circular motion, like a pitcher about to throw a ball. Never was man more lavish of his vital energy than this one. His face is white and tense and drawn; work such as this makes terrific draughts on a man's nerve force.

As the converts increase, he lifts a trapdoor in the platform, which permits him to stand three feet nearer the people. Still they come, often each led by some personal worker. I saw a Scandinavian led forward in one meeting; ten minutes later I saw him bringing his wife up the trail. Some of the faces are radiant with a new joy. Others are set at a nervous tension. Some jaws are grim and working, revealing the inner conflict which has resulted in this step.

A collarless, ragged, weak-faced slave of dissipation is next in line to a beautiful girl in the dew of her youth. An old, white-wooled negro, leaning on a staff, is led forward. Then a little child. Here are veritably all sorts and conditions of people.

In the particular session I am describing, a big delegation of railroad men is present, and the evangelist keeps turning to them, with an occasional "Come on, Erie!" The memories of his own days as a railroad brakeman are evidently working within him, and he seizes a green lantern and waves it. "A clear track ahead!" Toward these men he is most urgent, beckoning them also with a white railroad flag which he has taken from the decorations. When the master mechanic "hits the trail"

A COLLARLESS, WEAK-FACED SLAVE OF DISSIPATION IS NEXT IN LINE TO A BEAUTIFUL GIRL IN THE DEW OF HER YOUTH

there is cheering from the crowd, and Sunday himself shows a delight that was exhibited over none of the society folk who came forward.

Rare and remarkable as are these scenes in religious history, they occur nightly in the Sunday tabernacle. Two hundred, three hundred, five hundred, one thousand converts are common.

Anybody interested in life and in the phenomena of religion will find this occasion the most interesting scene at present to be witnessed in the whole world. As for the novelist, this is the human soul bared, and beyond the compass of his highest art.

For life is at its apex when, in new resolution, a mortal spirit makes compact with the Almighty.

CHAPTER XIV

The Service of Society

· A lot of people think a man needs a new grandfather, sanitation, and a new shirt, when what he needs is a new heart.—BILLY SUNDAY.

SOME day a learned university professor, with a string of titles after his name, will startle the world by breaking away from the present conventionalism in sociology, and will conduct elaborate laboratory experiments in human betterment on the field of a Billy Sunday campaign. His conclusion will surely be that the most potent force for the service of society—the shortest, surest way of bettering the human race—is by the fresh, clear, sincere and insistent preaching of the Gospel of Jesus Christ.

Of course, the New Testament has been teaching that for nearly twenty centuries, but the world has not yet comprehended the practicability of the program. Your learned professor may prove, by literally thousands of incidents, that honesty, chastity, brotherliness, and idealism have been more definitely promoted by revivals of religion than by legislative or educational programs. All that the social reformers of our day desire may be most quickly secured by straight-out preaching of the Gospel. The short-cut to a better social order is by way of converted men and women. And when a modern scholar comes to demonstrate this he will draw largely upon the aftermath of the Sunday campaigns for his contemporaneous evidence.

If there is one phrase which, better than another, can describe a Billy Sunday campaign it is "restitution and righteousness." In season and out, the evangelist insists upon a changed life as the first consequence of conversion. His message runs on this wise:

"You ought to live so that every one who comes near you will know that you are a Christian. Do you? Does your milkman know that you are a Christian?   Does the man who brings your laundry know that you belong to church?   Does the man who hauls away your ashes know that you are a Christian?   Does your newsboy know that you have religion?   Does the butcher know that you are on your way to heaven?   Some of you buy meat on Saturday night, and have him deliver it Sunday morning, just to save a little ice, and then you wonder why he doesn't go to church.

"If you had to get into heaven on the testimony of your washerwoman, could you make it?   If your getting into heaven depended on what your dressmaker knows about your religion, would you land?   If your husband had to gain admittance to heaven on the testimony of his stenographer, could he do it?   If his salvation depended on what his clerks tell about him, would he get there?   A man ought to be as religious in business as he is in church. He ought to be as religious in buying and selling as he is in praying.

"Dois Your Newsboy Know that You Have Religion?"

"There are so many church members who are not even known in their own neighborhood as Christians.   Out in Iowa where a meeting was held, a man made up his mind that he would try to get an old sinner into the Kingdom, and after chasing him around for three days he finally cornered him. Then he talked to that old fellow for two hours, and then the old scoundrel stroked his whiskers, and what do you think he said? 'Why, I've been a member of the church down there for fourteen years.' Just think of it! A member of the church fourteen years, and a man had to chase him three days, and talk with him two hours to find it out.

"You have let Jesus in? Yes, but you have put him in the spare-room. You don't want him in the rooms where you live. Take him down into the living-room. Take him into the dining-room. Take him into the parlor. Take him into the kitchen. Live with him. Make him one of the family."

Then follows a Sundayesque description of how Jesus would find beer in the refrigerator and throw it out; how he would find cards on the table and throw them out; how he would find nasty music on the piano and throw it out; how he would find cigarettes and throw them out.

"If you haven't Jesus in the rooms you live in, it's because you don't want him," he says. "You're afraid of one of two things: you're afraid because of the things he'll throw out if he comes in, or you're afraid because of the things he'll bring with him if he comes in."

Here is how a great newspaper, the Philadelphia *North American*, characterizes the ethical and political effectiveness of Mr. Sunday:

Billy Sunday, derided by many as a sensational evangelist, has created a political revolution in Allegheny County. What years of reform work could not do he has wrought in a few short weeks. Old line "practical" politicians, the men who did the dirty work for the political gang, are now zealous for temperance, righteousness and religion.

Judges on the bench, grand dames of society, millionaire business men, in common with the great host of undistinguished men and women in homes, mills, offices, and shops, have been fired by this amazing prophet with burning zeal for practical religion,

An unexpected, unpredicted and unprecedented social force has been unleashed in our midst. Not to reckon with this is to be blind to the phase of Sunday's work which bulks larger than his picturesque vocabulary or his acrobatic earnestness.

In the presence of this man's work all attempts to classify religious activities as either "evangelistic" or "social service" fall into confusion.

Sunday could claim for himself that he's an evangelist, and an evangelist only. He repudiates a Christian program that is merely palliative or ameliorative. To his thinking the Church has more fundamental business than running soup kitchens or gymnasiums or oyster suppers. All his peerless powers of ridicule are frequently turned upon the frail and lonely oyster in the tureen of a money-making church supper.

Nevertheless, the results of Sunday's preaching are primarily social and ethical. He is a veritable besom of righteousness sweeping through a community. The wife who neglects her cooking, mending and home-making; the employer who does not deal squarely with his workers; the rich man who rents his property for low purposes or is tied up in crooked business in any wise; the workman who is not on "his job"; the gossip and the slanderer; the idle creatures of fashion; the Christian who is not a good person to live with, the selfish, the sour, the unbrotherly—all these find themselves under the devastating harrow of this flaming preacher's biting, burning, excoriating condemnation. "A scourge for morality" is the way one minister described him; he is that, and far more.

After the whole field of philanthropy and reform have been traversed it still remains true that the fundamental reform of all is the cleaning up of the lives and the lifting up of the ideals of the people. That is indisputably what Sunday does. He sweetens life and promotes a wholesome, friendly, helpful and cheerful state of mind on the part of those whom he influences.

Assuredly it is basic betterment to cause men to quit their drunkenness and lechery and profanity. All the white-slave or social-evil commissions that have ever met have done less to put a passion for purity into the minds of men and women than this one man's preaching has done. The safest communities in the country for young men and young women are those which have been through a Billy Sunday revival.

One cannot cease to exult at the fashion in which the evangelist makes the Gospel synonymous with clean living. All the considerations that weigh to lead persons to go forward to grasp the evangelist's hand, also operate to make them partisans of purity and probity.

Put into three terse phrases, Sunday's whole message is: "Quit your meanness. Confess Christ. Get busy for him among men." There are no finely spun spiritual sophistries in Sunday's preaching. He sometimes speaks quite rudely of that conception of a "higher spiritual life" which draws Christians apart from the world in a self-complacent consciousness of superiority.

His is not a mystical, meditative faith. It is dynamic, practical, immediate. According to his ever-recurring reasoning, if one is not passing on the fruits of religion to somebody else—if one is not hitting hard blows at the devil or really doing definite tasks for God and the other man—then one has not the real brand of Christianity. Sunday's preaching has hands, with "punch" to them, as well as lift; and feet, with "kick" in them, as well as ministry.

Like a colliery mined on many levels, Sunday's preaching reaches all classes. Everybody can appreciate the social service value of converting a gutter bum and making him a self-supporting workman. Is it any less social service to convert a man—I cite an actual instance from Pittsburgh—who had lately lost a twelve-thousand-dollar-a-year position through dissipation, and so thoroughly to help him find himself that before the meetings were over he was back in his old office, once more drawing one thousand dollars a month?

To a student of these campaigns, it seems as if business has sensed, better than the preachers, the economic waste of of sin.

A careful and discriminating thinker, the Rev. Joseph H. Odell, D.D., formerly pastor of the Second Presbyterian Church of Scranton, wrote an estimate of Billy Sunday and his work for *The Outlook*, in which he explains why his church, which had been opposed to the coming of the evangelist, reversed its vote:

Testimony, direct and cumulative, reached the ears of the same refined and reverent men and women. The young business men, even those from the great universities, paused to consider. The testimony that changed the attitudes of the Church came from judges, lawyers, heads of corporations and well-known society leaders in their respective communities. The testimony was phenomenally concurrent in this: that, while it did not endorse the revivalist's methods, or accept his theological system, or condone his roughness and rudeness, it proved that the preaching produced results.

"Produced results!" Every one understood the phrase; in the business world it is talismanic. As the result of the Billy Sunday campaigns—anywhere and everywhere—drunkards became sober, thieves became honest, multitudes of people engaged themselves in the study of the Bible, thousands confessed their faith in Jesus Christ as the Saviour of the world, and all the quiescent righteousness of the community grew brave and belligerent against vice, intemperance, gambling, and political dishonesty.

During the last week of February I went to Pittsburgh for the purpose of eliciting interest in the candidacy of J. Benjamin Dimmick for the nomination of United States Senator. Billy Sunday had closed his Pittsburgh campaign a few days earlier. My task was easy. A group of practical politicians met Mr. Dimmick at dinner. They were the men who had worked the wards of Allegheny County on behalf of Penrose and the liquor interests for years. Together they were worth many thousands of votes to any candidate; in fact, they were the political balance of power in that county. They knew everything that men could know about the ballot, and some things that no man should know. Solidly, resolutely, and passionately they repudiated Penrose. "No one can get our endorsement in Allegheny County, even for the office of dog-catcher, who is not anti-booze and anti-Penrose," they asserted. When asked the secret of their crusader-like zeal against the alliance of liquor and politics, they frankly ascribed it to Billy Sunday; they had been born again—no idle phrase with them—in the vast whale-back tabernacle under the preaching of the base-ball evangelist.

Billy Sunday deals with the very springs of action; he seeks to help men get right back to the furthermost motives of the mind. "If you're born again, you won't live knowingly in sin. This does not mean that a Christian cannot sin, but that he does not want to sin." This truth the evangelist illustrates by the difference between a hog and a sheep. The sheep may fall into the mud, but it hates it and scrambles out. A hog loves the mud and wallows in it.

Nobody can measure the results of the social forces which this simple-thinking evangelist sets to work. His own figure of the dwarf who could switch on the electric lights in a room as easily as a giant, comes to mind. He has sent into Christian work men who can do a kind of service impossible to Sunday himself. Thus, one of Sunday's converts out in Wichita, two years ago, was Henry J. Allen, editor of *The Beacon* and Progressive candidate for governor. Mr. Allen became a member of one of the celebrated "Gospel Teams," which, since the Sunday meetings, have been touring Kansas and neighboring states and have won more than eleven thousand converts. It was in a meeting held by this band that William Allen White, the famous editor, author and publisher, took a definite stand for Christ and Christian work. One of the most interesting facts about Sunday's work is this one that the three greatest editors in the State of Kansas today are his direct or indirect converts. An "endless chain" letter would be easier to overtake than the effects of a Sunday revival campaign.

In the face of the mass of testimony of this sort is it any wonder that business men deem a Sunday campaign worth all it costs, merely as an ethical movement? The quickest and cheapest way to improve morals and the morale of a city is by a revival of religion. Thus it is illuminating to learn that there were 650 fewer inmates in the Allegheny County jail, during the period of the Sunday revival meetings, than during the same time in the preceding year.

From Pittsburgh also comes the remarkable story that the Cambria Steel Company, one of the largest steel concerns in the country, has established a religious department in connection with its plant, and placed a regularly ordained minister in charge of it. This as an avowed result of the Sunday campaign.

The Rev. Dr. Maitland Alexander, D.D., pastor of the First Presbyterian Church of Pittsburgh, is sponsor for this news, and he also declares that nine department stores of Pittsburgh are now holding prayer-meetings every morning at eight o'clock. These two statements are taken from Dr. Alexander's address to a body of ministers in New York City. He is reported to have said also:

Billy Sunday succeeded in moving the city of Pittsburgh from one end to the other. That, to my mind, was the greatest result of the meetings. It is easy to talk about religion now in Pittsburgh. Men especially are thinking of it as never before, and the great majority are no longer in the middle of the road. They are on one side or the other. I never knew a man who could speak to men with such telling effect as Billy Sunday. I covet his ability to make men listen to him.

It was necessary in my own church, which when packed, holds 3200 persons, to hold special meetings for different groups, such as lawyers, doctors, bankers, etc., and they were always crowded. In the big tabernacle, which was built for the campaign and holds more than 20,000 persons, the men from the big steel shops, after the second week, came in bodies of from one to three thousand, in many cases headed by their leading officers.

Dr. Alexander said that up to the time of this address the Sunday campaign had added 419 members to his own church.

One of the striking consequences of the Sunday campaign in Scranton was the development of the "Garage Bible Class." This was originally a Wilkes-Barre poker club. As the story was told by Mr. Thos. H. Atherton, a Wilkes-Barre attorney, to the same New York meeting that Dr. Alexander addressed, the Garage Bible Class was originally a group of wealthy men meeting at different homes every week for a poker game. One man bet a friend fifteen dollars that he wouldn't go to hear Billy Sunday. One by one, however, the men found themselves unable to resist the lure of the Tabernacle. As a result the poker club was abandoned, and in a garage belonging to one of the men they organized a Bible class which now has about a hundred members. They have adopted a rule that no Christian shall be added to their ranks. They make their own Christians out of the unconverted.

From this episode one gets some conception of the tug and pull of the Sunday Tabernacle. The temptation to attend becomes well nigh irresistible. All the streams of the community life flow toward the great edifice where the base-ball evangelist enunciates his simple message. A writer in *The Churchman* said, following the Pittsburgh campaign:

This evangelist made religion a subject of ordinary conversation. People talked about their souls as freely as about their breakfast. He went into the homes of the rich, dropped his wildness of speech, and made society women cry with shame and contrition. One's eternal welfare became the topic of the dinner table, not only in the slums but in the houses of fashion. It sounds incredible, and it is not a fact to be grasped by the mere reading of it, but the citizens of Pittsburgh forgot to be ashamed to mention prayer and forgiveness of sin; the name of Christ began to be used with simpleness and readiness and reverence by men who, two months ago, employed it only as a by-word. City politicians came forward in the meeting and asked for prayer. The daily newspapers gave more space to salvation than they did to scandal, not for one day, but for day after day and week after week. As a mere spectacle of a whole modern city enthralled by the Gospel it was astonishing, unbelievable, unprecedented, prodigious.

Because he preaches both to employers and to employed, Sunday is able to apply the healing salt of the gospel at the point of contact between the two. From Columbus it is reported that a number of business men voluntarily increased the wages of their helpers, especially the women, because of the evangelist's utterances.

A horse jockey out West reached the core of the matter when he said to a friend of mine concerning Billy Sunday, "He sets people to thinking about other people." There you have the genesis and genius and goal of social service. No other force that operates among men is equal to the inspirations and inhibitions of the Christian religion in the minds of individuals. The greatest service that can be done to any community is to set a considerable proportion of its people to endeavoring honestly to live out the ideals of Jesus Christ.

It is simply impossible to enumerate anything like a representative number of incidents of the community value of Billy Sunday's work. They come from every angle and in the most unexpected ways. A banker, who is not a member of any church, showed me the other day a letter he had received from a man who had defrauded him out of a small sum of money years before. The banker had never known anything about the matter and did not recall the man's name. What did amaze him, and set him to showing the letter to all of his friends, was this man's restitution, accompanied by an out-spoken testimony to his new discipleship to Jesus Christ, upon which he had entered at the inspiration of Billy Sunday.

The imagination is stirred by a contemplation of what

these individual cases of regeneration imply.   Consider the homes reunited; consider the happy firesides that once were the scene of misery; measure, if you can, the new joy that has come to tens of thousands of lives in the knowledge that they have given themselves unreservedly to the service of Jesus Christ.

The dramatic, human side of it strikes one ever and anon.   I chanced to see a young man "hit the trail" at Scranton whose outreachings I had later opportunity to follow.   The young man is the only son of his parents and the hope of two converging family lines.   Grandparents and parents, uncles and aunts, have pinned all of their expectations on this one young man.   He was a youth of parts and of force and a personality in the community. When, on the night of which I write, he came forward up the "saw-dust trail" to grasp the evangelist's hand, his aged grandfather and his mother wept tears of joy.   The grandfather himself also "hit the trail" at the Scranton meetings and has since spent his time largely in Christian work.   It is impossible to say how this young man's future might have spelled sorrow or joy for the family circle that had concentrated their hopes on him.   But now it is clear that his conversion has brought to them all a boon such as money could not have bought nor kings conferred

One of the countless instances that may be gleaned in any field of Sunday's sowing was related to me the other evening by a business man, who, like others, became a protagonist of Sunday by going through one of his campaigns.   In his city there was a cultivated, middle-aged German, a well-known citizen, who was an avowed atheist. He openly scoffed at religion.   He was unable, however, to resist the allurement of the Sunday meetings, and he went with his wife one night merely to "see the show." That one sermon broke down the philosophy of years, and the atheist and his wife became converts of Billy Sunday. His three sons followed suit, so that the family of five adults were led into the Christian life by this evangelist

12

untaught of the schools. One of the sons is now a member of the State Y. M. C. A. Committee.

. A western business man, who is interested in the Young Men's Christian Association, told me that one cold, rainy winter's day he happened into the Association Building in Youngstown, Ohio. He found a crowd of men streaming into a meeting, and because the day was so unpropitious, he asked the character of the gathering. He was told that it was the regular meeting of the Christian Workers' Band, gathered to report on the week's activities. The men had been converted to Christ, or to Christian work, by Billy Sunday, and their meeting had continued ever since, although it was more than a year since the evangelist's presence in Youngstown. Said my friend, "That room was crowded. One after another the men got up and told what definite Christian work they had been doing in the previous seven days. The record was wonderful. They had been holding all sorts of meetings in all sorts of places, and had been doing a variety of personal work besides, so that there were a number of converts to be reported at this meeting I attended." To have set that force in operation so that it would continue to work with undiminished zeal after twelve months of routine existence, was a greater achievement than to preach one of the Billy Sunday sermons.

There is a sufficient body of evidence to show that the work of Billy Sunday does not end when the evangelist leaves the community. He has created a vogue for religion and for righteousness. The crowd spirit has been called forth to the service of the Master. Young people and old have been given a new and overmastering interest in life. They have something definite to do for the world and a definite crowd with which to ally themselves.

One result has been a tremendous growth of Bible classes for men and women and a manifestation of the crusader spirit which makes itself felt in cleaned-up communities and in overthrown corruption in politics. So far as the Billy Sunday campaigns may be said to have a badge, it is the little red and white bull's eye of the Organized Adult Bible Classes.

Six months after the Scranton campaign five thousand persons attended a "Trail Hitters'" picnic, where the day's events were scheduled under two headings, "athletic" and "prayer." When wholesome recreation comes thus to be permeated with the spirit of clean and simple devotion something like an ideal state of society has come to pass for at least one group of people.

In more ways than the one meant by his critics, Sunday's work is sensational. What could be more striking than the visit on Sunday, October 25, 1914, of approximately a thousand trail-hitters from Scranton to the churches of Philadelphia, to help prepare them for their approaching Sunday campaign? Special trains were necessary to bring this great detachment of men the distance of three hundred miles. They went forth in bands of four, being distributed among the churches of the city, to hold morning and evening services, and in the afternoon conducting neighborhood mass meetings. These men were by no means all trained speakers, but they were witness-bearers; and their testimony could scarcely fail to produce a powerful influence upon the whole city. That, on a large scale, is what Sunday converts are doing in a multitude of places.

To close this chapter as it began, the truth stands out that Billy Sunday has set a host of people to thinking that this world's problems are to be solved, and its betterment secured, not by any new-fangled methods, but along the old and tested line of transforming individual characters through the redeeming power of the crucified Son of God. Salvation is surest social service.

The great evangelist's sermons are filled with the life stories of the men and women he has saved. The following is only one of many:

"I was at one time in a town in Nebraska and the

people kept telling me about one man. 'There is one man here, if you can get him he is good for one hundred men for Christ.' I said: 'Who is he?'

"'John Champenoy. He is the miller.' I said to Mr. Preston, who was then a minister: 'Have you been to see him?' 'No.' I asked another minister if he had been to see the fellow and he said no. I asked the United Presbyterian preacher (they have a college out there), and he said no, he hadn't been around to see him.

"I said: 'Well, I guess I'll go around to see him.' I found the fellow seated in a chair teetered back against the wall, smoking. I said: 'Is this Mr. Champenoy?' 'Yes, sir, that's my name.' He got up and took me by the hand. I said: 'My name is Sunday; I'm down at the church preaching. A good many have been talking to me about you and I came down to see you and ask you to give your heart to God.' He looked at me, walked to the cupboard, opened the door, took out a half-pint flask of whisky and threw it out on a pile of stones.

"He then turned around, took me by the hand, and as the tears rolled down his cheeks he said: 'I have lived in this town nineteen years and you are the first man that has ever asked me to be a Christian.'

"He said: 'They point their finger at me and call me an old drunkard. They don't want my wife around with their wives because her husband is a drunkard. Their children won't play with our babies. They go by my house to Sunday school and church, but they never ask us to go. They pass us by. I never go near the church. I am a member of the lodge. I am a Mason and I went to the church eleven years ago when a member of the lodge died, but I've never been back and I said I never would go.'

"I said: 'You don't want to treat the Church that way. God isn't to blame, is he?'

"'No.'

"'The Church isn't to blame, is it?'

"'No.'

"'Christ isn't to blame?'

"'No.'

"'You wouldn't think much of me if I would walk up and slap your wife because you kept a dog I didn't like, would you? Then don't slap God in the face because there are some hypocrites in the Church that you don't like and who are treating you badly. God is all right. He never treated you badly. Come up and hear me preach, will you, John?'

"'Yes, I'll come tonight.'

"I said: 'All right, the Lord bless you and I will pray for you.' He came; the seats were all filled and they crowded him down the side aisle. I can see him now standing there, with his hat in his hand, leaning against the wall looking at me. He never took his eyes off me. When I got through and gave the invitation he never waited for them to let him out. He walked over the backs of the seats, took his stand for Jesus Christ, and in less than a week seventy-eight men followed him into the kingdom of God. They elected that man chairman of the civic federation and he cleaned the town up for Jesus Christ and has led the hosts of righteousness from then until now. Men do care to talk about Jesus Christ and about their souls. 'No man cares for my soul.' That's what's the trouble. They are anxious and waiting for some one to come."

CHAPTER XV

Giving the Devil His Due

I know there is a devil for two reasons; first, the Bible declares it; and second I have done business with him.—BILLY SUNDAY.

THE Prince of Darkness was no more real to Martin Luther, when he flung his ink-well at the devil, than he is to Billy Sunday. He seems never long out of the evangelist's thought. Sunday regards him as his most personal and individual foe. Scarcely a day passes that he does not direct his attention publicly to the devil. He addresses him and defies him, and he cites Satan as a sufficient explanation for most of the world's afflictions.

There are many delicate shadings and degrees and differentiations in theology—but Billy Sunday does not know them. He never speaks in semitones, nor thinks in a nebulous way. His mind and his word are at one with his base-ball skill—a swift, straight passage between two points. With him men are either sheep or goats; there are no hybrids. Their destination is heaven or hell, and their master is God or the devil.

He believes in the devil firmly, picturesquely; and fights him without fear. His characterizations of the devil are hair-raising. As a matter of fact it is far easier for the average man, close down to the ruck and red realities of life, to believe in the devil, whose work he well knows, than it is for the cloistered man of books. The mass of the people think in the same sort of strong, large, elemental terms as Billy Sunday. The niceties of language do not bother them; they are the makers and users of that fluid speech called slang.

William A. Sunday is an elemental. Sophistication would spoil him. He is dead sure of a few truths of first magnitude. He believes without reservation or qualification in the Christ who saved him and reversed his life's direction.   Upon this theme he has preached to millions. Also he is sure that there is a devil, and he rather delights in telling old Satan out loud what he thinks of him.   Meanness, in Satan, sinner or saint, he hates and says so in the language of the street, which the common people understand.   He usually perturbs some fastidious folk who think that literary culture and religion are essentially interwoven.

Excoriation of the devil is not Sunday's masterpiece. He reaches his height in exaltation of Jesus Christ.   He is surer of his Lord than he is of the devil.   It is his bed-rock belief that Jesus can save anybody, from the gutter bum to the soul-calloused, wealthy man of the world, and make them both new creatures.   With heart tenderness and really yearning love he holds aloft the Crucified as the world's only hope.   That is why his gospel breaks hearts of stone and makes Bible-studying, praying church workers out of strange assortments of humanity.

The following passages will show how familiarly and frequently Sunday treats of the devil:

"DEVIL" PASSAGES

The devil isn't anybody's fool.   You can bank on that.   Plenty of folks will tell you there isn't any devil—that he is just a figure of speech; a poetic personification of the sin in our natures.   People who say that—and especially all the time-serving, hypocritical ministers who say it—are liars.   They are calling the Holy Bible a lie.   I'll believe the Bible before I'll believe a lot of time-serving, society-fied, tea-drinking, smirking preachers.   No, sir!   You take God's word for it, there is a devil, and a big one, too.

Oh, but the devil is a smooth guy!   He always was, and he is now.   He is right on his job all the time, winter and summer.   Just as he appeared to Christ in the wilderness, he is right in this tabernacle now, trying to make you sinners indifferent to Christ's sacrifice for your salvation.   When the invitation is given, and you start to get up, and then settle back into your seat, and say, "I guess I don't want to give way to a temporary impulse," that's the real, genuine, blazing-eyed, cloven-hoofed, forked-tailed old devil, hanging to your coat tail. He knows all your weaknesses, and how to appeal to them.

He knows about you and how you have spent sixty dollars in the last two years for tobacco, to make your home and the streets filthy, and that you haven't bought your wife a new dress in two years, because you "can't afford it"; and he knows about you, and the time and money you spend on fool hats and card parties, doing what you call "getting into society," while your husband is being driven away from home by badly cooked meals, and your children are running on the streets, learning to be hoodlums.

And he knows about you, too, sir, and what you get when you go back of the drug-store prescription counter to "buy medicine for your sick baby." And he knows about you and the lie you told about the girl across the street, because she is sweeter and truer than you are, and the boys go to see her and keep away from you, you miserable thrower of slime, dug out of your own heart of envy— yes, indeed, the devil knows all about you.

When the revival comes along and the Church of God gets busy, you will always find the devil gets busy, too. Whenever you find somebody that don't believe in the devil you can bank on it that he has a devil in him bigger than a woodchuck. When the Holy Spirit descended at Pentecost the devil didn't do a thing but go around and say that these fellows were drunk, and Peter got up and made him mad by saying that it was too early in the day. It was but the third hour. They had sense in those days; it was unreasonable to find them drunk at the third hour of the day. But now the fools sit up all night to booze.

When you rush forward in God's work, the devil begins to rush against you. There was a rustic farmer walking through Lincoln Park and he saw the sign, "Beware of pickpockets,"

"What do they want to put up a fool sign like that? Everybody looks honest to me." He reached for his watch to see what time it was and found it was gone. The pickpockets always get in the pockets of those who think there are no pickpockets around. Whenever you believe there is a devil around, you can keep him out, but if you say there isn't, he'll get you sure.

The Bible says there is a devil; you say there is no devil. Who knows the most, God or you? Jesus met a real foe, a personal devil. Reject it or deny it as you may. If there is no devil, why do you cuss instead of pray? Why do you lie instead of telling the truth? Why don't you kiss your wife instead of cursing her? You have just got the devil in you, that is all.

The devil is no fool; he is onto his job. The devil has been practicing for six thousand years and he has never had appendicitis, rheumatism or tonsilitis. If you get to playing tag with the devil he'll beat you every clip.

If I knew that all the devils in hell and all the devils in Pittsburgh were sitting out in the pews and sneering and jeering at me I'd shoot God's truth into their carcasses anyway, and I propose to keep firing away at the devils until by and by they come crawling out of their holes and swear that they were never in them, but their old hides would assay for lead and tan for chair bottoms.

Men in general think very little of the devil and his devices, yet he is the most formidable enemy the human race has to contend with. There is only one attitude to have toward him, and that is to hit him. Don't pick up a sentence and smooth it and polish it and sugar-coat it, but shy it at him with all the rough corners on.

The devil has more sense than lots of little preachers.

Jesus said: "It is written." He didn't get up and quote Byron and Shakespeare. You get up and quote that stuff, and the devil will give you the ha! ha! until you're gray-haired. Give him the Word of God, and he will take the count mighty quick. "It is written, thou shall not tempt the Lord thy God."

Don't you ever think for a minute that the devil isn't on the job all the time. He has been rehearsing for thousands of years, and when you fool around in his back yard he will pat you on the back and tell you that you are "IT."

I'll fight the devil in my own way and I don't want people to growl that I am not doing it right.

The devil comes to me sometimes. Don't think that because I am a preacher the devil doesn't bother me any. The devil comes around regularly, and I put on the gloves and get busy right away.

I owe God everything; I owe the devil nothing except the best fight I can put up against him.

I assault the devil's stronghold and I expect no quarter and I give him none.

"I AM AGAINST EVERYTHING THAT THE DEVIL IS IN FAVOR OF"

I am in favor of everything the devil is against, and I am against everything the devil is in favor of—the dance, the booze, the brewery, my friends that have cards in their homes. I am against everything that the devil is in favor of, and I favor everything the devil is against, no matter what it is. If you know which side the devil is on, put me down on the other side any time.

Hell is the highest reward that the devil can offer you for being a servant of his.

The devil's got a lot more sense than some of you preachers I know, and a lot of you old skeptics, who quote Shakespeare and Carlyle and Emerson and everybody and everything rather than the Bible.

When you hear a preacher say that he doesn't believe there is a devil, you can just bet your hat that he never preaches repentance. The men who do any preaching on repentance know there is a devil, for they hear him roar.

I drive the same kind of nails all orthodox preachers do. The only difference is that they use a tack hammer and I use a sledge.

The preacher of today who is a humanitarian question point is preaching to empty benches.

I do not want to believe and preach a lie. I would rather believe and preach a truth, no matter how unpleasant it is, than to believe and preach a pleasant lie. I believe there is a hell. If I didn't I wouldn't have the audacity to stand up here and preach to you. If there ever comes a time when I don't believe in hell I will leave the platform before I will ever preach a sermon with that unbelief in my heart. I would rather believe and preach a truth, no matter how unpleasant, than to believe and preach a lie simply for the friendship and favor of some people.

The man that preaches the truth is your friend. I have no desire to be any more broad or liberal than Jesus, not a whit, and nobody has any right, either, and claim to be a preacher. Is a man cruel that tells you the truth? The man that tells you there is no hell is the cruel man, and the man that tells you there is a hell is your friend. So it's a kindness to point out the danger. God's ministers have no business to hold back the truth.

I don't believe you can remember when you heard a sermon on hell. Well, you'll hear about hell while I am here. God Almighty put hell in the Bible and any preacher that sidesteps it because there are people sitting in the pews who don't like it, ought to get out of the pulpit. He is simply trimming his sails to catch a passing breeze of popularity.

CHAPTER XVI

Critics and Criticism

Some preachers need the cushions of their chairs upholstered oftener than they need their shoes half-soled.—BILLY SUNDAY.

IT is only when the bull's eye is hit that the bell rings. The preacher who never gets a roar out of the forces of unrighteousness may well question whether he is shooting straight. One of the most significant tributes to the Evangelist Sunday is the storm of criticism which rages about his head. It is clear that at least he and his message are not a negligible quantity.

This book certainly holds no brief for the impeccability and invulnerability of Billy Sunday. Yet we cannot be blind to the fact he has created more commotion in the camp of evil than any other preacher of his generation. Christians are bound to say "We love him for the enemies he has made." He hits harder at all the forces that hurt humanity and hinder godliness than any other living warrior of God.

The forces of evil pay Billy Sunday the compliment of an elaborately organized and abundantly financed assault upon him. He is usually preceded and followed in his campaigns by systematic attacks which aim to undermine and discredit him. A weekly paper, issued in Chicago, appears to be devoted wholly to the disparaging of Billy Sunday.

In rather startling juxtaposition to that statement is the other that many ministers have publicly attacked Sunday. This is clearly within their right. He is a public issue and fairly in controversy. As he claims the right of free speech for himself he cannot deny it to others. Some of his critics among the clergy object to evangelism in general, some to his particular methods, some to his forms of speech, some to his theology; but nobody apparently objects to his results.

During the past year there has arisen a tendency to abate this storm of clerical criticism, for it has been found that it is primarily serving the enemies of the Church. Whatever Billy Sunday's shortcomings, he is unquestionably an ally of the Kingdom of Heaven and an enemy of sin. His motives and his achievements are both aligned on the side of Christ and his Church. A host of ministers of fine judgment who are grieved by some of the evangelist's forms of speech and some of his methods, have yet withheld their voices from criticism because they do not want to fire upon the Kingdom's warriors from the rear. Sunday gets results for God; therefore, reason they, why should we attack him?

There is another side to this shield of criticism. There is no religious leader of our day who has such a host of ardent defenders and supporters as Billy Sunday. The enthusiasm of myriads for this man is second only to their devotion to Christ. Wherever he goes he leaves behind him a militant body of protagonists. He is championed valiantly and fearlessly.

So vigorous is this spirit which follows in the wake of a Sunday campaign that in a certain large city where the ministers of one denomination had publicly issued a statement disapproving of Mr. Sunday, their denomination has since suffered seriously in public estimation.

Some anonymous supporter of Billy Sunday has issued pamphlet made up exclusively of quotations from Scripture justifying Sunday and his message. He quotes such pertinent words as these:

And I, brethren, when I came to you, came not with excellency of speech or of wisdom, declaring unto you the testimony of God.

For I determined not to know any thing among you, save Jesus Christ, and him crucified.

And I was with you in weakness, and in fear, and in much trembling.

And my speech and my preaching was not with enticing words of man's wisdom, but in demonstration of the Spirit and of power;

That your faith should not stand in the wisdom of men, but in the power of God.

For Christ sent me not to baptize, but to preach the gospel: not with wisdom of words, lest the cross of Christ should be made of none effect.

For the preaching of the cross is to them that perish foolishness; but unto us which are saved it is the power of God.

For it is written, I will destroy the wisdom of the wise, and will bring to nothing the understanding of the prudent.

Where is the wise? where is the scribe? where is the disputer of this world? hath not God made foolish the wisdom of this world?

For after that in the wisdom of God the world by wisdom knew not God, it pleased God by the foolishness of preaching to save them that believe.

For the Jews require a sign, and the Greeks seek after wisdom:

But we preach Christ crucified, unto the Jews a stumblingblock, and unto the Greeks foolishness;

But unto them which are called, both Jews and Greeks, Christ the power of God, and the wisdom of God.

Because the foolishness of God is wiser than men; and the weakness of God is stronger than men.

For ye see your calling, brethren, how that not many wise men after the flesh, not many mighty, not many noble, are called:

But God hath chosen the foolish things of the world to confound the wise; and God hath chosen the weak things of the world to confound the things which are mighty;

And base things of the world, and things which are despised, hath God chosen, yea, and things which are not, to bring to nought things that are.

A great marvel is that this unconventional preacher has enlisted among his supporters a host of intellectual and spiritual leaders of our time. The churches of the country, broadly speaking, are for him, and so are their pastors. This might be attributed to partisanship, for certainly Sunday is promoting the work of the Church; but what is to be said when Provost Edgar F. Smith of the University of Pennsylvania comes out in an unqualified endorsement of the man and his work; or such an acute lawyer and distinguished churchman as George Wharton Pepper of Philadelphia, well known in the councils of the Protestant Episcopal Church, gives his hearty approval to Sunday?

Consider the letter which Secretary of State Bryan wrote to Sunday after hearing him at the Pittsburgh Tabernacle:

THE SECRETARY OF STATE.

Washington, January 12, 1914.

MY DEAR SUNDAY: Having about four hours in Pittsburgh last night, my wife and I attended your meeting and so we heard and felt the powerful sermon which you delivered. We noted the attention of that vast audience and watched the people, men and women, old and young, who thronged about you in response to your appeal. Mrs. Bryan had never heard you, and I had heard only a short afternoon address. Last night you were at your best. I cannot conceive of your surpassing that effort in effectiveness.

Do not allow yourself to be disturbed by criticism. God is giving you souls for your hire and that is a sufficient answer. Christ called attention to the fact that both he and John the Baptist had to meet criticism because they were so much unlike in manner. No man can do good without making enemies, but yours as a rule will be among those who do not hear you. Go on, and may the Heavenly Father use you for many years to come, as he has for many years past, and bring multitudes to know Christ as he presented himself when he said, "I am the way, the truth and the life."

Am sorry we could not see you personally, but we left because we found that we were discovered. Some insisted upon shaking hands and I was afraid I might become a cause of disturbance. Mrs. Bryan joins me in regards to Mrs. Sunday and yourself.

Yours truly,

W. J. BRYAN.

One need be surprised at nothing in connection with such a personality as Billy Sunday, yet surely there is no precedent for this resolution, adopted by the Pittsburgh City Council, while he was in that city:

WHEREAS, The Rev. William A. Sunday and his party have been in the city of Pittsburgh for the past eight weeks, conducting evangelistic services, and the Council of the city being convinced of the immense good which has been accomplished through his work for morality, good citizenship and religion, therefore be it

Resolved, That the Council of the city of Pittsburgh express its utmost confidence in Mr. Sunday and all of the members of his party; and be it further

Resolved, That it does hereby express to them its appreciation of all the work that has been done, and extends to Mr. Sunday its most cordial wishes for his future success.

While the adverse critics are doing all in their power to discredit him as he goes from place to place, Sunday's friends also are not idle. In Scranton, for instance, before the campaign opened, men in nearly all walks of life received letters from men in corresponding callings in Pittsburgh bearing tribute to Billy Sunday. Thus, bankers would inclose in their correspondence from Pittsburgh an earnest recommendation of Sunday and a suggestion that the bankers of Scranton stand squarely to his support. The local Scranton plumber heard from a plumbers' supply house; labor union men heard from their fellows in Pittsburgh; lawyers and doctors, and a host of business men, had letters from personal friends in Pittsburgh, telling what Sunday had done for that community, and in many cases bearing personal testimony to what his message had meant to the writers.

This is nearer to effective organization than the Christian forces of the country commonly get. This form of propaganda did not bulk large in the public eye, but it created a splendid undercurrent of sentiment; for Banker

Jones could say: "I have it straight from Banker Smith of Pittsburgh, whom I know to be a level-headed man, that Sunday is all right, and that he does nothing but good for the city."

Still more novel than this was the expedition sent by a great daily newspaper to hear the evangelist in Scranton. There is no parallel in the history of Christian work for the deputation of more than two hundred pastors who went to Scranton from Philadelphia. These went entirely at the charges of the Philadelphia *North American*, being carried in special trains. The railroad company recognized the significance of this unusual occasion, and both ways the train broke records for speed.

While in the city of Scranton the ministers were the guests of the Scranton churches. They had special space reserved for them in the Tabernacle and their presence drew the greatest crowds that were experienced during the Scranton campaign. Of course thousands were turned away. Nobody who saw and heard it will ever forget the way that solid block of Philadelphia pastors stood up and sang in mighty chorus "I Love to Tell the Story."

Between sessions these Philadelphia ministers were visiting their brethren in Scranton, learning in most detailed fashion what the effects of the Sunday campaign had been. Whenever they gathered in public assemblies they sounded the refrain, which grew in significance from day to day: "I Love to Tell the Story." Billy Sunday fired the evangelistic purpose of these pastors.

When this unique excursion was ended, and the company had de-trained at the Reading Terminal, the ministers, without pre-arrangement, gathered in a body in the train shed and lifted their voices in the refrain "I Love to Tell the Story," while hundreds and thousands of hurrying city folk, attracted by the unwonted music, gathered to learn what this could possibly mean.

A new militancy was put into the preaching of these clergymen by their Scranton visit; and many of them later reported that the largest congregations of all their ministerial experience were those which gathered to hear them report on the Sunday evangelistic campaign. Not a few of the preachers had to repeat their Billy Sunday sermons. Needless to say, an enthusiastic and urgent invitation to Sunday to come to Philadelphia to conduct a campaign, followed this demonstration on the part of the daily newspaper.

That there is a strategic value in rallying all the churches about one man was demonstrated by the Methodists of Philadelphia on this occasion. Bishop Joseph F. Berry had heartily indorsed the project, and had urged all of the Methodist pastors who could possibly do so to accept the *North American's* invitation. The Methodist delegation was an enthusiastic unit. When they returned to Philadelphia a special issue of the local Methodist paper was issued, and in this thirty-two articles appeared, each written by an aroused pastor who had been a member of the delegation. Incidentally, all of the city papers, as well as the religious press of a very wide region, reported this extraordinary pilgrimage of more than two hundred pastors to a distant city to hear an evangelist preach the gospel. A reflex of this was the return visit, some months later, of a thousand "trail-hitters" to speak in Philadelphia pulpits.

Before leaving the subject of the criticism of Sunday, pro and con, it should be insisted that no public man or institution should be free from the corrective power of public opinion, openly expressed. This is one of the wholesome agencies of democracy. Mr. Sunday himself is not slow to express his candid opinion of the Church, the ministry, and of society at large. It would be a sad day for him should all critical judgment upon his work give way to unreasoning adulation.

The best rule to follow in observing the evangelist's ministry is, "Never judge unfinished work." Only a completed campaign should pass in review before the critics; only the whole substance of the man's message; only the entire effect of his work upon the public. Partial judgments are sure to be incorrect judgments.

Billy Sunday succeeds in making clear to all his hearers—indeed he impresses them so deeply that the whole city talks of little else for weeks—that God has dealings with every man; and that God cares enough about man to provide for him a way of escape from the terrible reality of sin, that way being Jesus Christ.

When a preacher succeeds in lodging that conviction in the minds of the multitudes, he is heaven's messenger. Whether he speak in Choctaw, Yiddish, Bostonese or in the slang of Chicago, is too trivial a matter to discuss. We do not inspect the wardrobe or the vocabulary of the hero who rides before the flood, urging the people to safety in the hills.

PLAIN SPEECH FROM SUNDAY HIMSELF

The hour is come; come for something else. It has come for plainness of speech on the part of the preacher. If you have anything to antagonize, out with it; specify sins and sinners. You can always count on a decent public to right a wrong, and any public that won't right a wrong is a good one to get out of.

Charles Finney went to Europe to preach, and in London a famous free-thinker's wife went to hear him. The free-thinker's wife noticed a great change in him; he was more kind, more affectionate, more affable, less abusive and she said, "I know what is the matter with you; you have been to hear that man from America preach." And he said, "Wife, that is an insult; that man Finney don't preach; he just makes plain what the other fellows preach." Now the foremost preacher of his day was Paul. What he preached of his day was not so much idealism as practicality; not so much theology, homiletics, exegesis or didactics, but a manner of life. I tell you there was no small fuss about his way of teaching. When Paul was on the job the devil was awake. There is a kind of preaching that will never arouse the devil.

"He that believeth not is condemned already." He that has not believed in Jesus Christ, the only begotten son of God, is condemned where he sits.

Too much of the preaching of today is too nice; too pretty; too dainty; it does not kill. Too many sermons are just given for literary excellence of the production. They get a nice adjective or noun, or pronoun—you cannot be saved by grammar. A little bit of grammar is all right, but don't be a big fool and sit around and criticize because the preacher gets a word wrong—if you do that your head is filled with buck oysters and sawdust, if that is all that you can use it for.

They've been crying peace. There is no peace. Some people won't come to hear me because they are afraid to hear the truth. They want deodorized, disinfected sermons. They are afraid to be stuck over the edge of the pit and get a smell of the brimstone. You can't get rid of sin as long as you treat it as a cream puff instead of a rattlesnake. You can't brush sin away with a feather duster. Go ask the drunkard who has been made sober whether he likes "Bill." Go ask the girl who was dragged from the quagmire of shame and restored to her mother's arms whether she likes "Bill." Go ask the happy housewife who gets the pay envelope every Saturday night instead of its going to the filthy saloon-keeper whether she's for "Bill." Some people say, "Oh, he's sensational." Nothing would be more sensational than if some of you were suddenly to become decent. I would rather be a guide-post than a tombstone.

I repeat that everybody who is decent or wants to be decent, will admire you when you preach the truth, although you riddle them when you do it. The hour is come, my friend. The hour is come to believe in a revival. Some people do not believe in revivals; neither does the devil; so you are like your daddy.

I can see those disciples praying, and talking and having a big time. There are many fool short-sighted ministers who are satisfied if they can only draw a large crowd. Some are as crazy after sensations as the yellowest newspaper that ever came off the press. That's the reason we have these sermons on "The Hobble Skirt" and "The Merry Widow Hat" and other such nonsensical tommyrot. If there were not so many March-hare sort of fellows breaking into pulpits you would have to sweat more and work harder. There are some of you that have the devil in you. Maybe you don't treat your wife square. Maybe you cheat in your weights. Get rid of the devil. What does it matter if you pack a church to the roof if nothing happens to turn the devil pale? What is the use of putting chairs in the aisles and out the doors?

The object of the Church is to cast out devils.

The devil has more sense than lots of little preachers. I have been unfortunate enough to know D.D.'s and LL.D.'s sitting around whittling down the doctrine of the personality of the devil to as fine a point as they know how. You are a fool to listen to them. The devil is no fool, he is no four-flusher. He said to Christ: "If you are a God, act like it; if you are a man, and believe the Scriptures, act as one who believes."

John the Baptist wasn't that kind of a preacher. Jesus Christ wasn't that kind of a preacher. The apostles weren't that kind of preachers—except old Judas. John the Baptist opened the Bible right in the middle and preached the word of God just as he found it, and he didn't care whether the people liked it or not. That wasn't his business. I tell you, John the Baptist stirred up the devil. If any minister doesn't believe in a personal devil it's because he has never preached a sermon on repentance, or he'd have heard him roar. Yes, sir. If there's anything that will make the devil roar it is a sermon on repentance.

You can preach sociology, or psychology, or any other kind of ology, but if you leave Jesus Christ out of it you hit the toboggan slide to hell.

I'll preach against any minister who is preaching false doctrines. I don't give a rap who he is. I'll turn my guns loose against him, and don't you forget that.   Any man who is preaching false doctrines to the people and vomiting out false doctrines to them will hear from me.   I want to say that the responsibility for no revivals in our cities and towns has got to be laid at the doors of the ministry.   Preachers sit fighting their sham battles of different denominations, through their cussedness, inquiring into fol-da-rol and tommyrot, and there sits in the pews of the church that miserable old scoundrel who rents his property out for a saloon and is going to hell; and that other old scoundrel who rents his houses for houses of ill fame and is living directly on the proceeds of prostitution, and he doesn't preach against it. He is afraid he will turn the men against him.   He is afraid of his job.   They are a lot of backsliders and the whole bunch will go to hell together.   They are afraid to come out against it.

I'll tell you what's the matter.   Listen to me.   The Church of God has lost the spirit of concern today largely because of the ministry—that's what's the matter with them.   I'll allow no man or woman to go beyond me in paying tribute to culture.   I don't mean this miserable "dog" business, shaking hands with two fingers.   The less brains some people have the harder they try to show you that they have some, or think they have.   I allow no man to go beyond me in paying tribute to real, genuine culture, a tribute to intellectual greatness; but when a man stands in the pulpit to preach he has got to be a man of God.   He has got to speak with the passion for souls.   If you sleep in the time of a revival God Almighty will wake you up.

There are lots of preachers who don't know Jesus. They know about him, but they don't know him.   Experience will do more than forty million theories.   I can experiment with religion just the same as I can with water.   No two knew Him exactly alike, but all loved Him.   All would have something to say.

Now for you preachers.   When a man prays "Thy Kingdom Come" he will read the Bible to find out the way to make it come. The preacher who prays "Thy Kingdom Come" will not get all his reading from the new books or from the magazines. He will not try to please the high-brows and in pleasing them miss the masses. He will not try to tickle the palates of the giraffes and then let the sheep starve. He will put his cookies on the lower shelf. He will preach in a language that the commonest laborer can understand.

One of the prolific sources of unbelief and backsliding today is a bottle-fed church, where the whole membership lets the preacher do the studying of the Bible for them. He will go to the pulpit with his mind full of his sermon and they will come to the church with their minds filled with society and last night's card-playing, beer-and-wine-drinking and novel-reading party and will sit there half asleep. Many a preacher reminds me of a great big nursing bottle, and there are two hundred or three hundred rubber tubes, with nipples on the end, running into the mouths of two hundred or three hundred or four hundred great big old babies with whiskers and breeches on, and hair pins stuck in their heads and rats in their hair, sitting there, and they suck and draw from the preacher. Some old sister gets the "Amusement" nipple in her mouth and it sours her stomach, and up go her heels and she yells. Then the preacher has to go around and sing psalms to that big two-hundred-and-fifty-pound baby and get her good-natured so that she will go back to church some day.

By and by some old whisky-voting church member gets the "Temperance" nipple in his mouth and it sours his stomach and up go his heels and he lets out a yell, throws his hands across his abdominal region, and the preacher says, "Whatever is the matter? If I hit you any place but the heart or the head I apologize." The preacher has to be wet nurse to about two hundred and fifty big babies that haven't grown an inch since they came into the church.

One reason why some preachers are not able to bring many sinners to repentance is because they preach of a

God so impotent that he can only throw down card houses when all the signs are right! They decline to magnify his power for fear they will overdo it! And if they accidentally make a strong assertion as to his power, they immediately neutralize it by "as it were," or "in a measure, perhaps!"

You make a man feel as though God was stuck on him and you'll be a thirty-third degree sort of a preacher with that fellow.

If some preachers were as true to their trust as John the Baptist, they might be turned out to grass, but they'd lay up treasures for themselves in heaven.

Clergymen will find their authority for out-of-the-ordinary methods in the lowering of a paralytic through a roof, as told of in the Bible. If that isn't sensationalism, then trot some out.

"WE'VE GOT A BUNCH OF PREACHERS BREAKING THEIR NECKS TO PLEASE A LOT OF OLD SOCIETY DAMES"

If God could convert the preachers the world would be saved. Most of them are a lot of evolutionary hot-air merchants.

We've got churches, lots of them. We've got preachers, seminaries, and they are turning out preachers and putting them into little theological molds and keeping them there until they get cold enough to practice preaching.

The reason some ministers are not more interested in

their work is because they fail to realize that theirs is a God-given mission.

We've got a bunch of preachers breaking their necks to please a lot of old society dames.

Some ministers say, "If you don't repent, you'll die and go to a place, the name of which I can't pronounce." I can. You'll go to hell.

There is not a preacher on earth that can preach a better gospel than "Bill." I'm willing to die for the Church. I'm giving my life for the Church.

Your preachers would fight for Christ if some of you fossilated, antiquated old hypocrites didn't snort and snarl and whine.

A godless cowboy once went to a brown-stone church—with a high-toned preacher—I am a half-way house between the brown-stone church and the Salvation Army. They are both needed and so is the half-way house. Well, this fellow went to one of these brown-stone churches and after the preacher had finished the cowboy thought he had to go up and compliment the preacher, as he saw others doing, and so he sauntered down the aisle with his sombrero under his arm, his breeches stuck in his boots, a bandana handkerchief around his neck, his gun and bowie knife in his belt, and he walked over and said: "Hanged if I didn't fight shy of you fellows—but I'll tell you I sat here and listened to you for an hour and you monkeyed less with religion than any fellow I ever heard in my life." They have taken away the Lord and don't know where to find him.

You must remember that Jesus tells us to shine for God. The trouble with some people and preachers is that they try to shine rather than letting their light shine. Some preachers put such a big capital "I" in front of the cross that the sinner can't see Jesus. They want the glory. They would rather be a comet than stars of Bethlehem.

CHAPTER XVII

A Clean Man on Social Sins

There are a good many things worse than living and dying an old maid, and one of them is marrying the wrong man.—BILLY SUNDAY.

SUNDAY'S trumpet gives no uncertain sound on plain, every-day righteousness. He is like an Old Testament prophet in his passion for clean conduct. No phase of his work is more notable than the zeal for right living which he leaves behind him. His converts become partisans of purity.

Sunday's own mind is clean. He does not, as is sometimes the case, make his pleas for purity a real ministry of evil. In the guise of promoting purity he does not pander to pruriency. As outspoken as the Bible upon social sin, he yet leaves an impression so chaste that no father would hesitate to take his boy to the big men's meeting which Sunday holds in every campaign; and every woman who has once heard him talk to women would be glad to have her daughter hear him also.

The verdict of all Christians who have studied conditions in a community after one of the Sunday campaigns is that Sunday has been like a thunder storm that has cleared the moral atmosphere. Life is sweeter and safer and more beautiful for boys and girls after this man has dealt plainly with social sins and temptations. Of course, it is more important to clean up a neighborhood's mind than its streets.

Even in cold print one may feel somewhat of the power of the man's message on "The Moral Leper."

A PLAIN TALK TO MEN

"Rejoice, O young man, in thy youth; and let thy heart cheer thee in the days of thy youth, and walk in the ways of thine heart, and in the sight of thine eyes: but know thou that for all these things God will bring thee into judgment."

"Be not deceived; God is not mocked; for whatsoever a man soweth that shall he also reap."

In other words, do just as you please; lie if you want to, steal if you want to. God won't stop you, but he will hold you responsible in the end. Do just as you please until the end comes and the undertaker comes along and pumps the embalming fluid into you and then you are all in.

No one is living in ignorance of what will become of him if he does not go right and trot square. He knows there is a heaven for the saved and a hell for the damned, and that's all there is to it.

Many men start out on a life of pleasure. ʿ Please remember two things. First, pleasure soon has an end, and, second, there is a day of judgment coming and you'll get what's coming to you. God gives every man a square deal.

If a man stood up and told me he was going to preach on the things I am this afternoon, I'd want him to answer me several questions, and if he could do that I'd tell him to go ahead.

First—Are you kindly disposed toward me?

Second—Are you doing this to help me?

Third—Do you know what you're talking about?

Fourth—Do you practice what you preach?

That's fair. Well, for the first. God knows I am kindly disposed toward you. Second, God knows I would do anything in my power to help you be a better man. I want to make it easier for you to be square, and harder for you to go to hell. Third, I know what I'm talking about, for I have the Bible to back me up in parts and the statements of eminent physicians in other parts. And fourth, "Do I practice what I preach?" I will defy and challenge any man or woman on earth, and I'll look any man in the eye and challenge him, in the twenty-seven years I have been a professing Christian, to show anything against me. If I don't live what I preach, gentlemen, I'll leave the pulpit and never walk back here again. I live as I preach and I defy the dirty dogs who have insulted me and my wife and spread black-hearted lies and vilifications.

I was born and bred on a farm and at the age of eleven I held my place with men in the harvest field. When I was only nine years old I milked ten cows every morning. I know what hard knocks are. I have seen the seamy side of life. I have crawled out of the sewers and squalor and want. I have struggled ever since I was six years old, an orphan son of a dead soldier, up to this pulpit this afternoon. I know what it is to go to bed with an honest dollar in my overalls pocket, when the Goddess of Liberty became a Jenny Lind and the eagle on the other side became a nightingale and they'd sing a poor, homeless orphan boy to sleep. I'm not here to explode hot air and theories to you.

Some men here in town, if their wives asked them if they were coming down here, would say: "Oh no, I don't want to go anywhere I can't take you, dear." The dirty old dogs, they've been many a place they wouldn't take their wife and they wouldn't even let her know they were there.

If sin weren't so deceitful it wouldn't be so attractive. The effects get stronger and stronger while you get weaker and weaker all the time, and there is less chance of breaking away.

Many think a Christian has to be a sort of dish-rag proposition, a wishy-washy, sissified sort of a galoot that lets everybody make a doormat out of him. Let me tell you the manliest man is the man who will acknowledge Jesus Christ.

Christian Character

Christianity is the capital on which you build your character. Don't you let the devil fool you. You never

become a man until you become a Christian. Christianity
is the capital on which you do business. It's your character
that gets you anything. Your reputation is what people
say about you, but your character is what God and your
wife and the angels know about you. Many have reputa-
tions of being good, but their characters would make a
black mark on a piece of coal or tarred paper.

I was over in Terre Haute, Indiana, not long ago, and
I was in a bank there admiring the beauty of it when the
vice-president, Mr. McCormick, a friend of mine, said:
"Bill, you haven't seen the vault yet," and he opened up the
vaults there, carefully contrived against burglars, and let
me in. There were three, and I wandered from one to
another. No one watched me. I could have filled my
pockets with gold or silver, but no one watched me. Why
did they trust me? Because they knew I was preaching
the gospel of Jesus Christ, and living up to it. That's why
they trusted me. There was a time in my life when a man
wouldn't trust me with a yellow dog on a corner fifteen
minutes.

Before I was converted I could go five rounds so fast
you couldn't see me for the dust, and I'm still pretty handy
with my dukes and I can still deliver the goods with all
express charges prepaid. Before I was converted I could
run one hundred yards in ten seconds and circle the bases
in fourteen seconds, and I could run just as fast after I was
converted. So you don't have to be a dish-rag proposition at all.

When a person's acts affect only himself they can be
left to the conscience of the individual, but when they affect
others the law steps in. When a child has diphtheria, you
are not allowed personal liberty; you are quarantined,
because your personal liberty could endanger others if
exercised. So you haven't any right to live in sin. You say
you'll do it anyhow. All right, you'll go to hell, too. Adam
and Eve said they would eat the apple anyhow, and the
world became a graveyard, and here's the result today.

I look out into the world and see a man living in sin. I argue with him, I plead with him. I cry out warning words. I brand that man with a black brand, whose iniquities are responsible for the fall of others.

No man lives to himself alone. I hurt or help others by my life. When you go to hell you're going to drag some one else down with you and if you go to heaven you're going to take some one else with you. You say you hate sin. Of course you do if you have self-respect. But you never saw anyone who hates sin worse than I do, or loves a sinner more than I. I'm fighting for the sinners. I'm fighting to save your soul, just as a doctor fights to save your life from a disease. I'm your friend, and you'll find that I'll not compromise one bit with sin. I'll do anything to help you. No man will argue that sin is a good thing. Not a one who does not believe that the community would be better off if there was no sin. I preach against vice to show you that it will make your girl an outcast and your boy a drunkard. I'm fighting everything that will lead to this and if I have to be your enemy to fight it, God pity you, for I'm going to fight. People do not fight sin until it becomes a vice.

You say you're not afraid of sin. You ought to be, for your children. It doesn't take boys long to get on the wrong track, and while you are scratching gravel to make one lap, your boy makes ten. We've got kids who have not yet sprouted long breeches who know more about sin and vice than Methuselah. There are little frizzled-top sissies not yet sprouting long dresses who know more about vice than did their great-grandmothers when they were seventy-five years old. The girl who drinks will abandon her virtue. What did Methuselah know about smoking cigarettes? I know there are some sissy fellows out there who object to my talking plain and know you shirk from talking plain.

If any one ever tells you that you can't be virtuous and enjoy good health, I brand him as a low, infamous, black-hearted liar.

Ask any afflicted man you see on the street. If you

could only reveal the heart of every one of them! In most you would find despair and disease.

How little he thinks when he is nursing that lust that he is nursing a demon which, like a vampire, will suck his blood and wreck his life and blacken and blight his existence. And if any little children are born to him, they will be weak anemics without the proper blood in their veins to support them. Our young men ought to be taught that no sum they can leave to a charitable institution can blot out the deeds of an ignominious life. You don't have to look far for the reason why so many young men fail; why they go through life weak, ambitionless, useless.

Common Sense

Let's be common folks together today. Let's be men, and talk sense.

As a rule a man wants something better for his children than he has had for himself. My father died before I was born and I lived with my grandfather. He smoked, but he didn't want me to. He chewed, but he didn't want me to. He drank, but he didn't want me to. He cussed, but he didn't want me to. He made wine that would make a man fight his own mother after he had drunk it. I remember how I used to find the bottles and suck the wine through a straw or an onion top.

One day a neighbor was in and my grandfather asked him for a chew. He went to hand it back, and I wanted some. He said I couldn't have it. I said I wanted it anyhow, and he picked me up and turned me across his knee and gave me a crack that made me see stars as big as moons.

If there is a father that hits the booze, he doesn't want his son to. If he is keeping some one on the side, he doesn't want his son to. In other words, you would not want your son to live like you if you are not living right.

An old general was at the bedside of his dying daughter. He didn't believe in the Bible and his daughter said, "What shall I do? You don't believe in the Bible. Mamma does. If I obey one I'm going against the other." The old general put his arms around his daughter and said: "Follow your mother's way; it is the safest." Man wants his children to have that which is sure.

I have sometimes imagined that young fellow in Luke xv. He came to his father and said, "Dig up. I'm tired of this and want to see the world." His father didn't know what he meant. "Come across with the mazuma, come clean, divvy. I want the coin, see?" Finally the father tumbled, and he said, "I got you," and he divided up his share and gave it to the young man. Then he goes down to Babylon and starts out on a sporting life. He meets the young blood and the gay dame. I can imagine that young fellow the first time he swore. If his mother had been near he would have looked at her and blushed rose red. But he thought he had to cuss to be a man.

No man can be a good husband, no man can be a good father, no man can be a respectable citizen, no man can be a gentleman, and swear. You can hang out a sign of gentleman, but when you cuss you might as well take it in.

There are three things which will ruin any town and give it a bad name—open licensed saloons; a dirty, cussing, swearing gang of blacklegs on the street; and vile story tellers. Let a town be known for these three things, and these alone, and you could never start a boom half big enough to get one man there.

Old men, young men, boys, swear. What do you cuss for? It doesn't do you any good, gains you nothing in business or society; it loses you the esteem of men. God said more about cussing than anything. God said, "Thou shalt not kill," "Thou shalt not steal," "Thou shalt not bear false witness," but God said more about cussing than them all; and men are still cussing. "Thou shalt not take the name of the Lord thy God in vain, for the Lord will not hold him guiltless who taketh his name in vain."

No Excuse for Swearing

I can see how you can get out of anything but cussing. I can see how a man could be placed in such a position that he would kill and be exonerated by the law of God and man, if he killed to protect his life, or the life of another.

I can see how a man could be forced to steal if he stole to keep his wife from starving.

Up in Chicago several years ago there was a long-continued strike and the last division of the union treasury had given each man twenty-five cents. A man went into the railroad yards and got a bag of coal from one of the cars. They pinched him and he came up before a judge. He told the judge that he had only the twenty-five cents of the last division and he spent that for food. His wife and two children were at home starving and he had no fire. He stole the coal to cook their food. The judge thundered, "Get out of this room and get home and build that fire as quickly as you can."

Say, boys, if I was on a jury and you could prove to me that a father had stolen a loaf of bread to keep his wife from starving you could keep me in the room until the ants took me out through the keyhole before I'd stick him. That may not be law, I don't know; but you'll find there is a big streak of human nature in Bill.

There isn't a fellow in this crowd but what would be disgusted if his wife or sister would cuss and hit the booze like he does. If she would put fifteen or twenty beers under her belt, he'd go whining around a divorce court for a divorce right away and say he couldn't live with her. Why, you dirty dog, she has to live with you.

I heard of a fellow whose wife thought she would show him how he sounded around the house and give him a dose of his own medicine. So one morning he came down and asked for his breakfast. "Why you old blankety, blank, blank, bald-headed, blankety, blankety, blank, you can get your own breakfast." He was horrified, but every time he tried to say anything she would bring out a bunch of lurid

14

oaths until finally he said, "Wife, if you'll cut out that cussing I'll never swear again."

I have sometimes tried to imagine myself in Damascus on review day, and have seen a man riding on a horse richly caparisoned with trappings of gold and silver, and he himself clothed in garments of the finest fabrics, and the most costly, though with a face so sad and melancholy that it would cause the beholder to turn and look a second and third time. But he was a leper. And a man unaccustomed to such scenes might be heard to make a remark like this: "How unequally God seems to divide his favors! There is a man who rides and others walk; he is clothed in costly garments; they are almost naked while he is well fed," and they contrast the difference between the man on the horse and the others. If we only knew the breaking hearts of the people we envy we would pity them from the bottom of our souls.

I was being driven through a suburb of Chicago by a real estate man who wanted to sell me a lot. He was telling me who lived here and who lived there, and what an honor it would be for me and my children to possess a home there. We were driving past a house that must have cost $100,000 and he said: "That house is owned by Mr. So-and-So. He is one of our multi-millionaires, and he and his wife have been known to live in that house for months and never speak to each other. They each have separate apartments, each has a separate retinue of servants, each a dining-room and sleeping apartments, and months come and go by and they never speak to each other." My thoughts hurried back to the little flat we called our home, where we had lived for seventeen years. I have paid rent enough to pay for it. There wasn't much in it; I could load it in two furniture vans, maybe three, counting the piano, but I would not trade the happiness and the joy and the love of that little flat if I had to take that palatial home and the sorrow and the things that went with it.

Family Skeletons

Suppose you were driving along the street and a man who was intimately acquainted with the skeletons that are in every family, should tell you the secrets of them all, of that boy who has broken his father's heart by being a drunkard, a black-leg gambler, and that girl who has gone astray, and that wife who is a common drunkard, made so by society, and the father himself who is also a sinner.

Leprosy is exceedingly loathsome, and as I study its pathology I am not surprised that God used it as a type of sin. A man who is able to understand this disease, its beginning and its progress, might be approached by a man who was thus afflicted and might say to him, "Hurry! hurry! Show yourself to the priest for the cleansing of the Mosaic law."

"Why?" says the man addressed. "What is the trouble?" The other man would say, "Do hurry and show yourself to the priest." But the man says, "That is only a fester, only a water blister, only a pimple, nothing more. I say there is no occasion to be alarmed. You are unduly agitated and excited for my welfare."

Those sores are only few now, but it spreads, and it is first upon the hand, then upon the arm, and from the arm it goes on until it lays hold of every nerve, artery, vein with its slimy coil, and continues until the disintegration of the parts takes place and they drop off, and then it is too late. But the man who was concerned saw the beginning of that, not only the end, but the beginning. He looked yonder and saw the end too. If you saw a blaze you would cry, "Fire!" Why? Because you know that if let alone it will consume the building.

That is the reason why you hurry when you get evidence of the disease. So I say to you, young man, don't you go with that godless, good-for-nothing gang that blaspheme and sneer at religion, that bunch of character assassins; they will make of your body a doormat to wipe their feet upon. Don't go with that bunch. I heard you swear, I heard you sneer at religion. Stop, or you will become a staggering, muttering, bleary-eyed, foul-mouthed down-and-outer, on your way to hell. I say to you stop, or you will go reeling down to hell, breaking your wife's heart and wrecking your children's lives. And what have you got to show for it? What have you got to show for it? God pity you for all you got to show for selling your soul to the devil. You are a fool. You are a fool. Take it from "Bill," you are a fool.

Don't you go, my boy; don't you laugh at that smutty story with a double meaning. Don't go with that gang. But you say to me, "Mr. Sunday, you are unduly excited for my welfare. I know you smell liquor on my breath, but I never expect to become a drunkard. I never expect to become an outcast." Well, you are a fool. You are a fool. No man ever intended to become a drunkard. Every drunkard started out to be simply a moderate drinker. The fellow that tells me that he can leave it alone when he wants to lies. It is a lie. If you can, why don't you leave it alone? You will never let it alone. If you could, you would. My boy, hear me, I have walked along the shores of time and have seen them strewn with the wrecks of those who have drifted in from the seas of lust and passion and are fit only for danger signals to warn the coming race. You can't leave it alone or if you can, the time will come when it will get you. Take it from me.

My mother told me never to buy calico by lamplight, because you can't tell whether the colors will stand or run in the wash. Never ask a girl to be your wife when she's got her best bib and tucker on. Call on her and leave at ten o'clock and leave your glove on the piano, and go back the next morning about nine o'clock after your glove and ring the doorbell, and if she comes to the door with her hair done up in curl papers and a slipper on one foot and a shoe on the other foot, and that untied, and a Mother Hubbard on, take to the woods as fast as you can go. Never mind the glove, let the old man have that if he can wear it. But if she comes to the door nice and neat in a neat working

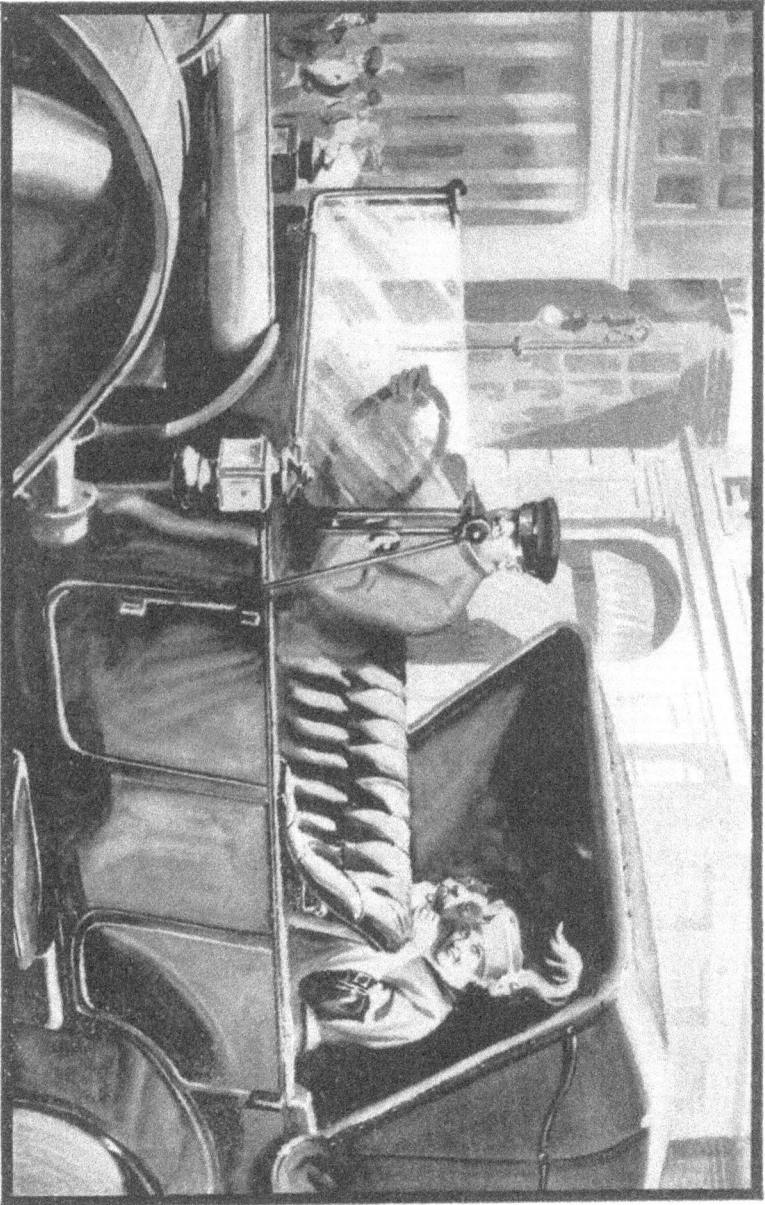

"Don't give a Pug-nosed Bulldog the Love a Baby ought to be Getting."

EVERY MUSCLE IN HIS BODY PREACHES IN ACCORD WITH HIS VOICE.

house dress, with her sleeves rolled up and her hair neatly done up, and a ribbon or a flower stuck in it, grab her quick.

Henry Clay Trumbull told me years ago that he was in Europe and in London he went to a theater to see a man who was going to give an exhibition of wild animals and serpents. He had a royal Bengal tiger and a Numidian lion, and he introduced a beast that seems to be least able of being tamed either by kindness or brutality, a black panther. He made him go through the various motions, and after a while a wire screen was put down in front of the stage between the audience and the performer, and to the weird strains of an oriental band the man approached from the left of the stage and a serpent from the right. The eyes of the serpent and the man met and the serpent quailed before the man. Man was master there. At his command the serpent went through various contortions, and the man stepped to the front of the stage and the serpent wound himself round and round and round the man, until the man and serpent seemed as one. His tongue shot out, his eyes dilated. The man gave a call, but the audience thought that part of the performance, and that horrified audience sat there and heard bone after bone in that man's body crack and break as the reptile tightened its grasp upon his body, and saw his body crushed before he could be saved.

He had bought that snake when it was only four feet long and he had watered and nursed it until it was thirty-five feet. At first he could have killed it; at last it killed him.

Nursing Bad Habits

Are you nursing a habit today? Is it drink? Are you nursing and feeding that which will wreck your life and wreck you upon the shores of passion, notwithstanding all the wrecks you have seen of those who have gone down the line?

I never got such a good idea of leprosy as I did by reading that wonderful book of the nineteenth century by General Lew Wallace, "Ben Hur." You remember the banishment of Ben Hur and the disintegration of that family life and estate, and the return of Ben Hur from his exile. He goes past his old home. The blinds are closed and drawn and all is deserted. He lies down upon the door-step and falls asleep. His mother and sister have been in the leper colony and are dying of leprosy and only waiting the time when they will be covered with the remains of others who have come there. So they have come to the city to get bread and secure water, and they see their son and brother lying on the door-step of their old home. They dare not awaken him for fear anguish at learning of their fate would be more than he could bear. They dare not touch him because it is against the law, so they creep close to him and put their leprous lips against his sandal-covered feet. They then go back again with the bread and water for which they had come.

Presently Ben Hur awakens and rubs his eyes and sees great excitement. (This part of the story is mine.) Along comes a blear-eyed, old, whisky-soaked degenerate and Ben Hur asks him what is the trouble, what is the excitement about, and he says: "A couple of lepers have been cleansed, but there is nothing to that, just some occult power, it's all a fake." Ben Hur goes farther on and hears about this wonder, and they say it is nothing; nothing, some long-haired evangelist who says his name is Jesus Christ; it's all a fake. Then Ben Hur goes farther and discovers that it is Jesus of Nazareth and that he has cleansed Ben Hur's own mother and sister. He hears the story and acknowledges the Nazarene.

The Leprosy of Sin

The lepers had to cry, "Unclean! Unclean!" in those days to warn the people. They were compelled by law to do that: also they were compelled by law to go on the side of the street toward which the wind was blowing lest the breeze bring the germs of their body to the clean and infect them with the disease. And the victim of this disease was compelled to live in a lonely part of the city, waiting until his teeth began to drop out, his eyes to drop from their sockets, and his fingers to drop from his hands, then he was compelled to go out in the tombs, the dying among the dead, there to live until at last he was gathered to the remains of the dead. That was the law that governed the leper in those days. All others shrank from him; he went forth alone. Alone! No man of all he loved or knew, was with him; he went forth on his way, alone, sick at heart, to die alone.

Leprosy is infectious. And so is sin. Sin begins in so-called innocent flirtation. The old, god-forsaken scoundrel of a libertine, who looks upon every woman as legitimate prey for his lust, will contaminate a community; one drunkard, staggering and maundering and muttering his way down to perdition, will debauch a town.

Some men ought to be hurled out of society; they ought to be kicked out of lodges; they ought to be kicked out of churches, and out of politics, and every other place where decent men live or associate. And I want to lift the burden tonight from the heads of the unoffending womanhood and hurl it on the heads of offending manhood.

Rid the world of those despicable beasts who live off the earnings of the unfortunate girl who is merchandising herself for gain. In some sections they make a business of it. I say commercialized vice is hell. I do not believe any more in a segregated district for immoral women than I would in having a section for thieves to live in where you could hire one any day or night in the week to steal for you. There are two things which have got to be driven out or they'll drive us out, and they are open licensed saloons and protected vice.

Society needs a new division of anathemas. You hurl the burden on the head of the girl; and the double-dyed scoundrel that caused her ruin is received in society with open arms, while the girl is left to hang her head and spend her life in shame. Some men are so rotten and vile that they ought to be disinfected and take a bath in carbolic acid and formaldehyde. Shut the lodge door in the face of every man that you know to be a moral leper; don't let him hide behind his uniform and his badge when you know him to be so rotten that the devil would duck up an alley rather than meet him face to face. Kick him out of church. Kick him out of society.

You don't live your life alone. Your life affects others. Some girls will walk the streets and pick up every Tom, Dick and Harry that will come across with the price of an ice-cream soda or a joy ride.

So with the boy. He will sit at your table and drink beer, and I want to tell you if you are low-down enough to serve beer and wine in your home, when you serve it you are as low down as the saloon-keeper, and I don't care whether you do it for society or for anything else. If you serve liquor or drink you are as low down as the saloon-keeper in my opinion. So the boy who had not grit enough to turn down his glass at the banquet and refuse to drink is now a blear-eyed, staggering drunkard, reeling to hell. He couldn't stand the sneers of the crowd. Many a fellow started out to play cards for beans, and tonight he would stake his soul for a show-down. The hole in the gambling table is not very big; it is about big enough to shove a dollar through; but it is big enough to shove your wife through; big enough to shove your happiness through; your home through; your salary, your character; just big enough to shove everything that is dear to you in this world through.

Listen to me. Bad as it is to be afflicted with physical leprosy, moral leprosy is ten thousand times worse. I don't care if you are the richest man in the town, the biggest tax-payer in the county, the biggest politician in the district, or in the state. I don't care a rap if you carry the political vote of Pennsylvania in your vest pocket, and if you can change the vote from Democratic to Republican in the convention—if after your worldly career is closed my text would make you a fitting epitaph for your tombstone and obituary notice in the papers, then what difference would it make what you had done—"he was a leper." He was a great politician—but "He was a leper." What difference would it make?

I'll tell you, I was never more interested in my life than in reading the story of an old Confederate colonel who was a stickler for martial discipline. One day he had a trifling case of insubordination. He ordered his men to halt, and he had the offender shot. They dug the grave and he gave the command to march, and they had stopped just three minutes by the clock. At the close of the war they made him chief of police of a Southern city, and he was so vile and corrupt that the people arose and ordered his dismissal. Then a great earthquake swept over the city, and the people rushed from their homes and thousands of people crowded the streets and there was great excitement. Some asked, "Where is the colonel?" and they said, "You will find him in one of two or three places." So they searched and found him in a den of infamy. He was so drunk that he didn't realize the danger he was in. They led him out, then put him upon a snow white-horse, put his spurs on his boots and his regimentals on; they pinned a star on his breast and put a cockade on his hat, and said to him: "Colonel, we command you as mayor of the city to quell this riot. You have supreme authority."

He rode out among the people to quell the riot, dug his spurs into the white side of the horse and the crimson flowed out, and he rode in and out among the surging mass of humanity.

He rode out among the people with commands here, torrents of obscenity there, and in twenty-five minutes the stillness of death reigned in city squares, so marvelously did they fear him, so wonderful was his power over men. He then rode out, dismounted, took off his cockade, tore the star from his breast and threw it down, threw off his regimentals, took off his sword; then he staggered back to the house of infamy, where three months later he died, away from his wife, away from virtue, away from morality, his name synonymous with all that is vile. What difference did it make that he had power over men when you might sum up his life in the words, "But he was a leper." What difference did it make?

I pity the boy or girl from the depths of my soul, who if you ask are you willing to be a Christian, will answer: "Mr. Sunday, I would like to be, but if I tell that at home my brothers will abuse me, my mother will sneer at me, my father will curse me. If I were, I would have no encouragement to stand and fight the battle." I pity from the depths of my soul that boy or girl, the boy who has a father like that; the girl that has a mother like that, who have a joint like that for a home.

Unclean! Suppose every young man who is a moral leper were impelled by some uncontrollable impulse over which he had no power to make public revelations of his sins! Down the street he comes in his auto and you speak to him from the curbstone and he will say: "Unclean! Unclean!" Yonder he comes walking down the street. Suppose that to every man and woman he meets he is impelled and compelled to make revelation of the fact that he is a leper.

Leprosy is an infectious disease; it is the germ of sin. If there is an evil in you the evil will dwell in others. When we do wrong we inspire others—and your lives scatter disease when you come in contact with others. If there is sin in the father there will be sin in the boy; if there is sin in the mother, there will be sin in the daughter; if there is sin in the sister, there will be sin in the brother; by your influence you will spread it. If you live the wrong way you will drag somebody else to perdition with you as you go, and kindred ties will facilitate it.

Supposing all your hearts were open. Supposing we had glass doors to our hearts, and we could walk down the street and look in and see where you have been, and with whom you have been and what you have been doing. A good many of you would want stained-glass windows and heavy tapestry to cover them.

" But the Lord Looketh on the Heart "

Suppose I could put a screen behind me, pull a string or push a button, and produce on that screen a view of the hearts of the people. I would say: "Here is Mr. and Mrs. A's life, as it is, and here, as the people think it is. Here is what he really is. Here is where he has been. Here is how much booze he drinks. Here is how much he lost last year at horse races." But these are the things that society does not take note of. Society takes no note of the flirtation on the street. It waits until the girl has lost her virtue and then it slams the door in her face. It takes no note of that young man drinking at a banquet table; it waits until he becomes a bleary-eyed drunkard and then it will slam the door in his face. It will take no note of the young fellow that plays cards for a prize; it waits until he becomes a blackleg gambler and then it slams the door in his face.

God says, "Look out in the beginning for that thing." Society takes no note of the beginning. It waits until it becomes vice, and then it organizes Civic Righteousness clubs. Get back to the beginning and do your work there. God has planned to save this world through the preaching of men and women, and God reaches down to save men; he pulls them out of the grog shops and puts them on the water wagon.

I never could imagine an angel coming down from heaven and preaching to men and women to save them. God never planned to save this world with the preaching of angels. When Jesus Christ died on the cross he died to redeem those whose nature he took. An angel wouldn't know what he was up against. Some one would say: "Good Angel, were you ever drunk?" "No!" "Good Angel, did you ever swear?" "Oh, no!" "Good Angel, did you ever try to put up a stove-pipe in the fall?" "Oh, no!" "Did you ever stub your toe while walking the floor with the baby at three A. M?" "Oh, no!"

'Well, then, Mr. Angel, you don't know. You say there is great mercy with God, but you are not tempted."

No. God planned to save the world by saving men and women and letting them tell the story.

The servant of Naaman entered the hut of the prophet Elisha and found him sitting on a high stool writing with a quill pen on papyrus. The servant bowed low and said, "The great and mighty Naaman, captain of the hosts of the king of Syria, awaits thee. Unfortunately he is a leper and cannot enter your august presence. He has heard of the miraculous cures that you have wrought and he hopes to become the recipient of your power." The old prophet of God replied:

"Tell him to dip seven times in the Jordan—beat it, beat it, beat it." The servant came out to Naaman, who was sitting on his horse.

"Well, is he at home?"

"He's at home, but he is a queer duck."

Naaman thought that Elisha would come out and pat the sores and say incantations, like an Indian medicine man. Naaman was wroth, like many a fool today. God reveals to the sinner the plan of salvation and, instead of thanking God for salvation and doing what God wants him to do, he condemns God and everybody else for bothering him.

Now here is a man who wants to be a Christian. What will he do? Will he go ask some old saloon-keeper? Will he go ask some of these old brewers? Will he ask some of the fellows of the town? Will he ask the County Liquor Dealers' Association? Where will he go? To the preacher, of course. He is the man to go to when you want to be a Christian. Go to a doctor when you are sick, to a blacksmith when your horse is to be shod, but go to the preacher when you want your heart set right.

So Naaman goes into the muddy water and the water begins to lubricate those old sores, and it begins to itch, and he says, "Gee whizz," like many a young fellow today who goes to a church and just gets religion enough to make him feel miserable. An old fellow in Iowa came to me and said,

"Bill, I have been to hear you every night and you have done me a lot of good. I used to cuss my old woman every day and I ain't cussed her for a week. I'm getting a little better."

The Joy of Religion

The trouble with many men is that they have got just enough religion to make them miserable. If there is no joy in religion, you have got a leak in your religion. Some haven't religion enough to pay their debts. Would that I might have a hook and for every debt that you left unpaid I might jerk off a piece of clothing. If I did some of you fellows would have not anything on but a celluloid collar and a pair of socks.

Some of you have not got religion enough to have family prayer. Some of you people haven't got religion enough to take the beer bottles out of your cellar and throw them in the alley. You haven't got religion enough to tell that proprietor of the red light, "No, you can't rent my house after the first of June;" to tell the saloon-keeper, "You can't rent my house when your lease runs out"; and I want to tell you that the man that rents his property to a saloon-keeper is as low-down as the saloon-keeper. The trouble with you is that you are so taken up with business, with politics, with making money, with your lodges, and each and every one is so dependent on the other, that you are scared to death to come out and live clean cut for God Almighty. You have not fully surrendered yourself to God.

The matter with a lot of you people is that your religion is not complete. You have not yielded yourself to God and gone out for God and God's truth. Why, I am almost afraid to make some folks laugh for fear that I will be arrested for breaking a costly piece of antique bric-à-brac. You would think that if some people laughed it would break their faces. To see some people you would think that the essential of orthodox Christianity is to have a face so long you could eat oatmeal out of the end of a gas pipe. Sister, that is not religion; I want to tell you that the happy, smiling, sunny-faced religion will win more people to Jesus Christ than the miserable old grim-faced kind will in ten years. I pity anyone who can't laugh. There must be something wrong with their religion or their liver. The devil can't laugh.

So I can see Naaman as he goes into the water and dips seven times, and lo! his flesh becomes again as a little child's. When? When he did what God told him to do.

I have seen men come down the aisle by the thousands, men who have drank whisky enough to sink a ship. I have seen fallen women come to the front by scores and hundreds, and I have seen them go away cleansed by the power of God. When? When they did just what God told them to do.

I wish to God the Church were as afraid of imperfection as it is of perfection.

I saw a woman that for twenty-seven years had been proprietor of a disorderly house, and I saw her come down the aisle, close her doors, turn the girls out of her house and live for God. I saw enough converted in one town where there were four disorderly houses to close their doors; they were empty; the girls had all fled home to their mothers.

Out in Iowa a fellow came to me and spread a napkin on the platform—a napkin as big as a tablecloth. He said: "I want a lot of shavings and sawdust."

"What for?"

"I'll tell you; I want enough to make a sofa pillow. Right here is where I knelt down and was converted and my wife and four children, and my neighbors. I would like to have enough to make a sofa pillow to have something in my home to help me think of God. I don't want to forget God, or that I was saved. Can you give me enough?"

I said, "Yes, indeed, and if you want enough to make a mattress, all right, take it; and if you want enough of the tent to make a pair of breeches for each of the boys, why take your scissors and cut it right out, if it will help you to keep your mind on God."

That is why I like to have people come down to the front and publicly acknowledge God. I like to have a man have a definite experience in religion—something to remember.

A PLAIN TALK TO WOMEN

And I say to you, young girl, don't go with that godless, God-forsaken, sneering young man that walks the streets smoking cigarettes. He would not walk the streets with you if you smoked cigarettes. But you say you will marry him and reform him; he would not marry you to reform you. Don't go to that dance. Don't you know that it is the most damnable, low-down institution on the face of God's earth, that it causes more ruin than anything this side of hell? Don't you go with that young man; don't you go to that dance. That is why we have so many whip-poor-will widows around the country: they married some of these mutts to reform them, and instead of doing that the undertaker got them. I say, young girl, don't go to that dance; it has proven to be the moral graveyard that has caused more ruination than anything that was ever spewed out of the mouth of hell. Don't go with that young fellow for a joy ride at midnight.

Girls, when some young fellow comes up and asks you the greatest question that you will ever be asked or called upon to answer, next to the salvation of your own soul, what will you say? "Oh, this is so sudden!" That is all a bluff; you have been waiting for it all the time.

But, girls, never mind now, get down to facts. When he asks you the greatest question, the most important one that any girl is ever asked, next to the salvation of her soul, just say, "Sit down and let me ask you three questions. I want to ask you these three questions and if I am satisfied with your answer, it will determine my answer to your question. 'Did you believe me to be virtuous when you came here to ask me to be your wife?" "Oh, yes, I believed you to be virtuous. That's the reason I came here. You are like violets dipped in dew." The second question: "Have you as a young man lived as you demand of me as a girl that I should have lived?" The third question: "If I, as a girl, had lived and done as you, as a young man, and you knew it, would you ask me to marry you?"

They will line up and nine times out of ten they will take the count. You can line them up, and I know what I am talking about, and I defy any man on God's earth successfully to contradict me. I have the goods. The average young man is more particular about the company he keeps than the average girl. I'll tell you. If he meets somebody on the street whom he doesn't want to meet he will duck into the first open doorway and avoid the publicity of meeting her, for fear she might smile or give an indication that she had seen him somewhere and sometime before that. Yet our so-called best girls keep company with young men whose character would make a black mark on a piece of anthracite. Their characters are foul and rotten and damnable.

I like to see a girl who has a good head, and can choose right because it is right, never minding the criticism. Choose the good and be careful of good company and good conduct, and keep company with a good young fellow. Don't go with the fellow whose reputation is bad. Everybody knows it is bad, and if you are seen with him you will lose your reputation as well, although your virtue is intact; and they might as well take you to the graveyard and bury you, when your reputation is gone. When a man like that asks you to go with him, say to him that if he will live the way you want him to you will go with him. If he would take a stand like that there wouldn't be so many wrecks. If our women and girls would take higher stands and say, "No, no, we will not keep company with you unless you live the way I want you to," there would be better men. A lot of you women hold yourselves too cheaply. You are scared to death for fear you will be what the world irreverently calls "an old maid."

Hospitality

You remember the prophet Elisha and his journey to the school of prophets up to Mount Carmel. There was a woman who noticed the actions and conduct of the man of God and she said to her husband, "Let us build a little room and place therein a bed, and bowl and pitcher, that he may make it his home."

The suggestion evidently met with the approval of the husband, because ever afterward the man of God enjoyed this hospitality. I sometimes thought she might have been a new woman of the olden times, because no mention is made of the husband. You never hear of some old lobsters unless they are fortunate enough to marry a woman who does things and their name is always mentioned in connection with what the wife does.

You know there are homes in which the advent of one, two and possibly three children is considered a curse instead of a blessing. God, in his providence, has often denied the honor of maternity to some women. But there are married women who shrink from maternity, not because of ill health, but simply because they love ease, because they love fine garments and ability to flirt like a butterfly at some social function.

Crimes have been and are being committed; hands are stained with blood; and that very crime has made France the charnel house of the world. And America, we of our boasted intelligence and wealth, we are fast approaching the same doom, until or unless it behooves somebody with grit and courage to preach against the prevailing sins and run the risk of incurring the displeasure of people who divert public attention from their own vileness rather than condemn themselves for the way they are living. They say the man who is preaching against it is vulgar, rather than the man who did it.

I am sure there is not an angel in heaven that would not be glad to come to earth and be honored with motherhood if God would grant her that privilege. What a grand thing

15

it must be, at the end of your earthly career, to look back upon a noble and godly life, knowing you did all you could to help leave this old world to God and made your contributions in tears and in prayers and taught your offspring to be God-fearing, so that when you went you would continue to produce your noble character in your children.

Maternity Out of Fashion

Society has just about put maternity out of fashion. When you stop to consider the average society woman I do not think maternity has lost anything. The humbler children are raised by their mothers instead of being turned over to a governess.

There are too many girls who marry for other causes than love. I think ambition, indulgence and laziness lead more girls to the altar than love—girls not actuated by love, but simply willing to pay the price of wifehood to wear fine clothes. They are not moved by the noble desires of manhood or womanhood.

Some girls marry for novelty and some girls marry for a home. Some fool mothers encourage girls to marry for ease so they can go to the matinee and buzz around. Some fool girls marry for money and some girls marry for society, because by connecting their name with a certain family's they go up a rung in the social ladder, and some girls marry young bucks to reform them—and they are the biggest fools in the bunch, because the bucks would not marry the girls to reform them.

"Society Has Just About Put Maternity Out of Fashion"

You mothers are worse fools to encourage your daughter to marry some old lobster because his father has money and when he dies, maybe your daughter can have good clothes and ride in an auto instead of hoofing it. Look at the

girls on the auction block today.   Look at the awful battle
the average stenographer and average clerk has to fight.
You cannot work for six dollars a week and wear fine duds
and be on the square as much as you are without having the
people suspicious.

In a letter to Miss Borson, President Roosevelt said:
"The man or woman who avoids marriage and has a heart
so cold as to know no passion and a brain so shallow as to
dislike having children is, in fact, a criminal."

Is it well with thee?   Is it well with your husband?
"The best man in the world," you answer.   Very well;
is it well with the child?   I think its responsibilities are equal,
if they don't outweigh its privileges, and when God is in
the heart of the child, I don't wonder that that home is a
haven of peace and rest.

I have no motive in preaching except the interest I have
in the moral welfare of the people.   There is not money
enough to hire me to preach.   I tell you, ladies, we have to
do something more than wipe our eyes, and blow our nose,
and say "Come to Jesus."   Go out and shell the woods and
make them let you know why they don't "come to Jesus."

I believe the time will come when sex hygiene will form
part of the high-school curriculum.   I would rather have
my children taught sex hygiene than Greek and Latin.   A
lot of the high-school curriculum is mere fad.   I think the
time will come when our girls will be taught in classes with
some graduated woman physician for an instructor.

Women live on a higher plane, morally, than men.   No
woman was ever ruined that some brute of a man did not
take the initiative.   Women have kept themselves purer than
men.   I believe a good woman is the best thing this side of
heaven and a bad woman the worst thing this side of hell.
I think woman rises higher and sinks lower than man.   I
think she is the most degraded on earth or the purest on
earth.

Our homes are on the level with women.   Towns are
on the level with homes.   What women are our homes will

be; and what the town is, the men will be, so you hold the destiny of the nation.

I believe there is something unfinished in the make-up of a girl who does not have religion. The average girl today no longer looks forward to motherhood as the crowning glory of womanhood. She is turning her home into a gambling shop and a social beer-and-champagne-drinking joint, and her society is made up of poker players, champagne, wine and beer drinkers, grass-widowers and jilted jades and slander-mongers—that comprises the society of many a girl today. She is becoming a matinee-gadder and fudge-eater.

The Girl Who Flirts

I wish I could make a girl that flirts see herself as others see her. If you make eyes at a man on the street he will pay you back. It doesn't mean that you are pretty. It means that if you don't care any more for yourself than that why should he? The average man will take a girl at her personal estimate of herself.

It takes a whole lot of nerve for a fellow to look a girl in the face and say, "Will you be my wife and partner, and help me fight the battle during life?" but I think it means a whole lot more to the girl who has to answer and fight that question. But the fool girl loafs around and waits to be chosen and takes the first chance she gets and seems to think that if they get made one, the laws of man can make them two again.

The divorce laws are damnable. America is first in many things that I love, but there are many things that are a disgrace. We lead the world in crime; and lead the world in divorce—we who boast of our culture.

Many a girl has found out after she is married that it would have been a good deal easier to die an old maid than to have said "yes," and become the wife of some cigarette-smoking, cursing, damnable libertine. They will launch the matrimonial boat and put the oars in and try it once for luck, anyway, and so we have many women praying for unconverted husbands.

I preached like this in a town once and the next day I heard of about five engagements that were broken. I can give you advice now, but if the knot is tied, the thing is done.

I am a Roman Catholic on divorce. There are a whole lot of things worse than living and dying an old maid and one of them is marrying the wrong man. So don't be one to do that.

Now, girls, don't simper and look silly when you speak about love. There is nothing silly about it, although some folks are silly because they are in love. Love is the noblest and purest gift of God to man and womankind. Don't let your actions advertise "Man Wanted, Quick." That is about the surest way not to get a man. You might get a thing with breeches on, but he is no man

Many a woman is an old maid because she wanted to do her share of the courting. Don't get excited and want to hurry things along. If a man begins to act as though he is after you, the surest way to get him is just to make him feel you don't want him, unless you drive him off by appearing too indifferent.

And, girls, don't worry if you think you are not going to get a chance to marry. Some of the noblest men in the world have been bachelors and some of the noblest women old maids. And, woman, for God's sake, when you do get married, don't transfer the love God gave you to bestow on a little child to a Spitz dog or a brindle pup.

The Task of Womanhood

All great women are satisfied with their common sphere in life and think it is enough to fill the lot God gave them in this world as wife and mother. I tell you the devil and women can damn this world, and Jesus and women can save this old world. It remains with womanhood today to lift our social life to a higher plane.

Mothers, be more careful of your boys and girls. Explain these evils that contaminate our social life today. I have had women say to me, "Mr. Sunday, don't you think there is danger of talking too much to them when they are so young?" Not much; just as soon as a girl is able to know the pure from the impure she should be taught. Oh, mothers, mothers, you don't know what your girl is being led to by this false and mock modesty.

Don't teach your girls that the only thing in the world is to marry. Why, some girls marry infidels because they were not taught to say "I would not do it." A girl is a big fool to marry an infidel. God says, "Be ye not unequally yoked with unbelievers."

I believe there is a race yet to appear which will be as far superior in morals to us as we are superior to the morals in the days of Julius Cæsar; but that race will never appear until God-fearing young men marry God-fearing girls and the offspring are God-fearing.

Culture will never save the world. If these miserable human vampires who feed and fatten upon the virtue of womanhood can get off with impunity; nay, more, be feasted and petted and coddled by society, we might as well back-pedal out and sink in shame, for we can never see to the heights nor command the respect of the great and good.

What paved the way for the downfall of the mightiest dynasties—proud and haughty Greece and imperial Rome? The downfall of their womanhood. The virtue of womanhood is the rampart wall of American civilization. Break that down and with the stones thereof you can pave your way to the hottest hell, and reeking vice and corruption.

CHAPTER XVIII

"Help Those Women"

If the womanhood of America had been no better than its manhood, the devil would have had the country fenced in long ago.—BILLY SUNDAY.

THE average American is somewhat of a sentimentalist. "Home, Sweet Home," is an American song. No people, except possibly the Irish, respond more readily to the note of "Mother" than the Americans. No other nation honors womanhood so greatly. We are really a chivalrous people.

In this respect, as in so many others, Sunday is true to type. His sermons abound with passages which express the best American sentiment toward womanhood. It is good for succeeding generations that such words as the following should be uttered in the ears of tens and hundreds of thousands of young people, and reprinted in scores and hundreds of newspapers.

"MOTHER"

The story of Moses is one of the most beautiful and fascinating in all the world. It takes a hold on us and never for an instant does it lose its interest, for it is so graphically told that once heard it is never forgotten.

I have often imagined the anxiety with which that child was born, for he came into the world with the sentence of death hanging over him, for Pharaoh had decreed that the male children should die. The mother defied even the command of the king and determined that the child should live, and right from the beginning the battle of right against might was fought at the cradle.

Moses' mother was a slave. She had to work in the brickyards or labor in the field, but God was on her side and she won, as the mother always wins with God on her

side. Before going to work she had to choose some hiding
place for her child, and she put his little sister, Miriam, on
guard while she kept herself from being seen by the soldiers
of Pharaoh, who were seeking everywhere to murder the
Jewish male children.   For three months she kept him
hidden, possibly finding a new hiding place every few days.
It is hard to imagine anything more difficult than to hide
a healthy, growing baby, and he was hidden for three
months.   Now he was grown larger and more full of life
and a more secure hiding place had to be found, and I can
imagine this mother giving up her rest and sleep to prepare
an ark for the saving of her child.

I believe the plan must have been formulated in
heaven.   I have often thought God must have been as
much interested in that work as was the mother of Moses,
for you can't make me believe that an event so important
as that, and so far-reaching in its results, ever happened by
luck or chance.   Possibly God whispered the plan to the
mother when she went to him in prayer and in her grief
because she was afraid the sword of Pharaoh would murder
her child.   And how carefully the material out of which
the ark was made had to be selected!   I think every twig
was carefully scrutinized in order that nothing poor might
get into its composition, and the weaving of that ark, the
mother's heart, her soul, her prayers, her tears, were interwoven.

Oh, if you mothers would exercise as much care over
the company your children keep, over the books they read
and the places they go, there would not be so many girls
feeding the red-light district, nor so many boys growing up
to lead criminal lives.   And with what thanksgiving she
must have poured out her heart when at last the work
was done and the ark was ready to carry its precious cargo,
more precious than if it was to hold the crown jewels of
Egypt.   And I can imagine the last night that baby was
in the home.   Probably some of you can remember when
the last night came when baby was alive; you can remem-

ber the last night the coffin stayed, and the next day the pall-bearers and the hearse came. The others may have slept soundly, but there was no sleep for you, and I can imagine there was no sleep for Moses' mother.

"There are whips and tops and pieces of string
And shoes that no little feet ever wear;
There are bits of ribbon and broken wings
And tresses of golden hair.

"There are dainty jackets that never are worn
There are toys and models of ships;
There are books and pictures all faded and torn
And marked by finger tips
Of dimpled hands that have fallen to dust—
Yet we strive to think that the Lord is just.

"Yet a feeling of bitterness fills our soul;
Sometimes we try to pray,
That the Reaper has spared so many flowers
And taken ours away.
And we sometimes doubt if the Lord can know
How our riven hearts did love them so

"But we think of our dear ones dead,
Our children who never grow old,
And how they are waiting and watching for us
In the city with streets of gold;
And how they are safe through all the years
From sickness and want and war.
We thank the great God, with falling tears,
For the things in the cabinet drawer."

A Mother's Watchfulness

Others in the house might have slept, but not a moment could she spare of the precious time allotted her with her little one, and all through the night she must have prayed that God would shield and protect her baby and bless the work she had done and the step she was about to take.

Some people often say to me: "I wonder what the angels

do; how they employ their time?" I think I know what some of them did that night. You can bet they were not out to some bridge-whist party. They guarded that house so carefully that not a soldier of old Pharaoh ever crossed the threshold. They saw to it that not one of them harmed that baby.

At dawn the mother must have kissed him good-bye, placed him in the ark and hid him among the reeds and rushes, and with an aching heart and tear-dimmed eyes turned back again to the field and back to the brickyards to labor and wait to see what God would do. She had done her prayerful best, and when you have done that you can bank on God to give the needed help. If we only believed that with God all things are possible no matter how improbable, what unexpected answers the Lord would give to our prayers! She knew God would help her some way, but I don't think she ever dreamed that God would help her by sending Pharaoh's daughter to care for the child. It was no harder for God to send the princess than it was to get the mother to prepare the ark. What was impossible from her standpoint was easy for God.

Pharaoh's daughter came down to the water to bathe, and the ark was discovered, just as God wanted it to be, and one of her maids was sent to fetch it. You often wonder what the angels are doing. I think some of the angels herded the crocodiles on the other side of the Nile to keep them from finding Moses and eating him up. You can bank on it, all heaven was interested to see that not one hair of that baby's head was injured. There weren't devils enough in hell to pull one hair out of its head. The ark was brought and with feminine curiosity the daughter of Pharaoh had to look into it to see what was there, and when they removed the cover, there was lying a strong, healthy baby boy, kicking up his heels and sucking his thumbs, as probably most of us did when we were boys, and probably as you did when you were a girl. The baby looks up and weeps, and those tears blotted out all that was against it and gave it a chance for its life.

I don't know, but I think an angel stood there and pinched it
to make it cry, for it cried at the right time. Just as God
plans. God always does things at the right time. Give
God a chance; he may be a little slow at times, but he will
always get around in time.

The tears of that baby were the jewels with which
Israel was ransomed from Egyptian bondage. The princess
had a woman's heart and when a woman's heart and a
baby's tears meet, something happens that gives the devil
cold feet. Perhaps the princess had a baby that had died,
and the sight of Moses may have torn the wound open
and made it bleed afresh. But she had a woman's heart,
and that made her forget she was the daughter of Pharaoh
and she was determined to give protection to that baby.
Faithful Miriam (the Lord be praised for Miriam) saw the
heart of the princess reflected in her face. Miriam had studied faces so much that she could read the princess' heart as
plainly as if written in an open book, and she said to her:
"Shall I go and get one of the Hebrew women to nurse the
child for you?" and the princess said, "Go."

I see her little feet and legs fly as she runs down the hot,
dusty road, and her mother must have seen her coming
a mile away, and she ran to meet her own baby put back
in her arms. And she was being paid Egyptian gold to take
care of her own baby. See how the Lord does things? "Now
you take this child and nurse it for me and I will pay you
your wages." It was a joke on Pharaoh's daughter, paying
Moses' mother for doing what she wanted to do more than
anything else—nurse her own baby.

How quickly the mother was paid for these long hours
of anxiety and alarm and grief, and if the angels know what
is going on what a hilarious time there must have been in
heaven when they saw Moses and Miriam back at home,
under the protection of the daughter of Pharaoh. I imagine
she dropped on her knees and poured out her heart to God,
who had helped her so gloriously. She must have said:
"Well, Lord, I knew you would help me. I knew you would

take care of my baby when I made the ark and put him in it and put it in the water, but I never dreamed that you would put him back into my arms to take care of, so I would not have to work and slave in the field and make brick and be tortured almost to death for fear that the soldiers of Pharaoh would find my baby and kill him. I never thought you would soften the stony heart of Pharaoh and make him pay me for what I would rather do than anything else in this world." I expect to meet Moses' mother in heaven, and I am going to ask her how much old Pharaoh had to pay her for that job. I think that's one of the best jokes, that old sinner having to pay the mother to take care of her own baby. But I tell you, if you give God a chance, he will fill your heart to overflowing. Just give him a chance.

A Mother's Bravery

This mother had remarkable pluck. Everything was against her but she would not give up. Her heart never failed. She made as brave a fight as any man ever made at the sound of the cannon or the roar of musketry.

"The bravest battle that was ever fought,
    Shall I tell you where and when?
On the maps of the world you'll find it not—
    'Twas fought by the mothers of men.

"Nay, not with cannon or battle shot,
    With sword or noble pen,
Nay, not with the eloquent word or thought,
    From the mouths of wonderful men.

"But deep in the walled-up woman's heart—
    Of women that would not yield.
But, bravely, silently bore their part—
    Lo, there is the battle-field.

"No marshaling troops, no bivouac song,
    No banner to gleam and wave;
But oh, these battles they last so long—
    From babyhood to the grave."

"HA! HA! OLD DEVIL, I'VE GOT YOU BEAT!"

"WHO WILL LEAD THE WAY?"

Copyright, 1908, by C. U. Williams.
"You Old Skeptic, We are Counting Time on You."

Copyright, 1908, by C. U. Williams.
"John, the Drunkard, Marching up to the Butcher's Shop."

Mothers are always brave when the safety of their children is concerned.

This incident happened out West. A mother was working in a garden and the little one was sitting under a tree in the yard playing. The mother heard the child scream; she ran, and a huge snake was wrapping its coils about the baby, and as its head swung around she leaped and grabbed it by the neck and tore it from her baby and hurled it against a tree.

Fathers often give up. The old man often goes to boozing, becomes dissipated, takes a dose of poison and commits suicide; but the mother will stand by the home and keep the little band together if she has to manicure her finger nails over a washboard to do it. If men had half as much grit as the women there would be different stories written about a good many homes. Look at her work! It is the greatest in the world; in its far-reaching importance it is transcendently above everything in the universe—her task in molding hearts and lives and shaping character. If you want to find greatness don't go to the throne, go to the cradle; and the nearer you get to the cradle the nearer you get to greatness. Now, when Jesus wanted to give his disciples an impressive object lesson he called in a college professor, did he? Not much. He brought in a little child and said: "Except ye become as one of these, ye shall in no wise enter the kingdom of God." The work is so important that God will not trust anybody with it but a mother. The launching of a boy or a girl to live for Christ is greater work than the launching of a battleship.

Moses was a chosen vessel of the Lord and God wanted him to get the right kind of a start, so he gave him a good mother. There wasn't a college professor in all Egypt that God would trust with that baby! so he put the child back in its mother's arms. He knew the best one on earth to trust with that baby was its own mother. When God sends us great men he wants to have them get the right kind of a start. So he sees to it that they have a good mother. Most

any old stick will do for a daddy.   God is particular about
the mothers.

Good Mothers Needed

And so the great need of this country, or any other
country, is good mothers, and I believe we have more good
mothers in America than any other nation on earth.   If
Washington's mother had been like a Happy Hooligan's
mother, Washington would have been a Happy Hooligan.

Somebody has said: "God could not be everywhere, so
he gave us mothers."   Now there may be poetry in it, but
it's true "that the hand that rocks the cradle rules the world,"
and if every cradle was rocked by a good mother, the world
would be full of good men, as sure as you breathe.   If every
boy and every girl today had a good mother, the saloons and
disreputable houses would go out of business tomorrow.

A young man one time joined a church and the preacher
asked him: "What was it I said that induced you to be a
Christian?"

Said the young man: "Nothing that I ever heard you
say, but it is the way my mother lived."   I tell you an ounce
of example outweighs forty million tons of theory and speculation.   If the mothers would live as they should, we preachers would have little to do.   Keep the devil out of the boys
and girls and he will get out of the world.   The old sinners
will die off if we keep the young ones clean.

The biggest place in the world is that which is being
filled by the people who are closely in touch with youth.
Being a king, an emperor or a president is mighty small
potatoes compared to being a mother or the teacher of children, whether in a public school or in a Sunday school, and
they fill places so great that there isn't an angel in heaven
that wouldn't be glad to give a bushel of diamonds to boot
to come down here and take their places.   Commanding
an army is little more than sweeping a street or pounding
an anvil compared with the training of a boy or girl.   The
mother of Moses did more for the world than all the kings

that Egypt ever had. To teach a child to love truth and hate a lie, to love purity and hate vice, is greater than inventing a flying machine that will take you to the moon before breakfast. Unconsciously you set in motion influences that will damn or bless the old universe and bring new worlds out of chaos and transform them for God.

God's Hall of Fame

A man sent a friend of mine some crystals and said: "One of these crystals as large as a pin point will give a distinguishable green hue to sixteen hogsheads of water." Think of it! Power enough in an atom to tincture sixteen hogsheads of water. There is power in a word or act to blight a boy and, through him, curse a community. There is power enough in a word to tincture the life of that child so that it will become a power to lift the world to Jesus Christ. The mothers will put in motion influences that will either touch heaven or hell. Talk about greatness!

Oh, you wait until you reach the mountains of eternity, then read the mothers' names in God's hall of fame, and see what they have been in this world. Wait until you see God's hall of fame; you will see women bent over the washtub.

I want to tell you women that fooling away your time hugging and kissing a poodle dog, caressing a "Spitz," drinking society brandy-mash and a cocktail, and playing cards, is mighty small business compared to molding the life of a child.

Tell me, where did Moses get his faith? From his mother. Where did Moses get his backbone to say: "I won't be called the son of Pharaoh's daughter?" He got it from his mother. Where did Moses get the nerve to say, "Excuse me, please," to the pleasures of Egypt? He got it from his mother. You can bank on it he didn't inhale it from his dad. Many a boy would have turned out better if his old dad had died before the kid was born. You tell your boy to keep out of bad company. Sometimes when he walks down the street with his father he's in the worst company in town. His dad smokes, drinks and chews. Moses got it from his mother. He was learned in all the wisdom of Egypt, but that didn't give him the swelled head.

When God wants to throw a world out into space, he is not concerned about it. The first mile that world takes settles its course for eternity. When God throws a child out into the world he is mighty anxious that it gets a good start. The Catholics are right when they say: "Give us the children until they are ten years old and we don't care who has them after that." The Catholics are not losing any sleep about losing men and women from their church membership. It is the only church that has ever shown us the only sensible way to reach the masses—that is, by getting hold of the children. That's the only way on God's earth that you will ever solve the problem of reaching the masses. You get the boys and girls started right, and the devil will hang a crape on his door, bank his fires, and hell will be for rent before the Fourth of July.

A friend of mine has a little girl that she was compelled to take to the hospital for an operation. They thought she would be frightened, but she said: "I don't care if mama will be there and hold my hand." They prepared her for the operation, led her into the room, put her on the table, put the cone over her face and saturated it with ether, and she said: "Now, mama, take me by the hand and hold it and I'll not be afraid." And the mother stood there and held her hand. The operation was performed, and when she regained consciousness, they said: "Bessie, weren't you afraid when they put you on the table?" She said: "No, mama stood there and held my hand. I wasn't afraid."

There is a mighty power in a mother's hand. There's more power in a woman's hand than there is in a king's scepter.

And there is a mighty power in a mother's kiss—inspiration, courage, hope, ambition, in a mother's kiss.

One kiss made Benjamin West a painter, and the memory of it clung to him through life. One kiss will drive away the fear in the dark and make the little one brave. It will give strength where there is weakness.

I was in a town one day and saw a mother out with her boy, and he had great steel braces on both legs, to his hips, and when I got near enough to them I learned by their conversation that that wasn't the first time the mother had had him out for a walk. She had him out exercising him so he would get the use of his limbs. He was struggling and she smiled and said: "You are doing finely today; better than you did yesterday." And she stooped and kissed him, and the kiss of encouragement made him work all the harder, and she said: "You are doing nobly, son." And he said: "Mama, I'm going to run; look at me." And he started, and one of his toes caught on the steel brace on the other leg and he stumbled, but she caught him and kissed him, and said: "That was fine, son; how well you did it!" Now, he did it because his mother had encouraged him with a kiss. He didn't do it to show off. There is nothing that will help and inspire life like a mother's kiss.

"If we knew the baby fingers pressed against the window pane,
Would be cold and still tomorrow, never trouble us again,
Would the bright eyes of our darling catch the frown upon our brow?

"Let us gather up the sunbeams lying all around our path,
Let us keep the wheat and roses, casting out the thorns and chaff!
We shall find our sweetest comforts in the blessings of today,
With a patient hand removing all the briars from our way."

A Mother's Song

There is power in a mother's song, too. It's the best music the world has ever heard. The best music in the world is like biscuits—it's the kind mother makes. There is no brass band or pipe organ that can hold a candle to mother's song. Calve, Melba, Nordica, Eames, Schumann-

Heinck, they are cheap skates, compared to mother. They can't sing at all. They don't know the rudiments of the kind of music mother sings. The kind she sings gets tangled up in your heart strings. There would be a disappointment in the music of heaven to me if there were no mothers there to sing. The song of an angel or a seraph would not have much charm for me. What would you care for an angel's song if there were no mother's song?

The song of a mother is sweeter than that ever sung by minstrel or written by poet. Talk about sonnets! You ought to hear the mother sing when her babe is on her breast, when her heart is filled with emotion. Her voice may not please an artist, but it will please any one who has a heart in him. The songs that have moved the world are not the songs written by the great masters. The best music, in my judgment, is not the faultless rendition of these high-priced opera singers. There is nothing in art that can put into melody the happiness which associations and memories bring. I think when we reach heaven it will be found that some of the best songs we will sing there will be those we learned at mother's knee.

A Mother's Love

There is power in a mother's love. A mother's love must be like God's love. How God could ever tell the world that he loved it without a mother's help has often puzzled me. If the devils in hell ever turned pale, it was the day mother's love flamed up for the first time in a woman's heart. If the devil ever got "cold feet" it was that day, in my judgment.

You know a mother has to love her babe before it is born. Like God, she has to go into the shadows of the valley of death to bring it into the world, and she will love her child, suffer for it, and it can grow up and become vile and yet she will love it. Nothing will make her blame it, and I think, women, that one of the awful things in hell will be that there will be no mother's love there. Nothing but black, bottomless, endless, eternal hate in hell—no mother's love.

> "And though he creep through the vilest caves of sin,
> And crouch perhaps, with bleared and blood-shot eyes,
> Under the hangman's rope—a mother's lips
> Will kiss him in his last bed of disgrace,
> And love him e'en for what she hoped of him."

I thank God for what mother's love has done for the world.

Oh, there is power in a mother's trust. Surely as Moses was put in his mother's arms by the princess, so God put the babes in your arms, as a charge from him to raise and care for. Every child is put in a mother's arms as a trust from God, and she has to answer to God for the way she deals with that child. No mother on God's earth has any right to raise her children for pleasure. She has no right to send them to dancing school and haunts of sin. You have no right to do those things that will curse your children. That babe is put in your arms to train for the Lord. No mother has any more right to raise her children for pleasure than I have to pick your pockets or throw red pepper in your eyes. She has no more right to do that than a bank cashier has to rifle the vaults and take the savings of the people. One of the worst sins you can commit is to be unfaithful to your trust.

A Mother's Responsibility

"Take this child and nurse it for me." That is all the business you have with it. That is a jewel that belongs to God and he gives it to you to polish for him so he can set it in a crown. Who knows but that Judas became the godless, good-for-nothing wretch he was because he had a godless, good-for-nothing mother? Do you know? I don't. What is more to blame for the crowded prisons than mothers? Who is more to blame for the crowded disreputable houses than you are, who let your children

gad the streets, with every Tom, Dick and Harry, or keep
company with some little jack rabbit whose character
would make a black mark on a piece of tar paper? I have
talked with men in prisons who have damned their mothers
to my face. Why? They blame their mothers for their
being where they are.

"Take the child and nurse it for me, and I will pay
you your wages." God pays in joy that is fire-proof,
famine-proof and devil-proof. He will pay you, don't you
worry. So get your name on God's pay-roll. "Take this
child and nurse it for me, and I will pay you your wages."
If you haven't been doing that, then get your name on
God's pay-roll.

"Take this child and nurse it for me, and I will pay
you your wages." Then your responsibility! It is so
great that I don't see how any woman can fail to be a
Christian and serve God. What do you think God will
do if the mother fails? I stagger under it. What, if
through your unfaithfulness, your boy becomes a curse
and your daughter a blight? What, if through your neglect,
that boy becomes a Judas when he might have been a John
or Paul?

Down in Cincinnati some years ago a mother went
to the zoological garden and stood leaning over the bear
pit, watching the bears and dropping crumbs and peanuts
to them. In her arms she held her babe, a year and three
months old. She was so interested in the bears that the
baby wriggled itself out of her arms and fell into the bear
pit, and she watched those huge monsters rip it to shreds.
What a veritable hell it will be through all her life to know
that her little one was lost through her own carelessness
and neglect!

"Take this child and raise it for me, and I will pay
you your wages." Will you promise and covenant with
God, and with me, and with one another, that from now
on you will try, with God's help, to do better than you
ever have done to raise your children for God?

"I once read the story of an angel who stole out of heaven and came to this world one bright, sunshiny day; roamed through field, forest, city and hamlet, and as the sun went down plumed his wings for the return flight. The angel said: "Now that my visit is over, before I return I must gather some mementos of my trip." He looked at the beautiful flowers in the garden and said: "How lovely and fragrant," and plucked the rarest roses, made a bouquet, and said: "I see nothing more beautiful and fragrant than these flowers." The angel looked farther and saw a bright-eyed, rosy-cheeked child, and said: "That baby is prettier than the flowers; I will take that, too," and looking behind to the cradle, he saw a mother's love pouring out over her babe like a gushing spring, and the angel said: "The mother's love is the most beautiful thing I have seen! I will take that, too."

And with these three treasures the heavenly messenger winged his flight to the pearly gates, saying: "Before I go I must examine the mementos of my trip to the earth." He looked at the flowers; they had withered. He looked at the baby's smile, and it had faded. He looked at the mother's love, and it shone in all its pristine beauty. Then he threw away the withered flowers, cast aside the faded smile, and with the mother's love pressed to his breast, swept through the gates into the city, shouting that the only thing he had found that would retain its fragrance from earth to heaven was a mother's love.

"Take this child and nurse it for me, and I will pay you your wages."

When Napoleon Bonaparte was asked, "What do you regard as the greatest need of France?" he replied, "Mothers, mothers, mothers." You women can make a hell of a home or a heaven of a home. Don't turn your old Gatling-gun tongue loose and rip everybody up and rip your husbands up and send them out of their homes. If I were going to investigate your piety I would ask the girl who works for you.

This talk about the land of the free is discounted when the children look like a rummage sale in a second-hand store; with uncombed hair, ripped pants, buttons off, stockings hanging down. It doesn't take the wisdom of truth to see that mother is too busy with her social duties, clubs, etc., to pay much attention to the kids.

Mothers of Great Men

The mother of Nero was a murderess, and it is no wonder that he fiddled while Rome burned. The mother of Patrick Henry was eloquent, and that is the reason why every school boy and girl knows, "Give me liberty or give me death." Coleridge's mother taught him Biblical stories from the old Dutch tile of the fireplace. In the home authority is needed today more than at any time in the history of this nation. I have met upon the arena of the conflict every form of man and beast imaginable to meet, and I am convinced that neither law nor gospel can make a nation without home authority and home example. Those two things are needed. The boy who has a wholesome home and surroundings and a judicious control included does not often find his way into the reformatory.

Susanna Wesley was the mother of nineteen children, and she held them for God. When asked how she did it she replied, "By getting hold of their hearts in their youth, and never losing my grip."

If it had not been for the expostulations of the mother of George Washington, George Washington would have become a midshipman in the British navy, and the name of that capital yonder would have been some other. John Randolph said in the House of Representatives, "If it had not been for my godly mother, I, John Randolph, would have been an infidel." Gray, who wrote the "Elegy in a Country Churchyard," said he was one of a large family of children that had the misfortune to survive their mother. And I believe the ideal mother is the product of a civilization that rose from the manger of Bethlehem.

I am sure there is not an angel in heaven that would not be glad to come to earth and be honored with motherhood if God would grant that privilege. What a grand thing it must be, at the end of your earthly career, to look back upon a noble and godly life, knowing you did all you could to help leave this old world to God, and made your contributions in tears and in prayers and taught your offspring to be God-fearing, so that when you went you would continue to produce your noble character in your children.

I believe in blood; I believe in good blood, bad blood, honest blood, and thieving blood; in heroic blood and cowardly blood; in virtuous blood, in licentious blood, in drinking blood and in sober blood. The lips of the Hapsburgs tell of licentiousness; those of the Stuarts tell of cruelty, bigotry and sensuality, from Mary, queen of Scots, down to Charles the First and Charles the Second, James the First—who showed the world what your fool of a Scotchman can be when he is a fool—down to King James the Second.

Scotch blood stands for stubbornness. They are full of stick-to-it-iveness. I know, Mrs. Sunday is full-blooded Scotch. English blood speaks of reverence for the English. That is shown by the fact that England spent $50,000,000 recently to put a crown on George's head. Danish blood tells of love of the sea. Welsh blood tells of religious fervor and zeal for God. Jewish blood tells of love of money, from the days of Abraham down until now.

You may have read this story: Down in New York was a woman who said to her drunken son: "Let's go down to the police court and have the judge send you over to the island for a few weeks. Maybe you'll straighten up then and I can have some respect for you again." Down they went to the police court and appeared before the judge. He asked who would make the charge and the mother sprang forward with the words on her lips. Then she stopped short, turned to her son and throwing her arms about his neck cried out: "I can't! I can't! He is my son, I love him and I can't." Then she fell at his feet dead. As dearly as she had loved her drunken, bloated, loafing son she couldn't stand in judgment.

CHAPTER XIX

Standing on the Rock

If a doctor didn't know any more about Materia Medica than the average church member knows about the Bible, he'd be arrested for malpractice. —BILLY SUNDAY.

A PUBLISHER remarked to me that a Billy Sunday campaign did not create a demand for religious books in general. With rather an air of fault-finding he said, "You can't sell anything but Bibles to that Billy Sunday crowd."

That remark is illuminating. Billy Sunday does not create a cult: he simply sends people back to the Bibles of their mothers. His converts do not become disciples of any particular school of interpretation: the Bible and the hymn book are their only armory. It cannot be gainsaid that it is better to read the Bible than to read books about the Bible. The work of Billy Sunday is not done with a convert until he has inspired that person to a love and loyalty for the old Book.

Such passages as this show the uncompromising loyalty of Sunday to the Bible:

"Here is a book, God's Word, that I will put up against all the books of all the ages. You can't improve on the Bible. You can take all the histories of all the nations of all the ages and cut out of them all that is ennobling, all that is inspiring, and compile that into a common book, but you cannot produce a work that will touch the hem of the garment of the Book I hold in my hand. It is said, 'Why cannot we improve on the Bible? We have advanced everything else.' No, sir. 'Heaven and earth shall pass away, but My Word shall not.' And so this old Book, which is the Word of God, the Word of Jesus Christ, is the book I intend to preach by everywhere. The religion that

(249)

THE STORY OF THE BRAZEN SERPENT

5. And the people spake against God and against Moses, Wherefore have ye brought us up out of Egypt to die in the wilderness? for there is no bread, neither is there any water; and our soul loatheth this light bread.

6. And the Lord sent fiery serpents among the people, and they bit the people; and much people of Israel died.

7. Therefore the people came to Moses and said, We have sinned, for we have spoken against the Lord, and against thee; pray unto the Lord that he take away the serpents from us. And Moses prayed for the people.

8. And the Lord said unto Moses, Make thee a fiery serpent, and set it upon a pole: and it shall come to pass that every one that is bitten, when he looketh upon it, shall live.

9. And Moses made a serpent of brass and put it upon a pole and it came to pass, that if a serpent had bitten any man, when he beheld the serpent of brass he lived.

The Jews were in Egyptian bondage for years. God said he would release them, but he hadn't come. But God never forgets. So he came and chose Moses to lead them, and when Moses got them out in the wilderness they began to knock and said, "Who is this Moses anyway? We don't know him. Were there not enough graves in Egypt?" and they said they didn't like the white bread they were getting and wanted the onions and the leeks and the garlic and melons of Egypt, and they found fault. And God sent the serpents and was going to kill them all, but Moses interceded and said, "Now see here, God." But the Lord said, "Get out of the way, Moses, and let me kill them all." But Moses said, "Hold on there, Lord. That bunch would have the laugh on you if you did that. They'd say you brought them out here and the commissary stores ran out and you couldn't feed them, so you just killed them all." So God said, "All right, for your sake, Moses, I won't," and he said, "Moses, you go and set up a brazen serpent in the wilderness and that will be the one thing that will save them if they are bitten. They must look or die."

has withstood the sophistry and the criticism of the ages, the sarcasm of Voltaire, the irony of Hume, the blasphemy of Ingersoll, the astronomer's telescope, the archæologist's spade and the physician's scalpel—they have all tried to prove the Bible false, but the old Book is too tough for the tooth of time, and she stands triumphant over the grave of all that have railed upon her. God Almighty is still on the job. Some people act as though they had sent for the undertaker to come to embalm God and bury him. But it is the truth; it is not an accident that places the Christian nations in the forefront of the world's battles. It is something more than race, color, climate, that causes the difference between the people that dwell on the banks of the Congo and those in this valley. The scale of civilization always ascends the line of religion; the highest civilization always goes hand in hand with the purest religion."

Rigid as he is in literal interpretation of the Bible, Sunday is celebrated for his paraphrases of favorite passages, a recasting of the familiar form of words into the speech of the day. Some of these "slang versions" of the old Book make one gasp; but generally the evangelist gets the innermost meaning of the Book itself. He is not an interpreter of the Bible but a popularizer of it. He does not expound the Scripture as much as he pounds in the Scripture. The Bible and its place in the life of the Christian are often on the Evangelist's lips.

Here, for instance, is his interpretation of the story of David and Goliath:

"All of the sons of Jesse except David went off to war; they left David at home because he was only a kid. After a while David's ma got worried. She wondered what had become of his brothers, because they hadn't telephoned to her or sent word. So she said to David, 'Dave, you go down there and see whether they are all right.'

"So David pikes off to where the war is, and the first morning he was there out comes this big Goliath, a big, strapping fellow about eleven feet tall, who commenced to shoot off his mouth as to what he was going to do.

"'Who's that big stiff putting up that game of talk?'
asked David of his brothers.

"'Oh, he's the whole works; he's the head cheese of the
Philistines. He does that little stunt every day.'

"'Say,' said David, 'you guys make me sick. Why
don't some of you go out and soak that guy? You let him
get away with that stuff.' He decided to go out and tell
Goliath where to head in.

"So Saul said, 'You'd better take my armor and sword.'
David put them on, but he felt like a fellow with a hand-me-
down suit about four times too big for him, so he took them
off and went down to the brook and picked up a half dozen
stones. He put one of them in his sling, threw it, and soaked
Goliath in the coco between the lamps, and he went down
for the count. David drew his sword and chopped off his
block, and the rest of the gang beat it."

SUNDAY UTTERANCES ON THE BIBLE

The Bible is the Word of God. Nothing has ever been
more clearly established in the world today, and God
blesses every people and nation that reverence it. It has
stood the test of time. No book has so endured through the
ages. No book has been so hated. Everything the cunning
of man, philosophy, brutality, could contrive has been
done, but it has withstood them all.

There is no book which has such a circulation today.
Bibles are dropping from the press like the leaves in autumn.
There are 200,000,000 copies. It is read by all nations. It
has been translated into five hundred languages and dia-
lects.

No book ever came by luck or chance. Every book
owes its existence to some being or beings, and within the
range and scope of human intelligence there are but three
things—good, bad, and God. All that originates in intellect,
all which the intellect can comprehend, must come from one
of the three. This book, the Bible, could not possibly be
the product of evil, wicked, godless, corrupt, vile men, for

it pronounces the heaviest penalties against sin. Like produces like, and if bad men were writing the Bible they never would have pronounced condemnation and punishment against wrong-doing. The holy men of old, we are told, "spake as they were moved by the Holy Ghost." Men do not attribute these beautiful and matchless and well-arranged sentences to human intelligence alone, but we are told that men spake as they were inspired by the Holy Ghost. The only being left, to whom you, or I, or any sensible person could ascribe the origin of the Bible, is God.

Men have been thrown to beasts and burned to death for having a Bible in their possession. There have been wars over the Bible; cities have been destroyed. Nothing ever brought such persecution as the Bible. Everything vile, dirty, rotten and iniquitous has been brought to bear against it because it reveals man's cussedness. But it's here, and its power and influence are greater today than ever.

Saloons, bawdy houses, gambling hells, every rake, every white-slaver, every panderer and everything evil has been against it, but it is the word of God, and millions of people know it.

This being true, it is of the highest importance that you should think of the truths in it. I'll bet my life that there are hundreds of you that haven't read ten pages of the Bible in ten years. Some of you never open it except at a birth, a marriage or a death, and then just to keep your family records straight. That's a disgrace and an insult. I repeat it, it's a disgrace and an insult. Don't blame God if you wind up in hell, after God warned you, because you didn't take time to read it and think about it.

It is the only book that tells us of a God that we can love, a heaven to win, a hell to shun and a Saviour that can save. Why did God give us the Bible? So that we might believe in Christ. No other book tells us this. It tells us why the Bible was written, that we might believe and be saved. You don't read a railroad guide to learn to raise buckwheat. You don't read a cook book to learn to shoe

horses.   You don't read an arithmetic to learn the history
of the United States.   A geography does not tell you about
how to make buckwheat cakes.   No, you read a railroad
guide to learn about the trains, a cook book to learn to make
buckwheat cakes, an arithmetic for arithmetic and a geography for geography.   If you want to get out of a book what
the author put in it, find out why it was written.   That's
the way to get good out of a book.   Read it.

It was written that you might read and believe that
Jesus is the Son of God.   The Bible wasn't intended for a
history or a cook book.   It was intended to keep me from
going to hell.

The greatest good can be had from anything by using
it for the purpose for which it was intended.   A loaf of
bread and a brick may look alike, but try and exchange them
and see.   You build a house with brick, but you can't eat
it.   The purpose of a time table is to give the time of trains,
the junctions, the different railroads.   A man that has been
over the road knows more about it than a man who has
never been over it.   A man who has made the journey of
life guided by the Bible knows more about it than any high-
browed lobster who has never lived a word of it.   Then whom
are you going to believe, the man who has tried it or the man
who knows nothing about it?

The Bible was not intended for a science any more than
a crowbar is intended for a toothpick.   The Bible was written
to tell men that they might live, and it's true today.

One man says: "I do not believe in the Bible because
of its inconsistencies."   I say the greatest inconsistency is
in your life—not in the Bible!   I bring up before you the
memory of some evil deed, and you immediately begin to
find fault with the Bible!   Go to a man and talk business or
politics and he talks sense.   Go to a woman and talk society,
clubs or dress, and she talks sense.   Talk religion to them,
and they will talk nonsense!

I want to say that I believe that the Bible is the Word
of God from cover to cover.   Not because I understand its

philosophy, speculation, or theory. I cannot; wouldn't attempt it; and I would be a fool if I tried. I believe it because it is from the mouth of God; the mouth of God has spoken it.

There is only one way to have the doubts destroyed. Read the Bible and obey it. You say you can't understand it. There's an A, B, C in religion, just as in everything else. When you go to school you learn the A, B, C's and pretty soon can understand something you thought you never could when you started out. So in religion. Begin with the simple things and go on and you'll understand. That's what it was written for, that you might read and believe and be saved. I'm willing to stand here and take the hand of any man or woman if you are willing to come and begin with the knowledge you have.

In South Africa there are diamond mines and the fact has been heralded to every corner of the world. But only those that dig for them get the diamonds. So it is with the Bible. Dig and you'll find gold and salvation. You have to dig out the truths.

Years ago in Sing Sing prison there was a convict by the name of Jerry McCauley and one day an old pal of his came back to the prison and told him how he had been saved, and quoted a verse of Scripture. McCauley didn't know where to find the verse in the Bible, so he started in at the first and read through until he came to it. It was away over in the ninth chapter of Hebrews. But he found Jesus Christ while he was reading it. He lived a godly life until the day he died.

Supposing a man should come to you and say, "The title to your property is no good and if some one contests it you will lose?" Would you laugh and go on about your business? No, sir! You would go to the court house and if you could find it in only one book there, the book in the recorder's office, you'd search and find it, and if the recorder said the deed was all right you could laugh at whatever any one else said.

There is only one book in the world that tells me about my soul. It says if you believe you're saved, if you don't you are damned. God said it and it's all true. Every man who believes in the Bible shall live forever. The Bible says heaven or hell, so why do you resist?

No words are put in the Bible for effect. The Bible talks to us so we can understand. God could use language that no one could understand. But we can not understand all by simply hearing and reading. When we see we will know.

"I stood one day beside a blacksmith's door,
  And heard the anvil beat and the bellows chime;
Looking in, I saw upon the floor
  Old hammers worn out with beating years and years of time.

"'How many anvils have you had?' said I,
  'To wear and batter all these hammers so?'
'Just one,' said he, then said with twinkling eye,
  'The anvil wears the hammers out, you know.'

"So methought, the anvils of God's word—
  Of Jesus' sacrifice—have been beat upon—
The noise of falling blows was heard—
  The anvil is unharmed—the hammers are all gone."

Julian the apostate was a hammer. Gone! Voltaire, Renan, hammers. Gone! In Germany, Goethe, Strauss, Schleiermacher—gone. In England, Mill, Hume, Hobbes, Darwin, Huxley and Spencer—the anvil remains; the hammer is gone. In America, Thomas Paine, Parker, Ingersoll, gone. The anvil remains.

Listen. In France a hundred years ago or more they were printing and circulating infidel literature at the expense of $4,500,000 a year. What was the result? God was denied, the Bible sneered at and ridiculed, and between 1792 and 1795 one million twenty thousand and fifty-one hundred people were brought to death. The Word of God stood unshaken amidst it all. Josh Billings said: "I would rather be an idiot than an infidel; because if I am an infidel I made myself so, but if I am an idiot somebody else did it." Oh, the wreckers' lights on the dangerous coasts that try to allure and drag us away from God have all gone out, but God's words shine on.

The vital truths of the Bible are more believed in the world today than at any other time. When a man becomes so intelligent that he can not accept the Bible, too progressive to be a Christian, that man's influence for good, in society, in business or as a companion, is at an end. Some think that being a doubter is an evidence of superior intellect. No!

I've never found a dozen men in my life who disbelieved in the Bible but what they were hugging some secret sin. When you are willing to give up that pet sin you will find it easy to believe in the Bible.

It explains to me why Saul of Tarsus, the murderer, was changed to Paul, the apostle. It explains to me why David Livingstone left his Highland home to go to darkest Africa. It explains to me why the Earl of Shaftesbury was made from a drunkard into a power for God in London for sixty-five years. It explains why missionaries leave home and friends to go into unknown lands and preach Jesus Christ, and perhaps to die at the hands of the natives.

I can see in this book God revealed to man and when I do and accept, I am satisfied. It is just what you need to be satisfied. God knows your every need.

This explains to me why Jesus Christ has such influence on men and women in the world today. No man ever had such influence to teach men and women virtue and goodness as Christ. This influence has been in the world from 2,000 years ago to the present time. The human heart is to Jesus like a great piano. First he plays the sad melodies of repentance and then the joyful hallelujahs.

The Bible has promises running all through it and God wants you to appropriate them for your use. They are like a bank note. They are of no value unless used. You might starve to death if you have money in your pockets,

17

but won't use it. So the promises may not do you any good because you will not use them. The Bible is a galaxy of promises like the Milky Way in the heavens.

When you are in trouble, instead of going to your Bible, you let them grow, and they grow faster than Jonah's gourd vine. You're afraid to step out on the promises.

There are many exceedingly great and precious promises in the Bible. Here is one:

"Whatsoever ye shall ask in my name, that will I do, that the Father may be glorified in the Son."

If some of you would receive such a promise from John D. Rockefeller or Andrew Carnegie, you'd sit up all night writing out checks to be cashed in the morning. And yet you let the Bible lie on the table.

But the infidel says: "Mr. Sunday, why are there so many intelligent people in the world that don't believe the Bible?"

Do you wonder that it was an infidel who started the question: "Is life worth living?" Do you wonder that it was some fool woman, an infidel woman, that first started the question: "Is marriage a failure?" A fool, infidel woman. Christians do not ask such fool questions. Would you be surprised to be reminded that infidel writers and speakers have always and do always advocate and condone and excuse suicide? Do you know that in infidelity the gospel is suicide? That is their theory and I don't blame them, and the sooner they leave the world the better the world will be.

The great men of the ages are on the side of the Bible. A good many infidels talk as though the great minds of the world were arrayed against Christianity and the Bible. Great statesmen, inventors, painters, poets, artists, musicians, have lifted up their hearts in prayer. Watt, the inventor of the steam engine, was a Christian; Fulton, the inventor of the steamboat, was a Christian; Cyrus McCormick, who first invented the self-binder, was a Christian; Morse, who invented the telegraph, and the first message that ever flashed over the wire was from Deuteron-

· omy—'What hath God wrought'. Edison, although a
doubter in some things, said that there was evidence enough
in chemistry to prove the existence of a God, if there was no
evidence besides that.   George Washington was a Christian.
Abraham Lincoln was a Christian, and with Bishop Simpson
knelt on his knees in the White House, praying God to give
victory to the Army of the Blue.   John Hay, the brightest
Secretary of State that ever managed the affairs of state, in
my judgment, was a Christian.   William Jennings Bryan,
a man as clean as a hound's tooth; Garfield, McKinley,
Grover Cleveland, Harrison, Theodore Roosevelt, Wood-
row Wilson—all Christians.

The poets drew their inspiration from the Bible. Dante's
"Inferno," Milton's "Paradise Lost," two of the greatest
works ever written, were inspired by the Word of God. Lord
Byron, although a profligate, drew his inspiration from the
Word of God.   Shakespeare's works abound with quotations
from the Bible.   John G. Whittier, Longfellow, Michael
Angelo, who painted "The Last Judgment," Raphael, who
painted the "Madonna of the Chair," DaVinci, who painted
"The Last Supper," all dipped their brushes in the light of
heaven and painted for eternity.   The great men of the
world of all ages, of science, art, or statesmanship, have all
believed in Jesus Christ as the Son of God.

Twenty-seven years ago, with the Holy Spirit for my
guide, I entered this wonderful temple that we call Christianity.   I entered through the portico of Genesis and walked
down through the Old Testament's art gallery, where I saw
the portraits of Joseph, Jacob, Daniel, Moses, Isaiah, Solomon and David hanging on the wall; I entered the music
room of the Psalms and the Spirit of God struck the key-
board of my nature until it seemed to me that every reed
and pipe in God's great organ of nature responded to the
harp of David, and the charm of King Solomon in his
moods.

I walked into the business house of Proverbs.

I walked into the observatory of the prophets and

there saw photographs of various sizes, some pointing to far-off stars or events—all concentrated upon one great Star which was to rise as an atonement for sin.

Then I went into the audience room of the King of Kings, and got a vision from four different points—from Matthew, Mark, Luke and John. I went into the correspondence room, and saw Peter, James, Paul and Jude, penning their epistles to the world. I went into the Acts of the Apostles and saw the Holy Spirit forming the Holy Church, and then I walked into the throne room and saw a door at the foot of a tower and, going up, I saw One standing there, fair as the morning, Jesus Christ, the Son of God, and I found this truest friend that man ever knew; when all were false I found him true.

In teaching me the way of life, the Bible has taught me the way to live, it taught me how to die.

So that is why I am here, sober and a Christian, instead of a booze-hoisting infidel.

CHAPTER XX

Making a Joyful Noise

Don't look as if your religion hurt you.—BILLY SUNDAY.

"HE hath put a new song in my mouth." That is real religion which sets the saints to singing. Gloomy Christians are a poor advertisement of the Gospel. There is nothing of gloom about a Billy Sunday revival.

Shrewd students of the campaigns have often remarked that there are so few tears and so much laughter at the evangelist's services. There is scarcely one of Sunday's sermons in which he does not make the congregation laugh. All of his work is attuned to the note of vitality, robustness and happiness. Concerning the long-faced Christian Sunday says:

"Some people couldn't have faces any longer if they thought God was dead. They ought to pray to stop looking so sour. If they smile it looks like it hurts them, and you're always glad when they stop smiling. If Paul and Silas had had such long faces as some church members have on them when they went into the Philippian jail, the jailer would never have been saved. There never was a greater mistake than to suppose that God wants you to be long-faced when you put on your good clothes. You'd better not fast at all if you give the devil all the benefit. God wants people to be happy.

"The matter with a lot of you people is that your religion is not complete. You have not yielded yourself to God and gone out for God and God's truth. Why, I am almost afraid to make some folks laugh for fear that I will be arrested for breaking a costly piece of antique bric-a-brac. You would think that if some people laughed it would break their faces. I want to tell you that the

(261)

happy, smiling, sunny-faced religion will win more people
to Jesus Christ than the miserable old grimfaced kind
will in ten years.   I pity any one who can't laugh.
There must be something wrong with their religion or
their liver.   The devil can't laugh.

> " 'Oh, laugh and the world laughs with you,
>   Weep and you weep alone;
>   'Tis easy enough to be pleasant
>   When life moves along like a song;
>   But the man worth while is the man who can smile
>   When everything goes dead wrong.'

"Don't look as if religion hurt you.   Don't look as if
you had on a number two shoe when you ought to be wearing a number five.   I see some women who look as if they
had the toothache.   That won't win anyone for Christ.
Look pleasant.   Look as if religion made you happy, when
you had it.

"Then there is music.   When you get to heaven you'll
find that not all have been preached there.   They have been
sung there.   God pity us when music is not for the glory of
God.   Some of you will sing for money and for honor, but
you won't sing in the church.   Much of the church music
today is all poppycock and nonsense.   Some of these high-
priced sopranos get up in church and do a little diaphragm
wiggle and make a noise like a horse neighing.   I don't
wonder the people in the congregation have a hard time
of it."

So Sunday sets the city to singing.   His sermons are
framed in music—and not music that is a performance by
some soloist, but music that ministers to his message.
His gospel is sung as well as preached.   The singing is as
essential a part of the service as the sermon.   Everybody
likes good music, especially of a popular sort.   Sunday sees
that this taste is gratified.

The Tabernacle music in itself is enough to draw the
great throngs which nightly crowd the building.   The choir

furnishes not only the melodies but also a rare spectacle. This splendid regiment of helpers seated back of the speaker affects both the eyes and the ears of the audiences. Without his choirs Sunday could scarcely conduct his great campaigns. These helpers are all volunteers, and their steadfast loyalty throughout weeks of strenuous meetings in all kinds of weather is a Christian service of the first order.

True, membership in a Sunday choir is in itself an avocation, a social and religious interest that enriches the lives of the choir members. They "belong" to something big and popular. They have new themes for conversation. New acquaintances are made. The associations first formed in the Sunday choir have in many cases continued as the most sacred relations of life. The brightest spot in the monotony of many a young person's life has been his or her membership in the Billy Sunday choir.

"SOME OF THESE HIGH-PRICED SOPRANOS GET UP IN CHURCH AND MAKE A NOISE LIKE A HORSE NEIGHING."

The choir also has the advantage of a musical drill and experience which could be secured in no other fashion. All the advantages of trained leadership are given in return for the volunteer service. Incidentally, the choir members know that they are serving their churches and their communities in a deep and far-reaching fashion.

Many visitors to the Sunday Tabernacle are surprised to find that the music is of such fine quality. There is less "religious rag-time" than is commonly associated with the idea of revival meetings. More than a fair half of the music sung is that which holds an established place in the hymnody of all churches.

There is more to the music of a campaign than the volume of singing by the choir, with an occasional solo by the chorister or some chosen person. A variety of ingenious devices are employed to heighten the impression of the music. Thus a common antiphonal effect is obtained by having the choir sing one line of a hymn and the last ten rows of persons in the rear of the Tabernacle sing the answering line. The old hymn "For You I am Praying" is used with electrical effect in this fashion. Part singing is employed in ways that are possible only to such a large chorus as the musical director of the Sunday campaigns has at his command.

A genius for mutuality characterizes the Sunday song services. The audiences are given a share in the music. Not only are they requested to join in the singing, but they are permitted to choose their favorite hymns, and frequently the choir is called upon to listen while the audience sings.

Various delegations are permitted to sing hymns of their own choice. Diversity, and variety and vim seem to be the objective of the musical part of the program. From half an hour to an hour of this varied music introduces each service. When the evangelist himself is ready to preach, the crowd has been worked up into a glow and fervor that make it receptive to his message.

If some stickler for ritual and stateliness objects that these services are entirely too informal, and too much like a political campaign, the partisan of Mr. Sunday will heartily assent. These are great American crowds in their every-day humor. These evangelistic meetings are not regular church services. It has already been made plain that there is no "dim religious light" about the Sunday Tabernacle meetings.

It is a tribute to the comprehensiveness of the Sunday method that they bring together the most representative gatherings imaginable every day under the unadorned rafters of the big wooden shell called the Tabernacle. Shrewdly, the evangelist has made sure of the democratic quality of his congregation. He has succeeded in having the gospel sing its way into the affection and interest of every-day folk.

It is no valid objection to the Sunday music that it is so thoroughly entertaining. The Tabernacle crowds sing, not as a religious duty, but for the sheer joy of singing. One of the commonest remarks heard amid the crowd is "I never expect to hear such singing again till I get to Heaven." It is real Christian ministry to put the melodies of the Gospel into the memories of the multitudes, and to brighten with the songs of salvation the gray days of the burden-bearers of the world. Boys and men on the street whistle Gospel songs. The echoes of Tabernacle music may be heard long after Mr. Sunday has gone from a community in ten thousand kitchens and in the shops and factories and stores of the community. This is the strategy of "the expulsive power of a new affection." These meetings give to Christians a new and jubilant affirmation, instead of a mere defense for their faith. The campaign music carries the campaign message farther than the voice of any man could ever penetrate.

Upon the place of music in the Christian life Sunday says: "For sixteen years there had been no songs in Jerusalem. It must have been a great loss to the Jews, for everywhere we read we find them singing. They sang all the way to the Red Sea, they sang when Jesus was born, they sang at the Last Supper and when Jesus was arisen.

"Song has always been inseparably associated with the advancement of God's word. You'll find when religion is at low ebb the song will cease. Many of the great revivals have been almost entirely song. The great Welsh revival was mostly song. In the movements of Martin Luther,

Wesley, Moody and Torrey you will find abundance of song. When a church congregation gets at such low ebb that they can't sing and have to hire a professional choir to sing for them, they haven't got much religion. And some of those choir members are so stuck up they won't sing in a chorus. If I had a bunch like that they'd quit or I would.

"Take the twenty-fourth Psalm, 'Lift up your heads, O ye gates,' and the thirty-third Psalm. They were written by David to be sung in the temple.

"I can imagine his singing them now. They were David's own experiences. Look at them. Now you hear an old lobster get up to give an experience, 'Forty years ago I started forth—.' The same old stereotyped form.

"There's many a life today which has no song. The most popular song for most of you would be,

> "'Where is that joy which once I knew,
> When first I loved the Lord?'"

Right behind you where you left it when you went to that card party; right where you left it when you began to go to the theater; right where you left it when you side-stepped and backslid; right where you left it when you began paying one hundred dollars for a dress and gave twenty-five cents to the Lord; right where you left it when you began to gossip."

CHAPTER XXI

The Prophet and His Own Time

There wouldn't be so many non-church goers if there were not so many non-going churches.—BILLY SUNDAY.

A PROPHET to his own generation is Billy Sunday. In the speech of today he arraigns the sins of today and seeks to satisfy the needs of today. A man singularly free and fearless, he applies the Gospel to the conditions of the present moment. Knowing life on various levels, he preaches with a definiteness and an appropriateness that echo the prophet Nathan's "Thou art the man." By the very structure of Billy Sunday's mentality it is made difficult for him to be abstract. He has to deal definitely with concrete sins.

Now a pastor would find it difficult to approach, in the ruthless and reckless fashion of Billy Sunday, the shortcomings of his members and neighbors. He has to live with his congregation, year in and year out; but the evangelist is as irresponsible as John the Baptist on the banks of the Jordan. He has no affiliations to consider and no consequences to fear, except the Kingdom's welfare. His only concern is for the truth and applicability of his message. He is perfectly heedless about offending hearers. Those well-meaning persons who would compare Billy Sunday with the average pastor should bear this in mind.

A rare gift of satire and scorn and invective and ridicule has been given to Sunday. He has been equipped with powerful weapons which are too often missing from the armory of the average Gospel soldier. His aptitude for puncturing sham is almost without a peer in contemporary life. Few orators in any field have his art of heaping up adjectives to a towering height that overwhelms their objective.

Nor does the Church escape Sunday's plain dealing. He treats vigorously her shortcomings and her imperfections. Usually, the persons who hear the first half dozen or dozen sermons in one of his campaigns are shocked by the reckless way in which the evangelist handles the Church and church members.

Others, forewarned, perceive the psychology of it. It is clear that in Sunday's thinking the purity of the Church is all-important. Complacency with any degree of corruption or inefficiency on her part he would regard as sin. So he unsparingly belabors the Church and her ministry for all the good that they have left undone and all amiss that they have done.

The net result of this is that the evangelist leaves on the minds of the multitudes, to whom the Church has been a negligible quantity, a tremendous impression of her preeminent importance. It is true that sometimes, after a Sunday campaign, a few ministers have to leave their churches, because of the new spirit of efficiency and spirituality which he has imparted. They have simply been unable to measure up to the new opportunity. On the whole, however, it is clear that he imparts a new sense of dignity and a new field of leadership to the ministers of the Gospel in the communities he has served. Testimony on this point seems to be conclusive.

Given prophets of today, with the conviction that both Church and social life should square with the teaching of Jesus Christ, and you have revolutionary possibilities for any community. Fair samples of Sunday's treatment of the Church and of society are these:

"There is but one voice from the faithful preacher about the Church—that is she is sick. But we say it in such painless, delicate terms; we work with such tender massage, that she seems to enjoy her invalidism. I'm coming with my scalpel to cut into the old sores and ulcers and drive them out. I feel the pulse and say it's pus temperature. The temperature's high. I'm trying to remove from the

Church the putrefying abscess which is boring into its vitals. About four out of every five who have their names on our church records are doing absolutely nothing to bring anybody to Christ and the Church is not a whit better for their having lived in it. Christians are making a great deal of Lent. I believe in Lent. I'll tell you what kind, though. I believe in a Lent that is kept 365 days in the year for Jesus Christ. That is the kind I like to see. Some people will go to hell sure if they die out of the Lenten season. I hate to see a man get enough religion in forty days to last him and then live like the devil the rest of the year. If you can reform for forty days you can reform for the year.

"The Jewish Church ran up against this snag and was wrecked. The Roman Catholic Church ran up against it and split. All of the churches today are fast approaching the same doom.

"The dangers to the Church, as I see them, are assimilation with the world, the neglect of the poor, substitution of forms for godliness; and all summed up mean a fashionable church with religion left out. Formerly Methodists used to attend class meetings. Now these are abandoned in many churches. Formerly shouts of praise were heard. Now such holy demonstration is considered undignified. Once in a while some good, godly sister forgets herself and pipes out in a falsetto, apologetic sort of a key: 'Amen, Brother Sunday.' I don't expect any of those ossified, petrified, dyed-in-the-wool, stamped-on-the-cork Presbyterians or Episcopalians to shout, 'Amen,' but it would do you good and loosen you up. It won't hurt you a bit. You are hidebound. I think about half the professing Christians amount to nothing as a spiritual force. They have a kind regard for religion, but as for evangelical service, as for a cheerful spirit of self-denial, as for prevailing prayer, willingness to strike hard blows against the devil, they are almost a failure. I read the other day of a shell which had been invented which is hurled on a ship and when it explodes it puts all on board asleep. I sometimes think one of these shells has hit the Church.

"What are some people going to do about the Judgment? Some are just in life for the money they get out of it. They will tell you north is south if they think they can get a dollar by it. They float get-rich-quick schemes and anything for money. I haven't a word to say about a man who has earned his money honestly, uses it to provide for his family and spends the surplus for good. You know there is a bunch of mutts that sit around on stools and whittle and spit and cuss and damn and say that every man who has an honest dollar ought to divide it with them, while others get out and get busy and work and sweat and toil and prepare to leave something for their wives and families when they die, and spend the rest for good.

"Old Commodore Vanderbilt had a fortune of over $200,000,000, and one day when he was ill he sent for Dr. Deems. He asked him to sing for him that old song:

'Come, ye sinners, poor and needy,
Come, ye wounded, sick and sore.'

The old commodore tossed from side to side, looked around at the evidence of his wealth, and he said: 'That's what I am, poor and needy.' Who? Commodore Vanderbilt poor and needy with his $200,000,000? The foundation of that fabulous fortune was laid by him when he poled a yawl from New York to Staten Island and picked up pennies for doing it. The foundation of the immense Astor fortune was laid by John Jacob Astor when he went out and bought fur and hides from trappers and put the money in New York real estate. The next day in the street one man said to another: 'Have you heard the news? Commodore Vanderbilt is dead.' 'How much did he leave?' 'He left it all.'

"Naked you came into this world, and naked you will crawl out of it. You brought nothing into the world and you will take nothing out, and if you have put the pack screws on the poor and piled up a pile of gold as big as a house you can't take it with you. It wouldn't do you any good if you could, because it would melt."

CHAPTER XXII

Those Billy Sunday Prayers

I never preach a sermon until I have soaked it in prayer.—BILLY SUNDAY.

CONCERNING the prayers of Sunday there is little to be said except to quote samples of them and let the reader judge for himself.

That they are unconventional no one will deny; many have gone farther and have said that they are almost sacrilegious. The charge has often been made that the evangelist addresses his prayers to the crowd instead of to God. No one criticism has oftener been made of Mr. Sunday by sensitive and thoughtful ministers of the Gospel, than that his public prayers seem to be lacking in fundamental reverence.

The defender of Sunday rejoins, "He talks to Jesus as familiarly as he talks to one of his associates." Really, though, there is deep difference. His fellow-workers are only fellow-workers, but of the Lord, "Holy and reverend is his name." Many of the warmest admirers of the evangelist do not attempt to defend all of his prayers.

Probably Sunday does not know that in all the Oriental, and some European, languages there is a special form of speech reserved for royalty; and that it would be an affront to address a king by the same term as the commoner. The outward signs of this mental attitude of reverence in prayer are unquestionably lacking in Sunday.

His usual procedure is to begin to pray at the end of a sermon, without any interval or any prefatory remarks, such as "Let us pray." For an instant, the crowd does not realize that he is praying. He closes his eyes and says, "Now Jesus, you know," and so forth, just as he would say to the chorister, "Rody, what is the name of that delegation?"   Indeed, I have heard him interject just this inquiry into a prayer.   Or he will mention "that Bible class over to my right, near the platform."   He will use the same colloquial figures of speech in a prayer—base-ball phrases, for instance—that he does in his sermons.   Sometimes it is really difficult to tell whether he is addressing the Lord or the audience.

More direct familiar, childish petitions were never addressed to the Deity than are heard at the Sunday meetings.   They run so counter to all religious conceptions of a reverential approach to the throne of grace that one marvels at the charity of the ministers in letting him go unrebuked.   But they say "It's Billy," and so it is.   That is the way the man prays in private, for I have heard him in his own room, before starting out to preach; and in entirely the same intimate, unconventional fashion he asks the help of Jesus in his preaching and in the meetings. But to the prayers themselves:

"O God, help this old world.   May the men who have been drunkards be made better; may the men who beat their wives and curse their children come to Jesus; may the children who have feared to hear the footsteps of their father, rejoice again when they see the parent coming up the steps of the home.   Bring the Church up to help the work.   Bless them, Lord.   Bless the preachers: bless the officials of the Church and bless everyone in them.   Save the men in the mines.   Save the poor breaker boys as they toil day by day in dangers; save them for their mothers and fathers and bring them to Jesus.   Bless the policemen, the newspapermen and the men, women and children; the men and girls from the plants, factories, stores and streets. Go into the stores every morning and have prayer meetings so that the clerks may hear the Word of God before they get behind the counters and sell goods to the trade.

"Visit this city, O Lord, its schools and scholars, and bless the school board.   Bless the city officials.   Go down into the city hall and bless the mayor, directors and all the rest. We thank thee that the storm has passed. We believe that we will learn a lesson of how helpless we are before thee. How chesty we are when the sun shines and the day is clear, but, oh! how helpless when the breath of God comes and the snowflakes start to fall; when the floods come we get on our knees and wring our hands and ask mercy from thee. Oh, help us, O Lord.

"When the people get to hell—I hope that nobody will ever go there and I am trying my best to save them—they will know that they are there because they lived against God. I am not here to injure them; I am not here to wreck homes; I am here to tell them of the blessing you send down when they are with you. We pray for the thousands and thousands that will be saved."

"Thank you, Jesus. I came to you twenty-seven years ago for salvation and I got salvation. Thank the Lord I can look in the face of every man and woman of God everywhere and say that for all those years I have lived in salvation. Not that I take any credit to myself for that; it was nothing inherent in me; it was the power of God that saved me and kept me.

"O Lord, sweep over this town and save the business men of this community, the young men and women. O God, save us all from the cesspools of hell and corruption. Help me, Lord, as I hurl consternation into the ranks of that miserable, God-forsaken crew who are feeding, fattening and gormandizing on the people! Get everybody interested in honesty and decency and sobriety and make them fight to the last ditch for God. There are too many cowards, four-flushers in the Church."

"O Jesus, we thank God that you came into this old world to save sinners. Keep us, Lord. Hear us, O God, ere we stumble on in darkness. Lead the hundreds here to thy throne. Help the professing Christians who have not

18

done as they should in the past, to come, down this trail and take a more determined stand for thee. Help the official boards, the trustees of our churches, to show the way to hundreds by themselves confessing sin. Help them to say, 'O Lord, I haven't been square with thee. It is possible for me to improve my business and I can certainly improve my service to thee. I know and I believe in God and I believe in hell and heaven.' Lead them down the trail, Lord."

"O Lord, there are a lot of people who step up to the collection plate at church and fan. And Lord, there are always people sitting in the grandstand and calling the batter a mutt. He can't hit a thing or he can't get it over the base, or he's an ice wagon on the bases, they say. O Lord, give us some coachers out at this Tabernacle so that people can be brought home to you. Some of them are dying on second and third base, Lord, and we don't want that. Lord, have the people play the game of life right up to the limit so that home runs may be scored. There are some people, Lord, who say, 'Yes, I have heard Billy at the Tabernacle and oh, it is so disgusting: really it's awful the way he talks.' Lord, if there weren't some grouches and the like in the city I'd be lost. We had a grand meeting last night, Lord, when the crowd come down from Dicksonville (or what was that place, Rody?), Dickson City, Lord, that's right. It was a great crowd. There's an undercurrent of religion sweeping through here, Lord, and we are getting along fine.

"There are some dandy folks in Scranton, lots of good men and women that are with us in this campaign, and Lord, we want you to help make this a wonderful campaign. It has been wonderful so far. Lord, it's great to see them pouring in here night after night. God, you have the people of the homes tell their maids to go to the meeting at the Y. W. C. A. Thursday afternoon, and God, let us have a crowd of the children here Saturday. Rody is going to talk to them, Lord. He can't preach and I can't sing, but the children will have a big time with him, Lord. Lord, I won't try to stop people from roasting and scoring me. I would not know what to do if I didn't get some cracks from people now and then."

"Well, Jesus, I don't know how to talk as I would like to talk. I am at a loss as to just what to say tonight. Father, if you hadn't provided salvation, we'd all be pretty badly off. Knowing the kind of life I live and the kind of lives other people live, I know you are very patient and kind, but if you can do for men and women what you did for me, I wish it would happen. I wouldn't dare stand up and say that I didn't believe in you. I'd be afraid you'd knock me in the head. I'd be afraid you'd paralyze me or take away my mind. I'm afraid you'd do that. There are hundreds here tonight who don't know you as their Saviour. The Bible class believes you are Jesus of Nazareth, but they don't know you as their personal Saviour. And these other delegations, Lord, help them all to come down. Well, well, well, it's wonderful—'I find no fault in Him.' Amen."

"Oh, devil, why do you hit us when we are down? Old boy, I know that you have no time for me and I guess you have about learned that I have no time for you. I will never apologize to you for anything I have done against you. If I have ever said anything that does not hurt you, tell me about it and I will take it out of my sermon."

"We thank thee, Jesus, for that manifestation of thy power in one of the big factories of the city. Lord, we are told that of eighty men who used to go to a saloon for their lunch seventy-nine go there no more. All these men heard the 'booze' sermon. Lord, they are working on the one man who is standing out and they'll get him, too. The saloon-keeper is standing with arms akimbo behind the bar, but his old customers give the place the go-by. Thank you, Jesus."

"Well, Jesus, I've been back in Capernaum tonight. I've been with you when you cast the devil out of that man. They all said, 'We know you're helping us, but you're hurting the hog business.' I've been with you when you got in the boat. And Jesus arose and said to the sea: 'Peace, be still.'

"Ah, look at her. Bless her heart. There comes that poor, crying woman.

"Say, Jesus, here are men who have been drunkards. They have been in our prayers. They have been in our sermons. If I could just touch Him. He's here."

"Well, thank you, Lord. It's all true. I expect this sermon has caused many men and women to look into their hearts. Perhaps they are powerless, helpless for the Church. O God, what it will mean to people in the cause of Christ all over this city! We appreciate their kind words, but we wish they would do more.

"O God, may some deacons, elders, vestrymen, come out for God this afternoon. May they come down these aisles and publicly acknowledge themselves for God. Help them, then, we pray, for Jesus' sake. Amen."

"Now, Lord, I'm not here to have a good time. I am here to show what you are doing for these people and to tell them that you are willing to save them and to bear their burdens if they will give their hearts to you."

"Well, Jesus, I'm not up in heaven yet. I don't want to go, not yet. I know it's an awful pretty place, Lord. I know you'll look after me when I get there. But, Jesus, I'd like to stay here a long time yet. I don't want to leave Nell and the children. I like the little bungalow we have out at the lake. I know you'll have a prettier one up there. If you'll let me, Jesus, I'd like to stay here, and I'll work harder for you if I can. I know I'll go there, Jesus, and I know there's lots of men and women here in this Tabernacle tonight who won't go.

"Solomon found it was all vanity and vexation of spirit. They're living that way today, Jesus. I say that to you here tonight, banker; to you, Commercial Club; to you, men from the stockyards. If you want to live right, choose Jesus as your Saviour, for man's highest happiness is his obedience to Jesus Christ. And now, while we're all still, who'll come down and say 'I'm looking above the world?' Solomon said it was all vanity. Why certainly, you poor fool. He knew. But I'm glad you saw the light, Solomon, and spread out your wings."

"O Lord, bend over the battlements of glory and hear the cry of old Pittsburgh. O Lord, do you hear us? Lord, save tens of thousands of souls in this old city. Lord, everybody is helping. Lord, they are keeping their churches closed so tight that a burglar couldn't get in with a jimmy. Lord, the angels will shout to glory and the old devil will say, 'What did they shut up the churches of Pittsburgh for, when they have so many good preachers, and build a Tabernacle and bring a man on here to take the people away from me? O Lord, we'll win this whisky-soaked, vice-ridden old city of Pittsburgh and lay it at your feet and purify it until it is like paraffine."

Sunday's sermon on prayer is entitled,

"TEACH US TO PRAY"

We live and develop physically by exercise. We are saved by faith, but we must work out our salvation by doing the things God wills. The more we do for God, the more God will do through us. Faith will increase by experience.

If you are a stranger to prayer you are a stranger to the greatest source of power known to human beings. If we cared for our physical life in the same lackadaisical way that we care for our spiritual, we would be as weak physically as we are spiritually. You go week in and week out without prayer. I want to be a giant for God. You don't even sing;

you let the choir do it.   You go to prayer-meeting and offer
no testimony.

You are a stranger to the great privilege that is offered
to human beings.   Some of the greatest blessings that
people enjoy come from prayer.   In earnest prayer you think
as the Lord directs, and lose yourself in him.

Some people say: "It's no use to pray.   The Lord
knows everything, anyway."   That's true.   He does.   He
is not limited, as I am limited.   He knows everything and
has known it since before the world was.   We don't know
everybody who is going to be converted at this revival, but
that doesn't relieve us of our duty.   We don't know, and we
must do the work he has commanded us to do.

Others say: "But I don't get what I pray for."   Well,
there's a cause for everything.   Get at the cause and you'll
be all right.   If you are sick and send for the doctor, he pays
no attention to the disease, but looks at what produced it.
If you have a headache, don't rub your forehead.   In Matthew it is written, "Ask and it shall be given you; seek and ye
shall find; knock and it shall be opened unto you."   If your
prayers are not answered you are not right with God.   If
you have no faith, if your motive is wrong, then your prayers
will be in vain.   Many times when people pray they are
selfish.   They are not gripping the word.   I believe that
when many a wife prays for the conversion of her husband
it isn't because she really desires the salvation of his soul,
but because she thinks if he were converted things would be
easier for her personally.   Pray for your neighbors as well
as your own family.   The pastor of one church does not
pray for the congregation of another denomination.   I'm
not saying anything against denominations.   I believe in
them.   I believe they are of God.   Denominations represent
different temperaments.   A man with warm emotions
would not make a good Episcopalian, but he would make a
crackerjack Methodist.   Oh, the curse of selfishness!   The
Church is dying for religion, for religion pure and undefiled.
Pure religion and undefiled is visiting the widow and the

fatherless and doing the will of God without so much thought of yourself. I tell you, a lot of people are going to be fooled the Day of Judgment.

Isaiah says the hand of God is not shortened and his ear is not deaf. No, his hand is not shortened so that it cannot save. He has provided agencies by which we can be saved. If he had made no provision for your salvation, then the trouble would be with God; but he has, so if you go to hell the trouble will be with you.

In Ezekiel we read that men have taken idols into their hearts and put stumbling-blocks before their faces. God is not going to hear you if you place clothes, money, pride of relationship before him. You know there is sin in your life. Many people know there is sin in their lives, yet ask God to bless them. They ought first to get down on their knees and pray, "God be merciful to me a sinner."

Some people are too contemptibly stingy for God to hear them. God won't hear you if you stop your ears to the cries of the poor. You drag along here for three weeks and raise a paltry sum that a circus would take out of town in two hours. When they give things to the poor they rip off the buttons and the fine braid. Some people pick out old clothes that the moths have made into sieves and give them to the poor and think they are charitable. That isn't charity, no sir; it's charity when you'll give something you'll miss. It's charity when you feel it to give.

And when you stand praying, forgive if you have aught against anyone. It's no use to pray if you have a mean, miserable disposition, if you are grouchy, if you quarrel in your home or with your neighbors.

It's no use to pray for a blessing when you have a fuss on with your neighbors. It doesn't do you any good. You go to a sewing society meeting to make mosquito netting for the Eskimo and blankets for the Hottentots, and instead you sit and chew the rag and rip some woman up the back. The spirit of God flees from strife and discord.

People say: "She is a good woman, but a worldly

Christian." What? Might as well speak of a heavenly devil. Might as well expect a mummy to speak and bear children as that kind to move the world God-ward. Prayer draws you nearer to God.

Learning of Christ

"Teach us to pray," implies that I want to be taught. It's a great privilege to be taught by Jesus. A friend of mine was preaching out in Cedar Rapids, Iowa, and had to go to a hospital in Chicago for an operation, and I was asked to go and preach in his place. Alexander was leading the singing, and one night Charles called a little girl out of the audience to sing. She didn't look over four or five years of age, though she might have been a little older. I thought, "What's the use? Her little voice can never be heard over this crowd." But Charlie stood her up in a chair by the pulpit and she threw back her head and out rolled some of the sweetest music I have ever heard. It was wonderful. I sat there and the tears streamed down my cheeks. That little girl was the daughter of a Northwestern engineer and he took her to Chicago when her mother was away. Some one took her to Patti. Patti took the little girl to one of her suite of rooms and told her to stand there and sing. Then she went to the other end of the suite and sat down on a divan and listened. The song moved her to tears. She ran and hugged and kissed the little girl and sat her down on the divan and said to her: "Now you sit here and I'll go over there and sing." She took up her position where the child had stood, and she lifted her magnificent voice and she sang "Home, Sweet Home" and "The Last Rose of Summer"— sang them for that little girl! And Patti used to get a thousand dollars for a song, too. She always knew how many songs she was to sing, for she had a check before she went on the platform. It was a great privilege the little daughter of that Northwestern engineer had, but it's a greater privilege to learn from Jesus Christ how to pray.

A friend of mine told me he went to hear Paganini, and

the great violinist broke one of the strings of his instrument, then another, then another, until he had only one left, and on that one he played so wonderfully that his audience burst into terrific applause. It was a privilege to hear that, but it's a greater privilege to have Jesus teach you to pray.

Let us take a few examples from the life of Christ. In Mark we learn that he rose up early in the morning and went out to a solitary place and prayed. He began every day with prayer. You never get up without dressing. You never forget to wash your face and comb your hair. You always think of breakfast. You feed your physical body. Why do you starve your spiritual body? If nine-tenths of you were as weak physically as you are spiritually, you couldn't walk.

When I was assistant secretary of the Y. M. C. A. at Chicago, John G. Paton came home from the New Hebrides and was lecturing and collecting money. He was raising money to buy a sea-going steam yacht, for his work took him from island to island and he had to use a row-boat, and sometimes it was dangerous when the weather was bad, so he wanted the yacht. We had him for a week, and it was my privilege to go to lunch with him. We would go out to a restaurant at noon and he would talk to us. Sometimes there would be as many as fifteen or twenty preachers in the crowd, and now and then some of us were so interested in what he told us of the work for Jesus in those far-away islands that we forgot to eat. I remember that he said one day: "All that I am I owe to my Christian father and mother. My father was one of the most prayerful men I ever knew. Often in the daytime he would slip into his closet, and he would drop a handkerchief outside the door, and when we children saw the white sentinel we knew that father was talking with his God and would go quietly away. It is largely because of the life and influence of that same saintly father that I am preaching to the cannibals in the South Seas." It is an insult to God and a disgrace to allow children to grow up without throwing Christian influences around them.   Seven-tenths of professing Christians have no family prayers and do not read the Bible.   It is no wonder boys and girls are going to hell.   It is no wonder the damnable ball-rooms are wrecking the virtue of our girls.

In the fourteenth chapter of Matthew it is told that when Jesus had sent the multitudes away he went up into the mountain and was there alone with God.   Jesus Christ never forgot to thank God for answering his prayers.   Jesus asked him to help him feed the multitude, and he didn't neglect to thank him for it.   Next time you pray don't ask God for anything.   Just try to think of all the things you have to be thankful for, and tell him about them.

Pride Hinders Prayer

Pride keeps us from proper prayer.   Being chesty and big-headed is responsible for more failures than anything else in this world.   It has spoiled many a preacher, just as it has spoiled many an employee.   Some fellows get a job and in about two weeks they think they know more about the business than the boss does.   They think he is all wrong. It never occurs to them that it took some brains and some knowledge to build that business up and keep it running till they got there.

Here's two things to guard against.   Don't get chesty over success, or discouraged over a seeming defeat.

"And when he prayed he said: 'Lazarus, come forth'; and he that was dead came forth."   If we prayed right we would raise men from sin and bring them forth into the light of righteousness.

"And as he prayed the fashion of his countenance was altered."   Ladies, do you want to look pretty?   If some of you women would spend less on dope and cold cream and get down on your knees and pray, God would make you prettier.   Why, I can look into your faces and tell what sort of lives you live.   If you are devoting your time and thoughts to society, your countenances will show it.   If you pray, I can see that.

Every man who has helped to light up the dark places of the world has been a praying man. I never preach a sermon until I've soaked it in prayer. Never. Then I never forget to thank God for helping me when I preach. I don't care whether you read your prayers out of a book or whether you just say them, so long as you mean them. A man can read his prayers and go to heaven, or he may just say his prayers and go to hell. We've got to face conditions. When I read I find that all the saintly men who have done things from Pentecost until today, have known how to pray. It was a master stroke of the devil when he got the church to give up prayer. One of the biggest farces today is the average prayer-meeting.

Praying in Secret

Matthew says, "But thou, when thou prayest, enter into thy closet, and when thou hast shut thy door, pray to thy Father, which is in secret; and thy Father which seeth in secret shall reward thee openly."

Two men came to the Temple to pray—the first was the Pharisee. He was nice and smooth, and his attitude was nice and smooth. He prayed: "God, I thank thee that I am not as other men are, extortioners, unjust, adulterers, or even as this publican. I fast twice in the week, I give tithes of all I possess," and he went out. I can imagine a lot of people sitting around the church and saying: "That is my idea of religion; that is it. I am no sensationalist; I don't want anything vulgar, no slang." Why don't you use a little, bud, so that something will come your way? And it will come as straight as two and two make four.

Services rendered in such opposite directions cannot meet with the same results. If two men were on the top of a tall building and one should jump and one come down the fire escape they couldn't expect to meet with the same degree of safety. The Pharisee said, "Thank God, I am not as other men are," and the publican said, "God be merciful to me, a sinner." The first man went to his house the same as when he came out of it. "God be merciful to me, a sinner." That man was justified. I am justified in my faith in Jesus Christ. I am no longer a sinner. I am justified as though I had never sinned by faith in the Son of God. That man went down to his house justified.

Praying in Humility

How many people pray in a real sense? How many people pray in humility and truth? Some men pray for humility when it is pride they want. Many a man gets down on his knees and says: "Our Father, who art in heaven, hallowed be thy name: thy kingdom come—" That is not so; they don't want God's kingdom to come. It is not so with half the people that pray. I say to you when you pray in the church pew and say that, it don't count a snap of my finger if you don't live it. You pray, "Thy kingdom come," and then you go out and do something to prevent that kingdom from coming. No man can get down and pray "Thy kingdom come," and have a beer-wagon back up to his door and put beer in the ice box. No man can get down on his knees and pray "Thy kingdom come," and look through the bottom of a beer glass. God won't stand for it. If you wanted God's will done you would do God's will, even if it took every drop of blood in your body to do it.

"Thy will be done on earth as it is in heaven." When you say this in your pew on Sunday it means nothing unless you live it on Monday. You say "Thy kingdom come," and then go out and do the very thing that will prevent God's kingdom from coming. Your prayers or anything you do in the church on Sunday mean nothing if you don't do the same thing in business on Monday. I don't care how loud your wind-jamming in prayer-meeting may be if you go out and skin somebody in a horse deal the next day.

The man who truly prays, "Thy kingdom come," cannot take his heart out of his prayer when he is out of the church. The man who truly prays "Thy kingdom come," will not be shrinking his measures at the store; the load of coal he sends to you won't be half slate. The man who truly prays "Thy kingdom come" won't cut off his yardstick when he measures you a piece of calico. It will not take the pure-food law to keep a man who truly prays "Thy kingdom come" from putting chalk in the flour, sand in the sugar, brick dust in red pepper, ground peanut shells in breakfast food.

The man who truly prays "Thy kingdom come" cannot pass a saloon and not ask himself the question, "What can I do to get rid of that thing that is blighting the lives of thousands of young men, that is wrecking homes, and that is dragging men and women down to hell?" You cannot pray "Thy kingdom come," and then rush to the polls and vote for the thing that is preventing that kingdom from coming. You cannot pray "Thy kingdom come" and then go and do the things that make the devil laugh. For the man who truly prays "Thy kingdom come" it would be impossible to have one kind of religion on his knees and another when he is behind the counter; it would be impossible to have one kind of religion in the pew and another in politics. When a man truly prays "Thy kingdom come" he means it in everything or in nothing.

A lot of church members are praying wrong. You should pray first, "God be merciful to me a sinner," and then "Thy kingdom come."

Saying a prayer is one thing: doing God's will is another. Both should be synonymous. Angels are angels because they do God's will. When they refuse to do God's will they become devils.

Many a man prays when he gets in a hole. Many a man prays when he is up against it. Many a man prays in the time of trouble, but when he can stick his thumbs in his armholes and take a pair of scissors and cut his coupons off, then it is "Good-bye, God; I'll see you later." Many a man will make promises to God in his extremity, but forget them in his prosperity. Many a man will make promises to God when the hearse is backed up to the door to carry the baby out, but will soon forget the promises made in the days of adversity.   Many a man will make promises when lying on his back, thinking he is going to die, and load up just the same when he is on his feet.

Men of Prayer

Every man and every woman that God has used to halt this sin-cursed world and set it going Godward has been a Christian of prayer.   Martin Luther arose from his bed and prayed all night, and when the break of day came he called his wife and said to her, "It has come."   History records that on that very day King Charles granted religious toleration, a thing for which Luther had prayed.

John Knox, whom his queen feared more than any other man, was in such agony of prayer that he ran out into the street and fell on his face and cried, "O God, give me Scotland or I'll die."   And God gave him Scotland and not only that, he threw England in for good measure.

When Jonathan Edwards was about to preach his greatest sermon on "Sinners in the Hands of an Angry God," he prayed for days; and when he stood before the congregation and preached it, men caught at the seats in their terror, and some fell to the floor; and the people cried out in their fear, "Mr. Edwards, tell us how we can be saved!"

The critical period of American history was between 1784 and 1789.   There was no common coinage, no common defense.   When the colonies sent men to a constitutional convention, Benjamin Franklin, rising with the weight of his four score years, asked that the convention open with prayer, and George Washington there sealed the bargain with God.   In that winter in Valley Forge, Washington led his men in prayer and he got down on his knees to do it.

When the battle of Gettysburg was on, Lincoln, old Abe Lincoln, was on his knees with God; yes, he was on his knees from five o'clock in the afternoon till four o'clock in the morning, and Bishop Simpson was with him.

"And whatsoever ye shall ask the Father in My name, that will I do, that the Father may be glorified in the Son."

No man can ever be saved without Jesus Christ. There's no way to God unless you come through Jesus Christ. It's Jesus Christ or nothing.

"Lord, teach us to pray."

CHAPTER XXIII

The Revival on Trial

One spark of fire can do more to prove the power of powder than a whole library written on the subject.—BILLY SUNDAY.

WHAT Evangelist Sunday says to his congregations is sometimes less significant than what he helps his congregation to say to the world. Let us take a sample meeting in the Pittsburgh campaign, with the tremendous deliverance which it made upon the subject of revivals and conversions.

A "sea of faces" is a petrified phrase, which means nothing to most readers. Anybody who will stand on the platform behind Billy Sunday at one of his great tabernacles understands it. More than twenty thousand faces, all turned expectantly toward one man, confront you. The faces rather than the hair predominate. There are no hats in sight.

Like the billows along the shore, which may be observed in detail, the nearer reaches of this human sea are individualized. What a Madonna-face yonder girl has! See the muscles of that young man's jaw working, in the intensity of his interest. The old man who is straining forward, so as not to miss a word, has put a black and calloused hand behind his ear. That gray-haired woman with the lorgnette and rolls of false hair started out with the full consciousness that she was a "somebody": watch her wilt and become merely a tired, heart-hungry old woman. And the rows and rows of undistinguished commonplace people, just like the crowds we meet daily in the street cars.

Somehow, though, each seems here engaged in an individual transaction. A revival meeting accents personality. Twenty or thirty rows down the big congregation begins to blurr in appearance, and individual faces are merged in the mass. The host, which is but an agglomeration of individuals, is impressive. The "sea of faces" is more affecting than old ocean's expanse.

Where else may one so see "the people"; or fundamental human nature so expressing itself? One compares these crowds with the lesser throngs that followed Jesus when he walked the earth, and recalls that "greater works than these shall they do." There is a sermon in every aspect of the Billy Sunday meetings.

Curiously, people will reveal more of themselves, be more candid concerning their inner experiences, in a crowd than when taken one by one. Thus this congregation is a rare laboratory. Tonight the evangelist is going to make an experiment upon revivals and their value.

It is common to object to revivals and to revivalists. Billy Sunday's reply to this is simply unanswerable: he appeals to the people themselves for evidence. By a show of hands—and he conducts this experiment in practically every community he visits—he gives a convincing demonstration that it is by special evangelistic efforts that most Christians have entered the Church of Christ. By the same method, he shows that youth is the time to make the great decision.

When this question is put to a test a dramatic moment, the significance of which the multitude quickly grasps, ensues. On this occasion there are more than twenty thousand persons within the Tabernacle. First the evangelist asks the confessed Christians to rise. The great bulk of the congregation stands on its feet. Then he asks for those who were converted in special meetings, revivals of some sort or other, to raise their hands. From three-fourths to four-fifths of the persons standing lift their hands in token that they were converted during revivals.

Then—each time elaborating his question so that there may be no misunderstanding—Sunday asks those who were converted before they were twenty to indicate it.

19

Here again the majority is so large as to be simply over-whelming. It almost seems that the whole body of Christians had become such before they attained their legal majority.

Of the few hundreds that are left standing, Sunday asks in turn for those who were converted before they were thirty, those who were converted before they were forty, before they were fifty, before they were sixty. When it comes to this point of age the scene is thrilling in its significance. Usually there are only one or two persons standing who have entered the Christian life after reaching fifty years of age.

The conclusion is irresistible. Unless a person accepts Christ in youth the chances are enormously against his ever accepting Him subsequently. The demonstration is an impressive vindication of revivals, and of the importance of an early decision for Christ.

After such a showing as this, everybody is willing to listen to a sermon upon revivals and their place in the economy of the Kingdom of Heaven.

"THE NEED OF REVIVALS"

Somebody asks: "What is a revival?" Revival is a purely philosophical, common-sense result of the wise use of divinely appointed means, just the same as water will put out a fire; the same as food will appease your hunger; just the same as water will slake your thirst; it is a philosophical common-sense use of divinely appointed means to accomplish that end. A revival is just as much horse sense as that.

A revival is not material; it does not depend upon material means. It is a false idea that there is something peculiar in it, that it cannot be judged by ordinary rules, causes and effects. That is nonsense. Above your head there is an electric light; that is effect. What is the cause? Why, the dynamo. Religion can be judged on the same basis of cause and effect. If you do a thing, results always come. The results come to the farmer. He has his crops.

That is the result. He has to plow and plant and take care of his farm before the crops come.

Religion needs a baptism of horse sense. That is just pure horse sense. I believe there is no doctrine more dangerous to the Church today than to convey the impression that a revival is something peculiar in itself and cannot be judged by the same rules of causes and effect as other things. If you preach that to the farmers—if you go to a farmer and say "God is a sovereign," that is true; if you say "God will give you crops only when it pleases him and it is no use for you to plow your ground and plant your crops in the spring," that is all wrong, and if you preach that doctrine and expect the farmers to believe it, this country will starve to death in two years. The churches have been preaching some false doctrines and religion has died out.

Some people think that religion is a good deal like a storm. They sit around and fold their arms, and that is what is the matter.

"You Sit in Your Pews so Easy that You Become Mildewed"

You sit in your pews so easy that you become mildewed. Such results will be sure to follow if you are persuaded that religion is something mysterious and has no natural connection between the means and the end. It has a natural connection of common sense and I believe that when divinely appointed means are used spiritual blessing will accrue to the individuals and the community in greater numbers than temporal blessings. You can have spiritual blessings as regularly as the farmer can have corn, wheat,

oats, or you can have potatoes and onions and cabbage in your garden. I believe that spiritual results will follow more surely than temporal blessings. I don't believe all this tommy-rot of false doctrines. You might as well sit around beneath the shade and fan yourself and say "Ain't it hot?" as to expect God to give you a crop if you don't plow the ground and plant the seed. Until the Church resorts to the use of divinely appointed means it won't get the blessing.

What a Revival Does

What is a revival? Now listen to me. A revival does two things. First, it returns the Church from her backsliding and second, it causes the conversion of men and women; and it always includes the conviction of sin on the part of the Church. What a spell the devil seems to cast over the Church today!

I suppose the people here are pretty fair representatives of the Church of God, and if everybody did what you do there were would never be a revival. Suppose I did no more than you do, then no people would ever be converted through my efforts; I would fold my arms and rust out. A revival helps to bring the unsaved to Jesus Christ.

God Almighty never intended that the devil should triumph over the Church. He never intended that the saloons should walk rough-shod over Christianity. And if you think that anybody is going to frighten me, you don't know me yet.

When is a revival needed? When the individuals are careless and unconcerned. If the Church were down on her face in prayer they would be more concerned with the fellow outside. The Church has degenerated into a third-rate amusement joint, with religion left out.

When is a revival needed? When carelessness and unconcern keep the people asleep. It is as much the duty of the Church to awaken and work and labor for the men and women of this city as it is the duty of the fire department to rush out when the call sounds. What would you think of

"I Never Look at a Child or an Older Person Without Thinking, 'There is a Casket of Locked-up
Possibilities. Only the Key of Salvation is Needed to Open it.'"

"Samson with the Holy Spirit could take the
Jawbone of an Ass and Lay Dead a Thousand
Philistines."

"Ha! Ha! Old Skeptic, I've got You Beat."

the fire department if it slept while the town burned? You would condemn them, and I will condemn you if you sleep and let men and women go to hell. It is just as much your business to be awake. The Church of God is asleep today; it is turned into a dormitory, and has taken the devil's opiates.

When may a revival be expected? When the wickedness of the wicked grieves and distresses the Christian. Sometimes people don't seem to mind the sins of other people. Don't seem to mind while boys and girls walk the streets of their city and know more of evil than gray-haired men. You are asleep.

When is a revival needed? When the Christians have lost the spirit of prayer.

When is a revival needed? When you feel the want of revival and feel the need of it. Men have had this feeling, ministers have had it until they thought they would die unless a revival would come to awaken their people, their students, their deacons and their Sunday-school workers, unless they would fall down on their faces and renounce the world and the works and deceits of the devil. When the Church of God draws its patrons from the theaters the theaters will close up, or else take the dirty, rotten plays off the stage.

When the Church of God stops voting for the saloon, the saloon will go to hell. When the members stop having cards in their homes, there won't be so many black-legged gamblers in the world. This is the truth. You can't sit around and fold your arms and let God run this business; you have been doing that too long here. When may a revival be expected? When Christians confess their sins one to another. Sometimes they confess in a general way, but they have no earnestness; they get up and do it in eloquent language, but that doesn't do it. It is when they break down and cry and pour out their hearts to God in grief, when the floodgates open, then I want to tell you the devil will have cold feet.

Revival Demands Sacrifice

When may a revival be expected? When the wickedness of the wicked grieves and distresses the Church. When you are willing to make a sacrifice for the revival; when you are willing to sacrifice your feelings. You say, "Oh, well, Mr. Sunday hurt my feelings." Then don't spread them all over his tabernacle for men to walk on. I despise a touchy man or woman. Make a sacrifice of your feelings; make a sacrifice of your business, of your time, of your money; you are willing to give to help to advance God's cause, for God's cause has to have money the same as a railroad or a steamship company. When you give your influence and stand up and let people know you stand for Jesus Christ and it has your indorsement and time and money. Somebody has got to get on the firing line. Somebody had to go on the firing line and become bullet meat for $13 a month to overcome slavery. Somebody has to be willing to make a sacrifice. They must be willing to get out and hustle and do things for God.

When may a revival be expected? A revival may be expected when Christian people confess and ask forgiveness for their sins. When you are willing that God shall promote and use whatever means or instruments or individuals or methods he is pleased to use to promote them. Yes. The trouble is he cannot promote a revival if you are sitting on the judgment of the methods and means that God is employing to promote a revival. The God Almighty may use any method or means or individual that he pleases in order to promote a revival. You are not running it. Let God have his way. You can tell whether you need a revival. You can tell if you will have one and why you have got one. If God should ask you sisters and preachers in an audible voice, "Are you willing that I should promote a revival by using any methods or means or individual language that I choose to use to promote it?" what would be your answer? Yes. Then don't growl if I use some things that you don't like. You have no business to. How can you promote a revival? Break up your fallow ground, the ground that produces nothing but weeds, briars, tin cans and brick-bats. Fallow ground is ground that never had a glow in it. Detroit had a mayor, Pingree, when Detroit had thousands and thousands of acres of fallow ground. This was taken over by the municipal government and planted with potatoes with which they fed the poor of the city.

There are individuals who have never done anything for Jesus Christ, and I have no doubt there are preachers as well, who have never done anything for the God Almighty. There are acres and acres of fallow ground lying right here that have never been touched. Look over your past life, look over your present life and future and take up the individual sins and with pencil and paper write them down. A general confession will never do. You have committed your sins, one by one, and you will have to confess them one by one. This thing of saying, "God, I am a sinner," won't do.

"God, I am a gossiper in my neighborhood. God, I have been in my ice-box while I am here listening to Mr. Sunday." Confess your sins.

How can you promote a revival? You women, if you found that your husband was giving his love and attention to some other woman and if you saw that some other woman was encroaching on his mind and heart, and was usurping your place and was pushing you out of the place, wouldn't you grieve? Don't you think that God grieves when you push him out of your life? You don't treat God square. You business men don't treat God fair. You let a thousand things come in and take the place that God Almighty had. No wonder you are careless. You blame God for things you have no right to blame him for. He is not to blame for anything. You judge God. The spirit loves the Bible; the devil loves the flesh.

If you don't do your part, don't blame God. How many times have you blamed God when you are the liar yourself. You are wont to blame him for the instances of unbelief that have come into your life. When should we promote a revival? When there is a neglect of prayer? When your prayers affect God? You never think of going out on the street without dressing. You would be pinched before you went a block. You never think of going without breakfast, do you? I bet there are multitudes that have come here without reading the Bible or praying for this meeting.

You can measure your desire for salvation by means of the amount of self-denial you are willing to practice for Jesus Christ. You have sinned before the Church, before the world, before God.

Don't the Lord have a hard time? Own up, now.

Persecution a Godsend

There are a lot of people in church, doubtless, who have denied themselves—self-denial for comfort and convenience. There are a lot of people here who never make any sacrifices for Jesus Christ. They will not suffer any reproaches for Jesus Christ. Paul says, "I love to suffer reproaches for Christ." The Bible says, "Woe unto you when all men shall speak well of you." "Blessed are you when your enemies persecute you." That is one trouble in the churches of God today. They are not willing to suffer reproach for God's sake. It would be a godsend if the Church would suffer persecution today; she hasn't suffered it for hundreds of years. She is growing rich and lagging behind. Going back.

Pride! How many times have you found yourself exercising pride? How many times have you attempted pride of wealth? Proud because you were related to some of the old families that settled in the Colonies in 1776. That don't get you anything; not at all. I have got as much to be proud of as to lineage as anyone; my great-grandfather was in the Revolutionary War, lost a leg at Brandywine; and my father was a soldier in the Civil War.

Envy! Envy of those that have more talent than you. Envious because someone can own a limousine Packard and you have to ride a Brush runabout; envious because some women can wear a sealskin coat and you a nearseal.

Then there is your grumbling and fault-finding. When speaking of people behind their backs, telling their faults, whether real or imaginary, and that is slander. When you sit around and rip people up behind their backs at your old sewing societies, when you rip and tear and discuss your neighbors and turn the affair into a sort of a great big gossiping society, with your fault-finding, grumbling and growling. There is a big difference between levity and happiness, and pleasure, and all that sort of thing. ·

Make up your mind that God has given himself up for you. I would like to see something come thundering along that I would have more interest in than I have in the cause of God Almighty! God has a right to the first place. God is first, remember that.

Multitudes of people are willing to do anything that doesn't require any self-denial on their part.

I am not a member of any lodge, and never expect to be, but if I were a member of a lodge and there were a prayer-meeting and a lodge-meeting coming on Wednesday night, I would be at the prayer-meeting instead of at the lodge-meeting. I am not against the lodges; they do some good work in the world, but that doesn't save anyone for God. God is first and the lodge-meeting is second. God is first and society second. God is first and business is second. "In the beginning, God!" That is the way the Bible starts out and it ought to be the way with every living being. "In the beginning, God." Seek you first God and everything else shall be added unto you. Christianity is addition; sin is subtraction. Christianity is peace, joy, salvation, heaven. Sin takes away peace, happiness, sobriety, and it takes away health. You are robbing God of the time that you misspend. You are robbing God when you spend time doing something that don't amount to anything, when you might do something for Christ. You are robbing God when you go to foolish amusements, when you sit around reading trashy novels instead of the Word of God.

"Oh, Lord, revive thy work!"

I have only two minutes more and then I am through. Bad temper. Abuse your wife and abuse your children; abuse your husband; turn your old gatling-gun tongue loose. A lady came to me and said, "Mr. Sunday, I know I have a bad temper, but I am over with it in a minute." So is the shotgun, but it blows everything to pieces.

And, finally, you abuse the telephone girl because she doesn't connect you in a minute. Bad temper. I say you abuse your wife, you go cussing around if supper isn't ready on time; cussing because the coffee isn't hot; you dig your fork into a hunk of beefsteak and put it on your plate and then you say: "Where did you get this, in the harness shop? Take it out and make a hinge for the door." Then you go to your store, or office, and smile and everybody thinks you are an angel about to sprout wings and fly to the imperial realm above. Bad temper! You growl at your children; you snap and snarl around the house until they have to go to the neighbors to see a smile. They never get a kind word —no wonder so many of them go to the devil quick.

CHAPTER XXIV

An Army with Banners

The man who is right with God will not be wrong with anything that is good.—BILLY SUNDAY.

THE oldest problem of the Christian Church, and the latest problem of democracy, is how to reach the great mass of the people. Frequently the charge is made that the Church merely skims the surface of society, and that the great uncaring masses of the people lie untouched beneath it. Commonly, a revival reaches only a short distance outside the circumference of church circles. The wonder and greatness of the Billy Sunday campaigns consist in the fact that they reach to the uttermost rim of a community, to its greatest height and its lowest depth. There can be no question that he stirs a city as not even the fiercest political campaign stirs it. Sunday touches life on all levels, bringing his message to bear upon the society woman in her parlor and the humblest day laborer in the trench.

This does not come to pass by any mere chance. Organized activity achieves it. The method which produces the greatest results is what is called the Delegation Idea, whereby detachments of persons from various trades, callings and organizations and communities attend in a body upon the services of the Sunday Tabernacle.

By prearrangement, seats are reserved every night for these visiting delegations. Sometimes there will be as many as a dozen delegations present in one evening. As the campaign progresses towards its conclusion real difficulty is experienced in finding open dates for all the delegations that apply. At the outset, Mr. Sunday's assistants have to "work up" these delegations. Later, the delegations themselves besiege the workers.

In variety the delegations range from a regiment of Boy Scouts to a post of old soldiers; from the miners of a specified colliery to the bankers of the city; from the telephone girls to the members of a woman's club; from an athletic club to a Bible class.

Not only the community in which the meetings are being held furnish these delegations, but the surrounding territory is drawn upon. It is by no means an unknown thing for a single delegation, numbering a thousand or fifteen hundred men, to come a distance of fifteen or twenty-five miles to attend a Sunday Tabernacle service. Almost every evening there are lines of special cars waiting for these deputations who have come from afar, with their banners and their badges and their bands, all bent upon hearing and being heard at the Tabernacle.

The crowd spirit is appealed to by this method. The every-day instinct of loyalty to one's craft or crowd is aroused. Each delegation feels its own identity and solidarity, and wants to make as good a showing as possible. There is considerable wholesome emulation among the delegations representing the same craft or community. Of course, the work of making ready the delegation furnishes a topic for what is literally "shop talk" among working men; and naturally each group zealously watches the effect of its appearance upon the great congregation. Delegations get a very good idea of what their neighbors think of them by the amount of applause with which they are greeted. Thus when the whole force of a daily newspaper appears in the Tabernacle 'its readers cheer vociferously. Every delegation goes equipped with its own battle cry, and prepared to make as favorable a showing as possible.

All this is wholesome for the community life. It fosters loyalty in the varied groups that go to make up our society. Any shop is the better for its workers, led by their heads of departments and by their employers, having gone in a solid phalanx to a Tabernacle meeting. Every incident of that experience becomes an unfailing source of conversation for long days and weeks to follow.

On Left: BIRTHPLACE OF BILLY SUNDAY AT AMES, IOWA. *On Right:* STANDING IN FRONT OF HOUSE IN WHICH HE WAS BORN IS BILLY SUNDAY WITH AUNT ROSETTA SIMMONS, WHO WAS WITH HIS MOTHER AT HIS BIRTH, AND HIS BROTHER, H. E. (ED) SUNDAY.

The Tabernacle at Scranton, Pennsylvania, Typical of the Auditoriums that are Erected Wherever Campaigns are Conducted. To Deaden Sound the Floor is Covered with Sawdust, whence the Name "Sawdust Trail." To Prevent the Possibility of a Panic, No Board is Fastened with More than Two Nails, and There is a Door at the End of Every Aisle.

Naturally, too, each delegation, delighted with the showing it has made at the Tabernacle, and with the part it has borne in the meeting, becomes one more group of partisans for the Billy Sunday campaign. Men who would not go alone to the Tabernacle, cannot in loyalty well refuse to stand by their own crowd. So it comes to pass that the delegation idea penetrates every level and every section of the community. A shrewder scheme for reaching the last man could scarcely be devised. Thousands who are impervious to religious appeals quickly respond to the request that they stand by their shop-mates and associates.

Participation in the meetings makes the people themselves feel the importance of their own part. They are not merely a crowd coming to be talked at; they share in the meetings. The newspapers comment upon them even as upon the sermon. All are uplifted by the glow of geniality and camaraderie which pervades the Tabernacle. For the songs and slogans and banners of the delegations greatly help to swell the interest of the meetings.

All this is wholesome, democratic and typically American. This good-natured crowd does not become unreal or artificial simply because it is facing the fundamental verities of the human soul.

Outspokenness in loyalty, a characteristic of Sunday converts, expresses itself through many channels. Taught by the delegation idea, as well as by the sermon, the importance of standing up to be counted, the friends and converts of the evangelist are always ready for the great parade which usually is held toward the close of the campaign. The simple basis for this street demonstration is found in the old Scripture, "Let the redeemed of the Lord say so." The idea of the Roman imperial triumph survives in the Billy Sunday parade. It is a testimony to the multitudes of the loyalty of Christians to the Gospel.

Beyond all question, a tremendous impression is made upon a city by the thousands of marching men whom the evangelist first leads and then reviews. A street parade i a visualization of the forces of the Church in a community. Many a man of the street, who might be unmoved by many arguments, however powerful, cannot escape the impression of the might of the massed multitudes of men who march through the streets, thousands strong. Some twenty thousand men were in the Sunday parade at Scranton. Nobody who witnessed them, be he never so heedless a scoffer, could again speak slightingly of the Church. Religion loses whatever traits of femininity it may have possessed, before the Sunday campaign is over.

Those most practical of men, the politicians, are quick to take cognizance of this new power that has arisen in the community's life. They know that every one of these men not only has a vote, but is a center of influence for the things in which he believes.

The heartening effect of such a great demonstration as this upon the obscure, lonely and discouraged saints is beyond calculation.

The great hosts of the Billy Sunday campaign are returning to first principles by taking religion out into the highways and making it talked about, even as the Founder of the Church created a commotion in the highways of Capernaum and Jerusalem. These marching men are a sermon one or two miles long. The impression made upon youth is not to be registered by any means in the possession of men. Every Christian the world around must be grateful to this evangelist and his associates for giving the sort of demonstration, which cannot be misunderstood by the world at large, of the virility and the immensity of the hosts of heaven on earth.

Many of the utterances of Billy Sunday are attuned to this note of valiant witness-bearing for Christ.

" SPIRITUAL POWER "

Samson didn't realize that the Spirit of the Lord had departed from him; he walked out and shook himself as aforetime; he weighed as much; he was as strong physically;

his mind was as active, but although he possessed all that, there was one thing that was necessary to make him as he had been: "He wist not that the Spirit of the Lord had left him."

A man may have a fine physique; he may have strength; he may have greatness; he may have a beautiful home; and a church may be magnificent and faultless in its equipment; the preacher may be able to reason; the choir may rival the angels in music; but if you have not the Spirit of the Lord you are, as Paul says, as sounding brass and tinklingcymbals, and the church is merely four walls with a roof over it.

Nothing in the world can be substituted for the Spirit of God; no wealth, culture nor anything in the world. By power we do not mean numbers; there never has been a time when there were more members in the Church than today; yet we haven't kept progress in the number of members in the Church with the increased number of people in the nation. Our nation has grown to over 90,000,000 of people, but we are not correspondingly keeping pace with the number of church members. God's Church has not increased correspondingly in power as it has in numbers; while increasing in numbers it has not increased in spiritual power. I am giving you facts, not fancies. We are not dealing with theories. I am not saying anything against the Church; you never had a man come into this community who would fight harder for the Church of God Almighty than I would. I am talking about her sins and the things that sap her power—and by power I do not mean numbers. If you had an army of 100,000 and increased it another 100,000 it ought to be doubled in power.

Derelicts in the Church

In the Church of God today you know there are a lot of people who are nothing but derelicts and nothing but driftwood.

By power I do not mean wealth. We are the richest people on the earth; nineteen-twentieths of all the wealth or all the money in the United States today is in the hands of professing Christians, Catholic and Protestant. That ought to mean that it is in God's hands; but it doesn't. They are robbing God. I was in a church in Iowa that had three members who were worth $200,000 each and they paid their preacher the measly salary of $600 a year, and I will be hornswaggled if they did not owe him $400 then. If I ever skinned any old fellows I did those old stingy coots. A man who doesn't pay to the church is as big a swindler as a man who doesn't pay his grocery bill and he is dead-beating his way to hell. You let somebody else pay your bills, you old dead-beat. God hasn't any more use today for a dead-beat in the church than he has for the man who doesn't pay his grocery bill—not a bit!

By power I do not mean culture. There never was a time when the people of America were better informed than they are today; they have newspapers, telephones, telegraphs, rural delivery, fast trains. You can leave home and in five days you are in Europe. If something happens in China or Japan tonight you can read it before you go to bed. The islands of the sea are our neighbors.

A stranger once asked: "What is the most powerful and influential church in this town?"

"That big stone Presbyterian church on the hill."

"How many members has it?"

"I don't know, my wife is a member."

"How many Sunday-school members?"

"I don't know; my children go."

"How many go to prayer-meetings?"

"I don't know; I have never been there."

"How many go to communion?"

"I don't know, I never go; my wife goes."

Then the stranger said: "Will you please tell me why you said it was the most powerful and influential church in the community?"

"Yes, sir; it is the only church in the town that has three millionaires in the church." That was why he thought it was a great church. The Church in America would die of dry rot and sink forty-nine fathoms in hell if all members were multimillionaires and college graduates. That ought not to be a barrier to spiritual power. By power I do not mean influence.

I'd hate to have to walk back nineteen hundred years to Pentecost. There were 120 at Pentecost who saved 3,000 souls.

Some of the most powerful churches I have ever worked with were not the churches that had the largest number or the richest members. Out in a town in Iowa there were three women who used to pray all night every Thursday night, one of them a colored woman. People used to come under her windows at night and listen to her pray. She murdered the king's English five times in every sentence, but oh, she knew God. They had 500 names on their list for prayer and when the meetings closed they had checked off 397 of them. Every Friday I would be called over the telephone or receive a letter or meet those women and they would tell me what assurances God gave them as to who would be saved. I have never met three women that were stronger in faith than those three. That town was Fairfield, Iowa, one of the brightest, cleanest, snappiest little towns I ever went into.

The Meaning of Power

Samson wist not the Spirit of the Lord had departed. So might we have money, so might we have members, so might we have increase in culture; but we have not increased in power. I mean spiritual power; power to bring things to pass by way of reform. What do I mean by power? I have told you what I did not mean.

By power I mean when the power of God comes upon you and enables you to do what you could not do without that power. That comes to you through confidence and faith in the Lord Jesus Christ. There was a time when the Church had more spiritual power than she has today; there never was a time when she had more members than she has

20

today; there never was a time when she had more money than she has today; more culture; but there was a time when she had more spiritual power than today.

And when she had more spiritual power she was a separate institution. She was not living for the devil as she is today. And the Church had not become a clearing house for the forces of evil. We are told that at Pentecost tongues of fire came upon the expectant worshipers.

I don't mean this gabby stuff they have got today that they call the things of the spirit; I don't mean that jabbering and froth and foaming at the mouth when you can't understand a word they say. Try the Spirit, whether it be of God, and in all ages when the Church has stood for something she has had power.

So few of us dream of the tremendous power at our command. At the World's Fair at Chicago the door to one of the great buildings was without doorknob or latch, for these were not needed. There was a great mat at the entrance, and as you stepped upon it your weight would cause an electrical connection to be made and the great doors would swing open. I take this old Book and stand upon it, and all the wonders of life and eternity are opened to me. The power of the Holy Spirit is at my command.

Church Needs Great Awakening

Let's quit fiddling with religion and do something to bring the world to Christ. We need a Pentecost today. The Church needs a great awakening. Now, I'll not stand anyone's saying anything against the Church as an institution; but I will rebuke its sins and point out its shortcomings. Nobody who loves the Church can be silent when so much needs to be said. I love the Church. I want to explode that old adage that "Love is blind"; I tell you, love has an eagle's eyes.

Lots of churches are wrong in their financial policy. It is a wrong that the churches have to resort to tricks that would shame the devil in order to filch a quarter out of a fellow's pocket to help pay the preacher's back salary. There is hardly a church in this country that couldn't have abundant funds if the people would only give of their means as they are commanded by God.

Then, too often you put the wrong men in places of authority in the church. You elect some old fellow who would look better in a penitentiary suit, just because he had a "drag" somewhere We must quit putting such men in church offices.

When I was a boy I was taught how to put glass knobs on the feet of a chair and charge the chair with electricity. So long as I didn't touch anything but the chair I was all right, but if I touched the wall or something else I got a shock. The power passed through and from me. As Christians we cannot come into touch with defiling things without suffering a loss of spiritual power. You can't go to the dance and the card party and the cheap-skate show without losing power. Yes, you can do those things and be a church member. But you can be a church member without being a Christian. There's a difference.

I read in the Bible that Lot first pitched his tents near Sodom. Next I read that Lot moved right into Sodom, and lived there for twenty years. He lost his power there, too. When God warned him to get out of the city he went and told his sons and daughters, but they wouldn't heed him. He had lost his power over them. He warned his sons-in-law, but they wouldn't heed him. He even lost power over his own wife, for he told her not to look back as they fled, and she rubbered.

If you have lost spiritual power it is because you have disobeyed some clear command of God. Maybe you're stingy. God requires tithes. He commands you to give one tenth of your income to him, and maybe you don't do it. It may be your temper. It may be that you have neglected to read the Bible and haven't prayed as you should.

The Church is a failure because she is compromising with the men that sit in the seats and own saloons whom she never rebukes; she is compromising with the men who rent their property for disorderly houses, and whom she never rebukes. They are living off the products of shame and if they buy food and clothes for their wives and children from such money, they, too, are living off this product of shame. We have lost our power because we have compromised.

When I played base ball I used to attend every theater in the country. Since I was converted I have not darkened a theater's door, except to preach the Gospel. We've lost our power because we've lost our faith.

Our leading members are leaders in nothing but card parties and society; they are not leaders in spiritual things. A man comes to me and says, "Mrs. So-and-So is one of my leading members."

I ask: "Does she get to prayer-meetings?"

"No."

"Does she visit the sick?"

"No."

"Does she put her arms around some poor sinner and try to save her for Christ?"

"No."

And I find she is a leader in nothing but society, card parties, dances and bridge-whist clubs. I don't call that kind a leading woman in the church; she is the devil's bell-wether. That is true. I tell you people what I call your leading woman: She is the one who gets down on her knees and prays; she is the one that can wrap her arms around a sinner and lead her to Christ; that is a leading church member. You have it doped out wrong.

Did Martin Luther trim his sails to the breeze of his day? If he had, you would never have had a Reformation. I will tell you why we have lost our power; I have told you what I don't mean by power.

Lost Power

We have lost our power because we have failed to insist on the separation of the Church from the world. The

Church is a separate body of men and women; we are to be in the world, but not of the world. She is all right in the world, all wrong when the world is in her, and the trouble with the Church today is that she has sprung a leak. The flood tides of the world have been swept in until even her pews are engulfed, yes, even the choir loft is almost submerged. We have become but a third-rate amusement bureau. The world has got to see a clean-cut line of demarkation between the Church and the world. So I believe.

If there's anything the Church of God needs it's to climb the stairs and get in an upper room.

Come out from the things of the world. When you hand out a pickle and a bunch of celery for the cause of good, then will my Father not be glorified; nor will he be glorified when you sell oyster soup at twenty-five cents a dish, when one lone oyster chases around the dish to find his brother. It doesn't require much power to do that, for two dollars would hire a girl to dish up ice-cream. That does not get you spiritual power.

There is deep heart hungering in the Church today for the old-time Pentecostal power.

Now, I do not know that the Spirit will ever come to us as he came to Pentecost, for you must remember that he came to usher in the new dispensation, or the dispensation of the Holy Ghost. It is true he was present in the Old Testament. He was in Abraham and Moses.

You'll have power when there is nothing questionable in your life.

You'll have power when you testify in a more positive manner.

Do as the disciples did, believe and receive the Holy Spirit by waiting. The Holy Spirit is ours. He is the promise of Jesus from the Father as a gift to the prayers of the Son. God can no more fill you with the Spirit if you are not right, willing and waiting to receive Him, than he can send the sunshine into your house if you have the blinds and shutters all closed. You can pray till you are black in the

face and bald-headed, but you're wasting your time unless
you agree with God.   There can be no wedding unless two
parties are agreed.   If the girl says "No," that ends it.
Don't think you are walking with God just because your
name is on a church record.   Walk in the path of righteousness even if it leads to a coffin and the graveyard.

Jesus gave his disciples power to perform miracles.   That
same power can be delegated to you and me today.   He
always spoke of the Holy Spirit in the future.   He was not
there.   He didn't have to be.   They had Jesus, but the
Church needs him today.   It needs a baptism of the Holy
Ghost.   There are no substitutes.   You can organize,
prepare, hire the best singers and preachers in the universe,
but you'll get no power.   No matter what Scriptural knowledge he may have, no matter if he prays so that it reaches
the stars, no matter if his sermons sway the congregation
with their word pictures, no matter if the singers warble
faultlessly and to beat the band—the preacher and the
singers will produce no more effect than the beating of a
drum or the running of a music box.   The preacher who
murders the king's English four times to every sentence and
has the Holy Ghost will get the revival.

The Church today needs power. It has plenty of wealth,
culture and numbers.   There is no substitute for the Holy
Spirit and you cannot have power without the Holy Spirit.
The Holy Spirit is ours by the promise of Christ.   To
receive him we must give up all sin and walk in the path of
righteousness even if it carries us to our graves or across
the seas as a missionary.   Give up everything the Lord
forbids even if it is as important to you as your hand or
your eye.

Dear Friend:

You have by this act of coming forward publicly acknowledged your faith in Jesus Christ as your personal Saviour. No one could possibly be more rejoiced that you have done this, or be more anxious for you to succeed and get the most joy out of the Christian life, than I. Therefore, I ask you to read carefully this little tract. Paste it in your Bible and read it frequently.

W. A. Sunday.

2 Tim: 2:15.

[Facsimile of Page One of Circular Handed to Every Convert.]

WHAT IT MEANS TO BE A CHRISTIAN

"A Christian is any man, woman or child who comes to God as a lost sinner, accepts the Lord Jesus Christ as their personal Saviour, surrenders to Him as their Lord and Master, confesses Him as such before the world, and strives to please Him in everything day by day."

Have **you** come to God realizing that you are a lost sinner? Have **you** accepted the Lord Jesus Christ as **your** personal Saviour; that is, do **you** believe with all your heart that God laid all **your** iniquity on Him? (Isa. 53:5-6) and that He bore the penalty of **your** sins (I Peter 2:24), and that **your** sins are forgiven because Jesus died in **your** stead?

Have **you** surrendered to Him as your Lord and Master? That is, are **you** willing to do His will even when it conflicts with your desire?

Have **you** confessed to Him as your Saviour and Master before the world?

Is it **your** purpose to strive to please Him in everything day by day?

If you can sincerely answer "YES" to the foregoing questions, then you may know on the authority of God's Word that **you** are NOW a child of God (John 1:12), that you have NOW eternal life (John 3:36); that is to say, if you have done **your** part (i. e., believe that Christ died in your place, and receive Him as your Saviour and Master) God has done HIS part and imparted to you His **own** nature (II Peter 1:4).

[Facsimile of Page Two of Circular Handed to Every Convert.]

HOW TO MAKE A SUCCESS OF THE CHRISTIAN LIFE

Now that you are a child of God **your** growth depends upon **yourself.**

It is impossible for you to become a useful Christian unless you are willing to do the things which are absolutely essential to your spiritual growth. To this end the following suggestions will be found to be of vital importance:

1. **STUDY THE BIBLE:** Set aside at least fifteen minutes a day for Bible Study. Let God talk to you fifteen minutes a day through His Word. Talk to God fifteen minutes a day in prayer. Talk for God fifteen minutes a day.

    "As new-born babes desire the sincere milk of the Word, that ye may grow thereby."—I Peter 2:2.

    The word of God is food for the soul.

    Commit to memory one verse of Scripture each day. Join a Bible class. (Psa. 119:11.)

2. **PRAY MUCH:** Praying is talking to God. Talk to Him about everything—your perplexities, joys, sorrows, sins, mistakes, friends, enemies.

    "Be careful for nothing, but in everything by prayer and supplication with thanksgiving let your requests be made known unto God." Phil. 4:6.

3. **WIN SOMEONE FOR CHRIST:** For spiritual growth you need not only food (Bible study) but exercise. Work for Christ. The only work Christ ever set for Christians is to win others.

    "Go ye into all the world and preach the Gospel to every creature." Mark 16:15.

    "When I say unto the wicked, thou shalt surely die; and thou givest him not warning, nor speakest to warn the wicked from his wicked way, to save his life; the same wicked man shall die in his iniquity; but his blood will I require at thine hand."—Ezek. 3:18.

[Facsimile of Page Three of Circular Handed to Every Convert]

4. **SHUN EVIL COMPANIONS:** Avoid bad people, bad books, bad thoughts. Read the First Psalm.

"Be ye not unequally yoked together with unbelievers: for what fellowship hath righteousness with unrighteousness, and what communion hath light with darkness—what part hath he that believeth with an infidel—wherefore come out from among them and be ye separate, saith the Lord."—II Cor. 6:14-17.

Try to win the wicked for God, but do not choose them for your companions.

5. **JOIN SOME CHURCH:** Be faithful in your attendance at the Sabbath and mid-week services.

"Not forsaking the assembling of ourselves together, as the manner of some is."—Heb. 10:25.

Co-operate with your pastor. God has appointed the pastor to be a shepherd over the church and you should give him due reverence and seek to assist him in his plans for the welfare of the church.

6. **GIVE TO THE SUPPORT OF THE LORD'S WORK:** Give as the Lord hath prospered you.—I Cor. 16:2.

"Give not grudgingly or of necessity, for God loveth a cheerful giver."—I Cor. 9:7.

7. **DO NOT BECOME DISCOURAGED:** Expect temptations, discouragement and persecution; the Christian life is warfare.

"Yea and all who will live godly in Christ Jesus shall suffer persecution."—II Tim. 3:12.

The eternal God is thy refuge. We have the promises that all things, even strange and hard unaccountable obstacles, work together for our good. Many of God's brightest saints were once as weak as you are, passed through dark tunnels and the hottest fire, and yet their lives were enriched by their experiences, and the world made better because of their having lived in it.

Read often the following passages of Scripture: Romans 8:18; James 1:12; I Corinthians 10:13.

[Facsimile of Page Four of Circular Handed to Every Convert.]

CHAPTER XXV

A Life Enlistment

When a man, after starting to be a Christian, looks back, it is only a question of time until he goes back.—BILLY SUNDAY.

PROFESSOR WILLIAM JAMES, the philosopher, contended that there was a scientific value to the stories of Christian conversions; that these properly belonged among the data of religion, to be weighed by the man of science. Harold Begbie's notable book, "Twice-Born Men," was recognized by Professor James as a contribution to the science of religion; for it was simply a collection of the stories of men whose lives had been transformed by the gospel which the Salvation Army had carried to them. A whole library of such books as "Twice-Born Men" could be written concerning the converts of Billy Sunday. His converts not only "right-about-face" but they keep marching in the new direction. Their enlistment is for life.

This point is one of the most critical in the whole realm of the discussion of revivals. Times without number it has been charged that the converts of evangelists lose their religion as quickly as they got it. A perfectly fair question to ask concerning these Billy Sunday campaigns is, "Are they temporary attacks of religious hysteria, mere effervescent moods of spiritual exaltation, which are dissipated by the first contact with life's realities?"

Here is opportunity for the acid test. Billy Sunday has been conducting revival meetings long enough to enable an investigator to go back over his trail and trace his results. After years have passed, are there still evidences of the presence and work of the evangelist? To this only one answer can be made. The most skeptical and antagonistic person cannot fail to find hundreds and thousands

of Billy Sunday converts in the churches of the towns where
the envangelist has conducted meetings during the past
twenty years.

Not all of the converts have held fast; we cannot forget that one of the Twelve was a complete renegade, and that
the others were for a time weak in the faith.   Alas, this
condition is true of Christian converts, however made.
The terrible record revealed in each year's church statistics,
of members who are missing—entirely lost to the knowledge
of the Church—is enough to restrain every pastor from
making uncharitable remarks upon the recruits won by an
evangelist. The fact to be stressed at this present moment
is that Billy Sunday converts are to be found in all departments of church work, in the ministry itself, and on the
foreign field.

One reason for the conservation of the results of the
Sunday campaigns is that all the powers of the evangelist
and his organization are exerted to lead those who have
confessed Christ in the tabernacles to become members of
the church of their choice, at the earliest possible date.
Sunday says candidly that converts cannot expect to grow
in grace and usefulness outside the organized Church of
Christ.   Thus it comes about that before a Sunday campaign closes, and for months afterwards, the church papers
report wholesale accessions to the local congregations of all
denominations.   Three thousand new church members were
added in a single Sunday in the city of Scranton.

What these campaigns mean in the way of rehabilitating
individual churches is illustrated by what a Scranton pastor
said to me toward the close of the Sunday campaign:
"You know my church burned down a short time ago.   We
have been planning to rebuild.   Now, however, we shall have
to rebuild to twice the size of our old church, and we have
enough new members already to make sure that our financial
problem will be a simple one."   In other words, the coming
of the evangelist had turned into a triumph and a new starting point for this congregation what might have otherwise
been a time of discouragement and temporary defeat.

For a moment the reader should take the viewpoint of the pastors who have been struggling along faithfully, year after year, at best getting but a few score of new members each year. Then Billy Sunday appears. The entire atmosphere and outlook of the church is transformed within a few days. Optimism reigns. Lax church members become Christian workers, and enthusiasm for the kingdom pervades the entire membership. The churches of the community find themselves bound together in a new solidarity of fellowship and service.

Then, to crown all, into the church membership come literally hundreds of men and women, mostly young, and all burning with the convert's ardent zeal to do service for the Master. Can anybody but a pastor conceive the thrill that must have come to the minister of a Wilkes-Barre church which added one thousand new members to its existing roll, as a result of the Billy Sunday campaign in that city?

Six months after the Sunday meetings in Scranton I visited Carbondale, a small town sixteen miles distant from Scranton, and talked with two of the resident pastors. There are four Protestant churches in Carbondale, which have already received a thousand new members within five months. All these converts are either the direct result of Billy Sunday's preaching, or else the converts of converts. Out of a Protestant population of nine thousand persons, the Carbondale churches have received one-ninth into their membership within six months. These bare figures do not express the greater total of Christian service and enthusiasm which permeates the community as an abiding legacy of the Billy Sunday campaign. These converts consider that they have been saved to serve.

Asked to fix a period after which he would expect a reaction from the Sunday meetings, a critic would probably say about one year. On this point we learn that when the evangelist visited the city of Scranton, which is within an hour's ride of Wilkes-Barre, he found that the influence of the meetings which he had held a year previously in Wilkes-Barre were perhaps the most potent single factor in preparing the people of Scranton for his coming. Night after night Wilkes-Barre sent delegations of scores and hundreds over to the Scranton Tabernacle. Investigators from afar who came to look into the Scranton meetings were advised to go to the neighboring city to ascertain what were the effects of the campaign after a year. The result was always convincing.

When the evangelist was in Pittsburgh, McKeesport, where he had been six years before, sent many delegations to hear him and on one occasion fifteen hundred persons made the journey from McKeesport to Pittsburgh to testify to the lasting benefits which their city had received from the evangelist's visit.

Usually some organization of the "trail-hitters" is effected after the evangelist's departure. These are bands for personal Christian work. The most remarkable of them all is reported from Wichita, Kansas, where the aftermath of the Sunday meetings has become so formidable as to suggest a new and general method of Christian service by laymen.

The Sunday converts organized themselves into "Gospel Teams," who announce that they are ready to go anywhere and conduct religious meetings, especially for men. They offer to pay their own expenses, although frequently the communities inviting them refuse to permit this. Sometimes these Gospel Teams travel by automobiles or street cars and sometimes they make long railway journeys.

The men have so multiplied themselves that there are now more than three hundred Gospel Teams in this work and they have formed "The National Federation of Gospel Teams" of which Claude Stanley of Wichita is president and West Goodwin of Cherryvale, Kansas, is secretary.

Up to date, the tremendous total of eleven thousand conversions is reported by these unsalaried, self-supporting gospel workers, who joyously acclaim Billy Sunday as their leader. They represent his teachings and his spirit in action.

The most celebrated of these gospel teams is "The Business Men's Team" of Wichita, an interdenominational group. It comprises such men as Henry Allen, the editor of the Wichita *Beacon* and one of the foremost public men of the state; the president of the Inter-urban Railway; the president of the Kansas Mutual Bank, and other eminent business men. This team has visited eleven states in its work, all without a penny of cost to the Church, and with results exceeding those achieved by many great and expensive organizations.

The Billy Sunday converts not only stick but they multiply themselves and become effective servants of the Church and the kingdom.

Nobody is left to conjecture as to the sort of counsel that Mr. Sunday gives his converts. Every man, woman and child who "hits the trail" is handed a leaflet, telling him how to make a success of the Christian life.

A trumpet call to Christian service by every confessed disciple of Jesus Christ is sounded by the evangelist. The following is an appeal of this sort:

"SHARP-SHOOTERS"

The twentieth century has witnessed two apparently contradictory facts: The decline of the Church and the growth of religious hunger in the masses. The world during the nineteenth and early twentieth centuries passed through a period of questioning and doubts, during which everything in heaven and earth was put into a crucible and melted down into constituent elements. During that period many laymen and preachers lost their moorings.

The definite challenging note was lost out of the life of the ministry. The preacher today is oftentimes a human interrogation point, preaching to empty pews. The hurrying, busy crowd in the street is saying to the preacher and the Church, "When you have something definite to say about the issues of life, heaven, hell and salvation, we will listen; till then we have no time for you." I believe we are on the eve of a great national revival. The mission of the Church is to carry the gospel of Christ to the world.

I believe that lack of efficient personal work is one of the curses of the Church today. The people of the Church are like squirrels in a cage. Lots of activity, but accomplishing nothing. It doesn't require a Christian life to sell oyster soup or run a bazaar or a rummage sale.

Last year many churches reported no new members on confession of faith. Why these meager results with this tremendous expenditure of energy and money? Why are so few people coming into the kingdom? I will tell you what is the matter—there is not a definite effort put forth to persuade a definite person to receive a definite Saviour at a definite time, and that definite time is now.

I tell you the Church of the future must have personal work and prayer. The trouble with some churches is that they think the preacher is a sort of ecclesiastical locomotive, who will snort and puff and pull the whole bunch through to glory.

A politician will work harder to get a vote than the Church of God will work to have men brought to Christ. Watch some of the preachers go down the aisles. They drag along as if they had grindstones tied to their feet.

No political campaign is won by any stump speaker or any spell-binder on the platform. It is won by a man-to-man canvass.

The Value of Personal Work

The children of this generation are wiser than the children of light. You can learn something from the world about how to do things. Personal work is the simplest and most effective form of work we can engage in. Andrew wins Peter. Peter wins three thousand at Pentecost. A man went into a boot and shoe store and talked to the clerk about Jesus Christ. He won the clerk to Christ. Do you know who

that young man was? It was Dwight L. Moody, and he
went out and won multitudes to Christ. The name of the
man who won him was Kimball, and Kimball will get as
much reward as Moody. Kimball worked to win Moody
and Moody worked and won the multitude. Andrew wins
Peter and Peter wins three thousand at Pentecost. That is
the way God works today. Charles G. Finney, after learning the name of any man or woman, would invariably ask:
"Are you a Christian?" There isn't any one here who hasn't
drag enough to win somebody to Christ.

  Personal work is a difficult form of work; more difficult
than preaching, singing, attending conventions, giving your
goods to feed the poor. The devil will let you have an easy
time until God asks you to do personal work. It is all right
while you sing in the choir, but just as soon as you get out
and work for God the devil will be on your back and you will
see all the flimsy excuses you can offer for not working for
the Lord. If you want to play into the hands of the devil
begin to offer your excuses.

There are many people who want to win somebody for
Jesus and they are waiting to be told how to do it. I believe
there are hundreds and thousands of people who are willing
to work and who know something must be done, but they
are waiting for help; I mean men and women of ordinary
ability. Many people are sick and tired and disgusted with
just professing religion; they are tired of trotting to church
and trotting home again. They sit in a pew and listen to a
sermon; they are tired of that, not speaking to anybody and
not engaging in personal work; they are getting tired of it
and the church is dying because of it. A lot should wake up
and go to the rescue and win souls for Jesus Christ.

I want to say to the deacons, stewards, vestrymen,
prudential committees, that they should work, and the
place to begin is at your own home. Sit down and write
the names of five or ten friends, and many of them members
of your own church, and two or three of those not members
of any church; yet you mingle with these people in the club,

in business, in your home in a friendly way. You meet them every week, some of them every day, and you never speak to them on the subject of religion; you never bring it to their attention at all; you should be up and doing something for God and God's truth. There are always opportunities for a Christian to work for God. There is always a chance to speak to some one about God. Where you find one that won't care, you'll find one thousand that will.

My Father's Business

Be out and out for God. Have a heart-to-heart talk with some people and win them to Christ. The first recorded words of Jesus are these: "Wist ye not that I must be about my Father's business?"

The trouble is we are too lackadaisical in religion, indifferent and dead and lifeless. That is the spirit of the committees today in the Church. I think the multitude in the Church will have to get converted themselves before they can lead any one else to Christ. It is my firm conviction, after many years of experience in the work, that half the people in the Church have never been converted, have never been born again. I take up a bottle of water, uncork it and take a drink. That is experimental. One sip of water can convince me more of its power to slake thirst than 40,000 books written on the subject. You know quinine is bitter because you have experimented; you know fire will burn because you have experimented; you know ice will freeze; it is cold; you have experimented.

A man must experience religion to know God. All you know of God is what you read in some book or what you heard somebody else talk about; you haven't lived so that you could learn first-handed, so most of your religion is second-handed. There is too much second-hand stuff in the Church. It is your privilege to know and to have salvation. Jesus said to Peter: "When you are converted strengthen your brethren." You are not in a position to help anybody else unless you have been helped yourself.

So many church members know nothing about the Bible. A preacher will take a text from the Bible and get as far from it as the East is from the West. A young preacher just out of the seminary said: "Must I confine myself in my preaching to the Bible?" Just like a shrimp who would say, "Must I confine my roaming to the Atlantic Ocean?" Imagine a little minnow saying: "Must I confine myself to the Atlantic Ocean?" "Must I confine myself to the Bible?" Just as if his intellect would exhaust it in two or three sermons.

We have cut loose from the Bible, and any man who is living contrary to the Bible is a sinner, whether he feels like a sinner or not. Every man who is living contrary to the laws is a criminal, whether he feels like it or not. A man who breaks the law of God is a sinner, and is on the road to hell, whether he feels like it or like a saint. Jesus came into the world to reveal God to man, and man reveals him to man. The only revelation we have of Jesus is through the Bible. You have got to know Jesus to know God; that's how I get through there. There is no revelation for God to make of himself greater than he has made through Jesus Christ. It is not possible for the human intellect to have a greater conception of God. Every man needs Christ. Jesus is the Saviour that he needs and he has got to know the Bible to show what it is that makes Jesus the Saviour. He needs a Saviour and now is the time to accept the Saviour and be saved. That's what the Bible says. Whatever the Bible says, write "finish" after it and stop.

Feeding the Spiritual Life

Then you need the Holy Spirit. Without him you cannot do anything. The spirit of God works through clean hands. There are too many dirty hands, too many dirty people trying to preach a clean gospel. I have known men that have preached the truth and God has honored the truth, although their lives were not as they should be. But God honored the truth and not the people who preached the truth. But if they had been Christians themselves then God would have honored them more, because he would have honored them and the truth.

Prayer. Three-fourths of the church members have no family prayer. They let spiritual life starve. That is the reason the pews are full of driftwood; that is the reason that religion is but a mirage to many.

Pray God to give you power. Pray God to give you power to carry on his work after you have become converted. I don't preach a sermon that I don't pray God for help, and I never finish a sermon that I don't thank God that I have preached it. Then I say: "Lord, you take care of the seed I have sown in that sermon." I think the Church needs a baptism of good, pure "horse sense."

Pure hearts. If I have any iniquity in my heart the Lord will not come in. We need a wise head. We need horse sense in preaching. We need horse sense in what we do. I think God is constantly looking for a company of men and women that are constantly alive. There are too many dead ones. He needs men and women that are always at it, not only during the revival; we need to be full of faith; dead in earnest, never give up, a bulldog tenacity and stick-to-it-iveness for the cause of God Almighty.

The Dignity of Personal Work

If it is beneath your dignity to do personal work then you are above your Master. If you are not willing to do what he did, then don't call him your Lord. The servant is not greater than the owner of the house. The chauffeur is not greater than the owner of the automobile. The servant on the railroad is not greater than the owners of the road. Certainly they are not greater than our Lord Jesus Christ.

It requires an effort to win souls to Christ. There is no harder work and none brings greater results than winning souls.

You'll need courage. It is hard to do personal work and

the devil will try to oppose you.   You'll seek excuses to try to get out of it.   Many people who attend the meetings regularly now will begin to stay at home when asked to do personal work.   It will surprise you to see them lie to get out of doing personal work.

We need enthusiasm for God.   If there is any place on God's earth that needs a baptism of enthusiasm, it is the church and the prayer-meetings.   It is not popular in some communities and in some churches to be enthusiastic for God.   You'll never accomplish anything without pure enthusiasm, and don't be afraid of being a religious enthusiast. Religion is too cold.   Formality is choking it in the pews.

There is nothing accomplished in war, politics or religion, without enthusiasm.   Admiral Decatur once gave this toast: "My country: May she always be right, but right or wrong, my country!"   That's enthusiasm.

Perseverance is needed to conquer in this old life.   Perseverance is contagious, not an epidemic.   Religion is contagious.   Roman soldiers shortened their swords and added to their kingdom.   You shorten the distance between you and the sinner and you'll add to the kingdom of God. The trouble is you have been trying to reach them with a ten-foot pole.   Drop your dignity and formality and walk up to them; take them by the hand.   You are too dignified. You sit in your fine homes and see the town going to hell.

We need carefulness to win souls.   The way to win souls is to be careful what you say.   Study the disposition of the person with whom you talk.

We need tact.   Personal work is the department of the church efficient to deal with the individual and not the masses. It is analogous to the sharpshooter in the army so dreaded by the opposing forces.   The sharpshooter picks out the pivotal individual instead of shooting at the mass.   The preacher shoots with a siege gun at long range.   You can go to the individual and dispose of his difficulties.   I shoot out there two or three hundred feet and you sit right beside people.   If I were a physician and you were sick I'd not

21

prescribe *en masse,* I'd go down and see you individually. I'd try to find out what was the matter and prescribe what you needed. All medicine is good for something, but not for everything.

We need sympathy. One of the noblest traits of the human character is sympathy. It levels mountains, warms the broken heart and melts the iceberg. Have sympathy with the sinner. Not with sin, but the fact that he is one. God hates sin and the devil. He will not compromise. Have sympathy with the girl who sins, but not with the sin that ruined her. Get down on the ground where the others are. You are away up there saved, but you must get down and help the sinner.

Five Classes of People

There are five classes of people and this classification will touch every man and woman, whether in Scranton, New York or London.

First, those who can not attend church, and you will always find some. Some are sick, shut in; some have to work in hotels and restaurants; the maids in your house have to get your meals, the railroad men have to go out, the furnaces must be kept going in the steel works.

Second, those who can attend and who do not attend church. There are millions of people that can and don't attend church. Some fellows never darken the church door until they die, and they carry their old carcass in to have a large funeral. It is no compliment to any man, and it is an insult to manhood, and disgrace to the individual, that he never darkens the church door. But he darkens the door of the grog shop any day.

Third, those who can and do attend church and who are not moved by the preaching. There are lots of people who come out of curiosity.

Fourth, those who can go to church and those who do go to church and are moved by the preaching and convicted but not converted. Every man that hears the truth is convicted. Talk to those men about Jesus Christ. Get them to take their stand for righteousness.

Fifth, those who can and do go to church and are convicted by the preaching and converted. They need strengthening. They are converted now, but they need the benefit of your experience. You say, "Where will I find these people to talk to them?" Where won't you find them? Where can you find a place where they are not? You will only find one place where they are not and that is in the cemetery. Right in your neighborhood, right in your block, how many are Christians? Is your husband a Christian? Are your children Christians? If they are, let them alone and get after somebody else's husband and children. Don't sit down and thank God that your husband and children are Christians. Suppose I were to say: "My family, my George, my Nell, my Paul, my Helen are Christians!" We are all Christians, let the rest of the world go to the devil. There is too much of that spirit in the Church today.

Go from house to house. Go to the people in your block, in your place of business. Have you said anything to the telephone girl when you called her up? You are quick enough to jump on her when she gives you the wrong number. Have you said anything to the delivery boy—to the butcher? Have you asked the milkman? Have you said anything to the newsboy who throws your paper on the doorstep at night? Have you called them up at the newspaper office? Have you said anything to the girl who waits on you at the store; to the servant who brings your dinner in at home; to the woman who scrubs your floors? Where will you find them?—where won't you find them?

The Privilege of Personal Work

Personal work is a great privilege. Not that God needs us, but that we need him. Jesus Christ worked. "I must do the works of Him that sent me." So must you. He didn't send me to work and you to loaf. Honor the God that gives you the privilege to do what he wants. Jesus worked.

324 A LIFE ENLISTMENT

Please God and see how it will delight your soul. If you'll win a soul you will have a blessing that the average church member knows nothing about. They are absolute strangers to the higher Christian life. We need an aroused church. An anxious church makes anxious sinners.

If all the Methodist preachers would each save a soul a month there would be 460,000 souls saved in a year. If all the Baptist preachers would each save a soul a month there would be 426,000 souls saved in a year. If all the other evangelical preachers would save a soul a month there would be 1,425,000 souls saved a year. Over 7,000 Protestant churches recently made report of no accessions on confession of faith. Christ said to preach the gospel to all the world and that means every creature in the world.

" My God, I've Got Two Boys Down There!"

Listen to this: There are 13,000,000 young men in this country between the ages of sixteen and thirty years; 12,000,000 are not members of any church, Protestant or Catholic; 5,000,000 of them go to church occasionally; 7,000,000 never darken a church door from one year's end to another. They fill the saloons and the houses of ill fame, the haunts of vice and corruption, and yet most young men have been touched by some Sunday-school influences; but you don't win them for God and they go into the world never won for God.

I want to tell you if you want to solve the problem for the future get hold of the young men now. Get them for

God now. Save your boys and girls. Save the young man and woman and you launch a life-boat.

At the Iroquois fire in Chicago six hundred people were burned to death. One young woman about seventeen years of age fought through the crowd, but her hair was singed from her head, her clothes were burned, her face blistered. She got on a street car to go to her home in Oak Park. She was wringing her hands and crying hysterically, and a woman said to her: "Why, you ought to be thankful you escaped with your life."

"I escaped—but I didn't save anybody; there are hundreds that died. To think that I escaped and didn't save anybody."

In Pennsylvania there was once a mine explosion, and the people were rushing there to help. Up came an old miner seventy or eighty years of age, tired, tottering and exhausted. He threw off his vest, his coat and hat and picked up a pick and shovel Some of them stopped him and said: "What is the matter? You are too old; let some of the younger ones do that. Stand back."

The old fellow said: "My God, I've got two boys down there!"

So you see it seems to make all the difference when you've got some boy down there.

Who is wise? You say Andrew Carnegie, the millionaire, is wise, the mayor, the judge, the governor, the educator, the superintendent of schools, the principal of the high school, the people who don't worry or don't live for pleasure, the inventor. But what does the Lord say? The Lord says, "He who winneth souls is wise."

CHAPTER XXVI

"A Good Soldier of Jesus Christ"

I'd rather undertake to save ten drunkards than one old financial Shylock—it would be easier.—BILLY SUNDAY.

SYMPATHETIC observers comment in distressed tones upon the physical exhaustion of Sunday after every one of his addresses. He speaks with such intensity and vigor that he is completely spent by every effort. To one who does not know that he has worked at this terrific pace for near a score of years it seems as if the evangelist is on the verge of a complete collapse. He certainly seems to speak "as a dying man to dying men." The uttermost ounce of his energy is offered up to each audience. Billy Sunday is an unsparing worker.

For a month or six weeks of every year he gives himself to rest. The remainder of the year he is under a strain more intense than that of a great political campaign. Even his Monday rest day, which is supposed to be devoted to recuperation, is oftener than not given to holding special meetings in some other city than the one wherein he is campaigning. Speaking twice or oftener every day, to audiences averaging many thousands, is a tax upon one's nerve force and vitality beyond all computation. In addition to this, Sunday has his administrative work, with its many perplexities and grave responsibilities.

Withal, the evangelist, like every other man preeminent in his calling, suffers a great loneliness; he has few intimates who can lead his mind apart from his work. What says Kipling, in his "Song of Diego Valdez," the lord high admiral of Spain, who pined in vain for the comradeship of his old companions, but who, in the aloneness of eminence, mourned his solitary state?

"They sold Diego Valdez
To bondage of great deeds."

(326)

The computable aggregate of Sunday's work is almost unbelievable. His associates say that his converts number more than a quarter of a million persons. That is a greater total than the whole membership of the entire Christian Church, decades after the resurrection of our Lord. Imagine a city of a quarter of a million inhabitants, every one of whom was a zealous disciple of Jesus Christ. What a procession these "trail-hitters" would make could they all be gathered into one great campaign parade!

Of course these converts are not all trophies of Billy Sunday's preaching power. He has not won them alone. He has merely stood in the forefront, as the agent of the Church, with vast co-operative forces behind him. Nevertheless, he has been the occasion and the instrument for this huge accomplishment in the Church's conquest.

When it comes to counting up the aggregate size of Sunday's audiences, one is tempted not to believe his own figures, for the total runs up into the millions, and even the tens of millions. Probably no living man has spoken to so great numbers of human beings as Billy Sunday.

More eloquent than any comment upon the magnitude and number of his meetings is the following summary of his campaigns gathered from various sources. Sunday himself does not keep records of his work. His motto seems to be, "Forgetting those things which are behind."

In 1904–5 Billy Sunday visited various cities of Illinois, where conversions ranged in numbers from 650 to 1,800; in Iowa, where conversions ranged from 400 to 1,000; and in a few other towns. In 1905–6 numerous campaigns in Illinois, Iowa and Minnesota produced converts ranging from 550 to 2,400, the highest number being reached in Burlington, Iowa. In 1906–7 the converts numbered over 12,000, with a maximum of 3,000 in Kewanee, Illinois. In 1907–8 campaigns in Illinois and Iowa, and one in Sharon, Pennsylvania, reported over 24,000 converts in all, with a maximum of 6,700 in Decatur, Illinois. In 1908–9 the total number of converts reached over 18,000, with 5,300 in Spokane, Wash-

In reading such a compiled record as the foregoing, it is to be remembered that in all things that affect spiritual values the only true record is that which is kept in another world. Enough has been shown, however, to make clear that Sunday practices what he preaches when he urges Christians to whole-hearted service.

SUNDAY'S " CONSECRATION " SERMON

"I beseech you, therefore, brethren, by the mercies of God, that ye present your bodies a living sacrifice, holy, acceptable unto God, which is your reasonable service."

The armies of God are never made up of drafted men and women, ordered into service whether willing or not. God never owned a slave. God doesn't want you to do anything that you can't do without protest. This is not a call to hard duty, but an invitation to the enjoyment of a privilege. It is not a call to hired labor to take the hoe and go into the field, but the appeal of a loving father to his children to partake of all he has to give.

If there is nothing in you that will respond to God's appeal when you think of his mercies, I don't think much of you. The impelling motive of my text is gratitude, not fear. It looks to Calvary, not to Sinai. We are being entreated, not threatened. That's the amazing thing to me. To think that God would entreat us—would stand to entreat us! He is giving me a chance to show I love him.

If you are not ready to offer it in gratitude, God doesn't want you to serve him through fear, but because you realize his love for you, and appreciate and respond to it.

A business man who loves his wife will never be too busy to do something for her, never too busy to stop sometimes to think of how good she has been and what she has done for him. If men would only think of the things God has done for them there would be less card-playing, less thought of dinners and of concerts and other diversions of the world. God wants us to sit down and think over his goodness to us. The man who doesn't isn't worth a nickel a punch. Has God done anything for us as a nation, has he done anything for us as individuals, that commands our gratitude?

Astronomers have counted three hundred and eighty million stars, and they have barely commenced. Why, you might as well try to count those countless stars as to try to count God's mercies. You might as well try to count the drops of water in the sea or the grains of sand upon the shore. If we only think, we shall say with David: "According to Thy tender mercies."

God's Mercies

An old lady said one morning that she would try to count all God's mercies for that one day, but at noon she was becoming confused, and at three o'clock she threw up her hands and said: "They come three times too fast for me to count."

Just think of the things we have to be thankful for! A visitor to an insane asylum was walking through the grounds and as he passed one of the buildings he heard a voice from a barred window high up in the wall and it said: "Stranger, did you ever thank God for your reason?" He had never thought of that before, but he says that he has thought of it every day since. Did you ever think that thousands of people who were just as good as you are, are beating their heads against the walls of padded cells? Did you ever think what a blessed thing it is that you are sane and you go about among men and follow your daily duties, and go home to be greeted by your wife and have your children climb about you?

Did you ever thank God for your eyes? Did you ever thank him that you can see the sunrise and the sunset and can see the flowers and the trees and look upon the storm? Did you ever thank God that you have two good eyes while so many others less fortunate than you must grope their way in blindness to the coffin?

Did you ever thank God for hearing? That you can hear music and the voices of friends and dear ones? That you can leave your home and business, and come here and hear the songs and the preaching of the word of God? Did you ever think what it would mean to be deaf?

Did you ever thank God for the blessing of taste? Some people can't tell whether they are eating sawdust and shavings or strawberries and ice cream. Think of the good things we enjoy! Others have tastes so vicious that they find it almost impossible to eat. God might have made our food taste like quinine.

Did you ever thank God that you can sleep? If not, you ought to be kept awake for a month. Think of the thousands who suffer from pain or insomnia so that they can sleep only under opiates. Did you ever wake up in the morning and thank God that you have had a good night's rest? If you haven't, God ought to keep you awake for a week, then you'd know you've had reason to be thankful.

Did you ever thank God for the doctors and nurses and hospitals? For the surgeon who comes with scalpel to save your life or relieve your sufferings? If it had not been for them you'd be under the grass. For the nurse who watches over you that you may be restored to health?

Did you ever thank God for the bread you eat, while so many others are hungry? Did you ever thank him for the enemy that has been baffled, for the lie against you that has failed?

Out in Elgin, Illinois, I was taken driving by a friend, and he said that he wanted me to go with him to see a man. He took me to see a man who was lying in bed, with arms most pitifully wasted by suffering. The poor fellow said he had been in bed for thirty-two years, but he wasn't worrying about that. He said he was so sorry for the well people who didn't know Jesus, I went out thanking God that I could walk. If your hearts are not made of stone or adamant they will melt with gratitude when you think of the many mercies, the tender mercies, of God.

The Living Sacrifice

"Brethren"—that's what God calls his true followers. No speaking from the loft. If there's any lesson we need to learn it is that of being "brethren."

Sinners are not called "brethren" in the Bible. God commands sinners. They are in rebellion. He entreats Christians. When Lincoln called for volunteers he addressed men as "citizens of the United States," not as foreigners.

The man who is appreciative of God's mercies will not have much mercy on himself. Don't stand up and say: "I'll do what Jesus bids me to do, and go where he bids me to go," then go to bed. Present your bodies—not mine—not those of your wives; you must present your own. Present your bodies; not your neighbor's; not your children's; it is their duty to do that. Do you trust God enough to let him do what he wants to do?

Henry Varley said to Moody, when that great American was in England, that God is waiting to show this world what one man could do for him. Moody said: "Varley, by the grace of God I'll be that man"; and God took hold of Moody and shook the world with him. God would shake the world with us today if only we would present our bodies as a living sacrifice to him, as Moody did. Are you willing to present yourself? I am tired of a church of five hundred or seven hundred members without power enough to bring one soul to Christ.

At the opening of the Civil War many a man was willing that the country should be saved by able-bodied male relatives of his wife, who made themselves bullet-men, but he didn't go himself. God isn't asking for other men's bodies. He's asking for yours. If you would all give to God what rightfully belongs to him, I tell you he would create a commotion on earth and in hell. If God had the feet of some of you he would point your toes in different ways from those you have been going for many years. If he had your feet he would never head you into a booze joint. If he had your feet he would never send you into a ball-room.

If he had the feet of some of you he would make you wear out shoe leather lugging back what you've taken that doesn't belong to you. If God had your feet he would take you to prayer-meeting. I'm afraid the preacher would have nervous prostration, for he hasn't seen some of you there in years. If God had your feet you'd find it harder to follow the devil. Some of you preachers have your children going to dancing school and I hear some of you go to dances. He would make your daily walk conform to the Golden Rule and the Sermon on the Mount.

Some people work only with their mouths. God wants that part that's on the ground. Some soldiers sit around and smell the coffee and watch the bacon frying.

If God had your hands he would make you let go a lot of things you hold on to with a death-like grip. If you don't let go of some of the things you hold so tightly they will drag you down to hell. He would have you let go some of the things you pay taxes on, but don't own, and he would make you let go of money to pay taxes on some that you do own. Some people are so busy muck-raking that they will lose a crown of glory hereafter. If God had your hands, how many countless tears you would wash away. A friend of mine bought a typewriter, and when he tried to use it his fingers seemed to be all sticks, but now he can write forty-five words a minute. Let God have your hands and he will make them do things that would make the angels wonder and applaud.

A Glass of Champagne

A young man went down to Thomasville, Alabama, and while there was invited to a dress ball—or rather an undress ball, if what I have read about such affairs properly describes the uniforms. A young lady—a young lady with eyes like the dove and with beautiful tresses—came up to him and said to the young man, "Won't you pledge a glass of champagne with me?"

The young man thanked her, but said: "No, I don't drink."

"Not with me?" she said, and smiled; and he repeated his answer, "No."

Then she said: "If I had thought you would refuse me I would not have asked you and exposed myself to the embarrassment of a refusal. I did not suppose you would think me bold for speaking to you in this way, and I thought you might be lonely."

A little later she came back to him and repeated her invitation. Again he said: "No."

Others came up and laughed. He took it and hesitated. She smiled at him and he gave in and drank the champagne, then drank another glass and another, until he was flushed with it. Then he danced.

At two o'clock the next morning a man with a linen duster over his other clothes walked back upon the railroad-station platform, waiting for a train for the North; and as he walked he would exclaim, "Oh God!" and would pull a pint flask from his pocket and drink. "My God," he would say, "what will mother say?" Four months later in his home in Vermont, with his weeping parents by him and with four strong men to hold him down, he died of delirium tremens.

The Epworth League's motto is: "Look up, lift up." But you'll never lift much up unless God has hold of your hands. Unless he has, you will never put your hands deep in your pocket, up to the elbows, and bring them up full of money for his cause. A man who was about to be baptized took out his watch and laid it aside; then he took out his knife and bank-book and laid them aside.

"Better give me your pocket-book to put aside for you," said the minister.

"No," said the man, "I want it to be baptized, too."

There's no such thing as a bargain-counter religion. Pure and undefiled religion will do more when God has something besides pennies to work with. God doesn't run any excursions to heaven. You must pay the full fare. Your religion is worth just what it cost you. If you get religion and then lie down and go to sleep, your joints will get stiff as Rip Van Winkle's did, and you'll never win the religious marathon.

Denying One's Self

A man said to his wife that he had heard the preacher say that religion is worth just what it costs, and that he had determined to give more for religion and to deny himself as well. "What will you give up?" she asked. He said that he would give up coffee—for he dearly loved coffee—used to drink several cups at every meal, the very best. She said that she would give up something, too—that she would give up tea. Then their daughter said she would give up some of her little pleasures, and the father turned to his son Tom, who was shoveling mashed potatoes, covered with chicken gravy, into his mouth. He said, "I'll give up salt mackerel. I never did like the stuff, anyway."

There are too many salt-mackerel people like that in the pews of our churches today. They will take something that they don't like, and that nobody else will have, and give it to the Lord. That isn't enough for God. He wants the best we have.

God wants your body with blood in it. Cain's altar was bigger than Abel's, but it had nothing valuable on it, while Abel's had real blood. God rejected Cain's and accepted Abel's. God turns down the man who merely lives a moral life and does not accept the religion of Jesus Christ. You must come with Jesus' blood. How thankful you are depends on how much you are willing to sacrifice.

I don't believe that the most honored angel in heaven has such a chance as we have. Angels can't suffer. They can't make sacrifices. They can claim that they love God, but we can prove it.

What would you think of a soldier if when he was ordered "Present arms," he would answer, "Tomorrow"; if he would say, "When the man next to me does"; if he would say, "When I get a new uniform"? "Present"—that means now. It is in the present tense. God wants us to make a present of our bodies to him—because we love him.

A little girl showed a man some presents she had received and he asked her, "How long may you keep them?"

"How long?" she answered. "Why, they were given to me. They are mine!"

Many a man gives his boy a colt or a calf, then when it has grown to a horse or a cow he sells it and pockets the money. Some of you fellows need to do a little thinking along that line. When we give our bodies, they ought to be His for keeps.

Thinking for God

If when you make a present you do not mean to give it outright, you are not honest. "Will a man rob God?" You bet he will—a heap quicker than he will rob any one else.

Your body, that takes the head as well as hands. God wants brains as well as bones and muscles. We ought to do our best thinking for God. God is in the greatest business there is, and he wants the best help he can get. Some of you old deacons and elders make me sick. If you used such methods in business as you do in the work of the Church the sheriff's sale flag would soon be hanging outside your door. I don't ask any of you business men to curtail any of your business activities, but I do ask that you give more of your energy to the things of religion. You want to use good business methods in religion. The Republicans and the Democrats and the Socialists use good business methods in politics. The farmer who hasn't any sense is still plowing with a forked stick. The farmer who has sense uses a modern plow. Use common sense.

Bishop Taylor promised God that he would do as much hard thinking and planning for him as he would do for another man for money. He did it. So did Wesley and Whitefield and Savonarola, and look what they did for God! If there is any better way of doing God's business than there

22

was one hundred years ago, for God's sake do it! He's entitled to the best there is. This thing of just ringing the church bell to get people to come in is about played out. In business, if they have a machine that is out of date and doesn't produce good results, it goes onto the scrap heap. If a man can produce a machine that can enlarge the product or better it, that machine is adopted at once. But in religion we have the same old flint-lock guns, smooth-bore; the same old dips and tallow candles; the same old stage coaches over corduroy roads; and if a protest is made some of you will roll your eyes as if you had on a hair shirt, and say: "Surely this is not the Lord's set time for work." I tell you any time is God's time. Now is God's time. It was God's time to teach us about electricity long before Franklin discovered it, but nobody had sense enough to learn.

It was God's time to give us the electric light long before Edison invented it, but nobody had sense enough to understand it. It was God's set time to give us the steam engine long before Watts watched the kettle boil and saw it puff the lid off, but nobody had sense enough to grasp the idea.

If God Almighty only had possession of your mouths, he'd stop your lying. If he had your mouths he'd stop your knocking. If he had your mouths, he'd stop your misrepresentations. If he had your mouths, he'd stop your swearing. If he had your mouths, he'd stop your back-biting. If he had your mouths, he'd stop your slanders. There would be no criticizing, no white lies, no black lies, no social lies, no talking behind backs.

If God had your mouths, so much money wouldn't go up in tobacco smoke or out in tobacco spit. If God had your mouths, there would be no thousands of dollars a year spent for whisky, beer and wine. You wouldn't give so much to the devil and you would give more to the Church. Many of you church pillars wouldn't be so noisy in politics and so quiet in religion. So many of you fellows wouldn't yell like Comanche Indians at a ratification meeting and sit like a bump on a log in prayer-meeting.

If God had our eyes he'd bring the millennium. His eyes run to and fro through the world seeking for men to serve him; and if he had our eyes, how our eyes would run to and fro looking for ways to help bring men to Christ. How hard it would be for sinners to get away. We would be looking for drunkards, and the prostitutes and down-and-outs, to lift and save them. How many sorrowful hearts we would find and soothe, how many griefs we would alleviate! Great God! How little you are doing. Don't you feel ashamed? Aren't you looking for a knot-hole to crawl through? If God had our eyes how many would stop looking at a lot of things that make us proud and unclean and selfish and critical and unchristian

What God Asks

God wants you to give your body. Are you afraid to give it to him? Are you afraid of the doctor when you are sick? Your body—that thing that sits out there in the seat, that thing that sits up there in the choir and sings, that thing that sits there and writes editorials, that body which can show Jesus Christ to fallen sons of Adam better than any angel—that's what God wants. God wants you to bring it to him and say: "Take it, God, it's yours." If he had your body, dissipation, overeating and undersleeping would stop, for the body is holy ground. We dare not abuse it.

A friend of mine paid $10,000 for a horse. He put him in a stable and there the animal had care-takers attending him day and night, who rubbed him down, and watched his feet to take care that they should not be injured, and put mosquito netting on the windows, and cooled him with electric fans, and sprinkled his oats and his hay. They wanted to keep him in shape, for he was worth $10,000 and they wanted him for the race-track. Give your body to God, and the devil will be welcome to anything he can find.

God wants your body as a living sacrifice, not a dead one. There are too many dead ones. A time was when God was satisfied with a dead sacrifice. Under old Jewish law a dead

CHAPTER XXVII

A Wonderful Day at a Great University

The higher you climb the plainer you are seen.—BILLY SUNDAY.

BILLY SUNDAY has had many great days in his life—mountain-top experiences of triumphant service; exalted occasions when it would seem that the climax of his ministry had been reached. Doubtless, though, the greatest day of his crowded life was the thirtieth of March, 1914, which he spent with the students of the University of Pennsylvania at Philadelphia.

The interest not alone of a great university but also of a great city was concentrated upon him on this occasion. An imposing group of discriminating folk took the opportunity to judge the much discussed evangelist and his work. In this respect, the day may be said to have proved a turning point in the public career of the evangelist. It silenced much of the widespread criticism which had been directed toward him up to this time; and it won for him the encomiums of a host of intellectual leaders.

What Sunday's own impressions of that day were may be understood from the prayer he offered at the close of the night meeting.

Oh, Jesus, isn't this a fine bunch? Did you ever look down on a finer crowd? I don't believe there is a mother who is any prouder of this lot of boys than I am tonight. I have never preached to a more appreciative crowd, and if I never preach another sermon, I am willing to go home to glory tonight, knowing that I have helped save the boys at the University of Pennsylvania. Help them to put aside temptations, and to follow in the paths in which Doctor Smith is trying to guide their feet.

Back of the visit of the evangelist to the University lies a story, and a great principle. The latter is that mate-

(343)

rialism has no message for the human soul or character. The authorities of the University, in common with a wide public, had been deeply disturbed over the suicide of several students during the winter of 1913–14. Sensational stories, largely unwarranted, in the daily press had reported an epidemic of suicides, due to infidelity.

Underneath all this "yellow" portrayal of conditions lay the truth, realized by nobody more clearly than by the University head, Provost Edgar Fahs Smith, that the character of young manhood needs to be fortified by spiritual ideals. In his rôle of religious leader of the University, and counselor to the young men, Provost Smith had heard confessions of personal problems which had wrung his soul. None knew better than he that it takes more than culture to help a man win the battle of life. Looking in every direction for succor in this deepest of all problems, the sight of Billy Sunday at Scranton indicated a possible ray of hope.

Led by Thomas S. Evans, the secretary of the Christian Association of the University, a deputation of student leaders went to Scranton, heard the evangelist, and conveyed to him an invitation to spend a day with the University. The call of the need of young men in particular is irresistible to Sunday, and he gladly accepted the invitation for a day in Philadelphia—going, it may be added parenthetically, entirely at his own expense, and insisting that the offering made be devoted to University Christian Association work.

There is a thorough organization of the Christian work of the University; so careful plans were laid for the visit of the evangelist. The meetings were made the subject of student prayer groups, and all that forethought could do to secure the smooth running of the day's services was carefully attended to. Students were to be admitted by their registration cards, and a few hundred other guests, mostly ministers and persons identified with the University, were given special admission cards.

There is no such rush for grand opera tickets in Philadelphia as was experienced for these coveted cards of admission to the Billy Sunday meetings at the University. The noon meeting and the night meetings were exclusively for men, but in the afternoon a few score favored women were admitted. The result was that in these three services the evangelist talked to representatives of the best life of the conservative old city of Philadelphia. He never before had faced so much concentrated culture as was represented that day within the walls of the great gymnasium.

This improvised auditorium could be made to hold about three thousand persons, especially when the hearers were students, and skilful in crowding and utilizing every inch of space, such as window sills and rafters. The line of ticket holders that gathered before the opening of the doors itself preached a sermon to the whole city. As one of the Philadelphia newspapers remarked, in the title it gave to a section of its whole page of Billy Sunday pictures, "Wouldn't think they were striving for admittance to a religious service, would you?" The newspapers, by pen and camera, chronicled this Billy Sunday day at the University as the city's most important news for that issue.

The evangelist's chorister, Homer Rodeheaver, led the introductory service of music. He set the college boys to singing and whistling familiar gospel hymns, and Mrs. De Armond's "If Your Heart Keeps Right"—a refrain which was heard for many weeks afterward in University corridors and campus.

From the first the students, than whom there are no more critical hearers alive, were won by Billy Sunday. Provost Smith, who has the men's hearts, introduced him in this happy fashion:

"Billy Sunday is a friend of men. He is a friend of yours and a friend of mine, and that's why we are glad to have him here today to tell us about his other friend, Jesus Christ. His is the spirit of friendship, and we are glad to extend to him our fellowship while we have the opportunity."

The three addresses given on that day were "What Shall I Do with Jesus?" "Real Manhood," and "Hot-cakes off the Griddle."

These fragments of the three addresses culled from the newspaper reports give the flavor of the messages heard by the students:

"What shall I do with Jesus?"

"This question is just as pertinent to the world today as it was to Pilate," he said. "Pilate had many things to encourage and discourage him, but no man ever sought to do anything without meeting difficulties.

"Pilate should have been influenced by his wife's dream," the speaker continued, whimsically suggesting that he didn't care what sort of wife Pilate had. "She may have been one of those miserable, pliable, plastic, two-faced, two-by-four, lick-spittle, toot-my-own-horn sort of women, but Pilate should have heeded her warning and set Jesus free," he asserted.

"Pilate had the personality of Jesus before him and should have been influenced by this. He had also heard of the miracles of Jesus, even if he had never seen them.

"Why, Jesus was cussed and discussed from one end of the land to the other. All he had to do was to say 'Come forth,' and the graves opened like chestnut burrs in the fall," he added.

"I have no use for the fellow that sneers and mocks at Jesus Christ. If the world is against Christ, I am against the world, with every tooth, nail, bit of skin, hair follicle, muscular molecule, articulation joint"—here the evangelist paused for breath before adding—"yes, and even my vermiform appendix.

"But Pilate was just one of those rat-hole, pin-headed, pliable, standpat, free-lunch, pie-counter politicians. He was the direct result of the machine gang in Jewish politics, and he was afraid that if he released Christ he would lose his job.

"Say, boys," he demanded, leaning so far over the

platform it seemed he must have fallen, "are you fellows willing to slap Jesus Christ in the face in order to have some one come up and slap you on the back and say you are a good fellow and a dead-game sport? That is the surest way to lose out in life. I am giving you the experience of a life that knows.

"Pilate had his chance and he missed it. His name rings down through the ages in scorn and contempt because he had not the courage to stand up for his convictions and Jesus Christ. Aren't you boys doing the same thing? You are convinced that Jesus Christ is the son of God, but you are afraid of the horse-laugh the boys will give you.

"God will have nothing to do with you unless you are willing to keep clean," he said. "Some people think they are not good enough to go to heaven and not bad enough to go to hell, and that God is too good to send them to hell, so they fix up a little religion of their own. God isn't keeping any half-way house for any one. The man who believes in that will change his theology before he has been in hell five minutes.

"There's just one enemy that keeps every one from accepting Christ, and that is your stubborn, miserable will power. You are not men enough to come clean for Jesus.

"I don't care whether you have brains enough to fill a hogshead or little enough to fill a thimble, you are up against this proposition: You must begin to measure Christ by the rules of God instead of the rules of men. Put him in the God class instead of in the man class; judge Christ by his task and the work he performed, and see if he was only a man."

The University of Pennsylvania would be turning out bigger men than Jesus Christ, he said, if Christ were not the son of God. The conditions and the opportunities are so much greater in these days, he showed, that a real superman should be the product of our day if education, society, business, politics and these varied interests could produce such a thing.

"Jesus Christ is just as well known today as old Cleopatra, the flat-nosed enchantress of the Nile, was known hundreds and hundreds of years ago.

"Don't swell up like a poisoned pup and say that 'it doesn't meet with my stupendous intellectual conception of what God intended should be understood.' God should have waited until you were born and then called you into counsel, I suppose. Say, fellows, I don't like to think that there are any four-flushing, excess-baggage, lackadaisical fools like that alive today, but there are a few.

"On the square, now, if you want to find a man of reason, would you go down in the red-light district, where women are selling their honor for money, or through the beer halls or fan-tan joints? You don't find intellect there," he continued.

In contrast to these places, the evangelist described with remarkable accuracy and emotion the scenes surrounding the death of President McKinley and the burial ceremony at Canton, Ohio; how the great men of the nation, all Christian men, passed by the flag-covered casket and paid their silent tribute to the man who had died with Christian confidence expressed in his last words.

"When I came out of that court-house at Canton, I said: 'Thank God, I'm in good company, for the greatest men of my nation are on the side of Jesus Christ,'" he added. From the farthest corner of the auditorium there came a fervent "Amen," which found many repetitions in the brief silence that followed.

Mr. Sunday reached a powerful climax when he described the possibilities of the Judgment Day, and the efforts of the evil one to lead into the dark, abysmal depths souls of men who have been popular in the world. To those who have accepted Christ, the Saviour will appear on that day as an advocate at the heavenly throne, he argued, and the saved ones can turn to the devil and say:

" 'Beat it, you old skin-flint. I have you skinned to a

frazzle. I have taken Jesus Christ and he's going to stand by me through all eternity.'

"Wherein does Jesus Christ fail to come up to your standard and the highest conception of the greatest Godlike spirit? Show me one flaw in his character. I challenge any infidel on earth to make good his claims that Christ was an ordinary man. The name of Jesus Christ, the son of God, is greater than any. It is the name that unhorsed Saul of Tarsus, and it is holding 500,000,000 of people by its majestic spell and enduring power.

"If you can't understand what this means, just take a walk out into some cemetery some day and look at the tomb-stones. You'll find that the name of the man who had a political drag twenty-five years ago is absolutely forgotten," continued the challenge.

"Do you fellows know what sacrifice means?" suddenly asked the speaker. "Some of your fathers are making sacrifices and wearing old clothes just to keep you here in school. He wants you to have an education because he can't even handle the multiplication table.

"If Jesus Christ should enter this gymnasium we would all fall to our knees. We have that much reverence in our hearts for him. I would run down and meet him, and would tell him how much I love him and that I am willing to go wherever he would have me go."

In closing, the evangelist told the story of a man who recklessly tossed a valuable pearl high into the air, reaching over the side of a ship to catch it as it fell. Time and again he was successful, but finally the ship swerved to one side and the gem disappeared beneath the waves.

"Boys, that man lost everything just to gain the plaudits of the crowd. Are you doing the same thing?

"That is the condition of thousands of people beneath the Stars and Stripes today—losing everything just to hear the clamor of the people, and get a little pat on the back for doing something the mob likes."

Mr. Sunday suddenly abandoned his dramatic attitude

and lowered his voice. There was an instantaneous bowing of heads, although he had given no suggestion of a prayer. It seemed proper at that time, and one of the evangelist's heart-to-heart talks with Christ, asking a blessing on the Christian workers of the University, and an earnest effort, on the part of every student, to live a Christian life, accompanied the great audience as it filed from the gymnasium.

Real Manhood

"Be thou strong, therefore, and show thyself a man," the Bible verse reads, and Mr. Sunday promptly added: "Don't be a mutt! Don't be a four-flusher—a mere cipher on the sea of human enterprise.

"God is a respecter of character, even if he isn't a respecter of persons," continued the speaker. "Abraham towers out, like a mountain above a molehill, and beside him some of our modern gimlet-eyed, heel-worn fellows shrink like Edward Hyde in Doctor Jekyll's clothes.

"When those fellows over in Babylon offered booze to Daniel, although he was only seventeen years old, he said, 'Nothing doing.' He told them where to head in. Moses pushed aside the greatest scepter of any kingdom and did what his heart told him was right. 'Be thou strong and show thyself a man.'

"David was a man of lofty purposes and his life was influenced by those that had preceded him. It wasn't an accident that made David a king. The big job is always looking for big men. A round peg will not fit into a square hole, even if he is a university professor.

"The young buck who inherits a big fortune without working for it," continued Mr. Sunday, "is going down the line so fast you can't see him for the fog. The man who has real, rich, red blood in his veins, instead of pink tea and ice water, when the lions of opposition roar, thinks it is only a call for dinner in the dining car, and he goes ahead and does things.

"There are some going around disguised as men who ought to be arrested," the evangelist interposed. "To know some men is an invitation to do right; to know others is an invitation to know dirty booze and to blot the family escutcheon, insult your mothers and sisters. The size of the man depends on his mind, not on his muscle. There is lots of bulk but little brains in some men.

"It's a sad day for a young man when Bill Taft's overcoat wouldn't make him a vest," he added, amid shouts of laughter, in which even staid, stern-faced professors joined with the students.

"Too many fellows look like men from across the street, but when you get close to them they shrivel up.

"It makes a difference what kind of an example you follow. If Thomas Edison should say to his boy, 'Be an inventor,' the boy would know what he meant, but if some red-nosed, beer-soaked old reprobate should tell his boy to 'be a man,' the boy would be all in. Lots of fellows today turn out bad because their fathers' talk and walk do not agree.

"The best thing that can happen to a young man," said Mr. Sunday, "is to come under the influence of a real man. Every one has a hero, whether it be on the football field or in the classroom, and if every one would lead right today, there would be no going astray tomorrow.

"There are some men in this world that when they are around you turn up your collar, feel chills running up and down your back and when you look at the thermometer, you find the temperature is about 60 degrees below zero."

Then followed the evangelist's famous story of how David killed Goliath, considerably tempered to suit the culture of his audience. He told how David boldly asked who the "big lobster was," and why he was "strutting around as if he was the whole cheese, the head guy of the opposition party.

"David put down the sword that Saul had given him,

for he felt like a fellow in à hand-me-down suit two sizes too large. He picked up one of his little pebbles, slung it across the river and hit poor old Goliath on the koko."

"Some fellows are working so hard to become angels they forget to be men. If you will study your Bible you will find that the men of old were subject to the same temptations as the men of today, but they didn't let their temptations get the best of them.

"If your manhood is buried in doubt and cheap booze, dig it out. You have to sign your own Declaration of Independence and fight your own Revolutionary wars before you can celebrate the Fourth of July over the things that try to keep you down.

"The best time for a man to sow his wild oats is between the age of eighty-five and ninety years. A six-ply drunk is about as good a passport into commercial life as a record for housebreaking, and the youth who goes to the mat with a half-pint of red-eye in his stomach, will be as beneficial to humanity as a one-legged man in a hurdle race."

'If I knew, when the undertaker pumps that pink stuff into me and embalms me, that the end of all had come, I would still be glad I lived a Christian life, because it meant a life of decency," he said. "I would rather go through the world without knowing the multiplication table than never to know the love of Christ. I don't underestimate the value of an education, boys, but just try living on oatmeal porridge. Get your education, but don't lose sight of Jesus."

"Once you have made your plan, cling to it. Be a man, even in situations of great danger. The man whose diet is swill will be at home with the hogs in any pen. He's bound to have bristles sticking through his skin. If Abraham Lincoln had read about Alkali Ike, or Three Fingered Pete, do you think he would ever have been President? While other young men were waking up with booze-headaches, he was pulling up his old-fashioned galluses and saying, 'I'm going to be a man.'

"And one morning the world awoke, rubbed its sleepy eyes and looked around for a man for a certain place. It found Abraham Lincoln and raised him from obscurity to the highest pinnacle of popular favor. He was a man and his example should be a guiding influence in the life of every American citizen."

Booze, evil women, licentious practices, cigarettes— all these came under the ban of Mr. Sunday's system of Christian living. He spared no words; he called a spade a spade and looked at modern affairs without colored glasses.

"You can't find a drunkard who ever intended to be a drunkard," argued Mr. Sunday. "He just intended to be a moderate drinker. He was up against a hard game, a game you can't beat."

He asserted that he could get more nourishment from a little bit of beef extract, placed on the edge of a knife blade, than can be obtained from 800 gallons of the best beer brewed.

Talking about riches, he suggested that King Solomon, with his wealth, could have hired Andrew Carnegie as a chauffeur or J. Pierpont Morgan to cut the lawns around his palace. "Money isn't all there is in this world, but neither is beer," he said. "I don't want to see you students get the booze habit, just because we are licensing men at so much per year to make you staggering, reeling, drunken sots, murderers, thieves and vagabonds."

The double standard of living was bitterly attacked by the revivalist, who said one of the crying needs of America was the recognition of a single standard of living.

"It makes no difference to God whether the sinner wears a plug hat and pair of suspenders or a petticoat and a willow plume. No man who deliberately drugs a girl and sends her into a life of shame ought to be permitted in good society. He ought to be shot at sunrise." This sentiment evoked a tremendous round of applause, and cries of "Amen!" and "Good, Bill!" were not infrequent.

23

"The avenging God is on his trail and the man who wrecks women's lives is going to crack brimstone on the hottest stone in hell, praise God," the speaker continued. "If we are to conciliate this unthinkable and unspeakable practice of vampires feeding on women's virtue, we might as well back-pedal in the progress of the nations. The virtue of womanhood is the rampart of our civilization and we must not let it be betrayed."

When the invitation was given after the night meeting, for men who wanted to dedicate themselves to cleaner, nobler manhood to rise, nearly the entire body, visibly moved by the words of the preacher, rose to its feet. Then, with a daring which prim and conservative Philadelphia had not thought possible in this citadel of intellectuality and conventionality, Sunday gave the invitation to the students who would begin a new life by confessing Christ to come forward. Accounts vary as to the number who went up and grasped the evangelist's hand. All reporters seemed to be carried away by the thrill of the occasion. Many reported that hundreds went forward. The most conservative report was that 175 young men took this open stand of confession of Jesus Christ.

The University weekly, *Old Penn*, in its issue of the following Saturday summarized the Billy Sunday visit in pages of contributions. These three paragraphs are the sober judgment of those best informed from the University standpoint:

The results of Mr. Sunday's visit within the University have been nothing short of marvelous. The Provost has been receiving congratulations from trustees, business men, lawyers, members of the faculty and prominent undergraduates. Several whole fraternities have taken action leading to higher living in every line. Drink has been completely excluded from class banquets. Students are joining the churches, and religion has been the paramount topic of conversation throughout the entire University.

Under the leadership of the University Christian

Association, the church leaders of Philadelphia of all denominations have been canvassing their own students in the University and have found most hearty response to everything that has to do with good living. The effect is really that of a religious crusade, and the result is of that permanent sort which expresses itself in righteousness of life. At the close of the night meeting on Monday, about 1,000 students arose to their feet in answer to Mr. Sunday's invitation to live the Christian life in earnest, or to join for the first time the Christian way of life. Those who have called upon the students who took this stand have found that it was genuine, and not in any sense due to a mere emotional movement. Mr. Sunday's appeal seems to be almost wholly to the will and conscience, but it is entirely based upon the movement of the Holy Spirit of God.

No one who has ever addressed the students of the University of Pennsylvania on vital religion has ever approached the success which was attained by Mr. Sunday in reaching the students, and without doubt this visit is only the opening up of a marvelous opportunity for Mr. Sunday to reach the students of the entire country, especially those of our great cosmopolitan universities.

The editor of *Old Penn* asked opinions from members of the faculty and undergraduate body. Dean Edward C. Kirk, M.D., D.D.S., of the Dental Department, said in his appraisal of the Sunday visit:

If, as according to some of the critics, the impression that he has made is but temporary and the enthusiasm which he has created is only a momentary impulse, even so, the success of his accomplishment lies in the fact that he has produced results where others have failed to make a beginning. The University ought to have the uplifting force not only of a Billy Sunday, but a Billy Monday, Tuesday, Wednesday and every other day in the week.

Of the students who testified in print, one, a prominent senior, wrote:

Mr. Sunday awoke in me a realization of my evil practices and sins so forcefully that I am going to make a determined effort to give them up and to make amends for the past. From my many conversations with fellow-students I find that this is what Mr. Sunday did. If he did not directly cause the student to come forward and take a stand, every student at least was aroused to think about this all-important question in a light that he had not seriously considered it in before. The undergraduate body, as a whole, is glad that Mr. Sunday came to Philadelphia.

A Christian worker from the Law School gave his opinion as follows:

I have been connected with the University of Pennsylvania for six years, and for the greater part of this time have been in close touch with the work of the Christian Association. The influence of the Association seems to be increasing constantly, but Billy Sunday accomplished in one day what the Association would be proud to have accomplished in one year. To my mind, Mr. Sunday's visit marks the beginning of a new epoch—the Renaissance of religious work of the University.

That is the sort of thing that occupied pages of the official publication of the University, following the evangelist's visit. This day's work attracted the attention not only of Philadelphia newspapers, but the religious press throughout the country quite generally commented upon it. Dr. Mosley H. Williams graphically reviewed it in the *Congregationalist.*

The University of Pennsylvania, founded by Benjamin Franklin in 1749, is the fourth in age of American universities, antedated only by Harvard, Yale, and Princeton by one year. It is located in a city of a million and three-quarters people. It now enrolls 6,632 students, representing every state in the Union, and fifty-nine foreign countries. There are 250 from Europe and Asia, and 150 from Latin America; so that in the cosmopolitanism of its make-up, probably no

American university equals it. Its Young Men's Christian Association employs twenty-seven secretaries, its Bible classes on week days gather 650 students, and every Fraternity House has its own Bible Class. But attendance upon daily prayers is not obligatory, and less than a hundred, on an average, are seen at those services.

Into this cosmopolitan University Billy Sunday came like a cyclone. After preaching in Scranton three times on the Sabbath, to audiences aggregating 30,000 people, he traveled all night, reached Philadelphia Monday morning, took an automobile spin to the baseball park, where he was a famous player twenty years ago, and preached three times in the University of Pennsylvania gymnasium, which was seated with chairs, and accommodated 3,000 hearers.

There were three services—noon, afternoon and evening. Tickets were issued, red, white and blue, each good for one service, and that one exclusively. Not a person was admitted without a ticket. The long lines reached squares away, and the police kept the people moving in order.

What does such a spectacle mean in a great old university, in a great city? Such a student body knows slang, and athleticism, and all sorts of side plays. No doubt there was plenty of criticism and questioning; but a spectator who had his eyes and ears and mind open, would say, that in getting a response to the religious appeal, Billy Sunday's Monday in the University of Pennsylvania scored high.

This effort for quickening religious interests in the University was not a spasmodic effort for one day; there had been the most careful preparations beforehand, in consultation with leading ministers of all denominations in the city, to seek out students of every denomination. Lists were carefully made and cards put in the hands of ministers and Christian workers, with the understanding that all the young men of the University should be visited in a friendly and Christian spirit by representatives of various churches. The results, of course, remain to be seen, but after this effort, no student need say, "No man cares for my soul."

The conclusion of the whole matter, of course, is that the old-time religion, the gospel of our fathers and our mothers, is still the deepest need of all sorts and conditions of men.   The religion that saved the outcast in the gutter is adequate to redeem the man in the university.

CHAPTER XXVIII

The Christian's Daily Helper

Too much of the work of the Church today is like a squirrel in a cage—lots of activity, but no progress.—BILLY SUNDAY.

IN the course of one of his campaigns, Sunday sweeps the arc of the great Christian doctrines. While he stresses ever and again the practical duties of the Christian life, yet he makes clear that the reliance of the Christian for all that he hopes to attain in character and in service is upon the promised Helper sent by our Lord, the ever-present Holy Spirit. One of the evangelist's greatest sermons is upon this theme, and no transcript of his essential message would be complete without it.

"THE HOLY SPIRIT"

The personality, the divinity and the attributes of the Holy Ghost afford one of the most inspiring, one of the most beneficial examples in our spiritual life. We are told that when the Holy Spirit came at Pentecost, he came as the rushing of a mighty wind and overurging expectancy. When Jesus was baptized in the River Jordan, of John, out from the expanse of heaven was seen to float the Spirit of God like a snowflake, and they heard a sound as of whirring wings, and the Holy Spirit in the form of a dove hovered over the dripping locks of Christ. Neither your eyes nor mine will ever behold such a scene; neither will our ears ever hear such a sound again. You cannot dissect or weigh the Holy Spirit, nor analyze him as a chemist may analyze material matter in his laboratory, but we can all feel the pulsing of the breath of his eternal love.

The Holy Spirit is a personality; as much a personality as Christ, or you or I. "Howbeit, when he, the Spirit of truth, is come, he will guide you into all truth: for he shall not speak of himself." He is to us what Jesus was when he was on earth. Jesus always speaks of the Holy Spirit in the future tense. He said, "It is expedient that I go away; if I go not away the Spirit will not come. It is expedient for you that I go away, but when I am gone, then I will send Him unto you who is from the Father." So we are living today in the beneficence of the Holy Spirit.

No Universal Salvation

I do not believe in this twentieth-century theory of the universal fatherhood of God and the brotherhood of man. We are all made of one blood—that is true, physically speaking; we are all related. I am talking about the spiritual, not the physical. You are not a child of God unless you are a Christian; then you are a child of God—if you are a Christian.

Samson with the Holy Spirit upon him could take the jawbone of an ass and lay dead a thousand Philistines. Samson without the Holy Spirit was as weak as a newborn babe, and they poked his eyes out and cut off his locks. And so with the Church and her members. Without the Holy Spirit you are as sounding brass and tinkling cymbals, simply four walls and a roof, and a pipe organ and a preacher to do a little stunt on Sunday morning and evening. I tell you, Christian people, that with the Holy Spirit there is no power on earth or in hell that can stand before the Church of Jesus Christ. And the damnable, hell-born, whisky-soaked, hog-jowled, rum-soaked moral assassins have damned this community long enough. Now it is time it was broken up and it is time to do something.

There are three classes in the Church, as I have looked at it from my standpoint. The first are those in the Church personally who want to be saved, but they are not concerned about other people. They do not give any help to other people; they don't lie awake at night praying for other people that they may be brought to the Lord.

The second class are going to depend upon human

wisdom.   There is no such thing as latent power, expressed or implied—power is just as distinctive in an individual as the electricity in these lights.   If these globes are without a current they would be nothing but glass bulbs, fit for nothing but the scrap heap.   Without the Holy Spirit you are as sounding brass and tinkling cymbals, and a third-rate amusement parlor, with religion left out.

The third class are church members not from might and honor and power, but from the Spirit.

While at Pentecost one sermon saved 3,000 people, now it takes 3,000 sermons to get one old buttermilk-eyed, whisky-soaked blasphemer.

Happiest Nation on Earth

We have our churches, our joss houses, our tabernacles; we have got the wisdom of the orientals, the ginger, vim, tabasco sauce, peppering of the twentieth century; we have got all of that, and I do not believe that there are any people beneath the sun who are better fed, better paid, better clothed, better housed, or any happier than we are beneath the stars and stripes—no nation on earth.   There are lots of things that could be eliminated to make us better than we are today.   We are the happiest people in God's world.

Out in Iowa, a fellow said to me: "Mr. Sunday, we ought to be better organized."   Just think of that, we ought to be better organized.   Now listen to me, my friends! Listen to me!   There is so much machinery in the churches today that you can hear it squeak.

Drop into a young people's meeting.   The leader will say in a weak, effeminate, apologetic, minor sort of way, that there was a splendid topic this evening but he had not had much time for preparation.   It is superfluous for him to say that; you could have told that.   He goes along and tells how happy he is to have you there to take part this evening, making this meeting interesting.   Some one gets up and reads a poem from the *Christian Endeavor World* and then they sing No. 38.   They get up and sing:

"Oh, to be nothing—nothing,
    Only to lie at His feet."

We used to sing that song, but I found out that people took it so literally that I cut it out.

Then a long pause, and some one says, "Let us sing No. 52." So they get up and then some one starts,

"Throw out the life line,
    Throw out the life line."

They haven't got strength enough to put up a clothes-line. Another long pause, and then you hear, "Have all taken part that feel free to do so? We have a few minutes left. So let us sing No. 23." Then another long pause. "I hear the organ prelude; it is time for us to close, now let us all repeat together, 'The Lord keep watch between me and thee, while we are absent one from another.'"

I tell you God has got a hard job on his hands. Ever hear anything like that?

Ambassadors of God

Believe that God Almighty can do something. Don't whine around as though God were a corpse, ready for the undertaker. God is still on the job. The Holy Spirit is needed to bring man into spiritual touch with God; to make man realize that he is a joint representative of God on earth today. Do you ever realize that you are God's representative—God's ambassador?

And as we are God's ambassadors why should we fear what the devil may do? Can it be that you fail to realize his power? Or are you so blind to the spiritual that you can't see that you need God's help? Let me ask you one question: Are you ready to surrender to him? A man said to me: "It was a mighty little thing to drive Adam and Eve out of the Garden of Eden because they ate an apple." It wasn't the fruit. It was the principle, whether man should bow to God or God bow to man. That act was an act of disobedience. You may say it was a mighty little thing for England to go to war with us because we threw some tea into Boston harbor. We didn't go to war over the tea. We said: "You can't brew tea in the East India Company and pour it down our throats." It was the principle we went to war about, not the price of tea, and we fought it out. Are you ready to surrender? You, who are in rebellion against God? You, who are in rebellion against the authority of God's government? Are you ready to do his will?

A good many people suppose that when they have accepted Jesus Christ as their Saviour and joined the Church that is all there is to the Christian life. As well might a student who has just matriculated imagine that he has finished his education. Nobody has reached a stage in the Christian life from which he cannot go further unless he is in the coffin—and then it's all over. To accept Christ, to join the Church, is only to begin. It is the starting of the race, not the reaching of the goal. There are constant and increasing blessings if you are willing to pay the price.

I don't care when or where you became a church member, if the Comforter, who is the Holy Ghost, is not with you, you are a failure.

This power of the Spirit is meant for all who are Christians. It is a great blessing for the Presbyterian elder as well as for the preacher. I know some Methodist stewards who need it. Deacons would "deak" better if they had it. It is a great blessing for the deacon and the members of the prudential committee, and it is just as great a blessing for the man in the pew who holds no office. To hear some people talk you would think that the Holy Spirit is only for preachers. God sets no double standard for the Christian life. There's nothing in the Bible to show that the people may live differently from the man in the pulpit.

Holy Spirit a Person

I once heard a doctor of divinity pray for the Holy Spirit, and he said: "Send it upon us now." He was wrong, doubly wrong. The Holy Spirit is not an impersonal thing. He is a person, not an "it." And the Holy Spirit has always been here since the days of Pentecost. He does not come and go. He is right here in the world and his power is at the command of all who will put themselves into position to use it.

A university professor was greeted by a friend of mine who took him by the hand, and said: "What do you think of the Holy Spirit?" The professor answered that he regarded the Holy Spirit as an influence for good, a sort of emanation from God. My friend talked to him and tried to show him his mistake, and a few months later he met him again. "What do you think of the Holy Spirit now?" he asked. The professor answered: "Well, I know that the Holy Spirit is a person. Since I talked with you and have come to that conviction, I have succeeded in bringing sixty-three students to Christ."

A great many people think the Holy Spirit comes and goes again, and quote from the Acts, where it says that Peter was filled with the Holy Spirit. Well, if you will find that Peter had been doing things right along, that showed he had been filled with the Holy Spirit all the time. Acts, second chapter and fourth verse, we read: "And they were all filled with the Holy Spirit." You have no right, nor have I, to say that the Holy Spirit ever left any one. We have no right to seek to find Scripture to bolster up some little theory of our own. We must take the Word of God for it, just as we find it written there. Now, at Pentecost, Peter had said: "Repent, and be baptized for the remission of sins." Then he promised them that the Holy Spirit would come and fill them. Now we have the fulfilment of the promise.

Who were filled with the Holy Spirit? Peter and James and John? No—the people. That is the record of the filling with the Holy Spirit of the three thousand who were converted at Pentecost, not the filling of Peter and James and John.

If the Spirit remains forever, why doesn't his power always show its   Why haven't you as much power with

God as the one hundred and twenty had at Pentecost? There are too many frauds, too much trash in the Church. It is because the people are not true to God. They are disobeying him. They are not right with him yet.

I don't know just how the Holy Spirit will come, but Jesus said we should do even greater works than he did. What are you doing? You are not doing such works now.

The Last Dispensation

We find the Holy Spirit in the Old Testament. When the prophets spoke they were moved by him. God seems to have spoken to man in three distinct dispensations. Once it was through the covenant with Abraham, then it was through Moses and under the Mosaic dispensation, and finally it is through his own son, Jesus Christ. Jesus Christ came into the world, proved that he is the Son of God, suffered, died and was buried, rose again, and sent his Holy Comforter. This is the last dispensation. There is no evidence that after the Holy Spirit once came, he ever left the world. He is here now, ready to help you to overcome your pride, and your diffidence that has kept you from doing personal work, and is willing and ready to lead you into a closer relationship with Jesus.

But you say, some are elected and some are not. On that point I agree with Henry Ward Beecher. He said: "The elect are those who will and the non-elect are those who won't."

But you go in for culture—"culchah." If you are too cultured to be a Christian, God pity you. You may call it culture. I have another name for it. Is there anything about Christianity that is necessarily uncultured? I think the best culture in the world is among the followers of Jesus Christ.

But you say: "Ignorance is a bar to some." No sir. Billy Bray, the Cornish miner, was an illiterate man. He was asked if he could read writing, and he answered: "No, I can't even read readin'. " Yet Billy Bray did a wonderful work for God in Wales and England. Ignorance is no bar to religion, or to usefulness for Jesus.

Some time ago, over in England, a man died in the poor house. He had had a little property, just a few acres of land, and it hadn't been enough to support him. After he died the new owner dug a well on it, and at a depth of sixty-five feet he found a vein of copper so rich that it meant a little fortune. If the man who died had only known of that vein, he need not have lived in poverty. There are many who are just as ignorant of the great riches within their reach. Lots of people hold checks on the bank of heaven, and haven't faith enough to present them at the window to have them cashed.

"Little Things"

You may say, "I have failed in something, but it is a little thing." Oh, these little things! Bugs are little things, but they cost this country $800,000,000 in one year. Birds are little enemies of the bugs, and birds are little things, and if it weren't for the birds we would starve in two years. If there's anything that makes me mad it is to see a farmer grab a shotgun and kill a chicken hawk. That hawk is worth a lot more than some old hen you couldn't cook tender if you boiled it for two days. That chicken hawk has killed all the gophers, mice and snakes it could get its claws on and it has come to demand from the farmer the toll that is rightfully due to it, for what it has done to rid the land of pests.

Why is it that with all our universities and colleges we haven't produced a book like the Bible? It was written long ago by people who lived in a little country no bigger than some of our states. The reason was that God was behind the writers. The book was inspired.

When good old Dr. Backus, of Hamilton College, lay dying the doctor whispered to Mrs. Backus, saying, "Dr. Backus is dying." The old man heard and looked up with a smile on his face and asked: "Did I understand you to say that I am dying?"

Sadly the doctor said: "Yes, I'm sorry, you have no more than half an hour to live."

Dr. Backus smiled again. "Then it will soon be over," he said. "Take me out of bed and put me on my knees. I want to die praying for the students of Hamilton College." They lifted him out and he knelt down and covered his face with his transparent hands, and prayed "Oh, God, save the students of Hamilton College."

For a time he continued to pray, then the doctor said, "He is getting weaker." They lifted him back upon the bed, and his face was whiter than the pillows. Still his lips moved. "Oh, God, save ——" Then the light of life went out, and he finished the prayer in the presence of Jesus. What did his dying prayer do? Why, almost the entire student body of Hamilton College accepted Jesus Christ.

If you haven't the power of the Spirit you have done something wrong. I don't know what it is—it's none of my business. It's between you and God. It is only my duty to call upon you to confess and get right with him.

A man went to a friend of mine and said: "I don't know what is wrong with me. I teach a Sunday-school class of young men, and I have tried to bring them to Jesus, and I have failed. Can you tell me why?"

"Yes," was the answer. "There's something wrong with you. You've done something wrong."

The man hesitated, but finally he said, "You're right. Years ago I was cashier in a big business house, and one time the books balanced and there was some money left over. I took that money and I have kept it. That was twelve years ago. Here is the money in this envelope."

"Take it back to the owner," said my friend. "It's not yours, and it's not mine."

"But I can't do that," said the man. "I am making a salary of $22,000 a year now, and I have a wife and daughters, and my firm will never employ a dishonest man."

"Well, that's your business," said my friend. "I have advised you, and that's all I can do; but God will never forgive you until you've given that money back."

The man sank into a chair and covered his eyes for a while. Then he got up and said, "I'll do it." He took a Chesapeake and Ohio train and went to Philadelphia, and went to a great merchant prince in whose employ he had been, and told his story. The merchant prince shut and locked the door. "Let us pray," he said. They knelt together, the great merchant's arm about his visitor; and when they got up the great merchant said: "Go in peace. God bless you."

On the next Sunday the man who had confessed took the Bible on his knee as he sat before his class and said to them: "Young men, I often wondered why I couldn't win any of you to Christ. My life was wrong, and I've repented and made it right." That man won his entire class for Christ, and they joined Dr. McKibben's church at Walnut Hills, Cincinnati, Ohio.

If you would get right with God what would be the result? Why, you would save your city.

"I'VE WALKED SIXTY MILES TO LOOK UPON HER FACE AGAIN"

The Fame of a Christian

Some time ago the funeral of a famous woman was held in London. Edward, who was king then, came with his consort, Alexandra, to look upon her face, and dukes and duchesses and members of the nobility came. Then the doors were opened and the populace came in by thousands.

Down the aisle came a woman whose face and dress bore the marks of poverty. By one hand she led a child, and in her arms she carried another. As she reached the coffin she set down the child she was carrying and bent her head upon the glass above the quiet face in the coffin, and her old fascinator fell down upon it.

"Come," said a policeman, "you must move on."

But the woman stood by the coffin. "I'll not move on," she said, "for I have a right here."

The policeman said, "You must move on. It's orders;" but the woman said, "No, I've walked sixty miles to look upon her face again. She saved my two boys from being drunkards." The woman in the coffin was Mrs. Booth, wife of the great leader of the Salvation Army.

I'd rather have some reclaimed drunkard, or some poor girl redeemed from sin and shame, stand by my coffin and rain down tears of gratitude upon it, than to have a monument of gold studded with precious stones, that would pierce the skies.

"If ye love me keep my commandments. And I will pray the Father, and he shall give you another Comforter, that he may abide with you forever."

CHAPTER XXIX

A Victorious Sermon

If you fall into sin and you're a sheep you'll get out; if you're a hog you'll stay there, just like a sheep and a hog when they fall into the mud.—
BILLY SUNDAY.

ON the walls of Sir Walter Scott's home at Abbottsford hangs the claymore of the redoubtable Rob Roy, one of the most interesting objects in that absorbing library of the great novelist. A peculiar interest attaches to the instruments of great achievement, as the scimitar of Saladin, or the sword of Richard the Lion-Hearted, or the rifle of Daniel Boone. Something of this same sort of interest clings to a particular form of words that has wrought wondrously. Apart altogether from its contents, Sunday's sermon on "The Unpardonable Sin" is of peculiar interest to the reader. This is the message that has penetrated through the indifference and skepticism and self-righteousness and shameless sin of thousands of men and women. Many thousands of persons have, under the impulse of these words, abandoned their old lives and crowded forward up the sawdust trail to grasp the preacher's hand, as a sign that they would henceforth serve the Lord Christ.

"The Unpardonable Sin" is a good sample of Sunday's sermons. It shows the character of the man's mind, and that quality of sound reasonableness which we call "common sense." There are no excesses, no abnormalities, no wrenchings of Scripture in this terrific utterance.

"THE UNPARDONABLE SIN"

"Wherefore I say unto you, All manner of sin and blasphemy shall be forgiven unto men: but the blasphemy against the Holy Ghost shall not be forgiven unto men.

"And whosoever speaketh a word against the Son of man, it shall be forgiven him: but whosoever speaketh against the Holy Ghost, it shall not be forgiven him, neither in this world, neither in the world to come."

I'd like to know where anybody ever found any authority for a belief in future probation. Jesus Christ was either human or he was divine. And if he was only human then I am not obligated to obey his word any more than I am that of any other philosopher.

The Pharisees charged Jesus with being in league with the devil. They said to him, "You have a devil." They grew bolder in their denunciation and said: "You do what you do through Beelzebub, the prince of devils." Jesus said: "How is that so? If what I do I do through the devil, explain why it is I am overthrowing the works of the devil. If I am a devil and if what I do is through the devil, then I wouldn't be working to hurt the works of the devil. I would not be doing what I am doing to destroy the works of the devil, but I would be working to destroy the works of God."

From that day forth they dared not ask him any questions.

I know there are various opinions held by men as to what they believe constitutes the sin against the Holy Ghost. There are those who think it could have been committed only by those who heard Jesus Christ speak and saw him in the flesh. If that be true then neither you nor I are in danger, for neither has ever seen Jesus in the flesh nor heard him. Another class think that it has been committed since the days of Jesus, but at extremely rare intervals; and still a third class think they have committed it and they spend their lives in gloom and dread and are perfectly useless to themselves and the community.

And yet I haven't the slightest doubt but that there are thousands that come under the head of my message, who are never gloomy, never depressed, never downcast; their conscience is at ease, their spirits are light and gay, they eat three meals a day and sleep as sound as a babe at night; nothing seems to disturb them, life is all pleasure and song.

What It Is

If you will lay aside any preconceived ideas or opinions which you may have had or still have as to what you imagine, think or believe constitutes the sin against the Holy Ghost, or the unpardonable sin, and if you will listen to me, for I have read every sermon I could ever get my hands upon the subject, and have listened to every man I have ever had an opportunity to hear preach, and have read everything the Bible has taught on the subject.

I do not say that my views on the subject are infallible, but I have wept and prayed and studied over it, and if time will permit and my strength will allow and your patience endure, I will try and ask and answer a few questions. What is it? Why will God not forgive it?

It is not swearing. If swearing were the unpardonable sin, lots of men in heaven would have to go to hell and there are multitudes on earth on their way to heaven who would have to go to hell. It is not drunkenness. There are multitudes in heaven that have crept and crawled out of the quagmires of filth and the cesspools of iniquity and drunkenness. Some of the brightest lights that ever blazed for God have been men that God saved from drunkenness.

It's not adultery. Jesus said to the woman committing adultery and caught in the very act: "Neither do I condemn thee; go and sin no more."

It isn't theft. He said to Zaccheus, "This day is salvation come upon thy house." Zaccheus had been a thief.

It's not murder. Men's hands have been red with blood and God has forgiven them. The Apostle Paul's hands were red with blood.

What is it? To me it is plain and simple. It is constant and continual, and final rejection of Jesus Christ as

Rev. L. K. Peacock, One of Mr. Sunday's Assistants, Preaching in a Machine Shop in One of the Noon-day Meetings that Form an Important Part of All Campaigns.

BILLY SUNDAY AND HIS FAMILY AT HOME, MOUNT HOOD, WINONA
LAKE, INDIANA.

your Saviour. God's offer of mercy and salvation comes to you and you say, "No," and you push it aside. I do know that there is such a thing as the last call to every man or woman. God says that his spirit will not always strive with man, and when a man or woman says "No" as God's spirit strives for the last time it forever seals your doom.

It is no special form of sin, no one act. It might be swearing, it might be theft. Any one becomes unpardonable if God keeps calling on you to forsake that sin and you keep on refusing to forsake it, and if you don't then he will withdraw and let you alone and that sin will become unpardonable, for God won't ask you again to forsake it.

It is no one glaring act, but the constant repetition of the same thing. There will come a time when you commit that sin once too often.

It is a known law of mind that truth resisted loses its power on the mind that resists it. You hear a truth the first time and reject it. The next time the truth won't seem so strong and will be easier to resist. God throws a truth in your face. You reject it. He throws again; you reject again. Finally God will stop throwing the truth at you and you will have committed the unpardonable sin.

> "There is a line by us unseen;
>   It crosses every path;
>   It is God's boundary between
>   His patience and his wrath.
>
> "To cross that limit is to die,
>   To die as if by stealth.
>   It may not dim your eye,
>   Nor pale the glow of health;
>
> "Your conscience may be still at ease;
>   Your spirits light and gay;
>   That which pleases still may please,
>   And care be thrown away;

"But on that forehead God hath set
    Indelibly a mark,
Unseen by man; for man as yet
    Is blind and in the dark.

"Indeed, the doomed one's path below
    May bloom as Edens bloom;
He does not, will not know,
    Nor believe that he is doomed."

Over in Scotland there are men who earn their living by gathering the eggs of birds, laid upon ledges on rocks away below the cliff top. They fasten a rope to a tree, also to themselves, then swing back and forth and in upon the ledge of rock. When a man was doing that same thing years ago, the rope beneath his arms became untied, and the protruding rock caused the rope to hang many feet beyond his reach.

The man waited for help to come, but none came. Darkness came, the light dawned, and he gave himself up to the fate of starvation, which he felt inevitably awaiting him, when a breeze freshened and the dangling rope began to vibrate. As the wind increased in velocity it increased the vibration of the rope and as it would bend in, he said: "If I miss it, I die; if I seize it, it's my only chance," and with a prayer to God as the rope bent in, he leaped out of the chasm and seized it and made his way hand over hand to the top, and when he reached it his hair was as white as the driven snow.

There is one cord that swings through this old world today—the Holy Spirit. With every invitation it swings farther away. We are living in the last dispensation, the dispensation of the Holy Spirit, and God is speaking to the world through the Holy Spirit today.

Resisting the Truth

By every known law of the mind, conversion must be effected by the influence of the truth on the mind. Every

time you resist the truth the next time you hear it, it loses
its force on your mind. And every time you hear a truth
and withstand it, then you become stronger in your power
to resist the truth. We all know this, that each resistance
strengthens you against the truth. When a man hears
the truth and he resists it, the truth grows weaker and he
grows stronger to resist it.

No matter what Jesus Christ did the Jews refused tc
believe. He had performed wonderful deeds but they
wouldn't believe, so when Lazarus was dead, he said:
"Lazarus, come forth," and then turned to the Jews and
said: "Isn't that evidence enough that I am the Son of
God?" and they cried: "Away with him." One day he
was walking down the hot dusty road and he met a funeral
procession. The mourners were bearing the body of a
young man and his mother was weeping. He told them
to place the coffin on the ground and said:

"Young man arise," and he arose. Then he asked
the Pharisees: "Is that not proof enough that I am the
Son of God, that I make the dead to arise?" and they
cried: "Away with him." So no matter what Jesus did,
the Jews refused to believe him. No matter what Jesus
Christ says or does today, you'll refuse to accept, and continue to rush pell-mell to eternal damnation.

"Too Late"

Jesus Christ gives you just as much evidence today.
Down in Indiana, my friend, Mrs. Robinson, was preaching.
I don't remember the town, but I think it was Kokomo,
and I remember the incident, and the last day she tried
to get the leader of society there to give her heart to God.
She preached and then went down in the aisle and talked
to her. Then she went back to the platform and made
her appeal from there. Again she went to the girl, but
she still refused. As Mrs. Robinson turned to go she saw
her borrow a pencil from her escort and write something
in the back of a hymn book.

A few years afterward Mrs. Robinson went back to the town and was told the girl was dying. They told her the physicians had just held a consultation and said she could not live until night. Mrs. Robinson hurried to her home. The girl looked up, recognized her and said: "I didn't send for you. You came on your own account, and you're too late." To every appeal she would reply: "You're too late." Finally she said: "Go look in the hymn book in the church."

They hurried to the church and looked over the hymn books and found in the back of one her name and address and these words, "I'll run the risk; I'll take my chance." That was the last call to her. Not any one sin is the unpardonable sin, but it may be that constant repetition, over and over again until God will say: "Take it and go to hell."

Who can commit it? I used to think that only the vile, the profane were the people who could commit it.

Whom did Jesus warn? The Pharisees. And who were they? The best men, morally, in Jerusalem.

Who can commit it? Any man or woman who says "No" to Jesus Christ. You may even defend the Bible. You may be the best man or woman, morally, in the world. Your name may be synonymous with virtue and purity, but let God try to get into your heart, let him try to get you to walk down the aisle and publicly acknowledge Jesus Christ, and your heart and lips are sealed like a bank vault, and God hasn't been able to pull you to your feet. And God won't keep on begging you to do it.

Something may say to you, "I ought to be a Christian." This is the dispensation of the Holy Spirit. God spoke in three dispensations. First, through the old Mosaic law. Then Jesus Christ came upon this earth and lived and the Jews and Gentiles conspired to kill him. Then the Holy Spirit came down at Pentecost and God is speaking through the Holy Spirit today. The Holy Spirit is pressing you to be a Christian. It takes the combined efforts of the Trinity to keep you out of hell—God the Father to provide the plan of salvation, the Holy Spirit to convict, Jesus Christ to redeem you through his blood, and your acceptance and repentance to save you. Sin is no trifle.

Representative of the Trinity

The only representative of the Trinity in the world today is the Holy Ghost. Jesus has been here, but he is not here now—that is, in flesh and blood. The Holy Ghost is here now. When he leaves the world, good-bye.

There was an old saint of God, now in glory. He was holding meetings one time and a young man came down the aisle and went so far as to ask him to pray for him. He said: "Let's settle it now," but the young man refused and told him to pray for him. Years afterwards, in Philadelphia, the old saint was in a hotel waiting for his card to be taken up to the man he wanted to see. He looked in the bar-room door. There was a young man ordering a drink. The two saw each other's reflections in the French plate behind the bar, and the young man came out and said: "How do you do?" The old man spoke to him.

The young fellow said: "I suppose you don't remember me?" and the old saint had to admit that he did not

The young fellow asked him if he remembered the meeting eleven years before in New York when a young man came down the aisle and asked him to pray for him. He said he was the young man. The old saint said: "From what I have just seen I would suppose that you did not settle it."

The young fellow said: "I did not and I never expect to. I believe there is a hell and I'm going there as fast as I can go."

The old man begged him to keep still, but he said: "It is true. If Jesus Christ would come through that door now I would spit in his face."

The old man said: "Don't talk that way. I would not stand to have you talk about my wife that way, and I will not stand it to have you talk about Christ that way." The young fellow said it was all true. The old fellow said: "Maybe it is all true, but I do not like to hear it." The young fellow said it was true, and that if he had a Bible he would tear it up. With a string of oaths he went to the bar, took two or three drinks and went out the door.

Sometimes it may be utter, absolute indifference. Some can hear any sermon and any song and not be moved. I'll venture that some of you have not been convicted of sin for twenty-five years. Back yonder the Spirit of God convicted you and you didn't yield. The first place I ever preached, in the little town of Garner, in Hancock county, Iowa, a man came down the aisle. I said, "Who's that?" and someone told me that he was one of the richest men in the county. I asked him what I had said to help him, and he said nothing. Then he told me that twenty-one years ago he had gone to Chicago and sold his stock four hours before he had to catch a train. Moody was in town and with a friend he had gone and stood inside the door, listening to the sermon. When Moody gave the invitation he handed his coat and hat to his friend and said he was going down to give Moody his hand. The friend told him not to do it, that he would miss his train, and then the railroad pass would be no good after that day. He said he could afford to pay his way home.

His friend told him not to go up there amid all the excitement, but to wait and settle it at home. He said he had waited thirty-five years and hadn't settled it at home, but the friend persisted against his going forward and giving his heart to God. Finally the time passed and they had to catch the train and the man hadn't gone forward. He told me that he had never had a desire to give his heart to God until that time, twenty-one years later, when he heard me preach. The Spirit called him when he heard Moody, and then the Spirit did not call him again until twenty-one years later, when he heard me.

I have never said and I never will say that all unbelievers died in agony.   Man ordinarily dies as he has lived.
If you have lived in unbelief, ninety-nine cases out of one
hundred you'll die that way.   If Christianity is a good
thing to die with it is a good thing to live with.

Death-bed Confessions

I don't go much on these death-bed confessions.   A
death-bed confession is like burning a candle at both ends
and then blowing the smoke in the face of Jesus.   A death-
bed confession is like drinking the cup of life and then offering the dregs to Christ.   I think it is one of the most con-
temptible, miserable, low-down, unmanly and unwomanly
things that you can do, to keep your life in your own control until the last moment and then try to creep into the
kingdom on account of the long-suffering and mercy of
Jesus Christ.   I don't say that none is genuine.   But
there is only one on record in the Bible, and that was the
first time the dying thief had ever heard of Christ, and he
accepted at once.   So your case is not analogous to this.
You have wagon loads of sermons dumped into you, but it's
a mighty hard thing to accept in the last moment. If you've
lived without conviction, your friends ought not to get
mad when the preacher preaches your funeral sermon, if
he doesn't put you in the front row in heaven, with a harp
in your hands and a crown on your head.

God can forgive sins but you have got to comply with
his requirements.   He is not willing that any shall perish, but
he has a right to tell me and you what to do to be saved.

A doctor had been a practitioner for sixty years and
he was asked how many Godless men he had seen show
any trace of concern on their death-bed.   He said he had
kept track of three hundred and only three had shown
any real concern.   That is appalling to me.   You ordinarily die as you have lived.

A minister was called to a house of shame to be with
a dying girl in her last moments.   He prayed and then

looked at her face and saw no signs of hope of repentance. He was led to pray again and this time he was led to put in a verse of scripture, Isaiah 1 : 18: "Come now and let us reason together, saith the Lord: Though your sins be as scarlet, they shall be as white as snow; though they be red like crimson, they shall be as wool."

"Is that what the Bible says?" the girl asked. He said it was. "Would you let me see it?" and the minister pointed it out to her.

"Would you pray again and put in that verse?" the girl asked and as he started she called, "Stop! Let me put my finger on that verse." The minister prayed and when he looked again, he saw hope and pardon and peace in the girl's face. "I'm so glad God made that 'scarlet,' " she said, "for that means me."

All manner of sins God will forgive. Then tell me why you will not come when God says, "All manner of sin and blasphemy shall be forgiven unto men." Great heavens! I can't understand how you sit still.

But a man says: "Bill, will He forgive a murderer? My hands are red with blood, although no one knows it." Didn't I say he forgave Paul?

A Forgiving God

A friend of mine was preaching in Lansing, Michigan, one time, and in the middle section of the church there was a man who made him so nervous he couldn't watch him and preach. Nothing seemed to attract him until he said, "Supposing there were a murderer here tonight, God would forgive him if he accepted Christ," and the man grabbed the chair in front of him at the word murderer and sat rigid throughout the sermon, never taking his eyes from my friend. At the end of the meeting my friend went down to him and asked him what was the matter, telling him that he had made him so nervous he could hardly preach. The man said: "I'm a murderer. I escaped through a technicality and I'm supporting the widow and

"Close that Window, Please."

"Break Away from the Old Bunch of the Damned."

SNOWBALLING IN JUNE. BILLY SUNDAY AND PARTY ON PIKE'S PEAK.

children, but I am a murderer." My friend brought him to Jesus Christ and now that man is a power in the Church. All manner of sins God says he will forgive.

Some say: "Mr. Sunday, why is it that so few aged sinners are converts?"

Infidels when asked this, seize upon it as a plan of attack. When God begins to show his power, then the devil and all of the demons of hell get busy. That's the best evidence in the world that these meetings are doing good, when that bunch of knockers gets busy. Infidels sneer and say: "How does it happen that when a man's mind has developed through age and experience and contact with the world, and he has passed the period of youthful enthusiasm,' how does it happen that so few of them are converted?"

Religion makes its appeal to your sensibility, not to your intellect. The way into the kingdom of heaven is heart first, not head first. God is not an explanation; God is a revelation.

A grain of corn is a revelation, but you can't explain it. You know that if you put the vegetable kingdom in the mineral kingdom the vegetable will be born again, but you can't explain it. Some of the greatest things are revelations. Therefore, instead of being an argument against religion, it is an argument for it.

Don't you know that sixteen out of twenty who are converted are converted before they are twenty years old? Don't you know that eighteen out of thirty who are converted are converted before they are thirty years old? Don't you know that?

What does that prove? It proves that if you are not converted before you are thirty years old the chances are about 100,000 to one that you never will be converted.

Power of Revivals

Most people are converted at special revival services. I want to hurl this in the teeth, cram it down the throats of those who sneer at revival efforts—preachers included. Almost nine-tenths of the Christians at this meeting were converted at a revival. What does that show? It shows that if you are thirty and have not been converted, the chances are that if you are not converted at this revival you never will be converted.

If it weren't for revivals, just think of what hell would be like. Then think of any low-down, God-forsaken, dirty gang knocking a revival.

God says: "You can spurn my love and trample the blood under your feet, but if you seek my pardon I will forgive you." You might have been indifferent to the appeals of the minister, you might have been a thief, or an adulterer, or a blasphemer, or a scoffer, and all that, but God says: "I will forgive you." You might have been indifferent to the tears of poor wife and children and friends, but if you will seek God he will forgive you.

But when He came down and revealed himself as the Son of God through the Holy Spirit, if you sneer and say it is not true, your sin may become unpardonable. If you don't settle it here you never will settle it anywhere else.

I will close with a word of comfort and a word of warning. If you have a desire to be a Christian it is proof that the devil hasn't got you yet. That is the comfort. Now for the warning: If you have that desire thank God for it and yield to it. You may never have another chance.

CHAPTER XXX

Eternity! Eternity!

I tell you a lot of people are going to be fooled on the Day of Judgment.
—BILLY SUNDAY.

ONLY a man to whom has been given eloquence and a dramatic instinct can drive home to the average mind the realities of eternity and its relation to right living in this world and time. Under the title "What Shall the End Be?" Sunday has widely circulated his message upon this theme:

"WHAT SHALL THE END BE?"

No book ever came by luck or chance. Every book owes its existence to some being or beings, and within the range and scope of human intelligence there are but three things—good, bad and God. All that originates in intellect; all which the intellect can comprehend, must come from one of the three. This book, the Bible, could not possibly be the product of evil, wicked, godless, corrupt, vile men, for it pronounces the heaviest penalties against sin. Like produces like, and if bad men were writing the Bible they never would have pronounced condemnation and punishment against wrong-doing. So that is pushed aside.

The holy men of old, we are told, spake as they were moved by the Holy Ghost. Men do not attribute these beautiful and matchless and well-arranged sentences to human intelligence alone, but we are told that men spake as they were inspired by the Holy Ghost.

The only being left, to whom you, or I or any sensible person could ascribe the origin of the Bible, is God, for here is a book, the excellence of which rises above other books, like mountains above molehills—a book whose brilliancy and life-giving power exceed the accumulated knowledge and combined efforts of men, as the sun exceeds the lamp, which is but a base imitation of the sun's glory. Here is a book that tells me where I came from and where I am going, a book without which I would not know of my origin or destiny, except as I might glean it from the dim outlines of reason or nature, either or both of which would be unsatisfactory to me. Here is a book that tells me what to do and what not to do.

Men Believe in God

Most men believe in God. Now and then you find a man who doesn't, and he's a fool, for "The fool hath said in his heart, there is no God." Most men have sense. Occasionally you will find a fool, or an infidel, who doesn't believe in God. Most men believe in a God that will reward the right and punish the wrong; therefore it is clear what attitude you ought to assume toward my message tonight, for the message I bring to you is not from human reason or intelligence, but from God's Book.

"What shall the end be of them that obey not the gospel of God?" Now listen, and I will try to help you. Israel's condition was desperate. Peter told them that if they continued to break God's law, they would merit his wrath. I can imagine him crying out in the words of Jeremiah: "What will you do in the swelling of the Jordan?" I hear him cry in the words of Solomon: "The way of the transgressor is hard." That seems to have moved him, and I can hear him cry in the words of my text: "What shall the end be of them that obey not the gospel of God?"

There are those who did obey. Peter knew what their end would be—blessings here and eternal life hereafter—but he said, "What shall the end be of them that obey not?"

A man said, "I cannot be a Christian. I cannot obey God." That is not true. That would make God out a demon and a wretch. God says if you are not a Christian you will be doomed. If God asked mankind to do something, and he knew when he asked them that they could

not do it, and he told them he would damn them if they
didn't do it, it would make God out a demon and a wretch,
and I will not allow you or any other man to stand up and
insult my God.   You can be a Christian if you want to,
and it is your cussedness that you are unwilling to give up
that keeps you away from God.

Supposing I should go on top of a building and say to my
little baby boy, "Fly up to me."   If he could talk, he would
say, "I can't."   And supposing I would say, "But you can;
if you don't, I'll whip you to death."   When I asked him to
do it, I knew he couldn't, yet I told him I would whip him to
death if he didn't, and in saying that I would, as an earthly
father, be just as reasonable as God would be if he should
ask you to do something you couldn't do, and though he
knew when he asked you that you couldn't do it, nevertheless would damn you if you didn't do it.

Don't tell God you can't.   Just say you don't want to be
a Christian, that's the way to be a man.   Just say, "I don't
want to be decent; I don't want to quit cussing; I don't
want to quit booze-fighting; I don't want to quit lying; I
don't want to quit committing adultery.   If I should be a
Christian I would have to quit all these things, and I don't
want to do it."   Tell God you are not man enough to be a
Christian.   Don't try to saddle it off on the Lord.   You
don't want to do it, that's all; that's the trouble with you.

At the Cross

A man in a town in Ohio came and handed one of the
ministers a letter, and he said, "I want you to read that
when you get home."   When the minister got home he
opened it and it read like this:

"I was at the meeting last night, and somehow or other,
the words 'What shall the end be?' got hold of me, and
troubled me.   I went to bed, but couldn't sleep.   I got up
and went to my library.   I took down my books on infidelity
and searched them through and searched through the writ-
ings of Voltaire, and Darwin, and Spencer, and Strauss, and

25

Huxley, and Tyndall, and through the lectures of Ingersoll, but none of them could answer the cry and longing of my heart, and I turn to you. Is there help? Where will I find it?" And that man found it where every man ever has, or ever will find it, down at the Cross of Jesus Christ, and I have been praying God that might be the experience of many a man and woman in this Tabernacle.

Ever since God saved my soul and sent me out to preach, I have prayed him to enable me to pronounce two words, and put into those words all they will mean to you; if they ever become a reality, God pity you. One word is "Lost," and the other is "Eternity."

Ten thousand years from now we will all be somewhere. Ten thousand times ten thousand times ten thousand years, the eternity has just begun. Increase the multiple and you will only increase the truth. If God should commission a bird to carry this earth, particle by particle, to yonder planet, making a round trip once in a thousand years, and if, after the bird had performed that task God should prolong its life, and it would carry the world back, particle by particle, making a round trip once in a thousand years, and put everything back as it was originally, after it had accomplished its task, you would have been five minutes in eternity; and yet you sit there with just a heart-beat between you and the judgment of God. I have been praying that God would enable me to pronounce those two words and put in them all they will mean to you, that I might startle you from your lethargy. I prayed God, too, that he might give me some new figure of speech tonight, that he might impress my mind, that I, in turn, might impress your mind in such a manner that I could startle you from your indifference and sin, until you would rush to Jesus.

The Judgment of God

What is your life? A hand's breadth—yes, a hair's breadth—yes, one single heart-beat, and you are gone, and yet you sit with the judgment of God hovering over you. "What shall the end be?"

I never met any man or woman in my life who disbelieved in Christianity but could not be classified under one of these two headings.

First—They who, because of an utter disregard of God's claims upon their lives, have, by and through that disregard, become poltroons, marplots or degenerate scoundrels, and have thrown themselves beyond the pale of God's mercy.

Second—Men and women with splendid, noble and magnificent abilities, which they have allowed to become absorbed in other matters, and they do not give to the subjects of religion so much as passing attention. They have the audacity to claim for themselves an intellectual superiority to those who believe the Bible, which they sneeringly term ' that superstition." But, listen! I will challenge you. If you will bring to religion or to the divinity of Jesus, or the salvation of your soul, the same honest inquiry you demand of yourself in other matters, you will know God is God; you will know the Bible is the Word of God, and you will know that Jesus Christ is the Son of God. You will know that you are a sinner on the road to hell, and you will turn from your sins. But you don't give to religion, you don't demand of yourself, the same amount of research that you would demand of yourself if you were going to buy a piece of property, to find out whether or not the title was perfect. You wouldn't buy it if you didn't know the title was without a flaw, and yet you will pass the Bible by and claim you have more sense than the person who does investigate and finds out, accepts and is saved.

Glad Tidings to All

What is the Gospel that the people ought to obey it? It is good news, glad tidings of salvation, through Jesus Christ.

Oh, but somebody says, do you call the news of that book that I am on the road to hell, good news? No, sir; that in itself is not good news, but since it is the truth, the sooner you find out the better it will be for you.

Supposing you are wandering, lost in a swamp, and a man would come to you and say: "You are lost." That wouldn't help you. But supposing the man said: "You are lost; I am a guide; I know the way out. If you put yourself in my care, I will lead you back to your home, back to your loved ones. " That would meet your condition.

Now God doesn't tell you that you are lost, and on the road to hell, and then leave you, but he tells you that you are on the road to hell, and he says, "I have sent a guide, my Son, to lead you out, and to lead you back to peace and salvation." That's good news, that God is kind enough to tell you that you are lost, and on the road to hell, and that he sends a guide, who, if you will submit, will lead you out of your condition and lead you to peace and salvation. That's gospel; that's good news that tells a man that he needn't go to hell unless he wants to.

When the Israelites were bitten by the serpents in the wilderness, wasn't if good news for them to know that Moses had raised up a brazen serpent and bid them all to look and be healed?

When the flood came, wasn't it good news for Noah to know that he would be saved in the ark?

When the city of Jericho was going to fall, wasn't it good news to Rahab. She had been kind and had hid two of God's servants who were being pursued as spies. They were running across the housetops to get away to the wall to drop down, and Rahab covered them, on top of her house, with grass and corn, and when the men came they could not find them. After the men had gone, Rahab gave them cord and lowered them down the wall, and God said to her, "Because you did that for my servants, I will save you and your household when I take the city of Jericho. What I want you to do is to hang a scarlet line out of your window and I will save all that are under your roof." Wasn't it good news to her to know that she and all her household would be saved by hanging a scarlet line out of the window? Never has such news been published. "Thou shalt call his name

Jesus, for he shall save his people from their sins." It was good news, but never has such news reached the world as that man need not go to hell, for God has provided redemption for them that will accept of it and be saved.

Supposing a man owed you $5,000 and he had nothing to pay it with. You would seize him and put him in jail, and supposing while there, your own son would come and say: "Father, how much does he owe you?" "Five thousand dollars." And your son would pay it and the man would be released.

Ah, my friends, hear me! We were all mortgaged to God, had nothing with which to pay, and inflexible justice seized upon us and put us in the prison of condemnation. God took pity on us. He looked around to find some one to pay our debts. Jesus Christ stepped forward and said: "I'll go; I'll become bone of their bone and flesh of their flesh." God gave man the Mosaic law. Man broke the law.

If a Jew violated the law he was compelled to bring a turtle dove, or pigeon, or heifer, or bullock to the high priest for a sacrifice, and the shedding of its blood made atonement for his sins. Once a year the high priest would kill the sacrifice, putting it on the altar. That made atonement for the sins of the people during the year. Then they would put their hand on the head of the scape-goat, and lead it out into the wilderness.

The Atonement of Christ

Jesus Christ came into the world, born of a woman. When he shed his blood, he made atonement for our sins. God says, "If you will accept Jesus Christ as your Saviour, I will put it to your credit as though you kept the law." And it's Jesus Christ or hell for every man or woman on God Almighty's dirt. There is no other way whereby you can be saved. It's good news that you don't have to go to hell, unless you want to.

When the North German Lloyd steamer, the *Elbe*, went

down in the North Sea, years and years ago, only nineteen of her passengers and crew were saved. Among them was a county commissioner who lived in Cleveland, Ohio, and when he reached the little English town he sent a cablegram to his wife, in which he said, "The *Elbe* is lost; I am saved." She crumpled that cablegram, ran down the street to her neighbors, and as she ran she waved it above her head and cried, "He's saved! He's saved!" That cablegram is framed, and hangs upon the walls of their beautiful Euclid Avenue home. It was good news to her that he whom she loved was saved.

Good news I bring you. Good news I bring you, people. You need not go to hell if you will accept the Christ that I preach to you.

"What shall the end be of them that obey not the gospel?" And the gospel of God is, "Repent or you will go to hell." "What shall the end be of them that obey not the gospel?" What is the gospel, and what is it to obey the gospel? We have seen that it is good news; now what is it to obey? What was it for Israel to obey? Look at the brazen serpent on the pole. What was it for Noah to obey? Build the ark and get into it. What was it for Rahab to obey? Hang a scarlet line out of the window, and God would pass her by when he took the city of Jericho. All that was obeying. It was believing God's message and obeying.

Ah! I see a man. He walks to the banks of the Seine, in Paris, to end his life. He walked to the bank four times, but he didn't plunge in. He filled a cup with poison, three times raised it to his lips, but he did not drink. He cocked the pistol, put it against his temple. He did that twice, but he didn't pull the trigger. He heard the story of Jesus Christ and dropped on his knees, and William Cowper wrote:

> "God moves in a mysterious way,
>   His wonders to perform;
> He plants his footsteps in the sea,
>   And rides upon the storm.

"There is a fountain filled with blood,
Drawn from Immanuel's veins;
And sinners plunged beneath that flood,
Lose all their guilty strains."

So that's what you found, is it, Cowper?

I go to Bridgeport, Connecticut. I rap at a humble home and walk into the presence of Fanny J. Crosby, the blind hymn-writer. She has written over six thousand hymns. She never saw the light of day, was born blind, and I say to her, "Oh, Miss Crosby, tell me that I may tell the people what you have found by trusting in the finished work of Jesus Christ? You have sat in darkness for ninety-four years; tell me, Miss Crosby." And that face lights up like a halo of glory; those sightless eyes flash, and she cries:

"Blessed assurance, Jesus is mine;
Oh, what a foretaste of glory divine!"

"Pass me not, O gentle Saviour,
Hear my humble cry!"

"Jesus keep me near the cross,
There's a precious fountain."

"Once I was blind, but now I can see,
The light of the world is Jesus."

"And I shall see Him, face to face,
And tell the story, Saved by Grace."

I go to Wesley as he walks along the banks of a stream, while the storm raged, the lightning flashed and the thunder roared. The birds were driven, in fright, from their refuge in the boughs of the trees. A little bird took refuge in his coat. Wesley held it tenderly, walked home, put it in a cage, kept it until morning, carried it out, opened the door and watched it as it circled around and shot off for its mountain home. He returned to his house and wrote:

"Jesus, lover of my soul,
Let me to thy bosom fly."

What have you found by trusting in the finished work of Jesus Christ?

God's Word

It is said of Napoleon that one day he was riding in review before his troops, when the horse upon which he sat became unmanageable, seized the bit in his teeth, dashed down the road and the life of the famous warrior was in danger. A private, at the risk of his life, leaped out and seized the runaway horse, while Napoleon, out of gratitude, raised in the stirrups, saluted and said, "Thank you, captain." The man said, "Captain of what, sir?" "Captain of my Life Guards, sir," said he.

The man stepped over to where the Life Guards were in consultation and they ordered him back into the ranks.

"CAPTAIN OF MY LIFE GUARDS, SIR"

He refused to go and issued orders to the officer by saying, "I am Captain of the Guards." Thinking him insane, they ordered his arrest and were dragging him away, when Napoleon rode up and the man said, "I am Captain of the Guards because the Emperor said so." And Napoleon arose and said, "Yes, Captain of my Life Guards. Loose him, sir; loose him."

I am a Christian because God says so, and I did what he told me to do, and I stand on God's Word and if that book goes down, I'll go down with it. If God goes down, I'll go with him, and if there were any other kind of God, except that God, I would have been shipwrecked long ago. Twenty-seven years ago in Chicago I piled all I had, my reputation, my character, my wife, children, home; I staked my soul, everything I had, on the God of that Bible, and the Christ of that Bible, and I won.

"What shall the end be of them that obey not the gospel of God?" Hear me! There are three incomprehensibilities to me. Don't think there are only three things I don't know, or don't you think that I think there are only three things I don't know. I say, there are three things that I cannot comprehend.

Eternity and Space

First—Eternity; that something away off yonder, somewhere. You will think it will end. It leads on, on, on and on. I can take a billion, I can subtract a million; I can take a million or a billion, or a quadrillion, or a septillion of years from eternity, and I haven't as much as disturbed its original terms. Minds trained to deal with intricate problems will go reeling back in their utter inability to comprehend eternity.

And there is space. When you go out tonight, look up at the moon, 240,000 miles away. Walking forty miles a day, I could reach the moon in seventeen years, but the moon is one of our near neighbors. Ah, you saw the sun today, 92,900,000 miles away. I couldn't walk to the sun. If I could charter a fast train, going fifty miles an hour, it would take the train two hundred and fifteen years to reach the sun.

In the early morn you will see a star, near the sun—Mercury—91,000,000 miles away; travels around the sun once in eighty-eight days, going at the speed of 110,000 miles an hour, as it swings in its orbit.

Next is Venus; she is beautiful; 160,000,000 miles away, travels around the sun once in 224 days, going at the rate of 79,000 miles an hour, as she swings in her orbit.

Then comes the earth, the planet upon which we live, and as you sit there, this old earth travels around the sun once in 365 days, or one calendar year, going at the speed of 68,000 miles an hour, and as you sit there and I stand here, this old planet is swinging in her orbit 68,000 miles an hour, and she is whirling on her axis nineteen miles a second. By force of gravity we are held from falling into illimitable space.

Yonder is Mars, 260,000,000 miles away. Travels around the sun once in 687 days, or about two years, going at the speed of 49,000 miles an hour. Who knows but that it is inhabited by a race unsullied by sin, untouched by death?

Yonder another, old Jupiter, champion of the skies, sashed and belted around with vapors of light. Jupiter, 480,000,000 miles away, travels around the sun once in twelve years, going at the speed of 30,000 miles an hour. I need something faster than an express train, going fifty miles an hour, or a cyclone, going one hundred miles an hour. If I could charter a Pullman palace car and couple it to a ray of light, which travels at the speed of 192,000 miles a second—if I could attach my Pullman palace car to a ray of light, I could go to Jupiter and get back tomorrow morning for breakfast at nine o'clock, but Jupiter is one of our near neighbors.

Yonder is old Saturn, 885,000,000 miles away. Travels around the sun once in twenty years, going at the speed of 21,000 miles an hour.

Away yonder, I catch a faint glimmer of another stupendous world, as it swings in its tireless and prodigious journey. Old Uranus, 1,780,000,000 miles away. Travels around the sun once in eighty-four years, going at the speed of two hundred and fifty miles an hour.

As the distance of the planets from the sun increases, their velocity in their orbit correspondingly decreases.

I say is that all? I hurry to Chicago and take the Northwestern. I rush out to Lake Geneva, Wisconsin, I climb into the Yerkes observatory, and I turn the most ponderous telescope in the world to the skies, and away out on the frontier of the universe, on the very outer rim of the world, I catch a faint glimmer of Neptune, 2,790,000,000 miles away. Travels around the sun once in one hundred and sixty-four years, going at the speed of two hundred and ten miles an hour. If I could step on the deck of a battleship and aim a 13-inch gun, and that projectile will travel 1,500 miles in a minute, it would take it three hundred and sixty years to reach that planet.

Away out yonder is Alpha Centauri. If I would attach my palace car to a ray of light and go at the speed of 192,000 miles a second, it would take me three years to reach that planet. An express train, going thirty miles an hour, would be 80,000,000 years pulling into Union depot at Alpha Centauri.

Yonder, the Polar or the North star. Traveling at a rate of speed of 192,000 miles a second, it would take me forty-five years to reach that planet. And if I would go to the depot and buy a railroad ticket to the North star, and pay three cents a mile, it would cost me $720,000,000 for railroad fare to go to that planet.

"Oh, God, what is man, that thou art mindful of him?" And the fool, the fool, the fool hath said in his heart, "There is no God." I'm not an infidel, because I am no fool. "The Heavens declare the glory of God and the firmament showeth his handiwork." I don't believe an infidel ever looked through a telescope or studied astronomy.

"What is man, that thou are mindful of him?" These are days when it is "Big man, little God." These are days when it is gigantic "I," and pigmy "God." These are days when it is "Ponderous man, infinitesimal God."

There are 1,400,000 people on earth. You are one of that number, so am I. None of us amount to much. What do you or I amount to out of 1,400,000,000 people? If I could take an auger and bore a hole in the top of the sun, I could pour into the sun 1,400,000,000 worlds the size of the planet upon which we live, and there would be room in the sun for more. Then think of the world, and God made that world, the God that you cuss, the God that wants to keep you out of hell, the God whose Son you have trampled beneath your feet.

If you take 1,400,000,000, multiply it by 1,400,000, multiply that by 1,000,000, multiply that by millions, multiply that by infinity, that's God. If you take 1,400,000,000, subtract 1,400,000, subtract millions, subtract, subtract, subtract, subtract on down, that's you. If ever a man appears like a consummate ass and an idiot, it's when he says he don't believe in a God or tries to tell God his plan of redemption don't appeal to him.

God's Infinite Love

And the third: The third is the love of God to a lost and sin-cursed world and man's indifference to God's love. How he has trampled God's love beneath his feet, I don't understand. I don't understand why you have grown gray-haired, and are not a Christian. I don't understand why you know right from wrong, and still are not a Christian. I don't understand it. Listen! What is it to obey the Gospel? The Gospel is good news, and to obey it is to believe in Jesus. What is it not to obey? What was the end of those who weren't in the ark with Noah? They found a watery grave. What was the end of those who didn't look at the brazen serpent in the wilderness? They died. What was the end of those who were not with Rahab when she hung out the scarlet line? They perished.

When a man starts on a journey he has one object in view—the end. A journey is well, if it ends well. We are all on a journey to eternity. What will be the end? My text doesn't talk about the present. Your present is, or may be, an enviable position in church, club life, or commercial life, lodge, politics; your presence may be sought after to grace every social gathering. God doesn't care about that. What shall the end be? When all that is gone, when pleasures pass away, and sorrow and weeping and wailing take their place, what shall the end be?

Some people deny that their suffering in the other world will be eternal fire. Do you think your scoffs can extinguish the flames of hell? Do you think you can annihilate hell because you don't believe in it? We have a few people who say, "Matter is non-existent," but that doesn't do away with the fact that matter is existent, just because we have some people who haven't sense enough to see it. You say, "I don't believe there is a hell." Well, there is, whether you believe it or not. You say, "I don't believe Jesus Christ is the Son of God." Well, he is, whether you believe it or not. Some people say, "I don't believe there is a heaven." There is, whether you believe it or not. You say, "I don't believe the Bible is the Word of God." Well, it is, and your disbelief does not change the fact, and the sooner you wake up to that the better for you. I might say that I don't believe George Washington ever lived. I never saw him, but it wouldn't do away with the fact that he did live, and George Washington lies buried on the banks of the Potomac. You say you don't believe there is a hell, but that doesn't do away with the fact that there is a hell.

What difference does it make whether the fire in hell is literal, or the fittest emblem God could employ to describe to us the terrible punishment? Do you believe the streets of heaven are paved with literal gold? Do you believe that? When we talk about gold we all have high and exalted ideas. How do you know but that God said "streets of gold" in order to convey to us the highest ideal our minds could conceive of beauty? It doesn't make any difference whether the gold on the streets in heaven is literal or not. What difference does it make whether the fire in hell is literal or not? When we talk about fire everybody shrinks from it. Suppose God used that term as figurative to convey to you the terror of hell. You are a fool to test the reality of it. It must be an awful place if God loved us well enough to give Jesus to keep us out of there. I don't want to go there.

Preparing for Eternity

I said to a fellow one time, "Don't you think that possibly there is a hell?"

He said, "Well, yes, possibly there may be a hell."

I said, "It's pretty good sense, then, to get ready for the maybe." Well, just suppose there is a hell. It's good sense to get ready, them, even for the "maybe." I don't look like a man that would die very quickly, do I? I have just as good a physique as you ever gazed at. I wouldn't trade with any man I know. A lot of you fellows are stronger than I, but I have as good a physique as ever you looked at. I have been preaching at this pace for fourteen years, and I've stood it, although I begin to feel myself failing a little bit. But I don't look like a man who would die quickly, do I? But I may die, and on that possibility I carry thousands of dollars of life insurance. I don't believe that any man does right to himself, his wife or his children if he doesn't provide for them with life insurance, so when he is gone they will not be thrown upon the charity of the world. And next to my faith, if I should die tonight, that which would give me the most comfort would be the knowledge that I have in a safe deposit vault in Chicago life insurance papers, paid up to date, and my wife could cash in and she and the babies could listen to the wolves howl for a good many years. I don't expect to die soon, but I may die, and on that "may" I carry thousands of dollars in life insurance.

I take a train to go home, I don't expect the train to be wrecked, but it may be wrecked, and on that "maybe" I carry $10,000 a year in an accident policy. It may go in the ditch. That's good sense to get ready for the "maybe." Are you a business man? Do you carry insurance on your stock? Yes. On the building? Yes. Do you expect it to burn? No, sir. But it may burn, so you are ready for it. Every ship is compelled, by law, to carry life-preservers and life-boats equal to the passenger capacity. They don't expect the ship to sink, but it may sink and they are ready for the "may." All right. There may be a hell. I'm ready;

where do you get off at? I have you beat any way you can look at it.

Suppose there is no hell? Suppose that when we die that ends it? I don't believe it does. I believe there is a hell and I believe there is a heaven, and just the kind of a heaven and hell that book says. But suppose there is no hell? Suppose death is eternal sleep? I believe the Bible; I believe its teachings; I have the best of you in this life. I will live longer, be happier, and have lost nothing by believing and obeying the Bible, even if there is no hell. But suppose there is a hell? Then I'm saved and you are the fool. I have you beat again.

"What shall the end be of them that obey not the gospel of God." What will some do? Some will be stoical, some will whimper, some will turn for human sympathy. Let God answer the question. You would quarrel with me. "A lake of fire" and "a furnace of fire." "In hell he lifted up his eyes, being in torment." "Eternal damnation." "The smoke of their torment ascendeth forever and ever." Let God answer the question. "What shall be the end of them that obey not the gospel of God"? Will you say, "God, I didn't have time enough"? "Behold! Now is the accepted time." Will you say, "God, I had no light?" But "light is come into the world, and men love darkness rather than light."

I stand on the shores of eternity and cry out, "Eternity! Eternity! How long, how long art thou?" Back comes the answer, "How long?"

"How long sometimes a day appears and weeks, how long are they?
They move as if the months and years would never pass away;
But months and years are passing by, and soon must all be gone,
Day by day, as the moments fly, eternity comes on.
All these must have an end; eternity has none,
It will always have as long to run as when it first begun."

"What shall be the end of them that obey not the Gospel of God?"

When Voltaire, the famous infidel, lay dying, he summoned the physician and said, "Doctor, I will give you all I have to save my life six months."

The doctor said, "You can't live six hours."

Then said Voltaire, "I'll go to hell and you'll go with me."

A Leap in the Dark

Hobbes, the famous English infidel, said: "I am taking a leap into the night."

When King Charles IX, who gave the order for the massacre of St. Bartholomew's day, when blood ran like water and 130,000 fell dead, when King Charles lay dying, he cried out, "O God, how will it end? Blood, blood, rivers of blood. I am lost!" And with a shriek he leaped into hell.

King Philip of Spain said; "I wish to God I had never lived," and then in a sober thought he said: "Yes, I wish I had, but that I had lived in the fear and love of God."

Wesley said, "I shall be satisfied when I awake in His likeness."

Florence A. Foster said, "Mother, the hilltops are covered with angels; they beckon me homeward; I bid you good-bye."

Frances E. Willard cried, "How beautiful to die and be with God."

Moody cried: "Earth recedes, heaven opens, God is calling me. This is to be my coronation day."

Going to the World's Fair in Chicago, a special train on the Grand Trunk, going forty miles an hour, dashed around a curve at Battle Creek, and headed in on a sidetrack where a freight train stood. The rear brakeman had forgotten to close the switch and the train rounded the curve, dashed into the open switch and struck the freight train loaded with iron, and there was an awful wreck. The cars telescoped and the flames rushed out. Pinioned in the wreck, with steel girders bent around her, was a woman who lived in New York. Her name was Mrs. Van Dusen. She removed her diamond ear-rings, took her gold watch and chain from about her neck, slipped her rings from her fingers and handing out her purse gave her husband's address, and then said: "Gentlemen, stand back! I am a Christian and I will die like a Christian."

They leaped to their task. They tore like demons to liberate her and she started to sing,

> "My heavenly home is bright and fair.
> I'm going to die no more." ∕

Strong men, who had looked into the cannon's mouth, fainted. She cried out, above the roar of the wind and the shrieks of the dying men, "Oh, men, don't imperil your lives for me. I am a Christian and I will die like a Christian! Stand back, men," and then she began to sing, "Nearer, My God, to Thee."

" The End Thereof "

"There is a way that seemeth right unto man, but the end thereof are the ways of death." Moses may have made some mistakes, but I want to tell you Moses never made a mistake when he wrote these words: "Their rock is not as our Rock, even our enemies themselves being the judges." He never made a mistake when he wrote these words. I say to you, you are going to live on and on until the constellations of the heavens are snuffed out. You are going to live on and on until the rocks crumble into dust through age. You are going to live on and on and on, until the mountain peaks are incinerated and blown by the breath of God to the four corners of infinity. "What shall the end be?" Listen! Listen!

I used to live in Pennsylvania, and of the many wonderful things for which this wonderful state has been noted, not the least is the fact that most always she has had godly men for governors, and one of the most magnificent examples of godly piety that ever honored this state was Governor

26

Pollock. When he was governor, a young man, in a drunken brawl, shot a companion. He was tried and sentenced to be executed. They circulated a petition, brought it to Harrisburg to the governor, and the committee that waited upon the governor, among them some of his own friends, pleaded with him to commute the sentence to life imprisoment. Governor Pollock listened to their pleadings and said, "Gentlemen, I can't do it. The law must take its course." Then the ministers—Catholic and Protestant—brought a petition, and among the committee was the governor's own pastor. He approached him in earnestness, put a hand on either shoulder, begged, prayed to God to give him wisdom to grant the request. Governor Pollock listened to their petition, tears streamed down his cheeks and he said, "Gentlemen, I can't do it. I can't; I can't."

At last the boy's mother came. Her eyes were red, her cheeks sunken, her lips ashen, her hair disheveled, her clothing unkempt, her body tottering from the loss of food and sleep. Broken-hearted, she reeled, staggered and dragged herself into the presence of the governor. She pleaded for her boy. She said, "Oh, governor, let me die. Oh, governor, let him go; let me behind the bars. Oh, governor, I beg of you to let my boy go; don't, don't hang him!" And Governor Pollock listened. She staggered to his side, put her arms around him. He took her arms from his shoulder, held her at arms' length, looked into her face and said to her: "Mother, mother, I can't do it, I can't," and he ran from her presence. She screamed and fell to the floor and they carried her out.

Governor Pollock said to his secretary, "John, if I can't pardon him I can tell him how to die." He went to the cell, opened God's Word, prayed, talked of Jesus. Heaven bent near, the angels waited, and then on lightning wing sped back to glory with the glad tidings that a soul was born again. And the governor left, wishing him well for the ordeal. Shortly after he had gone, the prisoner said to the watchman, "Who was that man that talked and prayed with me?" He said, "Great God, man, don't you know? That was Governor Pollock." He threw his hands to his head and cried: "My God! My God! The governor here and I didn't know it? Why didn't you tell me that was the governor and I would have thrown my arms about him, buried my fingers in his flesh and would have said, 'Governor, I'll not let you go unless you pardon me; I'll not let you go.'" A few days later, when he stood at the scaffold, feet strapped, hands tied, noose about his neck, black cap and shroud on, just before the trap was sprung he cried, "My God! The governor there and I —" He shot down.

You can't stand before God in the Judgment and say, "Jesus, were you down there in the tabernacle? In my home? In my lodge? Did you want to save me?" Behold! Behold! A greater than the governor is here. Jesus Christ, the Son of God, and he waits to be gracious.

"What shall the end be of them that obey not the gospel of God?"

CHAPTER XXXI

Our Long Home

Don't let God hang a "For Rent" sign on the mansion that has been prepared for you in heaven.—BILLY SUNDAY.

VIVID, literal and comforting, is Sunday's portrayal of the Christian's long home. He is one of the few preachers who depict heaven so that it ministers to earth. Countless thousands of Christians have been comforted by his realistic pictures of "the land that is fairer than day."

"HEAVEN"

What do I want most of all? A man in Chicago said to me one day, "If I could have all I wanted of any one thing I would take money." He would be a fool, and so would you if you would make a similar choice. There's lots of things money can't do. Money can't buy life; money can't buy health. Andrew Carnegie says, "Anyone who can assure men ten years of life can name his price."

If you should meet with an accident which would require a surgical operation or your life would be despaired of, there is not a man here but would gladly part with all the money he has if that would give him the assurance that he could live twelve months longer.

If you had all the money in the world you couldn't go to the graveyard and put those loved ones back in your arms and have them sit once more in the family circle and hear their voices and listen to their prattle.

A steamer tied up at her wharf, having just returned from an expedition, and as the people walked down the plank their friends met them to congratulate them on their success or encourage them through their defeat. Down came a man I used to know in Fargo, S. D. Friends rushed up and said, "Why, we hear that you were very fortunate."

"Yes, wife and I left here six months ago with hardly anything. Now we have $350,000 in gold dust in the hold of the ship."

Then somebody looked around and said, "Mr. L——, where is your little boy?"

The tears rolled down his cheeks and he said, "We left him buried on the banks of the Yukon beneath the snow and ice, and we would gladly part with all the gold, if we only had our boy."

But all the wealth of the Klondike could not open the grave and put that child back in their arms. Money can't buy the peace of God that passeth understanding. Money can't take the sin out of your life.

Is there any particular kind of life you would like? If you could live one hundred years you wouldn't want to die, would you? I wouldn't. I think there is always something the matter with a fellow that wants to die. I want to stay as long as God will let me stay, but when God's time comes for me to go I'm ready, any hour of the day or night. God can waken me at midnight or in the morning and I'm ready to respond. But if I could live a million years I'd like to stay. I don't want to die. I'm having a good time. God made this world for us to have a good time in. It's nothing but sin that has damned the world and brought it to misery and corruption. God wants you to have a good time. Well, then, how can I get this life that you want and everybody wants, eternal life?

If you are ill the most natural thing for you to do is to go for your doctor. You say, "I don't want to die. Can you help me?"

He looks at you and says, "I have a hundred patients on my hands, all asking the same thing. Not one of them wants to die. They ask me to use my skill and bring to bear all I have learned, but I can't fight back death. I can prescribe for your malady, but I can't prevent death."

"I, Too, Must Die"

Well, go to your philosopher. He it is that reasons out the problems and mysteries of life by the application of reason. Say to him, "Good philosopher, I have come to you for help. I want to live forever and you say that you have the touch-stone of philosophy and that you can describe and solve. Can you help me?"

He says to you, "Young man, my hair and my beard have grown longer and as white as snow, my eyes are dim, my brows are wrinkled, my form bent with the weight of years, my bones are brittle and I am just as far from the solution of that mystery and problem as when I started. I, too, sir, must soon die and sleep beneath the sod."

In my imagination I have stood by the bedside of the dying Pullman-palace-car magnate, George M. Pullman, whose will was probated at $25,000,000, and I have said, "Oh, Mr. Pullman, you will not die, you can bribe death." And I see the pupils of his eyes dilate, his breast heaves, he gasps—and is no more. The undertaker comes and makes an incision in his left arm, pumps in the embalming fluid, beneath whose mysterious power he turns as rigid as ice, and as white as alabaster, and they put his embalmed body in the rosewood coffin, trimmed with silver and gold, and then they put that in a hermetically sealed casket.

The grave-diggers go to Graceland Cemetery, on the shore of Lake Michigan, and dig his grave in the old family lot, nine feet wide, and they put in there Portland cement four and a half feet thick, while it is yet soft, pliable and plastic. A set of workmen drop down into the grave a steel cage with steel bars one inch apart. They bring his body, in the hermetically sealed casket all wrapped about with cloth, and they lower it into the steel cage, and a set of workmen put steel bars across the top and another put concrete and a solid wall of masonry and they bring it up within eighteen inches of the surface; they put back the black loamy soil, then they roll back the sod and with a whisk broom and dust pan they sweep up the dirt, and you would never know that there sleeps the Pullman-palace-car magnate, waiting for the trumpet of Gabriel to sound; for the powers of God will snap his steel, cemented sarcophagus as though it were made of a shell and he will stand before God as any other man.

What does your money amount to? What does your wealth amount to?

I summon the three electrical wizards of the world to my bedside and I say, "Gentlemen, I want to live and I have sent for you to come," and they say to me, "Mr. Sunday, we will flash messages across the sea without wires; we can illuminate the homes and streets of your city and drive your trolley cars and we can kill men with electricity, but we can't prolong life."

And I summon the great Queen Elizabeth, queen of an empire upon which the sun never sets. Three thousand dresses hung in her wardrobe. Her jewels were measured by the peck. Dukes, kings, earls fought for her smiles. I stand by her bedside and I hear her cry "All my possessions for one moment of time!"

I go to Alexander the Great, who won his first battle when he was eighteen, and was King of Macedonia when he was twenty. He sat down on the shore of the Ægean sea, wrapped the drapery of his couch about him and lay down to eternal sleep, the conqueror of all the known world, when he was thirty-five years of age.

I go to Napoleon Bonaparte. Victor Hugo called him the archangel of war. He arose in the air of the nineteenth century like a meteor. His sun rose at Austerlitz; it set at Waterloo. He leaped over the slain of his countrymen to be first consul; and then he vaulted to the throne of the emperor of France. But it was the cruel wanton achievement of insatiate and unsanctified ambition and it led to the barren St. Helena isle. As the storm beat upon the rock, once more he fought at the head of his troops at Austerlitz, at Mt. Tabor, and the Pyramids. Once more he cried, "I'm still the head of the army," and he fell back, and the greatest warrior the world has known since the days of Joshua, was no more. Tonight on the banks of the Seine he lies in his magnificent tomb, with his marshals sleeping where he can summon them, and the battle flags he made famous draped around him, and from the four corners of the earth students and travelers turn aside to do homage to the great military genius.

I want to show you the absolute and utter futility of pinning your hope to a lot of fool things that will damn your soul to hell. There is only one way: "As Moses lifted up the serpent in the wilderness, even so must the Son of Man be lifted up, that whosoever believeth in him should not perish, but have eternal life. For God so loved the world that he gave his only begotten Son, that whosoever believeth in him should not perish, but have everlasting life." Search the annals of time and the pages of history and where do you find promises like that? Only upon the pages of the Bible do you find them.

You want to live and so do I. You want eternal life and so do I, and I want you to have it. The next question I want to ask is, how can you get it? You have seen things that won't give it to you. How can you get it? All you have tonight or ever will have you will come into possession of in one of three ways—honestly, dishonestly, or as a gift. Honestly: You will work and sweat and therefore give an honest equivalent for what you get. Dishonestly: You will steal. Third, as a gift, you will inherit it. And eternal life must come to you in one of these three ways.

No Substitute for Religion

A great many people believe in a high moral standard. They deal honestly in business and are charitable, but if you think that is going to save you, you are the most mistaken man on God's earth, and you will be the biggest disappointed being that ever lived. You can't hire a substitute in religion. You can't do some deed of kindness or act of philanthropy and substitute that for the necessity of repentance and faith in Jesus Christ. Lots of people will acknowledge their sin in the world, struggle on without Jesus Christ, and do their best to live honorable, upright lives. Your morality will make you a better man or woman, but it will never save your soul in the world.

Supposing you had an apple tree that produced sour apples and you wanted to change the nature of it, and you would ask the advice of people. One would say prune it, and you would buy a pruning hook and cut off the superfluous limbs. You gather the apples and they are still sour. Another man says to fertilize it, and you fertilize it and still it doesn't change the nature of it. Another man says spray it to kill the caterpillars, but the apples are sour just the same. Another man says introduce a graft of another variety.

When I was a little boy, one day my grandfather said to me: "Willie, come on," and he took a ladder, and beeswax, a big jackknife, a saw and some cloth, and we went into the valley. He leaned the ladder against a sour crab-apple tree, climbed up and sawed off some of the limbs, split them and shoved in them some little pear sprouts as big as my finger and twice as long, and around them he tied a string and put in some beeswax. I said, "Grandpa, what are you doing?" He said, "I'm grafting pear sprouts into the sour crab." I said, "What will grow, crab apples or pears?" He said, "Pears; I don't know that I'll ever live to eat the pear—I hope I may—but I know you will." I lived to see those sprouts which were no longer than my finger grow as large as any limb and I climbed the tree and picked and ate the pears. He introduced a graft of another variety and that changed the nature of the tree.

And so you can't change yourself with books. That which is flesh is flesh, no matter whether it is cultivated flesh, or ignorant flesh or common, ordinary flesh. That which is flesh is flesh, and all your lodges, all your money on God Almighty's earth can never change your nature. Never. That's got to come by and through repentance and faith in Jesus Christ. That's the only way you will ever get it changed. We have more people with fool ways trying to get into heaven, and there's only one way to do and that is by and through repentance and faith in Jesus Christ.

Here are two men. One man born with hereditary tendencies toward bad, a bad father, a bad mother and bad grandparents. He has bad blood in his veins and he turns as naturally to sin as a duck to water. There he is, down and out, a booze fighter and the off-scouring scum of the earth. I go to him in his squalor and want and unhappiness, and say to him: "God has included all that sin that he may have mercy on all. All have sinned and come short of the glory of God. Will you accept Jesus Christ as your Saviour?"

"Whosoever cometh unto me I will in no wise cast out," and that man says to me, "No, I don't want your Christ as my Saviour."

Here is a man with hereditary tendencies toward good, a good father, a good mother, good grandparents, lived in a good neighborhood, was taught to go to Sunday school and has grown up to be a good, earnest, upright, virtuous, responsible business man; his name is synonymous with all that is pure and kind, and true. His name is as good as a government bond at any bank for a reasonable amount. Everybody respects him. He is generous, charitable and kind. I go to your high-toned, cultured, respectable man and say to him: "God hath included all under sin that he might have mercy upon all. All have sinned and come short of the glory of God. Whosoever cometh unto me I will in no wise cast out. Will you accept Jesus Christ as your Saviour? Will you give me your hand?" He says: "No, sir; I don't want your Christ."

What's the difference between those two men? Absolutely none. They are both lost. Both are going to hell.

God hasn't one way of saving the one and another way of saving the other fellow. God will save that man if he accepts Christ and he will do the same for the other fellow. That man is a sinner and this man is a sinner. That man is lower in sin than this man, but they both say, "No" to Jesus Christ and they are both lost or God is a liar.

You don't like it? I don't care a rap whether you do or not. You'll take it or go to hell. Stop doing what you think will save you and do what God says will save you.

Morality Not Enough

Morality doesn't save anybody. Your culture doesn't save you. I don't care who you are or how good you are, if you reject Jesus Christ you are doomed. God hasn't one plan of salvation for the millionaire and another for the hobo. He has the same plan for everybody. God isn't going to ask you whether you like it or not, either. He isn't going to ask you your opinion of his plan. There it is and we'll have to take it as God gives it.

You come across a lot of fools who say there are hypocrites in the Church. What difference does that make? Are you the first person that has found that out and are you fool enough to go to hell because they are going to hell? If you are, don't come to me and expect me to think you have any sense. Not at all. Not for a minute.

A good many people attend church because it adds a little bit to their respectability. That is proof positive to me that the Gospel is a good thing. This is a day when good things are counterfeited. You never saw anybody counterfeiting brown paper. No, it isn't worth it. You have seen them counterfeiting Christians? Yes. You have seen counterfeit money? Yes. You never saw a counterfeit infidel. They counterfeit religion. Certainly. A hypocrite is a counterfeit.

But there is one class of these people that I haven't very much respect for. They are so good, so very good,

that they are absolutely good for nothing. A woman
came to me and said: "Mr. Sunday, I haven't sinned in
ten years."

I said: "You lie, I think."

Well, a man says: "Look here, there must be something in morality, because so many people trust in it."
Would vice become virtue because more people follow it?
Simply because more people follow it doesn't make a
wrong right; not at all.

The Way of Salvation

There was an old Spaniard, Ponce de Leon, who
searched through the glades of Florida. He thought away
out there in the midst of the tropical vegetation was a
fountain of perpetual youth, which, if he could only find
and dip beneath its water would smooth the wrinkles from
his brow and make his gray hair turn like the raven's
wing. Did he ever find it? No, it never existed. It
was all imagination. And there are people today search-
ing for something that doesn't exist. Salvation doesn't
exist in morality, in reformation, in paying your debts.
It doesn't exist in being true to your marriage vows. It is
only by repentance and faith in the atoning blood of Jesus
Christ, and some of you fellows have searched for it until
you are gray-haired, and you will never find it because
it only exists in one place—repentance and faith in Jesus
Christ.

Supposing I had in one hand a number of kernels of
wheat and a number of diamonds equal in number and
size to the kernels of wheat. I would say: "Take your
choice." Nine of ten would take the diamonds. I would
say: "Diamonds are worth more than wheat." So they
are now, but you take those diamonds, they will never
grow, never add. But I can take a handful of wheat, sow
it, and, fecundated by the rays of the sun and the moisture,
it will grow and in a few years I have what's worth all the
diamonds in the world, for wheat contains the power of

life; wheat can reproduce and diamonds can't; they're not life. A diamond is simply a piece of charcoal changed by the mysterious process of nature, but it has no life. Wheat has life. Wheat can grow. You can take a moral man; he may shine and glisten and sparkle like a diamond. He may outshine in his beauty the Christian man. But he will never be anything else. His morality can never grow. It has no life, but the man who is a Christian has life. He has eternal life. Your morality is a fine thing until death comes, then it's lost and you are lost. Your diamond is a fine thing to carry until it's lost, and of what value is it then? Of what value is your morality when your soul is lost?

Supposing I go out in the spring and I see two farmers, living across the road from each other. One man plows his field and then harrows and puts on the roller, gets it all fine and then plants the corn or drills in the oats. I come back in the fall and that man has gathered his crop into the barn and the granaries and has hay stacked around the barn.

The other fellow is plowing and puts the roller on and gets his ground in good shape. I come back in the fall and he is still doing the same thing. I say, "What are you doing?" He says: "Well, I believe in a high state of cultivation." I say: "Look at your neighbor, see what he has." "A barn full of grain." "Yes." "More stock." "Yes." But he says: "Look at the weeds. You don't see any weeds like that on my place. Why, he had to burn the weeds before he could find the potatoes to dig them. The weeds were as big as the corn." I said: "I'll agree with you that he has raised some weeds, but he has raised corn as well." What is that ground worth without seed in it? No more than your life is worth without having Jesus Christ in it. You will starve to death if you don't put seed in the ground. Plowing the ground without putting in the seed doesn't amount to a snap of the finger.

Rewards of Merit

When I was a little boy out in Iowa, at the end of the term of school it was customary for the teachers to give us little cards, with a hand in one corner holding a scroll, and in that scroll was a place to write the name: "Willie Sunday, good boy." Willie Sunday never got hump-shouldered lugging them home, I can tell you. I never carried off the champion long-distance belt for verse-quoting, either. If you ever saw an American kid, I was one.

I feel sorry for the little Lord Fauntleroy boys with long curly hair and white stockings. Yank 'em off and let them go barefoot.

A friend of mine told me he was one time being driven along the banks of the Hudson and they went past a beautiful farm, and there sitting on the fence in front of a tree, in which was fastened a mirror about twelve inches square, sat a bird of paradise that was looking into the mirror, adjusting his plumage and admiring himself, and the farmer who had driven my friends out said that every time he passed those birds were doing that.

"I FEEL SORRY FOR THE LIT-TLE LORD FAUNTLEROY BOYS WITH LONG CURLY HAIR AND WHITE STOCKINGS"

I thought, "Well, that reminds me of a whole lot of fools I'm fortunate enough to meet everywhere. They sit before the mirror of culture, and their mirror of money, and their mirror of superior education and attainments; they are married into some old families. What does God care about that?" I suppose some of you spent a whole lot of money to plant a family tree, but I warrant you keep to the back the limbs

on which some of your ancestors were hanged for stealing horses.

You are mistaken in God's plan of salvation. Some people seem to think God is like a great big bookkeeper in heaven and that he has a whole lot of angels as assistants. Every time you do a good thing he writes it down on one page and every time you do a bad deed he writes it down on the opposite page, and when you die he draws a line and adds them up. If you have done more good things than bad, you go to heaven; more bad things than good, go to hell. You would be dumfounded how many people have sense about other things that haven't any sense about religion. As though that was God's plan of redemption. Your admission into heaven depends upon your acceptance of Jesus Christ; reject him and God says you will be damned.

Back in the time of Noah, I have no doubt there were a lot of good folks. There was Noah. God says: "Look here, Noah, I'm going to drown this world with a flood and I want you to go to work and make an ark." And Noah started to make it according to God's instructions and he pounded, and sawed, and drove nails and worked for 120 years, and I have often imagined the comments of the gang in an automobile going by. They say: "Look at the old fool Noah building an ark. Does he ever expect God's going to get water enough to flood that?" Along comes another crowd and' one says: "That Noah bunch is getting daffy on religion. I think we'd better take them before the commission and pass upon their sanity." Along comes another crowd and they say: "Well, there's that Noah crowd. I guess we won't invite them to our card party after Lent is over." They said: "Why, they're too religious. We'll just let them alone."

Noah paid no heed to their criticism, but went on working until he got through. God gave the crowd a chance, but they didn't heed. It started to rain and it rained and rained until the rivers and creeks leaped their banks and the lowlands were flooded. Then the people began to move to the hilltops. The water began to creep up the hills. Then I can see the people hurrying off to lumber yards to buy lumber to build little rafts of their own, for they began to see that Noah wasn't such a fool after all. The hilltops became inundated and it crept to the mountains and the mountains became submerged. Until the flood came that crowd was just as well off as Noah, but when the flood struck them Noah was saved and they were lost, because Noah trusted God and they trusted in themselves. You moral men, you may be just as well off as the Christian until death knocks you down, then you are lost, because you trust in your morality. The Christian is saved because he trusts in Jesus. Do you see where you lose out?

"Without the shedding of blood there is no remission of sin." You must accept the atonement Christ made by shedding his blood or God will slam the gate of heaven in your face.

Some people, you know, want to wash their sins and they whitewash them, but God wants them white, and there's a lot of difference between being "white-washed" and "washed white."

Supposing I was at one of your banks this morning and they gave me $25 in gold. Supposing I would put fifty of your reputable citizens on this platform and they would all substantiate what I say, and supposing I would be authorized by bank to say that they would give every man and woman that stands in line in front of the bank at 9 o'clock in the morning, $25 in gold. If I could stand up there and make that announcement in this city with confidence in my word, people would line the streets and string away back on the hills, waiting for the bank to open.

I can stand here and tell you that God offers you salvation through repentance and faith in Jesus Christ and that you must accept it or be lost, and you will stand up and argue the question, as though your argument can change God's plan. You never can do it. Not only has God promised you salvation on the grounds of your acceptance of Jesus Christ as your Saviour, but he has promised to give you a home in which to spend eternity. Listen! "In my Father's house are many mansions; if it were not so I would have told you. I go to prepare a place for you." Some people say heaven is a state or condition. I don't believe it. It might possibly be better to be in a heavenly state than in a heavenly place. It might be better to be in hell in a heavenly state than to be in heaven in a hellish state. That may be true. Heaven is as much a place as the home to which you are going when I dismiss the meeting is a place. "I go to prepare a place for you." Heaven is a place where there are going to be some fine folks. Abraham will be there and I'm going up to see him. Noah, Moses, Joseph, Jacob, Isaiah, Daniel, Jeremiah the weeping prophet, Paul, John, Peter, James, Samuel, Martin Luther, Spurgeon, Calvin, Moody. Oh, heaven is a place where there will be grand and noble people, and all who believe in Jesus will be there.

Suppose instead of turning off the gas at bedtime I blew it out. Then when Nell and I awoke choking, instead of opening the window and turning off the gas I got a bottle of cologne and sprinkled ourselves. The fool principle of trying to overcome the poison of gas with perfumery wouldn't work. The next day there would be a coroner's jury in the house. Your principle of trying to overcome sin by morality won't work either.

I'm going to meet David and I'll say: "David, I'm not a U. P., but I wish you'd sing the twenty-third psalm for me."

A Place of Noble People

The booze fighter won't be in heaven; he is here. The skeptic won't be there; he is here. There'll be nobody to run booze joints or gambling hells in heaven. Heaven

27

will be a place of grand and noble people, who love Jesus. The beloved wife will meet her husband. Mother, you will meet your babe again that you have been separated from for months or years. Heaven will be free from everything that curses and damns this old world here. Wouldn't this be a grand old world if it weren't for a lot of things in it? Can you conceive anything being grander than this world if it hadn't a lot of things in it? The only thing that makes it a decent place to live in is the religion of Jesus Christ. There isn't a man that would live in it if you took religion out. Your mills would rot on their foundations if there were no Christian people of influence here.

There will be no sickness in heaven, no pain, no sin, no poverty, no want, no death, no grinding toil. "There remaineth therefore a rest to the people of God." I tell you there are a good many poor men and women that never have any rest. They have had to get up early in the morning and work all day, but in heaven there remaineth a rest for the people of God. Weary women that start out early to their daily toil, you won't have to get out and toil all day. No toil in heaven, no sickness. "God shall wipe away all tears from their eyes." You will not be standing watching with a heart filled with expectation, and doubt, and hope. No watching the undertaker screw the coffin lid over your loved one, or watching the pall-bearers carrying out the coffin and hearing the preacher say, "Ashes to ashes, dust to dust." None of that in heaven. Heaven—that is a place He has gone to prepare for those who will do his will and keep his commandments and turn from their sin. Isn't it great?

Everything will be perfect in heaven. Down here we only know in part, but there we will know as we are known. It is a city that hath foundation. Here we have no continuing state. Look at your beautiful homes. You admire them. The next time you go up your avenues and streets look at the homes. But they are going to rot on their foundations. Every one of them. Where are you tonight, old Eternal City of Rome on your seven hills? Where are you? Only a memory of your glory. Where have they all gone? The homes will crumble.

"Enoch walked with God and was not, for God took him." That is a complete biography of Enoch.

Elijah was carried to heaven in a chariot of fire and Elisha took up the mantle of the prophet Elijah and smote the Jordan and went back to the seminary where Elijah had taught and told the people there. They would not believe him, and they looked for Elijah, but they found him not. Centuries later it was the privilege of Peter, James and John in the company of Jesus Christ, on the Mount of Transfiguration, to look into the face of that same Elijah who centuries before had walked the hilltops and slain four hundred and fifty of the prophets of Baal.

"A Place for You"

Stephen, as they stoned him to death, with his face lighted up saw Jesus standing on the right of God the Father, the place which he had designated before his crucifixion would be his abiding place until the fulfilment of the time of the Gentiles in the world. Among the last declarations of Jesus is, "In my Father's house are many mansions." What a comfort to the bereaved and afflicted. Not only had God provided salvation through faith in Jesus Christ as a gift from God's outstretched hand, but he provided a home in which you can spend eternity. He has provided a home for you. Surely, surely, friends, from the beginning of the history of man, from the time Enoch walked with God and was not, until John on the island of Patmos saw the new Jerusalem let down by God out of heaven, we have ample proof that heaven is a place. Although we cannot see it with the natural eyes, it is a place, the dwelling place of God and of the angels and of the redeemed through faith in the Son of God.

He says, "I go to prepare a place for you."

People sometimes ask me, "Who do you think will die first, Mr. Sunday, you or your wife, or your children or your mother?" I don't know. I think I will. I never expect to be an old man, I work too hard. I burn up more energy preaching in an hour than any other man will burn up in ten or twelve hours. I never expect to live to be an old man. I don't expect to, but I know this much, if my wife or my babies should go first this old world would be a dark place for me and I would be glad when God summoned me to leave it; and if I left first I know they would be glad when God called them home. If I go first, I know after I go up and take Jesus by the hand and say, "Jesus, thank you. I'm glad you honored me with the privilege of preaching your Gospel; I wish' I could have done it better, but I did my best, and now, Jesus, if you don't care, I'd like to hang around the gate and be the first to welcome my wife and the babies when they come. Do you care, Jesus, if I sit there?" And he will say, "No, you can sit right there, Bill, if you want to; it's all right." I'll say, "Thank you, Lord."

If they would go first, I think after they would go up and thank Jesus that they are home, they would say, "Jesus, I wish you would hurry up and bring papa home. He doesn't want to stay down there because we are up here." They would go around and put their grips away in their room, wherever it is, and then they would say, "Can we sit here, Jesus?" "Yes, that's all right."

I don't know where I'll live when I get to heaven. I don't know whether I'll live on a main street or an avenue or a boulevard. I don't know where I'll live when I get to heaven. I don't know whether it will be in the back alley or where, but I'll just be glad to get there. I'll be thankful for the mansion wherever God provides it. I never like to think about heaven as a great, big tenement house, where they put hundreds of people under one roof, as we do in Chicago or other big cities. "In my Father's house are many mansions." And so it will be up in heaven, and I'll be glad, awfully glad, and I tell you I think if my wife and children go first, the children might be off some place playing, but wife would be right there, and I would meet her and say, "Why, wife, where are the children?" She would say, "Why, they are playing on the banks of the river." (We are told about the river that flows from the throne of God.) We would walk down and I would say, "Hello, Helen! Hey, George. Hey, Willsky; bring the baby; come on." And they would come tearing as they do now.

I would say, "Now, children, run away and play a little while. I haven't seen mother for a long time and we have lots of things to talk about," and I think we would walk away and sit down under a tree and I would put my head in her lap as I do now when my head is tired, and I would say, "Wife, a whole lot of folks down there in our neighborhood in Chicago have died; have they come to heaven?"

The Missing

"Well, I don't know. Who has died?"

"Mr. S. Is he here?"

"I haven't seen him."

"No? His will probated five million. Bradstreet and Dun rated him AaG. Isn't he here?"

"I haven't seen him."

"Is Mr. J. here?"

"I haven't seen him."

"Haven't seen him, wife? That's funny. He left years before I did. Is Mrs. N here?"

"No."

"You know they lived on River street. Her husband paid $8,000 for a lot and $60,000 for a house. He paid $2,000 for a bathroom. Mosaic floor and the finest of fixtures. You know, wife, she always came to church late and would drive up in her carriage, and she would sweep down the aisle and you would think all the perfume of

Arabia had floated in, and she had diamonds in her ears as big as pebbles. Is she here?"

"I haven't seen her."

"Well! Well! Well! Is Aunty Griffith here?"

"Yes; aunty lives next to us."

"I knew she would be here. God bless her heart! She had two big lazy, drunken louts of boys that didn't care for her, and the church supported her for sixteen years to my knowledge and they put her in the home for old people. Hello, yonder she comes. How are you, Aunty?"

She will say, "How are you, William?"

"I'm first rate."

"Mon, ye look natural just the same."

"Yes."

"And when did ye leave Chicago, Wally?"

"Last night, Aunty."

"I'm awfully glad to see you, and, Wally, I live right next door to you, mon."

"Good, Aunty, I knew God would let you in. My, where's mother, wife?"

"She's here."

"I know she's here; I wish she would come. Helen, is that mother coming down the hill?"

"Yes."

I would say, "Have you seen Fred, or Rody, or Peacock, or Ackley, or any of them?"

"Yes. They live right around near us."

"George, you run down and tell Fred I've come, will you? Hunt up Rody, and Peacock and Ackley and Fred, and see if you can find Frances around there and tell them I've just come in." And they would come and I would say, "How are you? Glad to see you. Feeling first-rate."

And, oh, what a time we'll have in heaven. In heaven they never mar the hillsides with spades, for they dig no graves. In heaven they never telephone for the doctor, for nobody gets sick. In heaven no one carries handkerchiefs, for nobody cries. In heaven they never telephone for the undertaker, for nobody dies. In heaven you will never see a funeral procession going down the street, nor crêpe hanging from the doorknob. In heaven, none of the things that enter your home here will enter there. Sickness won't get in; death won't get in, nor sorrow, because "Former things are passed away," all things have become new. In heaven the flowers never fade, the winter winds and blasts never blow. The rivers never congeal, never freeze, for it never gets cold. No, sir.

Say, don't let God be compelled to hang a "For Rent" sign in the window of the·mansion he has prepared for you. I would walk around with him and I'd say, "Whose mansion is that, Jesus?"

"Why, I had that for one of the rich men, but he passed it up."

"Who's that one for?"

"That was for a doctor, but he did not take it."

"That was for one of the school teachers, but she didn't come."

"Who is that one for, Jesus?"

"That was for a society man, but he didn't want it."

"Who is that one for?"

"That was for a booze fighter, but he wouldn't pass up the business."

Don't let God hang a "For Rent" sign in the mansion that he has prepared for you. Just send up word and say, "Jesus, I've changed my mind; just put my name down for that, will you? I'm coming. I'm coming." "In my Father's house are many mansions; if it were not so I would have told you; I go to prepare a place for you."

CHAPTER XXXII

Glorying in the Cross

It's Jesus Christ or nothing.—BILLY SUNDAY.

PAULINE in more than one characteristic is Billy Sunday. But in none so much as in his devotion to the cross of Jesus Christ. His life motto may well be Paul's, "I am resolved to know nothing among you, save Jesus Christ and him crucified." His preaching is entirely founded on the message that "the blood of Jesus Christ cleanseth us from all sin." There are no modern theories of the atonement in his utterances. To the learned of the world, as to the Greeks of old, the Cross may seem foolishness, but Sunday knows and preaches it as the power of God unto salvation. As his closing and most characteristic message to the readers of this book we commend his sermon on "Christ and him crucified."

"ATONEMENT"

"For if the blood of bulls and of goats and the ashes of an heifer sprinkling the unclean, sanctifieth to the purifying of the flesh"—Paul argued in his letter to the Hebrews —"how much more shall the blood of Christ, who through the eternal Spirit offered himself without spot to God, purge your conscience from dead works to serve the living God."

No more of this turtle-dove business, no more offering the blood of bullocks and heifers to cleanse from sin.

The atoning blood of Jesus Christ—that is the thing about which all else centers. I believe that more logical, illogical, idiotic, religious and irreligious arguments have been fought over this than all others. Now and then when a man gets a new idea of it he goes out and starts a new denomination. He has a perfect right to do this under the thirteenth amendment, but he doesn't stop here.   He makes war on all of the other denominations that do not interpret as he does.   Our denominations have multiplied by this method until it would give one brain fever to try to count them all.

The atoning blood!   And as I think it over I am reminded of a man who goes to England and advertises that he will throw pictures on the screen of the Atlantic coast of America.   So he gets a crowd and throws pictures on the screen of high bluffs and rocky coasts and waves dashing against them until a man comes out of the audience and brands him a liar and says that he is obtaining money under false pretense, as he has seen America and the Atlantic coast and what the other man is showing is not America at all.   The men almost come to blows and then the other man says that if the people will come tomorrow he will show them real pictures of the coast.   So the audience comes back to see what he will show, and he flashes on the screen pictures of a low coast line, with palmetto trees and banana trees and tropical foliage and he apologizes to the audience, but says these are the pictures of America.   The first man calls him a liar and the people don't know which to believe.   What was the matter with them?

They were both right and they were both wrong, paradoxical as it may seem.   They were both right as far as they went, but neither went far enough.   The first showed the coast line from New England to Cape Hatteras, while the second showed the coast line from Hatteras to Yucatan.   They neither could show it all in one panoramic view, for it is so varied it could not be taken in one picture. God never intended to give you a picture of the world in one panoramic view.   From the time of Adam and Eve down to the time Jesus Christ hung on the cross he was unfolding his views.   When I see Moses leading the people out of bondage where they for years had bared their backs to the taskmaster's lash; when I see the lowing herds and the high priest standing before the altar severing the jugular vein of the rams and the bullocks on until Christ cried out from the cross, "It is finished," God was preparing the picture for the consummation of it in the atoning blood of Jesus Christ.

A sinner has no standing with God. He forfeits his standing when he commits sin and the only way he can get back is to repent and accept the atoning blood of Jesus Christ.

I have sometimes thought that Adam and Eve didn't understand as fully as we do when the Lord said, "Eat and you shall surely die." They had never seen any one die. They might have thought it simply meant a separation from God. But no sooner had they eaten and seen their nakedness than they sought to cover themselves, and it is the same today. When man sees himself in his sins, uncovered, he tries to cover himself in philosophy or some fake. But God looked through the fig leaves and the foliage and God walked out in the field and slew the beasts and took their skins and wrapped them around Adam and Eve, and from that day to this when a man has been a sinner and has covered himself it has been by and through faith in the shed blood of Jesus Christ. Every Jew covered his sins and received pardon through the blood of the rams and bullocks and the doves.

An old infidel said to me once, "But I don't believe in atonement by blood. It doesn't come up to my ideas of what is right."

I said, "To perdition with your ideas of what is right. Do you think God is coming down here to consult you with your great intellect and wonderful brain, and find out what you think is right before he does it?" My, but you make me sick. You think that because you don't believe it that it isn't true.

I have read a great deal—not everything, mind you, for a man would go crazy if he tried to read everything—but I have read a great deal that has been written against the atonement from the infidel standpoint—Voltaire, Huxley,

Spencer, Diderot, Bradlaugh, Paine, on down to Bob Inger-soll—and I have never found an argument that would stand the test of common sense and common reasoning. And if anyone tells me he has tossed on the scrap heap the plan of atonement by blood I say, "What have you to offer that is better?" and until he can show me something that is better I'll nail my hopes to the cross.

Suffering for the Guilty

You say you don't believe in the innocent suffering for the guilty. Then I say to you, you haven't seen life as I have seen it up and down the country. The innocent suffer with the guilty, by the guilty and for the guilty. Look at that old mother waiting with trembling heart for the son she has brought into the world. And see him come staggering in and reeling and staggering to bed while his mother prays and weeps and soaks the pillow with her tears over her godless boy. Who suffers most? The mother or that godless, maudlin bum? You have only to be the mother of a boy like that to know who suffers most. Then you won't say anything about the plan of redemption and of Jesus Christ suffering for the guilty.

Look at that young wife, waiting for the man whose name she bears, and whose face is woven in the fiber of her heart, the man she loves. She waits for him in fright and when he comes, reeking from the stench of the breaking of his marriage vows, from the arms of infamy, who suffers most? That poor, dirty, triple extract of vice and sin? You have only to be the wife of a husband like that to know whether the innocent suffers for the guilty or not. I have the sympathy of those who know right now.

This happened in Chicago in a police court. A letter was introduced as evidence for a criminal there for vagrancy. It read, "I hope you won't have to hunt long to find work. Tom is sick and baby is sick. Lucy has no shoes and we have no money for the doctor or to buy any clothes. I manage to make a little taking in washing, but we are living in one room in a basement. I hope you won't have to look long for work," and so on, just the kind of a letter a wife would write to her husband. And before it was finished men cried and policemen with hearts of adamant were crying and fled from the room. The judge wiped the tears from his eyes and said: "You see, no man lives to himself alone. If he sins others suffer. I have no alternative. I sympathize with them, as does every one of you, but I have no alternative. I must send this man to Bridewell." Who suffers most, that woman manicuring her nails over a washboard to keep the little brood together or that drunken bum in Bridewell getting his just deserts from his acts? You have only to be the wife of a man like that to know whether or not the innocent suffer with the guilty.

So when you don't like the plan of redemption because the innocent suffer with the guilty, I say you don't know what is going on. It's the plan of life everywhere.

From the fall of Adam and Eve till now it has always been the rule that the innocent suffer with the guilty. It's the plan of all and unless you are an idiot, an imbecile and a jackass, and gross flatterer at that, you'll see it.

Jesus' Atoning Blood

Jesus gave his life on the cross for any who will believe. We're not redeemed by silver or gold. Jesus paid for it with his blood. When some one tells you that your religion is a bloody religion and the Bible is a bloody book, tell them yes, Christianity is a bloody religion, the gospel is a bloody gospel, the Bible is a bloody book, the plan of redemption is bloody. It is. You take the blood of Jesus Christ out of Christianity and that book isn't worth the paper it is written on. It would be worth no more than your body with the blood taken out. Take the blood of Jesus Christ out and it would be a meaningless jargon and jumble of words.

If it weren't for the atoning blood you might as well rip the roofs off the churches and burn them down. They aren't worth anything. But as long as the blood is on the mercy seat the sinner can return, and by no other way. There is nothing else. It stands for the redemption. You are not redeemed by silver or gold, but by the blood of Jesus Christ. Though a man says to read good books, do good deeds, live a good life and you'll be saved, you'll be damned. That's what you will. All the books in the world won't keep you out of hell without the atoning blood of Jesus Christ. It's Jesus Christ or nothing for every sinner on God's earth.

Without it not a sinner will ever be saved. Jesus has paid for your sins with his blood. The doctrine of universal salvation is a lie. I wish every one would be saved, but they won't. You will never be saved if you reject the blood.

I remember when I was in the Y. M. C. A. in Chicago I was going down Madison Street and had just crossed Dearborn

"SAY, BOSS, WHY DIDN'T YOU CHUCK THAT NICKEL IN THE SEWER?"

Street when I saw a newsboy with a young sparrow in his hand. I said: "Let that little bird go."

He said, "Aw, g'wan with you, you big mutt."

I said, "I'll give you a penny for it," and he answered, "Not on your tintype."

"I'll give you a nickel for it," and he answered, "Boss, I'm from Missouri; come across with the dough."

I offered it to him, but he said, "Give it to that guy there," and I gave it to the boy he indicated and took the sparrow.

I held it for a moment and then it fluttered and struggled and finally reached the window ledge in a second story

across the street. And other birds fluttered around over my head and seemed to say in bird language, "Thank you, Bill."

The kid looked at me in wonder and said: "Say, boss, why didn't you chuck that nickel in the sewer?"

I told him that he was just like that bird. He was in the grip of the devil, and the devil was too strong for him just as he was too strong for the sparrow, and just as I could do with the sparrow what I wanted to after I had paid for it because it was mine. God paid a price for him far greater than I had for the sparrow, for he had paid it with the blood of his Son and he wanted to set him free.

No Argument Against Sin

So, my friend, if I had paid for some property from you with a price, I could command you, and if you wouldn't give it to me I could go into court and make you yield. Why do you want to be a sinner and refuse to yield? You are withholding from God what he paid for on the cross. When you refuse you are not giving God a square deal.

I'll tell you another. It stands for God's hatred of sin. Sin is something you can't deny. You can't argue against sin. A skilful man can frame an argument against the validity of religion, but he can't frame an argument against sin. I'll tell you something that may surprise you. If I hadn't had four years of instruction in the Bible from Genesis to Revelation, before I saw Bob Ingersoll's book, and I don't want to take any credit from that big intelligent brain of his, I would be preaching infidelity instead of Christianity. Thank the Lord I saw the Bible first. I have taken his lectures and placed them by the side of the Bible, and said, "You didn't say it from your knowledge of the Bible." And I have never considered him honest, for he could not have been so wise in other things and such a fool about the plan of redemption. So I say I don't think he was entirely honest.

But you can't argue against the existence of sin, simply because it is an open fact, the word of God. You can argue against Jesus being the Son of God. You can argue about there being a heaven and a hell, but you can't argue against sin. It is in the world and men and women are blighted and mildewed by it.

Some years ago I turned a corner in Chicago and stood in front of a police station. As I stood there a patrol dashed up and three women were taken from some drunken debauch, and they were dirty and blear-eyed, and as they were taken out they started a flood of profanity that seemed to turn the very air blue. I said, "There is sin." And as I stood there up dashed another patrol and out of it they took four men, drunken and ragged and bloated, and I said, "There is sin." You can't argue against the fact of sin. It is in the world and blights men and women. But Jesus came to the world to save all who accept him.

"How Long, O God?"

It was out in the Y. M. C. A. in Chicago. "What is your name and what do you want?" I asked.

"I'm from Cork, Ireland," said he, "and my name is James O'Toole." Here is a letter of introduction." I read it and it said he was a good Christian young man and an energetic young fellow.

I said, "Well, Jim, my name is Mr. Sunday. I'll tell you where there are some good Christian boarding houses and you let me know which one you pick out." He told me afterwards that he had one on the North Side. I sent him an invitation to a meeting to be held at the Y. M. C. A., and he had it when he and some companions went bathing in Lake Michigan. He dived from the pier just as the water receded unexpectedly and he struck the bottom and broke his neck. He was taken to the morgue and the police found my letter in his clothes, and told me to come and claim it or it would be sent to a medical college. I went and they had the body on a slab, but I told them I would send a cablegram to his folks and asked them to hold it. They put it in a glass case and turned on the cold air, by which they freeze bodies by chemical processes, as they freeze ice, and said they would save it for two months, and if I wanted it longer they would stretch the rules a little and keep it three.

I was just thinking of what sorrow that cablegram would cause his old mother in Cork when they brought in the body of a woman. She would have been a fit model of Phidias, she had such symmetry of form. Her fingers were manicured. She was dressed in the height of fashion and her hands were covered with jewels and as I looked at her, the water trickling down her face, I saw the mute evidence of illicit affection. I did not say lust, I did not say passion, I did not say brute instincts. I said, "Sin." Sin had caused her to throw herself from that bridge and seek repose in a suicide's grave. And as I looked, from the saloon, the fan-tan rooms, the gambling hells, the opium dens, the red lights, there arose one endless cry of "How long, O God, how long shall hell prevail?"

You can't argue against sin. It's here. Then listen to me as I try to help you.

When the Standard Oil Company was trying to refine petroleum there was a substance that they couldn't dispose of. It was a dark, black, sticky substance and they couldn't bury it, couldn't burn it because it made such a stench; they couldn't run it in the river because it killed the fish, so they offered a big reward to any chemist who would solve the problem. Chemists took it and worked long over the problem, and one day there walked into the office of John D. Rockefeller, a chemist and laid down a pure white substance which we since know as paraffine.

You can be as black as that substance and yet Jesus Christ can make you white as snow. "Though your sins be as scarlet they shall be as white as snow."